Charles Kingsley

At last a Christmas in the West Indies

Charles Kingsley

At last a Christmas in the West Indies

ISBN/EAN: 9783741179303

Manufactured in Europe, USA, Canada, Australia, Japa

Cover: Foto ©Andreas Hilbeck / pixelio.de

Manufactured and distributed by brebook publishing software (www.brebook.com)

Charles Kingsley

At last a Christmas in the West Indies

THE BOTANIC GARDENS, PORT OF SPAIN.

A CHRISTMAS IN THE WEST INDIES

BY

CHARLES KINGSLEY

ILLUSTRATED

London
MACMILLAN AND CO., Limited
NEW YORK: THE MACMILLAN COMPANY
1905

TO HIS EXCELLENCY

THE HON. SIR ARTHUR GORDON,

GOVERNOR OF MAURITIUS

My Dear Sir Arthur Gordon,

To whom should I dedicate this book, but to you, to whom I owe my visit to the West Indies? I regret that I could not consult you about certain matters in Chapters XIV and XV; but you are away again over sea; and I can only send the book after you, such as it is, with the expression of my hearty belief that you will be to the people of Mauritius what you have been to the people of Trinidad.

I could say much more. But it is wisest often to be most silent on the very points on which one longs most to speak.

Ever yours,

C. KINGSLEY.

CONTENTS

CHAP.		PAGE
I.	OUTWARD BOUND	1
II.	DOWN THE ISLANDS	21
III.	TRINIDAD	55
IV.	PORT OF SPAIN	70
V.	A LETTER FROM A WEST INDIAN COTTAGE ORNÉE	77
VI.	MONOS	94
VII.	THE HIGH WOODS	120
VIII.	LA BREA	142
IX.	SAN JOSEF	166
X.	NAPARIMA AND MONTSERRAT	181
XI.	THE NORTHERN MOUNTAINS	214
XII.	THE SAVANNA OF ARIPO	253
XIII.	THE COCAL	264
XIV.	THE 'EDUCATION QUESTION' IN TRINIDAD	285
XV.	THE RACES—A LETTER	303
XVI.	A PROVISION GROUND	309
XVII.	HOMEWARD BOUND	323

LIST OF ILLUSTRATIONS

	PAGE
THE BOTANIC GARDENS, PORT OF SPAIN	*Frontispiece*
VIRGIN GORDA, ST. JOHN'S, TORTOLA	1
GULF-WEED	7
SEASIDE GRAPE	14
FRANGIPANI	15
THE BOCAS	21
ST. EUSTATIUS	23
THE PITONS OF ST. LUCIA	42
THE MONOS BOCA	53
CHINESE MAN AND WOMAN	73
GROO-GROOS	80
SANDBOX	82
TAMARIND	84
THE LITTLE ANT-EATER	92
COOLIES A-FIELD	97
COOLIES COOKING	100
MONOS	108
CACAO	126
THE HIGH WOODS	130
CEIBA	141
CASHEW NUT	147

LIST OF ILLUSTRATIONS

	PAGE
THE PITCH LAKE	151
COOLIE AND NEGRO	166
A MANGROVE SWAMP	169
A COOLIE FAMILY	190
BANANA	197
TORTUGA	208
COOLIE GROUP	211
FILLETTE	223
AVOCADO PEAR	224
CANNON-BALL TREE	226
A TROPIC BEACH	251
YOUNG COCO PALM	271
THE COCAL	272
COOLIE SACRIFICING	301
WAITING FOR THE RACES	304
THE LAST OF THE GIANTS	310
BREAD-FRUIT	311
YAM	313
SWEET POTATO	314
GUAVA	321

FIRST SIGHT OF THE TROPICS. VIRGIN GORDA, ST. JOHN'S, TORTOLA.

CHAPTER I

OUTWARD BOUND

At last we, too, were crossing the Atlantic. At last the dream of forty years, please God, would be fulfilled, and I should see (and happily, not alone) the West Indies and the Spanish Main. From childhood I had studied their Natural History, their charts, their Romances, and alas! their Tragedies; and now, at last, I was about to compare books with facts, and judge for myself of the reported wonders of the Earthly Paradise. We could scarce believe the evidence of our own senses when they told us that we were surely on board a West Indian steamer, and could by no possibility get off it again, save into the ocean, or on the farther side of the ocean; and it was not till the morning of the second day, the 3d of December, that we began to be thoroughly aware that we were on the old route of Westward-Ho, and far out in the high seas, while the Old World lay behind us like a dream.

Like dreams seemed now the last farewells over the taffrel, beneath the chill low December sun; and the shining calm of Southampton water, and the pleasant and well-beloved old shores and woods and houses sliding by; and the fisher-boats at anchor off Calshot, their brown and olive sails reflected in the dun water, with dun clouds overhead tipt with dull red from off the setting sun—a study for Vandevelde or Backhuysen in the tenderest moods. Like a dream seemed the twin lights of Hurst Castle and the Needles, glaring out of the gloom behind us, as if old England were watching us to the last with careful eyes, and bidding us good speed upon our way. Then had come—still like a dream—a day of pouring rain, of lounging on the main-deck, watching the engines, and watching, too (for it was calm at night), the water from the sponson behind the paddle-boxes; as the live flame-beads leaped and ran amid the swirling snow, while some fifteen feet beyond the untouched oily black of the deep sea spread away into the endless dark.

It took a couple of days to arrange our little cabin Penates; to discover who was on board; and a couple of days, too, to become aware, in spite of sudden starts of anxiety, that there was no post, and could be none; that one could not be wanted, or, if one was wanted, found and caught; and it was not till the fourth morning that the glorious sense of freedom dawned on the mind, as through the cabin port the sunrise shone in, yellow and wild through flying showers, and great north-eastern waves raced past us, their heads torn off in spray, their broad backs laced with ripples, and each, as it passed, gave us a friendly onward lift away into the 'roaring forties,' as the sailors call the stormy seas between 50 and 40 degrees of latitude.

These 'roaring forties' seem all strangely devoid of animal life—at least in a December north-east gale; not a whale did we see—only a pair of porpoises; not a sea-bird, save a lonely little kittiwake or two, who swung round our stern in quest of food: but the seeming want of life was only owing to our want of eyes; each night the wake teemed more bright with flame-atomies. One kind were little brilliant sparks, hurled helpless to and fro on the surface, probably Noctilucæ; the others (what they may be we could not guess at first) showed patches of soft diffused light, paler than the sparks, yet of the same yellow-white hue, which floated quietly past, seeming a foot or two below the foam. And at the bottom, far beneath, deeper under our feet than the summit of the Peak of Teneriffe was above our heads—for we were now in more than two thousand fathoms water—what exquisite forms might there not be? myriads on myriads, generations on generations, people the eternal darkness, seen only by Him to whom the darkness is as light as day: and to be seen hereafter, a few of them—but how few—when future men of science shall do for this mid-Atlantic sea-floor what Dr. Carpenter and Dr. Wyville Thomson have done for the North Atlantic, and open one more page of that book which has, to us creatures of a day, though not to Him who wrote it as the Time-pattern of His timeless mind, neither beginning nor end.

So, for want of animal life to study, we were driven to study the human life around us, pent up there in our little iron world. But to talk too much of fellow-passengers is (though usual enough just now) neither altogether fair nor kind. We see in travel but the outside of people, and as we know nothing of their inner history, and little, usually, of their antecedents, the pictures which we might sketch of them would be probably as untruthfully as rashly drawn. Crushed together, too, perforce, against each other, people are apt on board ship to make little hasty confidences, to show unawares little weaknesses, which should be forgotten all round the moment they step on shore and return to something like a normal state of society. The wisest and most humane rule for a traveller toward his companions is to

'Be to their faults a little blind;
Be to their virtues very kind;'

and to consider all that is said and done on board, like what passes among the members of the same club, as on the whole private and confidential. So let it suffice that there were on board the good steamship *Shannon*, as was to be expected, plenty of kind, courteous, generous, intelligent people; officials, travellers—one, happy man! away to discover new birds on the yet unexplored Rio Magdalena, in New Grenada; planters, merchants, what not, all ready, when once at St. Thomas's, to spread themselves over the islands, and the Spanish Main, and the Isthmus of Panama, and after that, some of them, down the Pacific shore to Callao and Valparaiso. The very names of their different destinations, and the imagination of the wonders they would see (though we were going to a spot as full of wonders as any), raised something like envy in our breasts, all the more because most of them persisted in tantalising us, in the hospitable fashion of all West Indians, by fruitless invitations to islands and ports, which to have seen were 'a joy for ever.'

But almost the most interesting group of all was one of Cornish miners, from the well-known old Redruth and Camborne county, and the old sacred hill of Carn-brea, who were going to seek their fortunes awhile in silver mines among the Andes, leaving wives and children at home, and hoping, 'if it please God, to do some good out there,' and send their earnings home. Stout, bearded, high-cheek-boned men they were, dressed in the thick coats and rough caps, and, of course, in the indispensable black cloth trousers, which make a miner's full dress; and their faces lighted up at the old pass-word of 'Down-Along'; for whosoever knows Down-Along, and the speech thereof, is at once a friend and a brother. We had many a pleasant talk with them ere we parted at St. Thomas's.

And on to St. Thomas's we were hurrying; and, thanks to the north-east wind, as straight as a bee-line. On the third day we ran two hundred and fifty-four miles; on the fourth two hundred and sixty; and on the next day, at noon, where should we be? Nearing the Azores; and by midnight, running past them, and away on the track of Columbus, towards the Sargasso Sea.

We stayed up late on the night of December 7, in hopes of seeing, as we passed Terceira, even the loom of the land: but the moon was down; and a glimpse of the 'Pico' at dawn next morning was our only chance of seeing, at least for this voyage, those wondrous Isles of the Blest—Isles of the Blest of old; and why not still? They too are said to be earthly paradises in soil, climate, productions; and yet no English care to settle there, nor even to go thither for health, though the voyage from Lisbon is but a short one, and our own mail steamers, were it made worth their while, could as easily touch at Terceira now as they did a few years since.

And as we looked out into the darkness, we could not but recollect, with a flush of pride, that yonder on the starboard beam lay Flores, and the scene of that great fight off the Azores, on August 30, 1591, made ever memorable by the pen of Walter Raleigh—and of late by Mr. Froude; in which the *Revenge*, with Sir Richard Grenville for her captain, endured for twelve hours, before she struck, the attack of eight great Spanish armadas, of which two (three times her own burden) sank at her side; and after all her masts were gone, and she had been three times boarded without success, defied to the last the whole fleet of fifty-one sail, which lay around her, waiting, 'like dogs around the dying forest-king,' for the Englishman to strike or sink. Yonder away it was, that, wounded again and again, and shot through body and through head, Sir Richard Grenville was taken on board the Spanish Admiral's ship to die; and gave up his gallant ghost with those once-famous words: 'Here die I, Richard Grenville, with a joyful and quiet mind; for that I have ended my life as a true soldier ought, fighting for his country, queen, religion, and honour; my soul willingly departing from this body, leaving behind the lasting fame of having behaved as every valiant soldier is in his duty bound to do.'

Yes; we were on the track of the old sea-heroes; of Drake and Hawkins, Carlile and Cavendish, Cumberland and Raleigh, Preston and Sommers, Frobisher and Duddeley, Keymis and Whiddon, which last, in that same Flores fight, stood by Sir Richard Grenville all alone, and, in 'a small ship called the *Pilgrim,* hovered all night to see the successe: but in the morning, bearing with the *Revenge,* was hunted like a hare amongst many ravenous houndes, but escaped'[1]—to learn, in after years, in company with hapless Keymis, only too much

---

[1] Raleigh's *Report of the Truth of the Fight about the Iles of Azores.*

about that Trinidad and Gulf of Paria whither we were bound.

Yes. There were heroes in England in those days. Are we, their descendants, degenerate from them? I, for one, believe not. But they were taught—what we take pride in refusing to be taught—namely, to obey.

The morning dawned: but Pico, some fifty miles away, was taking his morning bath among the clouds, and gave no glimpse of his eleven thousand feet crater cone, now capped, they said, with winter snow. Yet neither last night's outlook nor that morning's was without result. For as the steamer stopped last night to pack her engines, and slipped along under sail at some three knots an hour, we made out clearly that the larger diffused patches of phosphorescence were Medusæ, slowly opening and shutting, and rolling over and over now and then, giving out their light, as they rolled, seemingly from the thin limb alone, and not from the crown of their bell. And as we watched, a fellow-passenger told how, between Ceylon and Singapore, he had once witnessed that most rare and unexplained phenomenon of a 'milky sea,' of which Dr. Collingwood writes (without, if I remember right, having seen it himself) in his charming book, *A Naturalist's Rambles in the China Seas*. Our friend described the appearance as that of a sea of shining snow rather than of milk, heaving gently beneath a starlit but moonless sky. A bucket of water, when taken up, was filled with the same half-luminous whiteness, which stuck to its sides when the water was drained off. The captain of the Indiaman was well enough aware of the rarity of the sight to call all the passengers on deck to see what they would never see again; and on asking our captain, he assured us that he had not only never seen, but never heard of the appearance in the West Indies. One curious fact, then, was verified that night.

The next morning gave us unmistakable tokens that we were nearing the home of the summer and the sun. A north-east wind, which would in England keep the air at least at freezing in the shade, gave here a temperature just over 60°; and gave clouds, too, which made us fancy for a moment that we were looking at an April thunder sky, soft, fantastic, barred, and feathered, bright white where they ballooned out above into cumuli, rich purple in their massive shadows, and dropping from their under edges long sheets of inky rain. Thanks to the brave North-Easter, we had gained in five days thirty degrees of heat, and had slipped out of December into May. The North-Easter, too, was transforming itself more and more into the likeness of a south-west wind; say, rather, renewing its own youth, and becoming once more what it was when it started on its long journey from the Tropics towards the Pole. As it rushes back across the ocean, thrilled and expanded by the heat, it opens its dry and thirsty lips to suck in the damp from below, till, saturated once more with steam, it will reach the tropic as a gray rain-laden sky of North-East Trade.

So we slipped on, day after day, in a delicious repose which yet was not monotonous. Those, indeed, who complain of the monotony of a voyage must have either very few resources in their own minds, or much worse company than we had on board the *Shannon*. Here, every hour brought, or might bring, to those who wished, not merely agreeable conversation about the Old World behind us, but fresh valuable information about the New World before us. One morning, for instance, I stumbled on a merchant returning to Surinam, who had fifty things to tell of his own special business—of the woods, the drugs, the barks, the vegetable oils, which he was going back to procure —a whole new world of yet unknown wealth and use. Most cheering, too, and somewhat unexpected, were the facts we heard of the improving state of our West India Colonies, in which the tide of fortune seems to have turned at last, and the gallant race of planters and merchants, in spite of obstacle on obstacle, some of them unjust and undeserved, are winning their way back (in their own opinion) to a prosperity more sound and lasting than that which collapsed so suddenly at the end of the great French war. All spoke of the emancipation of the slaves in Cuba (an event certain to come to pass ere long) as the only condition which they required to put them on an equal footing with any producers whatsoever in the New World.

However pleasant, though, the conversation might be, the smallest change in external circumstances, the least break in the perpetual—

'Quocumque adspicias, nil est nisi pontus et aer,'

even a passing bird, if one would pass, which none would do save once or twice a stately tropic-bird, wheeling round aloft like an eagle, was hailed as an event in the day; and, on the 9th of December, the appearance of the first fragments of gulf-weed caused quite a little excitement, and set an enthusiastic pair of naturalists—a midland hunting squire, and a travelled scientific doctor who had been twelve years in the Eastern Archipelago — fishing eagerly over the bows, with an extemporised grapple of wire, for gulf-weed, a specimen of which they did not catch. However, more and more still would come in a day or two, perhaps whole acres, even whole leagues, and then (so we hoped, but hoped in vain) we should have our feast of zoophytes, crustacea, and what not.

Meanwhile, it must be remembered that this gulf-weed has not, as some of the uninitiated fancy from its name, anything to do with the Gulf Stream, along the southern edge of which we were steaming. Thrust away to the south by that great ocean-river, it lies in a vast eddy, or central pool of the Atlantic, between the Gulf Stream and the equatorial current, unmoved save by surface-drifts of wind, as floating weeds collect and range slowly round and round in the still corners of a tumbling-bay or salmon pool. One glance at a bit of the weed, as it floats past, showed that it is like no Fucus of our shores, or anything we ever saw before. The difference of look is undefinable in words, but clear enough. One sees in a moment that the Sargassos, of which there are several species on Tropical shores, are a genus of themselves and by themselves; and a certain awe may, if the beholder be at once scientific and poetical, come over him at the first sight of this famous and unique variety thereof, which has lost ages since the habit of growing on rock or sea-bottom, but propagates itself for ever floating; and feeds among its branches a whole family of fish, crabs, cuttle-fish, zoophytes, mollusks, which, like the plant which shelters them, are found nowhere else in the world. And that awe, springing from 'the scientific use of the imagination,' would be increased if he recollected the theory—not altogether impossible—that this sargasso (and possibly some of the animals which cling to it) marks the site of an Atlantic continent, sunk long ages since; and that, transformed by the necessities of life from a rooting to a floating plant,

GULF-WEED.

'Still it remembers its august abodes,'

and wanders round and round as if in search of the rocks where it once grew. We looked eagerly day by day for more and more gulf-weed, hoping that

'Slimy things would crawl with legs
Upon that slimy sea,'

and thought of the memorable day when Columbus's ship first plunged her bows into the tangled 'ocean meadow,' and the sailors, naturally enough, were ready to mutiny, fearing hidden shoals, ignorant that they had four miles of blue water beneath their keel, and half recollecting old Greek and Phœnician legends of a weedy sea off the coast of Africa, where the vegetation stopped the ships and kept them entangled till all on board were starved.

Day after day we passed more and more of it, often in long processions, ranged in the direction of the wind; while, a few feet below the surface, here and there floated large fronds of a lettuce-like weed, seemingly an ulva, the bright green of which, as well as the rich orange hue of the sargasso, brought out by contrast the intense blue of the water.

Very remarkable, meanwhile, and unexpected, was the opacity and seeming solidity of the ocean when looked down on from the bows. Whether sapphire under the sunlight, or all but black under the clouds, or laced and streaked with beads of foam, rising out of the nether darkness, it looks as if it could resist the hand; as if one might almost walk on it; so unlike any liquid, as seen near shore or inland, is this leaping, heaving plain, reminding one, by its innumerable conchoidal curves, not of water, not even of ice, but rather of obsidian.

After all we got little of the sargasso. Only in a sailing ship, and in calms or light breezes, can its treasures be explored. Twelve knots an hour is a pace sufficient to tear off the weed, as it is hauled alongside, all living things which are not rooted to it. We got, therefore, no Crustacea; neither did we get a single specimen of the Calamaries,[1] which may be described as cuttle-fish carrying hooks on their arms as well as suckers, the lingering descendants of a most ancient form, which existed at least as far back as the era of the shallow oolitic seas, x or y thousand years ago. A tiny curled Spirorbis, a Lepraria, with its thousand-fold cells, and a tiny polype belonging to the Campanularias, with a creeping stem, which sends up here and there a yellow-stalked bell, were all the parasites we saw. But the sargasso itself is a curious instance of the fashion in which one form so often mimics another of a quite different family. When fresh out of the water it resembles not a sea-weed so much as a sprig of some willow-leaved shrub, burdened with yellow berries, large and small; for every broken bit of it seems growing, and throwing out ever new berries and leaves—or what, for want of a better word, must be called leaves in a sea-weed. For it must be remembered that the frond of a sea-weed is not merely leaf, but root also; that it not only breathes air, but feeds on water; and that even the so-called root by which a sea-weed holds to the rock is really only an anchor, holding mechanically to the stone, but not deriving, as the root of a land-plant would, any nourishment from it. Therefore it is, that to grow while uprooted and floating, though impossible to most land plants, is easy enough to many sea-weeds, and especially to the sargasso.

The flying-fish now began to be a source of continual amuse-

---

[1] *Chiroteuthi* and *Onychoteuthi*.

ment, as they scuttled away from under the bows of the ship, mistaking her, probably, for some huge devouring whale. So strange are they when first seen, though long read of and long looked for, that it is difficult to recollect that they are actually fish. The first little one was mistaken for a dragon-fly, the first big one for a gray plover. The flight is almost exactly like that of a quail or partridge—flight, I must say ; for, in spite of all that has been learnedly written to the contrary, it was too difficult as yet for the English sportsmen on board to believe that their motion was not a true flight, aided by the vibration of the wings, and not a mere impulse given (as in the leap of the salmon) by a rush under water. That they can change their course at will is plain to one who looks down on them from the lofty deck, and still more from the paddle-box. The length of the flight seems too great to be attributed to a few strokes of the tail ; while the plain fact that they renew their flight after touching, and only touching, the surface, would seem to show that it was not due only to the original impetus, for that would be retarded, instead of being quickened, every time they touched. Such were our first impressions : and they were confirmed by what we saw on the voyage home.

The nights as yet, we will not say disappointed us,—for to see new stars, like Canopus and Fomalhaut, shining in the far south, even to see Sirius, in his ever-changing blaze of red and blue, riding high in a December heaven, is interesting enough ; but the brilliance of the stars is not, at least at this season, equal to that of a frosty sky in England. Nevertheless, to make up for the deficiency, the clouds were glorious ; so glorious, that I longed again and again, as I did afterwards in the West Indies, that Mr. Ruskin were by my side, to see and to describe, as none but he can do. The evening skies are fit weeds for widowed Eos weeping over the dying Sun ; thin, formless, rent—in carelessness, not in rage ; and of all the hues of early autumn leaves, purple and brown, with green and primrose lakes of air between : but all hues weakened, mingled, chastened into loneliness, tenderness, regretfulness, through which still shines, in endless vistas of clear western light, the hope of the returning day. More and more faint, the pageant fades below towards the white haze of the horizon, where, in sharpest contrast, leaps and welters against it the black jagged sea ; and richer and richer it glows upwards, till it cuts the azure overhead : until, only too soon—

> 'The sun's rim dips, the stars rush out,
> At one stride comes the dark,'

to be succeeded, after the long balmy night, by a sunrise which repeats the colours of the sunset, but this time gaudy, dazzling, triumphant, as befits the season of faith and hope. Such imagery, it may be said, is hackneyed now, and trite even to impertinence. It might be so at home; but here, in presence of the magnificent pageant of tropic sunlight, it is natural, almost inevitable; and the old myth of the daily birth and death of Helios, and the bridal joys and widowed tears of Eos, re-invents itself in the human mind, as soon as it asserts its power—it may be, its sacred right—to translate nature into the language of the feelings.

And, meanwhile, may we not ask—have we not a right—founded on that common sense of the heart which often is the deepest reason—to ask, If we, gross and purblind mortals, can perceive and sympathise with so much beauty in the universe, then how much must not He perceive, with how much must not He sympathise, for whose pleasure all things are, and were created? Who that believes (and rightly) the sense of beauty to be among the noblest faculties of man, will deny that faculty to God, who conceived man and all besides?

Wednesday, the 15th, was a really tropic day; blazing heat in the forenoon, with the thermometer at 82° in the shade, and in the afternoon stifling clouds from the south-west, where a dark band of rain showed, according to the planters' dictum, showers over the islands, which we were nearing fast. At noon we were only two hundred and ten miles from Sombrero, 'the Spanish Hat,' a lonely island, which is here the first outlier of the New World. We ought to have passed it by sunrise on the 16th, and by the afternoon reached St. Thomas's, where our pleasant party would burst like a shell in all directions, and scatter its fragments about all coasts and isles—from Demerara to Panama, from Mexico to the Bahamas. So that day was to the crew a day of hard hot work—of lifting and sorting goods on the main-deck, in readiness for the arrival at St. Thomas's, and of moving forwards two huge empty boilers which had graced our spar-deck, filled with barrels of onions and potatoes, all the way from Southampton. But in the soft hot evening hours, time was found for the usual dance on the quarter-deck, with the band under the awning, and lamps throwing fantastic shadows, and waltzing couples, and the crew clustering aft to see, while we old folks looked on, with our 'Ludite dum lubet, pueri,' till the captain bade the sergeant-at-arms leave the lights burning for an extra half hour; and 'Sir Roger de Coverley' was danced out, to the great amusement of the foreigners, at actually half-past eleven. After which unexampled dissipation, all went off to rest, promising to themselves and their partners that they would get up at sunrise to sight Sombrero.

But, as it befell, morning's waking brought only darkness, the heavy pattering of a tropic shower, and the absence of the everlasting roll of the paddle-wheels. We were crawling slowly along, in thick haze and heavy rain, having passed Sombrero unseen; and were away in a gray shoreless world of waters, looking out for Virgin Gorda; the first of those numberless isles which Columbus, so goes the tale, discovered on St. Ursula's day, and named them after the Saint and her eleven thousand mythical virgins. Unfortunately, English buccaneers have since then given to most of them less poetic names. The Dutchman's Cap, Broken Jerusalem, The Dead Man's Chest, Rum Island, and so forth, mark a time and a race more prosaic, but still more terrible, though not one whit more wicked and brutal, than the Spanish Conquistadores, whose descendants, in the seventeenth century, they smote hip and thigh with great destruction.

The farthest of these Virgin Islands is St. Thomas's. And there ended the first and longer part of a voyage unmarred by the least discomfort, discourtesy, or dulness, and full of enjoyment, for which thanks are due alike to captain, officers, crew, and passengers, and also to our much-maligned friend the North-East wind, who caught us up in the chops of the Channel, helped us graciously on nearly to the tropic of Cancer, giving us a more prosperous passage than the oldest hands recollect at this season, and then left us for a while to the delicious calms of the edge of the tropic, to catch us up again as the North-East Trade.

Truly, this voyage had already given us much for which to thank God. If safety and returning health, in an atmosphere in which the mere act of breathing is a pleasure, be things for which to be thankful, then we had reason to say in our hearts that which is sometimes best unsaid on paper.

Our first day in a tropic harbour was spent in what might be taken at moments for a dream, did not shells and flowers remain to bear witness to its reality. It was on Friday morning, December 17th, that we first sighted the New World; a rounded hill some fifteen hundred feet high, which was the end of Virgin Gorda. That resolved itself, as we ran on, into a cluster of long, low islands; St. John's appearing next on the horizon, then Tortola, and last of all St. Thomas's; all pink and purple in the sun, and warm-gray in the shadow, which again became, as we neared them one after the other, richest green, of scrub and down, with bright yellow and rusty rocks, plainly lava, in low cliffs along the shore. The upper outline of the hills reminded me, with its multitudinous little coves and dry gullies, of the Vivarais or Auvergne Hills; and still more of the sketches of the Chinese Tea-mountains in Fortune's book. Their water-line has been exposed, evidently for many ages, to the gnawing of the sea at the present level. Everywhere the lava cliffs are freshly broken, toppling down in dust and boulders, and leaving detached stacks and skerries, like that called the 'Indians,' from its supposed likeness to a group of red-brown savages afloat in a canoe. But, as far as I could see, there has been no upheaval since the land took its present shape. There is no trace of raised beaches, or of the terraces which would have inevitably been formed by upheaval on the soft sides of the lava hills. The numberless deep channels which part the isles and islets would rather mark depression still going on. Most beautiful meanwhile are the winding channels of blue water, like land-locked lakes, which part the Virgins from each other; and beautiful the white triangular sails of the canoe-rigged craft, which beat up and down them through strong currents and cockling seas. The clear air, the still soft outlines, the rich and yet delicate colouring, stir up a sense of purity and freshness, and peace and cheerfulness, such as is stirred up by certain views of the Mediterranean and its shores; only broken by one ghastly sight—the lonely mast of the ill-fated *Rhone*, standing up still where she sank with all her crew, in the hurricane of 1867.

At length, in the afternoon, we neared the last point, and turning inside an isolated and crumbling hummock, the Dutchman's Cap, saw before us, at the head of a little narrow harbour, the scarlet and purple roofs of St. Thomas's, piled up among orange-trees, at the foot of a green corrie, or rather couple of corries, some eight hundred feet high. There it was, as veritable a Dutch-oven for cooking fever in, with as veritable a dripping-pan for the poison when concocted in the tideless basin below the town, as man ever invented. And we were not sorry when the superintendent, coming on board, bade us steam back again out of the port, and round a certain Water-island, at the back of which is a second and healthier harbour, the Gri-gri channel. In the port close to the town we could discern another token of the late famous hurricane, the funnels and masts of the hapless *Columbia*, which lies still on the top of the sunken floating dock, immovable, as yet, by the art of man.

But some hundred yards on our right was a low cliff, which was even more interesting to some of us than either the town or the wreck; for it was covered with the first tropic vegetation which we had ever seen. Already on a sandy beach outside, we had caught sight of unmistakable coco-nut trees; some of them, however, dying, dead, even snapped short off, either by the force of the hurricane, or by the ravages of the beetle, which seems minded of late years to exterminate the coco-nut throughout the West Indies; belonging, we are told, to the Elaters—fire-fly, or skip-jack beetles. His grub, like that of his cousin, our English wire-worm, and his nearer cousin, the great wire-worm of the sugar-cane, eats into the pith and marrow of growing shoots; and as the palm, being an endogen, increases from within by one bud, and therefore by one shoot only, when that is eaten out nothing remains for the tree but to die. And so it happens that almost every coco-nut grove which we have seen has a sad and shabby look as if it existed (which it really does) merely on sufferance.

But on this cliff we could see, even with the naked eye, tall Aloes, gray-blue Cerei like huge branching candelabra, and bushes the foliage of which was utterly unlike anything in Northern Europe; while above the bright deep green of a patch of Guinea-grass marked cultivation, and a few fruit trees round a cottage told, by their dark baylike foliage, of fruits whose names alone were known to us.

Round Water-island we went, into a narrow channel between steep green hills, covered to their tops, as late as 1845, with sugar-cane, but now only with scrub, among which the ruins of mills and buildings stood sad and lonely. But Nature in this land of perpetual summer hides with a kind of eagerness every scar which man in his clumsiness leaves on the earth's surface; and all, though relapsing into primeval wildness, was green, soft, luxuriant, as if the hoe had never torn the ground, contrasting strangely with the water-scene; with the black steamers snorting in their sleep; the wrecks and condemned hulks, in process of breaking up, strewing the shores with their timbers; the boatfuls of Negroes gliding to and fro; and all the signs of our hasty, irreverent, wasteful, semi-barbarous mercantile system, which we call (for the time being only, it is to be hoped) civilisation. The engine had hardly stopped, when we were boarded from a fleet of negro boats, and huge bunches of plantains, yams, green oranges, junks of sugar-cane, were displayed upon the deck; and more than one of the ladies went through the ceremony of initiation into West Indian ways, which consisted in sucking sugar-cane, first pared for the sake of their teeth. The Negro's stronger incisors tear it without paring. Two amusing figures, meanwhile, had taken up their station close to the companion. Evidently privileged personages, they felt themselves on their own ground, and looked round patronisingly on the passengers, as ignorant foreigners who were too certain to be tempted by the treasures which they displayed to need any solicitations. One went by the name of Jamaica Joe, a Negro blacker than the night, in smart white coat and smart black trousers; a tall courtly gentleman, with the organ of self-interest, to judge from his physiognomy, very highly developed. But he was thrown into the shade by a stately brown lady, who was still very handsome—beautiful, if you will—and knew it, and had put on her gorgeous turban with grace, and plaited her short locks under it with care, and ignored the very existence of a mere Negro like Jamaica Joe, as she sat by her cigars, and slow-match, and eau-de-cologne at four times the right price, and mats, necklaces, bracelets, made of mimosa-seeds, white negro hats, nests of Curaçoa baskets, and so forth. They drove a thriving trade among all newcomers: but were somewhat disgusted to find that we, though new to the West Indies, were by no means new to West Indian wares, and therefore not of the same mind as a gentleman and lady who came fresh from the town next day, with nearly a bushel of white branching madrepores, which they were going to carry as coals to Newcastle, six hundred miles down the islands. Poor Joe tried to sell us a nest of Curaçoa baskets for seven shillings; retired after a firm refusal; came up again to R——, after a couple of hours, and said, in a melancholy and reproachful voice, 'Da—— take dem for four shillings and sixpence. I give dem you.'

But now——. Would we go on shore? To the town? Not we, who came to see Nature, not towns. Some went off on honest business; some on such pleasure as can be found in baking streets, hotel bars, and billiard-rooms: but the one place on which our eyes were set was a little cove a quarter of a mile off, under the steep hill, where a white line of sand shone between blue water and green wood. A few yards broad of sand, and then impenetrable jungle, among which we could see, below, the curved yellow stems of the coco-nuts; and higher up the straight gray stems and broad fan-leaves of Carat palms; which I regret to say we did not reach. Oh for a boat to get into that paradise! There was three-quarters of an hour left, between dinner and dark; and in three-quarters of an hour what might not be seen in a world where all was new? The kind chief officer, bidding us not trust negro boats on such a trip, lent us one of the ship's, with four honest fellows, thankful enough to escape from heat and smoke; and away we went with two select companions—the sportsman and our scientific friend —to land, for the first time, in the New World.

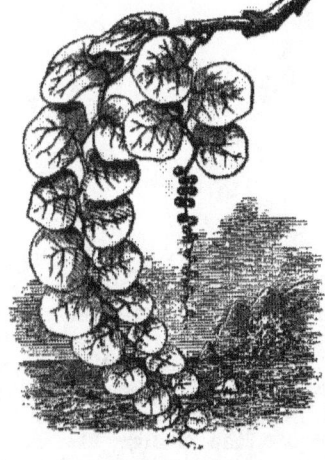
SEASIDE GRAPE.

As we leaped on shore on that white sand, what feelings passed through the heart of at least one of us, who found the dream of forty years translated into fact at last, are best, perhaps, left untold here. But it must be confessed that ere we had stood for two minutes staring at the green wall opposite us, astonishment soon swallowed up, for the time, all other emotions. Astonishment, not at the vast size of anything, for the scrub was not thirty feet high; nor at the gorgeous colours, for very few plants or trees were in flower; but at the wonderful wealth of life. The massiveness, the strangeness, the variety, the very length of the young and still growing shoots was a wonder. We tried, at first in vain, to fix our eyes on some one dominant or typical form, while every form was clamouring, as it were, to be looked at, and a fresh Dryad gazed out of every bush, and with wooing eyes asked to be wooed again. The first two plants, perhaps, we looked steadily at were the *Ipomœa pes capræ*, lying along the sand in straight shoots thirty feet long, and growing longer, we fancied, while we looked at it, with large bilobed green leaves at every joint, and here and there a great purple convolvulus flower; and next, what we knew at once for the 'shore-grape.'[1] We had fancied it (and correctly) to be a mere low bushy tree with roundish leaves. But what a bush! with drooping boughs, arched over and through each other, shoots already six feet long, leaves as big as the hand shining like dark velvet, a crimson mid-rib down each, and tiled over each other — 'imbricated,' as the botanists would say, in that fashion, which gives its peculiar solidity and richness of light and shade to the foliage of an old sycamore; and among these noble shoots and noble leaves, pendent

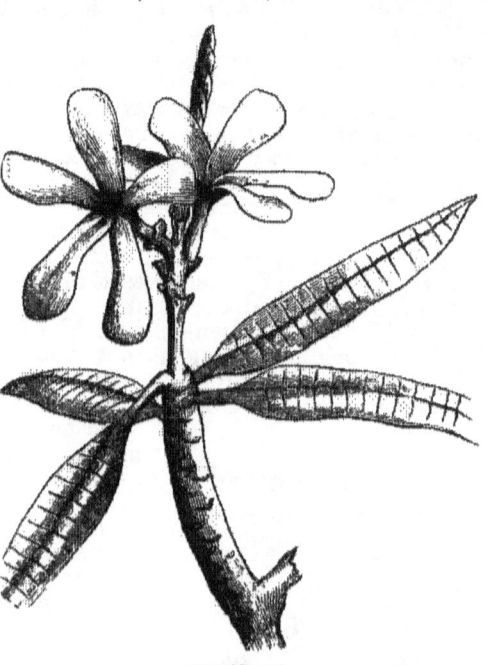

FRANGIPANI.

everywhere, long tapering spires of green grapes. This shore-grape, which the West Indians esteem as we might a bramble, we found to be, without exception, the most beautiful broad-leafed plant which we had ever seen. Then we admired the Frangipani,[2] a tall and almost leafless shrub with thick fleshy shoots, bearing, in this species, white flowers, which have the fragrance peculiar to certain white blossoms, to the jessamine, the tuberose, the orange, the Gardenia, the night-flowering Cereus; then the Cacti and Aloes; then the first coco-nut, with its last year's leaves pale yellow, its new leaves deep green, and its trunk ringing, when struck,

---

[1] *Coccoloba uvifera.*   [2] *Plumieria.*

like metal; then the sensitive plants; then creeping lianes of a dozen different kinds. Then we shrank back from our first glimpse of a little swamp of foul brown water, backed up by the sand-brush, with trees in every stage of decay, fallen and tangled into a doleful thicket, through which the spider-legged Mangroves rose on stilted roots. We turned, in wholesome dread, to the white beach outside, and picked up—amid, alas! wreck, everywhere wreck—shells—old friends in the cabinets at home —as earnests to ourselves that all was not a dream: delicate prickly Pinnæ; 'Noah's-arks' in abundance; great Strombi, their lips and outer shell broken away, disclosing the rosy cameo within, and looking on the rough beach pitifully tender and flesh-like; lumps and fragments of coral innumerable, reminding us by their worn and rounded shapes of those which abound in so many secondary strata; and then hastened on board the boat; for the sun had already fallen, the purple night set in, and from the woods on shore a chorus of frogs had commenced chattering, quacking, squealing, whistling, not to cease till sunrise.

So ended our first trip in the New World; and we got back to the ship, but not to sleep. Already a coal-barge lay on either side of her, and over the coals we scrambled, through a scene which we would fain forget. Black women on one side were doing men's work, with heavy coal-baskets on their heads, amid screaming, chattering, and language of which, happily, we understood little or nothing. On the other, a gang of men and boys, who, as the night fell, worked, many of them, altogether naked, their glossy bronze figures gleaming in the red lamplight, and both men and women singing over their work in wild choruses, which, when the screaming cracked voices of the women were silent, and the really rich tenors of the men had it to themselves, were not unpleasant. A lad, seeming the poet of the gang, stood on the sponson, and in the momentary intervals of work improvised some story, while the men below took up and finished each verse with a refrain, piercing, sad, running up and down large and easy intervals. The tunes were many and seemingly familiar, all barbaric, often ending in the minor key, and reminding us much, perhaps too much, of the old Gregorian tones. The words were all but unintelligible. In one song we caught 'New York' again and again, and then 'Captain he heard it, he was troubled in him mind.'

'Ya-he-ho-o-hu'—followed the chorus.

'Captain he go to him cabin, he drink him wine and whisky——'

'Ya-he,' etc.

'You go to America? You as well go to heaven.'

'Ya-he,' etc.

These were all the scraps of negro poetry which we could

overhear; while on deck the band was playing quadrilles and waltzes, setting the negro shoveller dancing in the black water at the barge-bottom, shovel in hand; and pleasant white folks danced under the awning, till the contrast between the refinement within and the brutality without became very painful. For brutality it was, not merely in the eyes of the sentimentalist, but in those of the moralist; still more in the eyes of those who try to believe that all God's human children may be somewhen, somewhere, somehow, reformed into His likeness. We were shocked to hear that at another island the evils of coaling are still worse; and that the white authorities have tried in vain to keep them down. The coaling system is, no doubt, demoralising in itself, as it enables Negroes of the lowest class to earn enough in one day to keep them in idleness, even in luxury, for a week or more, till the arrival of the next steamer. But what we saw proceeded rather from the mere excitability and coarseness of half-civilised creatures than from any deliberate depravity; and we were told that, in the island just mentioned, the Negroes, when forced to coal on Sunday, or on Christmas Day, always abstain from noise or foul language, and, if they sing, sing nothing but hymns. It is easy to sneer at such a fashion as formalism. It would be wiser to consider whether the first step in religious training must not be obedience to some such external positive law; whether the savage must not be taught that there are certain things which he ought never to do, by being taught that there is one day at least on which he shall not do them. How else is man to learn that the Laws of Right and Wrong, like the laws of the physical world, are entirely independent of him, his likes or dislikes, knowledge or ignorance of them; that by Law he is environed from his cradle to his grave, and that it is at his own peril that he disobeys the Law? A higher religion may, and ought to, follow, one in which the Law becomes a Law of Liberty, and a Gospel, because it is loved, and obeyed for its own sake; but even he who has attained to that must be reminded again and again, alas! that the Law which he loves does not depend for its sanction on his love of it, on his passing frames or feelings; but is as awfully independent of him as it is of the veriest heathen. And that lesson the Sabbath does teach as few or no other institutions can. The man who says, and says rightly, that to the Christian all days ought to be Sabbaths, may be answered, and answered rightly, 'All the more reason for keeping one day which shall be a Sabbath, whether you are in a sabbatical mood or not. All the more reason for keeping one day holy, as a pattern of what all days should be.' So we will be glad if the Negro has got thus far, as an earnest that he may some day get farther still.

That night, however, he kept no Sabbath, and we got no sleep; and were glad enough, before sunrise, to escape once more to the cove we had visited the evening before; not that it was prettier or more curious than others, but simply because it is better, for those who wish to learn accurately, to see one thing twice than many things once. A lesson is never learnt till it is learnt over many times, and a spot is best understood by staying in it and mastering it. In natural history the old scholar's saw of 'Cave hominem unius libri' may be paraphrased by 'He is a thoroughly good naturalist who knows one parish thoroughly.'

So back to our little beach we went, and walked it all over again, finding, of course, many things which had escaped us the night before. We saw our first Melocactus, and our first nightblowing Cereus creeping over the rocks. We found our first tropic orchid, with white, lilac, and purple flowers on a stalk three feet high. We saw our first wild pines (*Tillandsias*, etc.) clinging parasitic on the boughs of strange trees, or nestling among the angular limb-like shoots of the columnar Cereus. We learnt to distinguish the poisonous Manchineel; and were thankful, in serious earnest, that we had happily plucked none the night before, when we were snatching at every new leaf; for its milky juice, by mere dropping on the skin, burns like the poisoned tunic of Nessus, and will even, when the head is injured by it, cause blindness and death. We gathered a nosegay of the loveliest flowers, under a burning sun, within ten days of Christmas; and then wandered off the shore up a little path in the red lava, toward a farm where we expected to see fresh curiosities, and not in vain. On one side of the path a hedge of Pinguin (*Bromelia*)—the plants like huge pine-apple plants without the fruit—was but three feet high, but from its prickles utterly impenetrable to man or beast; and inside the hedge, a tree like a straggling pear, with huge green calabashes growing out of its bark—here was actually *Crescentia Cujete*—the plaything of one's childhood—alive and growing. The other side was low scrub—prickly shrubs like acacias and mimosas, covered with a creeping vine with brilliant yellow hair (we had seen it already from the ship, gilding large patches of the slopes), most like European dodder. Among it rose the tall *Calotropis procera*, with its fleshy gray stems and leaves, and its azure of lovely lilac flowers, with curious columns of stamens in each—an Asclepiad introduced from the Old World, where it ranges from tropical Africa to Afghanistan; and so on, and so on, up to a little farmyard, very like a Highland one in most things, want of neatness included, save that huge spotted Trochi were scattered before the door, instead of buckies or periwinkles; and in the midst of the yard grew, side by side, the common accompaniment of a West India kitchen door, the magic trees, whose leaves rubbed on the toughest meat make it tender on the spot, and whose fruit makes the best of sauce or pickle to be eaten therewith—namely, a male and female Papaw (*Carica Papaya*), their stems some fifteen feet high, with a flat crown of mallow-like leaves, just beneath which, in the male, grew clusters of fragrant flowerets, in the female, clusters of unripe fruit. On through the farmyard, picking fresh flowers at every step, and down to a shady cove (for the sun, even at eight o'clock in December, was becoming uncomfortably fierce), and again into the shore-grape wood. We had already discovered, to our pain, that almost everything in the bush had prickles, of all imaginable shapes and sizes ; and now, touching a low tree, one of our party was seized as by a briar, through clothes and into skin, and, in escaping, found on the tree (*Guilandina Bonducella*) rounded prickly pods, which, being opened, proved to contain the gray horse-nicker-beads of our childhood.

Up and down the white sand we wandered, collecting shells, as did the sailors, gladly enough, and then rowed back, over a bottom of white sand, bedded here and there with the short manati-grass (*Thalassia Testudinum*), one of the few flowering plants which, like our *Zostera*, or grass-wrack, grows at the bottom of the sea. But, wherever the bottom was stony, we could see huge prickly sea-urchins, huger brainstone corals, round and gray, and branching corals likewise, such as, when cleaned, may be seen in any curiosity shop. These, and a flock of brown and gray pelicans sailing over our head, were fresh tokens to us of where we were.

As we were displaying our nosegay on deck, on our return, to some who had stayed stifling on board, and who were inclined (as West Indians are) at once to envy and to pooh-pooh the superfluous energy of newcome Europeans, R—— drew out a large and lovely flower, pale yellow, with a tiny green apple or two, and leaves like those of an Oleander. The brown lady, who was again at her post on deck, walked up to her in silence, uninvited, and with a commanding air waved the thing away. 'Dat manchineel. Dat poison. Throw dat overboard.' R——, who knew it was not manchineel, whispered to a bystander, 'Ce n'est pas vrai.' But the brown lady was a linguist. 'Ah! mais c'est vrai,' cried she, with flashing teeth ; and retired, muttering her contempt of English ignorance and impertinence.

And, as it befell, she was, if not quite right, at least not quite wrong. For when we went into the cabin, we and our unlucky yellow flower were flown at by another brown lady, in another gorgeous turban, who had become on the voyage a friend and an intimate ; for she was the nurse of the baby who had been the light of the eyes of the whole quarter-deck ever since we left Southampton—God bless it, and its mother, and beautiful Mon Nid, where she dwells beneath the rock, as exquisite as one of her own humming-birds. We were so scolded about this poor little green apple that we set to work to find out what it was, after promising at least not to eat it. And it proved to be *Thevetia neriifolia*, and a very deadly poison.

This was the first (though by no means the last) warning

which we got not to meddle rashly with 'poison-bush,' lest that should befall us which befell a scientific West Indian of old. For hearing much of the edible properties of certain European toadstools, he resolved to try a few experiments in his own person on West Indian ones; during the course of which he found himself one evening, after a good toad-stool dinner, raving mad. The doctor was sent for, and brought him round, a humbled man. But a heavier humiliation awaited him, when his negro butler, who had long looked down on him for his botanical studies, entered with his morning cup of coffee. 'Now, Massa,' said he, in a tone of triumphant pity, 'I think you no go out any more cut bush and eat him.'

If we had wanted any further proof that we were in the Tropics, we might have had it in the fearful heat of the next few hours, when the *Shannon* lay with a steamer on each side, one destined for 'The Gulf,' the other for 'The Islands'; and not a breath of air was to be got till late in the afternoon, when (amid shaking of hands and waving of handkerchiefs, as hearty as if we the 'Island-bound,' and they the 'Gulf-bound,' and the officers of the *Shannon* had known each other fourteen years instead of fourteen days) we steamed out, past the Little Saba rock, which was said (but it seems incorrectly) to have burst into smoke and flame during the earthquake, and then away to the south and east for the Islands: having had our first taste, but, thank God, not our last, of the joys of the 'Earthly Paradise.'

THE BOCAS.

CHAPTER II

DOWN THE ISLANDS

I HAD heard and read much, from boyhood, about these 'Lesser Antilles.' I had pictured them to myself a thousand times: but I was altogether unprepared for their beauty and grandeur. For hundreds of miles, day after day, the steamer carried us past a shifting diorama of scenery, which may be likened to Vesuvius and the Bay of Naples, repeated again and again, with every possible variation of the same type of delicate loveliness.

Under a cloudless sky, upon a sea, lively yet not unpleasantly rough, we thrashed and leaped along. Ahead of us, one after another, rose high on the southern horizon banks of gray cloud, from under each of which, as we neared it, descended the shoulder of a mighty mountain, dim and gray. Nearer still the gray changed to purple; lowlands rose out of the sea, sloping upwards with those grand and simple concave curves which betoken, almost always, volcanic land. Nearer still, the purple changed to green. Tall palm-trees and engine-houses stood out against the sky; the surf gleamed white around the base of isolated rocks. A little nearer, and we were under the lee, or western side, of the island. The sea grew smooth as glass; we entered the shade of the island-cloud, and slid along in still unfathomable blue water, close under the shore of what should have been one of the Islands of the Blest.

It was easy, in presence of such scenery, to conceive the exaltation which possessed the souls of the first discoverers of the West Indies. What wonder if they seemed to themselves to have burst into Fairyland—to be at the gates of The Earthly Paradise? With such a climate, such a soil, such vegetation, such fruits, what luxury must not have seemed possible to the dwellers along those shores? What riches too, of gold and jewels, might not be hidden among those forest-shrouded glens and peaks? And beyond, and beyond again, ever new islands, new continents perhaps, an inexhaustible wealth of yet undiscovered worlds.

No wonder that the men rose above themselves, for good and for evil; that having, as it seemed to them, found infinitely, they hoped infinitely, and dared infinitely. They were a dumb generation and an unlettered, those old Conquistadores. They did not, as we do now, analyse and describe their own impressions: but they felt them nevertheless; and felt them, it may be, all the more intensely, because they could not utter them; and so went, half intoxicated, by day and night, with the beauty and the wonder round them, till the excitement overpowered alike their reason and their conscience; and, frenzied with superstition and greed, with contempt and hatred of the heathen Indians, and often with mere drink and sunshine, they did deeds which, like all wicked deeds, avenge themselves, and are avenging themselves, from Mexico to Chili, unto this very day.

I said that these islands resembled Vesuvius and the Bay of Naples. Like causes have produced like effects; and each island is little but the peak of a volcano, down whose shoulders lava and ash have slidden toward the sea. Some carry several crater cones, complicating at once the structure and scenery of the island; but the majority carry but a single cone, like that little island, or rather rock, of Saba, which is the first of the Antilles under the lee of which the steamer passes. Santa Cruz, which is left to leeward, is a long, low, ragged island, of the same form as St. Thomas's and the Virgins, and belonging, I should suppose, to the same formation. But Saba rises sheer out of the sea some 1500 feet or more, without flat ground, or even harbour. From a little landing-place to leeward a stair runs up 800 feet into the bosom of the old volcano; and in that hollow live some 1200 honest Dutch, and some 800 Negroes, who were, till of late years, their slaves, at least in law. But in Saba, it is said, the whites were really the slaves, and the Negroes the masters. For they went off whither and when they liked; earned money about the islands, and brought it home; expected their masters to keep them when out of work: and not in vain. The island was, happily for it, too poor for sugar-growing and the 'Grande Culture'; the Dutch were never tempted to increase the number of their slaves; looked upon the few they had as friends and children; and when emancipation came, no change whatsoever ensued, it is said, in the semi-feudal relation between the black men and the white. So these good Dutch live peacefully aloft in their volcano, which it is to be hoped will not explode again. They grow garden crops; among which, I understand, are several products of the temperate zone, the air being, at that height, pleasantly cool. They sell their produce about the islands. They build boats up in the crater—the best boats in all the West Indies—and lower them down the cliff to the sea. They hire themselves out too, not having lost their forefathers' sea-going instincts, as sailors about all those seas, and are, like their boats, the best in those parts. They all speak English; and though they are nominally Lutherans, are glad of the services of the excellent Bishop of Antigua, who pays them periodical visits. He described them as virtuous, shrewd, simple, healthy folk, retaining, in spite of the tropic sun, the same clear white and red complexions which their ancestors brought from Holland two hundred years ago—a proof, among many, that the white man need not degenerate in these isles.

Saba has, like most of these islands, its 'Somma' like that of Vesuvius; an outer ring of lava, the product of older eruptions, surrounding a central cone, the product of some newer one. But even this latter, as far as I could judge by the glass, is very ancient. Little more than the core of the central cone is left. The rest has been long since destroyed by rains and winds. A

ST. EUSTATIUS.

white cliff at the south end of the island should be examined by geologists. It belongs probably to that formation of tertiary calcareous marl so often seen in the West Indies, especially at Barbadoes: but if so, it must, to judge from the scar which it makes seaward, have been upheaved long ago, and like the whole island—and indeed all the islands—betokens an immense antiquity.

Much more recent—in appearance at least—is the little isle of St. Eustatius, or at least the crater-cone, with its lip broken down at one spot, which makes up five-sixths of the island. St.

Eustatius may have been in eruption, though there is no record of it, during historic times, and looks more unrepentant and capable of misbehaving itself again than does any other crater-cone in the Antilles; far more so than the Souffrière in St. Vincent which exploded in 1812.

But these two are mere rocks. It is not till the traveller arrives at St. Kitts that he sees what a West Indian island is.

The 'Mother of the Antilles,' as she is called, is worthy of her name. Everywhere from the shore the land sweeps up, slowly at first, then rapidly, toward the central mass, the rugged peak whereof goes by the name of Mount Misery. Only once, and then but for a moment, did we succeed in getting a sight of the actual summit, so pertinaciously did the clouds crawl round it. 3700 feet aloft a pyramid of black lava rises above the broken walls of an older crater, and is, to judge from its knife-edge, flat top, and concave eastern side, the last remnant of an inner cone which has been washed, or more probably blasted, away. Beneath it, according to the report of an islander to Dr. Davy (and what I heard was to the same effect), is a deep hollow, longer than it is wide, without an outlet, walled in by precipices and steep declivities, from fissures in which steam and the fumes of sulphur are emitted. Sulphur in crystals abounds, encrusting the rocks and loose stones; and a stagnant pool of rain-water occupies the bottom of the Souffrière. A dangerous neighbour—but as long as he keeps his temper, as he has done for three hundred years at least, a most beneficent one—is this great hill, which took, in Columbus's imagination, the form of the giant St. Christopher bearing on his shoulder the infant Christ, and so gave a name to the whole island.

From the lava and ash ejected from this focus, the whole soils of the island have been formed; soils of still unexhausted fertility, save when—as must needs be in a volcanic region—patches of mere rapilli and scoriæ occur. The mountain has hurled these out; and everywhere, as a glance of the eye shows, the tropic rains are carrying them yearly down to the lowland, exposing fresh surfaces to the action of the air, and, by continual denudation and degradation, remanuring the soil. Everywhere, too, are gullies sawn in the slopes, which terminate above in deep and narrow glens, giving, especially when alternated with long lava-streams, a ridge-and-furrow look to this and most other of the Antilles. Dr. Davy, with his usual acuteness of eye and soundness of judgment, attributes them rather to 'water acting on loose volcanic ashes' than to 'rents and fissures, the result of sudden and violent force.' Doubtless he is in the right. Thus, and thus only, has been formed the greater part of the most beautiful scenery in the West Indies; and I longed again and again, as I looked at it, for the company of my friend and teacher, Colonel George Greenwood, that I might show him, on island after island, such manifold corroborations of his theories in *Rain and Rivers*.

But our eyes were drawn off, at almost the second glance, from mountain-peaks and glens to the slopes of cultivated lowland, sheeted with bright green cane, and guinea-grass, and pigeon pea; and that not for their own sakes, but for the sake of objects so utterly unlike anything which we had ever seen, that it was not easy, at first, to discover what they were. Gray pillars, which seemed taller than the tallest poplars, smooth and cylindrical as those of a Doric temple, each carrying a flat head of darkest green, were ranged along roadsides and round fields, or stood, in groups or singly, near engine-works, or towered above rich shrubberies which shrouded comfortable country-houses. It was not easy, as I have said, to believe that these strange and noble things were trees: but such they were. At last we beheld, with wonder and delight, the pride of the West Indies, the Cabbage Palms—Palmistes of the French settlers—which botanists have well named *Oreodoxa*, the 'glory of the mountains.' We saw them afterwards a hundred times in their own native forests; and when they rose through tangled masses of richest vegetation, mixed with other and smaller species of palms, their form, fantastic though it was, harmonised well with hundreds of forms equally fantastic. But here they seemed, at first sight, out of place, incongruous, and artificial, standing amid no kindred forms, and towering over a cultivation and civilisation which might have been mistaken, seen from the sea, for wealthy farms along some English shore. Gladly would we have gone on shore, were it but to have stood awhile under those Palmistes; and an invitation was not wanting to a pretty tree-shrouded house on a low cliff a mile off, where doubtless every courtesy and many a luxury would have awaited us. But it could not be. We watched kind folk rowed to shore without us; and then turned to watch the black flotilla under our quarter.

The first thing that caught our eye on board the negro boats which were alongside was, of course, the baskets of fruits and vegetables, of which one of us at least had been hearing all his life. At St. Thomas's we had been introduced to bananas (figs, as they are miscalled in the West Indies); to the great green oranges, thick-skinned and fragrant; to those junks of sugar-cane, some two feet long, which Cuffy and Cuffy's ladies delight to gnaw, walking, sitting, and standing; increasing thereby the size of their lips, and breaking out, often enough, their upper front teeth. We had seen, and eaten too, the sweet sop[1]—a passable fruit, or rather congeries of fruits, looking like a green and purple strawberry, of the bigness of an orange. It is the cousin of the prickly sour-sop;[2] of the really delicious, but to me unknown, Chirimoya;[3] and of the custard apple,[4] containing

---

[1] *Anona squamosa.*   [2] *A. muricata.*   [3] *A. cherimolia.*   [4] *A. reticulata.*

a pulp which (as those who remember the delectable pages of *Tom Cringle* know) bears a startling likeness to brains. Bunches of grapes, at St. Kitts, lay among these; and at St. Lucia we saw with them, for the first time, Avocado, or Alligator pears, *alias* midshipman's butter;[1] large round brown fruits, to be eaten with pepper and salt by those who list. With these, in open baskets, lay bright scarlet capsicums, green coco-nuts tinged with orange, great roots of yam[2] and cush-cush,[3] with strange pulse of various kinds and hues. The contents of these vegetable baskets were often as gay-coloured as the gaudy gowns, and still gaudier turbans, of the women who offered them for sale.

Screaming and jabbering, the Negroes and Negresses thrust each other's boats about, scramble from one to the other with gestures of wrath and defiance, and seemed at every moment about to fall to fisticuffs and to upset themselves among the sharks. But they did neither. Their excitement evaporated in noise. To their 'ladies,' to do them justice, the men were always civil, while the said 'ladies' bullied them and ordered them about without mercy. The negro women are, without doubt, on a more thorough footing of equality with the men than the women of any white race. The causes, I believe, are two. In the first place there is less difference between the sexes in mere physical strength and courage; and watching the average Negresses, one can well believe the stories of those terrible Amazonian guards of the King of Dahomey, whose boast is, that they are no longer women, but men. There is no doubt that, in case of a rebellion, the black women of the West Indies would be as formidable, cutlass in hand, as the men. The other cause is the exceeding ease with which, not merely food, but gay clothes and ornaments, can be procured by light labour. The negro woman has no need to marry and make herself the slave of a man, in order to get a home and subsistence. Independent she is, for good and evil; and independent she takes care to remain; and no schemes for civilising the Negro will have any deep or permanent good effect which do not take note of, and legislate for, this singular fact.

Meanwhile, it was a comfort to one fresh from the cities of the Old World, and the short and stunted figures, the mesquin and scrofulous visages, which crowd our alleys and back wynds, to see everywhere health, strength, and goodly stature, especially among women. Nowhere in the West Indies are to be seen those haggard down-trodden mothers, grown old before their time, too common in England, and commoner still in France. Health, 'rude' in every sense of the word, is the mark of the negro woman, and of the negro man likewise. Their faces shine with fatness; they seem to enjoy, they do enjoy, the mere

---

[1] *Persea gratissima.*   [2] *Dioscorea.*   [3] *Colocasia esculenta.*

act of living, like the lizard on the wall. It may be said—it must be said—that, if they be human beings (as they are), they are meant for something more than mere enjoyment of life. Well and good: but are they not meant for enjoyment likewise? Let us take the beam out of our own eye, before we take the mote out of theirs; let us, before we complain of them for being too healthy and comfortable, remember that we have at home here tens of thousands of paupers, rogues, whatnot, who are not a whit more civilised, intellectual, virtuous, or spiritual than the Negro, and are meanwhile neither healthy nor comfortable. The Negro may have the *corpus sanum* without the *mens sana*. But what of those whose souls and bodies are alike unsound?

Away south, along the low spit at the south end of the island, where are salt-pans which, I suspect, lie in now extinguished craters; and past little Nevis, the conical ruin, as it were, of a volcanic island. It was probably joined to the low end of St. Kitts not many years ago. It is separated from it now only by a channel called the Narrows, some four to six miles across, and very shallow, there being not more than four fathoms in many places, and infested with reefs, whether of true coral or of volcanic rock I should be glad to know. A single peak, with its Souffrière, rises to some 2000 feet; right and left of it are two lower hills, fragments, apparently, of a Somma, or older and larger crater. The lava and ash slide in concave slopes of fertile soil down to the sea, forming an island some four miles by three, which was in the seventeenth century a little paradise, containing 4000 white citizens, who had dwindled down in 1805, under the baneful influences of slavery, to 1300; in 1832 (the period of emancipation) to 500; and in 1854 to only 170.[1] A happy place, however, it is said still to be, with a population of more than 10,000, who, as there is happily no Crown land in the island, cannot squat, and so return to their original savagery; but are well-ordered and peaceable, industrious, and well-taught, and need, it is said, not only no soldiers, but no police.

One spot on the little island we should have liked much to have seen: the house where Nelson, after his marriage with Mrs. Nisbet, a lady of Nevis, dwelt awhile in peace and purity. Happier for him, perhaps, though not for England, had he never left that quiet nest.

And now, on the leeward bow, another gray mountain island rose; and on the windward another, lower and longer. The former was Montserrat, which I should have gladly visited, as I had been invited to do. For little Montserrat is just now the scene of a very hopeful and important experiment.[2] The Messrs. Sturge have established there a large plantation of

[1] Dr. Davy's *West Indies.*
[2] An account of the Souffrière of Montserrat is given by Dr. Nugent, Geological Society's *Transactions,* vol. i., 1811.

limes, and a manufactory of lime-juice, which promises to be able to supply, in good time, vast quantities of that most useful of all sea-medicines.

Their connection with the Society of Friends, and indeed the very name of Sturge, is a guarantee that such a work will be carried on for the benefit, not merely of the capitalists, but of the coloured people who are employed. Already, I am assured, a marked improvement has taken place among them; and I, for one, heartily bid God-speed to the enterprise: to any enterprise, indeed, which tends to divert labour and capital from that exclusive sugar-growing which has been most injurious, I verily believe the bane, of the West Indies. On that subject I may have to say more in a future chapter. I ask the reader, meanwhile, to follow, as the ship's head goes round to windward toward Antigua.

Antigua is lower, longer, and flatter than the other islands. It carries no central peak: but its wildness of ragged uplands forms, it is said, a natural fortress, which ought to be impregnable; and its loyal and industrious people boast that, were every other West Indian island lost, the English might make a stand in Antigua long enough to enable them to reconquer the whole. I should have feared, from the look of the island, that no large force could hold out long in a country so destitute of water as those volcanic hills, rusty, ragged, treeless, almost sad and desolate—if any land could be sad and desolate with such a blue sea leaping around and such a blue sky blazing above. Those who wish to know the agricultural capabilities of Antigua, and to know, too, the good sense and courage, the justice and humanity, which have enabled the Antiguans to struggle on and upward through all their difficulties, in spite of drought, hurricane, and earthquake, till permanent prosperity seems now become certain, should read Dr. Davy's excellent book, which I cannot too often recommend. For us, we could only give a hasty look at its southern volcanic cliffs; while we regretted that we could not inspect the marine strata of the eastern parts of the island, with their calcareous marls and limestones, hardened clays and cherts, and famous silicified trees, which offer important problems to the geologist, as yet not worked out.[1]

We could well believe, as the steamer ran into English Harbour, that Antigua was still subject to earthquakes; and had been shaken, with great loss of property though not of life, in the Guadaloupe earthquake of 1843, when 5000 lives were lost in the town of Point-à-Pitre alone. The only well-marked effect which Dr. Davy could hear of, apart from damage to artificial structures, was the partial sinking of a causeway leading to Rat Island, in the harbour of St. John. No wonder:

[1] For what is known of these, consult Dr. Nugent's 'Memoir on the Geology of Antigua,' *Transactions* of Geological Society, vol. v., 1821. See also Humboldt, *Personal Narrative*, book v. cap. 14.

if St. John's harbour be—as from its shape on the map it probably is—simply an extinct crater, or group of craters, like English Harbour. A more picturesque or more uncanny little hole than that latter we had never yet seen: but there are many such harbours about these islands, which nature, for the time being at least, has handed over from the dominion of fire to that of water. Past low cliffs of ash and volcanic boulder, sloping westward to the sea, which is eating them fast away, the steamer runs in through a deep crack, a pistol-shot in width. On the east side a strange section of gray lava and ash is gnawn into caves. On the right, a bluff rock of black lava dips sheer into water several fathoms deep; and you anchor at once inside an irregular group of craters, having passed through a gap in one of their sides, which has probably been torn out by a lava flow. Whether the land, at the time of the flow, was higher or lower than at present, who can tell? This is certain, that the first basin is for half of its circumference circular, and walled with ash beds, which seem to slope outward from it. To the left it leads away into a long creek, up which, somewhat to our surprise, we saw neat government-houses and quays; and between them and us, a noble ironclad and other ships of war at anchor close against lava and ash cliffs. But right ahead, the dusty sides of the crater are covered with strange bushes, its glaring shingle spotted with bright green Manchineels; while on the cliffs around, aloes innumerable, seemingly the imported American Agave, send up their groups of huge fat pointed leaves from crannies so arid that one would fancy a moss would wither in them. A strange place it is, and strangely hot likewise; and one could not but fear a day—it is to be hoped long distant—when it will be hotter still.

Out of English Harbour, after taking on board fruit and bargaining for beads, for which Antigua is famous, we passed the lonely rock of Redonda, toward a mighty mountain which lay under a sheet of clouds of corresponding vastness. That was Guadaloupe. The dark undersides of the rolling clouds mingled with the dark peaks and ridges, till we could not see where earth ended and vapour began; and the clouds from far to the eastward up the wind massed themselves on the island, and then ceased suddenly to leeward, leaving the sky clear and the sea brilliant.

I should be glad to know the cause of this phenomenon, which we saw several times among the islands, but never in greater perfection than on nearing Nevis from the south on our return. In that case, however, the cloud continued to leeward. It came up from the east for full ten miles, an advancing column of tall ghostly cumuli, leaden, above a leaden sea; and slid toward the island, whose lines seemed to leap up once to meet them; fail; then, in a second leap, to plunge the crater-peak high into the mist; and then to sink down again into the western sea, so gently that the line of shore and sea was indistinguishable. But above, the cloud-procession passed on, shattered by its contact with the mountain, and transfigured as it neared the setting sun into long upward streaming lines of rack, purple and primrose against a saffron sky, while Venus lingered low between cloud and sea, a spark of fire glittering through dull red haze.

And now the steamer ran due south, across the vast basin which is ringed round by Antigua, Montserrat, and Guadaloupe, with St. Kitts and Nevis showing like tall gray ghosts to the north-west. Higher and higher ahead rose the great mountain mass of Guadaloupe, its head in its own canopy of cloud. The island falls into the sea sharply to leeward. But it stretches out to windward in a long line of flat land edged with low cliff, and studded with large farms and engine-houses. It might be a bit of the Isle of Thanet, or of the Lothians, were it not for those umbrella-like Palmistes, a hundred feet high, which stand out everywhere against the sky. At its northern end, a furious surf was beating on a sandy beach ; and beyond that, dim and distant, loomed up the low flat farther island, known by the name of Grande Terre.

Guadaloupe, as some of my readers may know, consists, properly speaking, of two islands, divided by a swamp and a narrow salt-water river. The eastward half, or Grande Terre, which is composed of marine strata, is hardly seen in the island voyage, and then only at a distance, first behind the westward Basse Terre, and then behind other little islands, the Saintes and Mariegalante. But the westward island, rising in one lofty volcanic mass which hides the eastern island from view, is perhaps, for mere grandeur, the grandest in the Archipelago. The mountains—among which are, it is said, fourteen extinct craters—range upward higher and higher toward the southern end, with corries and glens, which must be, when seen near, hanging gardens of stupendous size. The forests seem to be as magnificent as they were in the days of Père Labat. Tiny knots on distant cliff-tops, when looked at through the glass, are found to be single trees of enormous height and breadth. Gullies hundreds of feet in depth, rushing downwards toward the sea, represent the rush of the torrents which have helped, through thousands of rainy seasons, to scoop them out and down.

But all this grandeur and richness culminates, toward the southern end, in one great crater-peak 5000 feet in height, at the foot of which lies the Port of Basse Terre, or Bourg St. François.

We never were so fortunate as to see the Souffrière entirely free from cloud. The lower, wider, and more ancient crater was generally clear : but out of the midst of it rose a second cone buried in darkness and mist. Once only we caught sight of part of its lip, and the sight was one not to be forgotten,

The sun was rising behind the hills. The purple mountain was backed by clear blue sky. High above it hung sheets of orange cloud lighted from underneath; lower down, and close upon the hill-tops, curved sheets of bright white mist

> 'Stooped from heaven, and took the shape,
> With fold on fold, of mountain and of cape.'

And under them, again, the crater seethed with gray mist, among which, at one moment, we could discern portions of its lip; not smooth, like that of Vesuvius, but broken into awful peaks and chasms hundreds of feet in height. As the sun rose, level lights of golden green streamed round the peak right and left over the downs: but only for a while. As the sky-clouds vanished in his blazing rays, earth-clouds rolled up below from the valleys behind; wreathed and weltered about the great black teeth of the crater; and then sinking among them, and below them, shrouded the whole cone in purple darkness for the day; while in the foreground blazed in the sunshine broad slopes of cane-field; below them again the town, with handsome houses and old-fashioned churches and convents, dating possibly from the seventeenth century, embowered in mangoes, tamarinds, and palmistes; and along the beach a market beneath a row of trees, with canoes drawn up to be unladen, and gay dresses of every hue. The surf whispered softly on the beach. The cheerful murmur of voices came off the shore, and above it the tinkling of some little bell, calling good folks to early mass. A cheery, brilliant picture as man could wish to see: but marred by two ugly elements. A mile away on the low northern cliff, marked with many a cross, was the lonely cholera cemetery, a remembrance of the fearful pestilence which a few years since swept away thousands of the people: and above frowned that black giant, now asleep; but for how long?

In 1797 an eruption hurled out pumice, ashes, and sulphureous vapours. In the great crisis of 1812, indeed, the volcano was quiet, leaving the Souffrière of St. Vincent to do the work; but since then he has shown an ugly and uncertain humour. Smoke by day, and flame by night—or probably that light reflected from below which is often mistaken for flame in volcanic eruptions—have been seen again and again above the crater; and the awful earthquake of 1843 proves that his capacity for mischief is unabated. The whole island, indeed, is somewhat unsafe; for the hapless town of Point-à-Pitre, destroyed by that earthquake, stands not on the volcanic Basse Terre, but on the edge of the marine Grande Terre, near the southern mouth of the salt-water river. Heaven grant these good people of Guadaloupe a long respite; for they are said to deserve it, as far as human industry and enterprise goes. They have, as well, I understand, as the gentlemen of Martinique, discovered the worth of the 'division of labour.' Throughout the West Indies the planter is usually not merely a sugar-grower, but a sugar-maker also. He requires, therefore, two capitals, and two intellects likewise, one for his cane-fields, the other for his 'ingenio,' engine-house, or sugar-works. But he does not gain thereby two profits. Having two things to do, neither, usually, is done well. The cane-farming is bad, the sugar-making bad; and the sugar, when made, disposed of through merchants by a cumbrous, antiquated, and expensive system. These shrewd Frenchmen, and, I am told, even small proprietors among the Negroes, not being crippled, happily for them, by those absurd sugar-duties which, till Mr. Lowe's budget, put a premium on the making of bad sugar, are confining themselves to growing the canes, and sell them raw to 'Usines Centrales,' at which they are manufactured into sugar. They thus devote their own capital and intellect to increasing the yield of their estates; while the central factories, it is said, pay dividends ranging from twenty to forty per cent. I regretted much that I was unable to visit in crop-time one of these factories, and see the working of a system which seems to contain one of the best elements of the co-operative principle.

But (and this is at present a serious inconvenience to a traveller in the Antilles) the steamer passes each island only once a fortnight; so that to land in an island is equivalent to staying there at least that time, unless one chooses to take the chances of a coasting schooner, and bad food, bugs, cockroaches, and a bunk which—but I will not describe. 'Non ragionam di lor, ma guarda' (down the companion) 'e passa.'

I must therefore content myself with describing, as honestly as I can, what little we saw from the sea, of islands at each of which we would gladly have stayed several days.

As the traveller nears each of them—Guadaloupe, Dominica, Martinique (of which two last we had only one passing glance), St. Vincent, St. Lucia, and Grenada—he will be impressed, not only by the peculiarity of their form, but by the richness of their colour.

All of them do not, like St. Kitts, Guadaloupe, and St. Vincent, slope up to one central peak. In Martinique, for instance, there are three separate peaks, or groups of peaks—the Mont Pelée, the Pitons du Carbet, and the Piton du Vauclain. But all have that peculiar jagged outline which is noticed first at the Virgin Islands.

Flat 'vans' or hog-backed hills, and broad sweeps of moorland, so common in Scotland, are as rare as are steep walls of cliff, so common in the Alps. Pyramid is piled on pyramid, the sides of each at a slope of about 45°, till the whole range is a congeries of multitudinous peaks and peaklets, round the base of which spreads out, with a sudden sweep, the smooth lowland of volcanic ash and lava. This extreme raggedness of outline is easily explained. The mountains have never been, as in

Scotland, planed smooth by ice. They have been gouged out, in every direction, by the furious tropic rains and tropic rain-torrents. Had the rocks been stratified and tolerably horizontal, these rains would have cut them out into tablelands divided by deep gullies, such as may be seen in Abyssinia, and in certain parts of the western United States. But these rocks are altogether amorphous and unstratified, and have been poured or spouted out as lumps, dykes, and sheets of lava, of every degree of hardness; so that the rain, in degrading them, has worn them, not into tables and ranges, but into innumerable cones. And the process of degradation is still going on rapidly. Though a cliff, or sheet of bare rock, is hardly visible among the glens, yet here and there a bright brown patch tells of a recent landslip; and the masses of debris and banks of shingle, backed by a pestilential little swamp at the mouth of each torrent, show how furious must be the downpour and down-roll before the force of a sudden flood, along so headlong an incline.

But in strange contrast with the ragged outline, and with the wild devastation of the rainy season, is the richness of the verdure which clothes the islands, up to their highest peaks, in what seems a coat of green fur; but when looked at through the glasses, proves to be, in most cases, gigantic timber. Not a rock is seen. If there be a cliff here and there, it is as green as an English lawn. Steep slopes are gray with groo-groo palms,[1] or yellow with unknown flowering trees. High against the sky-line, tiny knots and lumps are found to be gigantic trees. Each glen has buried its streamlet a hundred feet in vegetation, above which, here and there, the gray stem and dark crown of some palmiste towers up like the mast of some great admiral. The eye and the fancy strain vainly into the green abysses, and wander up and down over the wealth of depths and heights, compared with which European parks and woodlands are but paltry scrub and shaugh. No books are needed to tell that. The eye discovers it for itself, even before it has learnt to judge of the great size of the vegetation, from the endless variety of form and colour. For the islands, though green intensely, are not of one, but of every conceivable green, or rather of hues ranging from pale yellow through all greens into cobalt blue; and as the wind stirs the leaves, and sweeps the lights and shadows over hill and glen, all is ever-changing, iridescent, like a peacock's neck; till the whole island, from peak to shore, seems some glorious jewel—an emerald with tints of sapphire and topaz, hanging between blue sea and white surf below, and blue sky and white cloud above.

If the reader fancies that I exaggerate, let him go and see. Let him lie for one hour off the Rosseau at Dominica. Let him

[1] *Acrocomia.*

sail down the leeward side of Guadaloupe, down the leeward side of what island he will, and judge for himself how poor, and yet how tawdry, my words are, compared with the luscious yet magnificent colouring of the Antilles.

The traveller, at least so I think, would remark also, with some surprise, the seeming smallness of these islands. The Basse Terre of Guadaloupe, for instance, is forty miles in length. As you lie off it, it does not look half, or even a quarter, of that length; and that, not merely because the distances north and south are foreshortened, or shut in by nearer headlands. The causes, I believe, are more subtle and more complex. First, the novel clearness of the air, which makes the traveller, fresh from misty England, fancy every object far nearer, and therefore far smaller, than it actually is. Next the simplicity of form. Each outer line trends upward so surely toward a single focus; each whole is so sharply defined between its base-line of sea and its background of sky, that, like a statue, each island is compact and complete in itself, an isolated and self-dependent organism; and therefore, like every beautiful statue, it looks much smaller than it is. So perfect this isolation seems, that one fancies, at moments, that the island does not rise out of the sea, but floats upon it; that it is held in place, not by the roots of the mountains, and deep miles of lava-wall below, but by the cloud which has caught it by the top, and will not let it go. Let that cloud but rise, and vanish, and the whole beautiful thing will be cast adrift; ready to fetch way before the wind, and (as it will seem often enough to do when viewed through a cabin-port) to slide silently past you, while you are sliding past it.

And yet, to him who knows the past, a dark shadow hangs over all this beauty; and the air—even in clearest blaze of sunshine—is full of ghosts. I do not speak of the shadow of negro slavery, nor of the shadow which, though abolished, it has left behind, not to be cleared off for generations to come. I speak of the shadow of war, and the ghosts of gallant soldiers and sailors. Truly here

> 'The spirits of our fathers
> Might start from every wave;
> For the deck it was their field of fame,
> And ocean was their grave,'

and ask us: What have you done with these islands, which we won for you with precious blood? What could we answer? We have misused them, neglected them; till now, ashamed of the slavery of the past, and too ignorant and helpless to govern them now slavery is gone, we are half-minded to throw them away again, or to allow them to annex themselves, in sheer weariness at our imbecility, to the Americans, who, far too wise to throw them away in their turn, will accept them gladly as an

instalment of that great development of their empire, when
'The stars and stripes shall float upon Cape Horn.'

But was it for this that these islands were taken and retaken,
till every gully held the skeleton of an Englishman ? Was it for
this that these seas were reddened with blood year after year, till
the sharks learnt to gather to a sea-fight, as eagle, kite, and
wolf gathered of old to fights on land ? Did all those gallant souls
go down to Hades in vain, and leave nothing for the Englishman but the sad and proud memory of their useless valour?
That at least they have left.

However we may deplore those old wars as unnecessary ;
however much we may hate war in itself, as perhaps the worst
of all the superfluous curses with which man continues to deface
himself and this fair earth of God, yet one must be less than
Englishman, less, it may be, than man, if one does not feel a
thrill of pride at entering waters where one says to oneself,—
Here Rodney, on the glorious 12th of April 1782, broke Count
de Grasse's line (teaching thereby Nelson to do the same in like
case), took and destroyed seven French ships of the line and
scattered the rest, preventing the French fleet from joining the
Spaniards at Hispaniola ; thus saving Jamaica and the whole
West Indies, and brought about by that single tremendous
blow the honourable peace of 1783. On what a scene of crippled
and sinking, shattered and triumphant ships, in what a sea,
must the conquerors have looked round from the *Formidable's*
poop, with De Grasse at luncheon with Rodney in the cabin
below, and not, as he had boastfully promised, on board his own
Ville de Paris. Truly, though cynically, wrote Sir Gilbert Blane,
'If superior beings make a sport of the quarrels of mortals, they
could not have chosen a better theatre for this magnificent
exhibition, nor could they ever have better entertainment than
this day afforded.'

Yon lovely roadstead of Dominica—there it was that Rodney
first caught up the French on the 9th of April, three days before,
and would have beaten them there and then, had not a great
part of his fleet lain becalmed under these very highlands, past
which we are steaming through water smooth as glass. You
glance, again, running down the coast of Martinique, into a
deep bay, ringed round with gay houses embowered in mango
and coco-nut, with the Piton du Vauclain rising into the
clouds behind it. That is the Cul-de-sac Royal, for years the
rendezvous and stronghold of the French fleets. From it Count
de Grasse sailed out on the fatal 8th of April ; and there, beyond
it, opens an isolated rock, of the shape, but double the size, of
one of the great Pyramids, which was once the British sloop of
war *Diamond Rock.*

For, in the end of 1803, Sir Samuel Hood saw that French ships
passing to Fort Royal harbour in Martinique escaped him by
running through the deep channel between Pointe du Diamante

and this same rock, which rises sheer out of the water 600 feet, and is about a mile round, and only accessible at a point to the leeward, and even then only when there is no surf. He who lands, it is said, has then to creep through crannies and dangerous steeps, round to the windward side, where the eye is suddenly relieved by a sloping grove of wild fig-trees, clinging by innumerable air-roots to the cracks of the stone.

So Hood, with that inspiration of genius so common then among sailors, laid his seventy-four, the *Centaur*, close alongside the Diamond; made a hawser, with a traveller on it, fast to the ship and to the top of the rock; and in January 1804 got three long 24's and two 18's hauled up far above his masthead by sailors who, as they 'hung like clusters,' appeared 'like mice hauling a little sausage. Scarcely could we hear the Governor on the top directing them with his trumpet; the *Centaur* lying close under, like a cocoa-nut shell, to which the hawsers are affixed.'[1] In this strange fortress Lieutenant James Wilkie Maurice (let his name be recollected as one of England's forgotten worthies) was established, with 120 men and boys, and ammunition, provisions, and water, for four months; and the rock was borne on the books of the Admiralty as His Majesty's ship *Diamond Rock*, and swept the seas with her guns till the 1st of June 1805, when she had to surrender, for want of powder, to a French squadron of two 74's, a frigate, a corvette, a schooner, and eleven gunboats, after killing and wounding some seventy men on the rock alone, and destroying three gunboats, with a loss to herself of two men killed and one wounded. Remembering which story, who will blame the traveller if he takes off his hat to His Majesty's quondam corvette, as he sees for the first time its pink and yellow sides shining in the sun, above the sparkling seas over which it domineered of old? You run onwards toward St. Lucia. Across that channel Rodney's line of frigates watched for the expected reinforcement of the French fleet. The first bay in St. Lucia is Gros islet; and there is the Gros islet itself—Pigeon Rock, as the English call it—behind which Rodney's fleet lay waiting at anchor, while he himself sat on the top of the rock, day after day, spy-glass in hand, watching for the signals from his frigates that the French fleet was on the move.

And those glens and forests of St. Lucia—over them and through them Sir John Moore and Sir Ralph Abercrombie fought, week after week, month after month, not merely against French soldiers, but against worse enemies; 'Brigands,' as the poor fellows were called; Negroes liberated by the Revolution of 1792. With their heads full (and who can blame them?) of the Rights of Man, and the democratic teachings of that valiant and able friend of Robespierre, Victor Hugues,

---

[1] *Naval Chronicles*, vol. xii. p. 206.

they had destroyed their masters, man, woman, and child, horribly enough, and then helped to drive out of the island the invading English, who were already half destroyed, not with fighting, but with fever. And now 'St. Lucia the faithful,' as the Convention had named her, was swarming with fresh English; and the remaining French and the drilled Negroes made a desperate stand in the earthworks of yonder Morne Fortunée, above the harbour, and had to surrender, with 100 guns and all their stores; and then the poor black fellows, who only knew that they were free, and intended to remain free, took to the bush, and fed on the wild cush-cush roots and the plunder of the plantations, man-hunting, murdering French and English alike, and being put to death in return whenever caught. Gentle Abercrombie could not coax them into peace: stern Moore could not shoot and hang them into it; and the 'Brigand war' dragged hideously on, till Moore—who was nearly caught by them in a six-oared boat off the Pitons, and had to row for his life to St. Vincent, so saving himself for the glory of Corunna—was all but dead of fever; and Colonel James Drummond had to carry on the miserable work, till the whole 'Armée Française dans les bois' laid down their rusty muskets, on the one condition, that free they had been, and free they should remain. So they were formed into an English regiment, and sent to fight on the coast of Africa; and in more senses than one 'went to their own place.' Then St. Lucia was ours till the peace of 1802; then French again, under the good and wise Nogués; to be retaken by us in 1803 once and for all.

I tell this little story at some length, as an instance of what these islands have cost us in blood and treasure. I have heard it regretted that we restored Martinique to the French, and kept St. Lucia instead. But in so doing, the British Government acted at least on the advice which Rodney had given as early as the year 1778. St. Lucia, he held, would render Martinique and the other islands of little use in war, owing to its windward situation and its good harbours; for from St. Lucia every other British island might receive speedy succour. He advised that the Little Carenage should be made a permanent naval station, with dockyard and fortifications, and a town built there by Government, which would, in his opinion, have become a metropolis for the other islands. And indeed, Nature had done her part to make such a project easy of accomplishment. But Rodney's advice was not taken—any more than his advice to people the island, by having a considerable quantity of land in each parish allotted to ten-acre men (*i.e.* white yeomen), under penalty of forfeiting it to the Crown should it be ever converted to any other use than provision ground (*i.e.* thrown into sugar estates). This advice shows that Rodney's genius, though, with the prejudices of his time, he supported not only slavery, but the slave-trade itself, had perceived one of the most fatal weaknesses of the slaveholding and sugar-growing system. And well it would have been for St. Lucia if his advice had been taken. But neither ten-acre men nor dockyards were ever established in St. Lucia. The mail-steamers, if they need to go into dock, have, I am ashamed to say, to go to Martinique, where the French manage matters better. The admirable Carenage harbour is empty; Castries remains a little town, small, dirty, dilapidated, and unwholesome; and St. Lucia itself is hardly to be called a colony, but rather the nucleus of a colony, which may become hereafter, by energy and good government, a rich and thickly-peopled garden up to the very mountain-tops.

We went up 800 feet of steep hill, to pay a visit on that Morne Fortunée which Moore and Abercrombie took, with terrible loss of life, in May 1796; and wondered at the courage and the tenacity of purpose which could have contrived to invest, and much more to assault, such a stronghold, 'dragging the guns across ravines and up the acclivities of the mountains and rocks,' and then attacking the works only along one narrow neck of down, which must be fat, to this day, with English blood.

All was peaceful enough now. The forts were crumbling, the barracks empty, and the 'neat cottages, smiling flower gardens, smooth grass-plats and gravel-walks,' which were once the pride of the citadel, replaced for the most part with Guava-scrub and sensitive plants. But nothing can destroy the beauty of the panorama. To the north and east a wilderness of mountain peaks; to the west the Grand Cul-de-sac and the Carenage, mapped out in sheets of blue between high promontories; and, beyond all, the open sea. What a land: and in what a climate: and all lying well-nigh as it has been since the making of the world, waiting for man to come and take possession. But there, as elsewhere, matters are mending steadily; and in another hundred years St. Lucia may be an honour to the English race.

We were, of course, anxious to obtain at St. Lucia specimens of that abominable reptile, the Fer-de-lance, or rat-tailed snake,[1] which is the pest of this island, as well as of the neighbouring island of Martinique, and, in Père Labat's time, of lesser Martinique in the Grenadines, from which, according to Davy, it seems to have disappeared. It occurs also in Guadaloupe. In great Martinique—so the French say—it is dangerous to travel through certain woodlands on account of the Fer-de-lance, who lies along a bough, and strikes, without provocation, at horse or man. I suspect this statement, however, to be an exaggeration. I was assured that this was not the case in St. Lucia; that the snake attacks no oftener than other venomous

[1] *Craspedocephalus lanceolatus.*

snakes,—that is, when trodden on, or when his retreat is cut off. At all events, it seems easy enough to kill him: so easy, that I hope yet it may be possible to catch him alive, and that the Zoological Gardens may at last possess—what they have long coveted in vain—the hideous attraction of a live Fer-de-lance. The specimens which we brought home are curious enough, even from this æsthetic point of view. Why are these poisonous snakes so repulsive in appearance, some of them at least, and that not in proportion to their dangerous properties? For no one who puts the mere dread out of his mind will call the Cobras ugly, even anything but beautiful; nor, again, the deadly Coral snake of Trinidad, whose beauty tempts children, and even grown people, to play with it, or make a necklace of it, sometimes to their own destruction. But who will call the Puff Adder of the Cape, or this very Fer-de-lance, anything but ugly and horrible: not only from the brutality signified, to us at least, by the flat triangular head and the heavy jaw, but by the look of malevolence and craft signified, to us at least, by the eye and the lip? 'To us at least,' I say. For it is an open question, and will be one, as long as the nominalist and the realist schools of thought keep up their controversy—which they will do to the world's end—whether this seeming hideousness be a real fact: whether we do not attribute to the snake the same passions which we should expect to find—and to abhor—in a human countenance of somewhat the same shape, and then justify our assumption to ourselves by the creature's bites, which are actually no more the result of craft and malevolence than the bite of a frightened mouse or squirrel. I should be glad to believe that the latter theory were the true one; that nothing is created really ugly, that the Fer-de-lance looks an hideous fiend, the Ocelot a beautiful fiend, merely because the outlines of the Ocelot approach more nearly to those which we consider beautiful in a human being: but I confess myself not yet convinced. 'There is a great deal of human nature in man,' said the wise Yankee; and one's human nature, perhaps one's common-sense also, will persist in considering beauty and ugliness as absolute realities, in spite of one's efforts to be fair to the weighty arguments on the other side.

These Fer-de-lances, be that as it may, are a great pest in St. Lucia. Dr. Davy says that he 'was told by the Lieutenant-Governor that as many as thirty rat-tailed snakes were killed in clearing a piece of land, of no great extent, near Government House.' I can well believe this, for about the same number were killed only two years ago in clearing, probably, the same piece of ground, which is infested with that creeping pest of the West Indies, the wild Guava-bush, from which guava-jelly is made. The present Lieutenant-Governor has offered a small reward for the head of every Fer-de-lance killed: and the number brought in, in the first month, was so large that I do not like to quote it merely from memory. Certainly, it was high time to make a crusade against these unwelcome denizens. Dr. Davy, judging from a Government report, says that nineteen persons were killed by them in one small parish in the year 1849; and the death, though by no means certain, is, when it befalls, a hideous death enough. If any one wishes to know what it is like, let him read the tragedy which Sir Richard Schomburgk tells—with his usual brilliance and pathos, for he is a poet as well as a man of science—in his *Travels in British Guiana*, vol. ii. p. 255—how the *Craspedocephalus*, coiled on a stone in the ford, let fourteen people walk over him without stirring, or allowing himself to be seen: and at last rose, and, missing Schomburgk himself, struck the beautiful Indian bride, the 'Liebling der ganzen Gesellschaft;' and how she died in her bridegroom's arms, with horrors which I do not record.

Strangely enough, this snake, so fatal to man, has no power against another West Indian snake, almost equally common, namely, the Cribo.[1] This brave animal, closely connected with our common water-snake, is perfectly harmless, and a welcome guest in West Indian houses, because he clears them of rats. He is some six or eight feet long, black, with more or less bright yellow about the tail and under the stomach. He not only faces the Fer-de-lance, who is often as big as he, but kills and eats him. It was but last year, I think, that the population of Carenage turned out to see a fight in a tree between a Cribo and a Fer-de-lance, of about equal size, which, after a two hours' struggle, ended in the Cribo swallowing the Fer-de-lance, head foremost. But when he had got his adversary about one-third down, the Creoles—just as so many Englishmen would have done—seeing that all the sport was over, rewarded the brave Cribo by killing both, and preserving them as a curiosity in spirits. How the Fer-de-lance came into the Antilles is a puzzle. The black American scorpion—whose bite is more dreaded by the Negroes than even the snake's—may have been easily brought by ship in luggage or in cargo. But the Fer-de-lance, whose nearest home is in Guiana, is not likely to have come on board ship. It is difficult to believe that he travelled northward by land at the epoch—if such a one there ever was—when these islands were joined to South America: for if so, he would surely be found in St. Vincent, in Grenada, and most surely of all in Trinidad. So far from that being the case, he will not live, it is said, in St. Vincent. For (so goes the story) during the Carib war of 1795-96, the savages imported Fer-de-lances from St. Lucia or Martinique, and turned them loose, in hopes of their destroying the white men: but they did not breed, dwindled away, and were soon extinct. It is possible

---

[1] *Coluber variabilis.*

that they, or their eggs, came in floating timber from the
Orinoco : but if so, how is it that they have never been stranded
on the east coast of Trinidad, whither timber without end drifts
from that river? In a word, I have no explanation whatsoever
to give ; as I am not minded to fall back on the medieval one,
that the devil must have brought them thither, to plague the
inhabitants for their sins.

Among all these beautiful islands, St. Lucia is, I think, the
most beautiful ; not indeed on account of the size or form of its
central mass, which is surpassed by that of several others, but
on account of those two extraordinary mountains at its south-
western end, which, while all conical hills in the French
islands are called Pitons, bear the name of The Pitons *par excel-
lence*. From most elevated points in the island their twin
peaks may be seen jutting up over the other hills, like, according to irreverent English sailors, the tips of a donkey's ears.
But, as the steamer runs southward along the shore, these two
peaks open out, and you find yourself in deep water close to the
base of two obelisks, rather than mountains, which rise sheer
out of the sea, one to the height of 2710, the other to that of
2680 feet, about a mile from each other. Between them is the
loveliest little bay ; and behind them green wooded slopes rise
toward the rearward mountain of the Souffrière. The whole
glitters clear and keen in blazing sunshine : but behind, black
depths of cloud and gray sheets of rain shroud all the central
highlands in mystery and sadness. Beyond them, without a
shore, spreads open sea. But the fantastic grandeur of the
place cannot be described in words. The pencil of the artist
must be trusted. I can vouch that he has not in the least
exaggerated the slenderness and steepness of the rock-masses.
One of them, it is said, has never been climbed ; unless a myth
which hangs about it is true. Certain English sailors, probably
of Rodney's men—and numbering, according to the pleasure of
the narrator, three hundred, thirty, or three—are said to have
warped themselves up it by lianes and scrub ; but they found
the rock-ledges garrisoned by an enemy more terrible than any
French. Beneath the bites of the Fer-de-lances, and it may be
beneath the blaze of the sun, man after man dropped ; and lay,
or rolled down the cliffs. A single survivor was seen to reach
the summit, to wave the Union Jack in triumph over his head,
and then to fall a corpse. So runs the tale, which, if not true,
has yet its value, as a token of what, in those old days, English
sailors were believed capable of daring and of doing.

At the back of these two Pitons is the Souffrière, probably
the remains of the old crater, now fallen in, and only 1000 feet
above the sea : a golden egg to the islanders, were it but used.
In case of war, and any difficulty occurring in obtaining
sulphur from Sicily, a supply of the article to almost any
amount might be obtained from this and the other like Solfa-

PITONS OF ST. LUCIA.

terras of the British Antilles; they being, so long as the natural distillation of the substance continues active as at present, inexhaustible. But to work them profitably will require a little more common-sense than the good folks of St. Lucia have as yet shown. In 1836 two gentlemen of Antigua,[1] Mr. Bennett and Mr. Wood, set up sulphur works at the Soufrière of St. Lucia, and began prosperously enough, exporting 540 tons the first year. 'But in 1840,' says Mr. Breen, 'the sugar-growers took the alarm,' fearing, it is to be presumed, that labour would be diverted from the cane-estates, 'and at their instigation the Legislative Council imposed a tax of 16s. sterling on every ton of purified sulphur exported from the colony.' The consequence was that 'Messrs. Bennett and Wood, after incurring a heavy loss of time and treasure, had to break up their establishment and retire from the colony.' One has heard of the man who killed the goose to get the golden egg. In this case the goose, to avoid the trouble of laying, seems to have killed the man.

The next link in the chain, as the steamer runs southward, is St. Vincent; a single volcano peak, like St. Kitts, or the Basse Terre of Guadaloupe. Very grand are the vast sheets, probably of lava covered with ash, which pour down from between two rounded mountains just above the town. Rich with green canes, they contrast strongly with the brown ragged cliffs right and left of them, and still more with the awful depths beyond and above, where, underneath a canopy of bright white clouds, scowls a purple darkness of cliffs and glens, among which lies, unseen, the Soufrière.

In vain, both going and coming, by sunlight, and again by moonlight, when the cane-fields gleamed white below and the hills were pitch-black above, did we try to catch a sight of this crater-peak. One fact alone we ascertained, that like all, as far as I have seen, of the West Indian volcanoes, it does not terminate in an ash-cone, but in ragged cliffs of blasted rock. The explosion of April 27, 1812, must have been too violent, and too short, to allow of any accumulation round the crater. And no wonder; for that single explosion relieved an interior pressure upon the crust of the earth, which had agitated sea and land from the Azores to the West Indian islands, the coasts of Venezuela, the Cordillera of New Grenada, and the valleys of the Mississippi and Ohio. For nearly two years the earthquakes had continued, when they culminated in one great tragedy, which should be read at length in the pages of Humboldt.[2] On March 26, 1812, when the people of Caraccas were assembled in the churches, beneath a still and blazing sky, one minute of earthquake sufficed to bury, amid the ruins of churches and houses, nearly 10,000 souls. The same earthquake wrought

[1] Breen's *St. Lucia*, p. 295.
[2] *Personal Narrative*, book v. cap. 14.

terrible destruction along the whole line of the northern Cordilleras, and was felt even at Santa Fé de Bogota, and Honda, 180 leagues from Caraccas. But the end was not yet. While the wretched survivors of Caraccas were dying of fever and starvation, and wandering inland to escape from ever-renewed earthquake shocks, among villages and farms, which, ruined like their own city, could give them no shelter, the almost forgotten volcano of St. Vincent was muttering in suppressed wrath. It had thrown out no lava since 1718; if, at least, the eruption spoken of by Moreau de Jonnés took place in the Souffrière. According to him, with a terrific earthquake, clouds of ashes were driven into the air with violent detonations from a mountain situated at the eastern end of the island. When the eruption had ceased, it was found that the whole mountain had disappeared. Now there is no eastern end to St. Vincent, nor any mountain on the east coast; and the Souffrière is at the northern end. It is impossible, meanwhile, that the wreck of such a mountain should not have left traces visible and notorious to this day. May not the truth be, that the Souffrière had once a lofty cone, which was blasted away in 1718, leaving the present crater-ring of cliffs and peaks; and that thus may be explained the discrepancies in the accounts of its height, which Mr. Scrope gives as 4940 feet, and Humboldt and Dr. Davy at 3000, a measurement which seems to me to be more probably correct? The mountain is said to have been slightly active in 1785. In 1812 its old crater had been for some years (and is now) a deep blue lake, with walls of rock around 800 feet in height, reminding one traveller of the Lake of Albano.[1] But for twelve months it had given warning, by frequent earthquake shocks, that it had its part to play in the great subterranean battle between rock and steam; and on the 27th of April 1812 the battle began.

A negro boy—he is said to be still alive in St. Vincent—was herding cattle on the mountain-side. A stone fell near him; and then another. He fancied that other boys were pelting him from the cliffs above, and began throwing stones in return. But the stones fell thicker: and among them one, and then another, too large to have been thrown by human hand. And the poor little fellow woke up to the fact that not a boy, but the mountain, was throwing stones at him; and that the column of black cloud which was rising from the crater above was not harmless vapour, but dust, and ash, and stone. He turned, and ran for his life, leaving the cattle to their fate, while the steam mitrailleuse of the Titans—to which all man's engines of destruction are but pop-guns—roared on for three days and nights, covering the greater part of the island in ashes, burying crops, breaking branches off the trees, and spreading ruin from

[1] Dr. Davy.

which several estates never recovered ; and so the 30th of April dawned in darkness which might be felt.

Meanwhile, on that same day, to change the scene of the campaign two hundred and ten leagues, 'a distance,' as Humboldt says, 'equal to that between Vesuvius and Paris,' 'the inhabitants, not only of Caraccas, but of Calabozo, situate in the midst of the Llanos, over a space of four thousand square leagues, were terrified by a subterranean noise, which resembled frequent discharges of the loudest cannon. It was accompanied by no shock : and, what is very remarkable, was as loud on the coast as at eighty leagues' distance inland ; and at Caraccas, as well as at Calabozo, preparations were made to put the place in defence against an enemy who seemed to be advancing with heavy artillery.' They might as well have copied the St. Vincent herd-boy, and thrown their stones, too, at the Titans ; for the noise was, there can be no doubt, nothing else than the final explosion in St. Vincent far away. The same explosion was heard in Venezuela, the same at Martinique and Guadaloupe : but there, too, there were no earthquake shocks. The volcanoes of the two French islands lay quiet, and left their English brother to do the work. On the same day a stream of lava rushed down from the mountain, reached the sea in four hours, and then all was over. The earthquakes which had shaken for two years a sheet of the earth's surface larger than half Europe were stilled by the eruption of this single vent.

No wonder if, with such facts on my memory since my childhood, I looked up at that Souffrière with awe, as at a giant, obedient though clumsy, beneficent though terrible, reposing aloft among the clouds when his appointed work was done.

The strangest fact about this eruption was, that the mountain did not make use of its old crater. The original vent must have become so jammed and consolidated, in the few years between 1785 and 1812, that it could not be reopened, even by a steam-force the vastness of which may be guessed at from the vastness of the area which it had shaken for two years. So when the eruption was over, it was found that the old crater-lake, incredible as it may seem, remained undisturbed, as far as has been ascertained. But close to it, and separated only by a knife-edge of rock some 700 feet in height, and so narrow that, as I was assured by one who had seen it, it is dangerous to crawl along it, a second crater, nearly as large as the first, had been blasted out, the bottom of which, in like manner, is now filled with water. I regretted much that I could not visit it. Three points I longed to ascertain carefully — the relative heights of the water in the two craters ; the height and nature of the spot where the lava stream issued ; and lastly, if possible, the actual causes of the locally famous Rabacca, or 'Dry River,' one of the largest streams in the island, which was swallowed up during the eruption, at a short distance from its source, leaving its bed an arid gully to this day. But it could not be, and I owe what little I know of the summit of the Souffrière principally to a most intelligent and gentleman-like young Wesleyan minister, whose name has escaped me. He described vividly as we stood together on the deck, looking up at the volcano, the awful beauty of the twin lakes, and of the clouds which, for months together, whirl in and out of the cups in fantastic shapes before the eddies of the trade-wind.

The day after the explosion, 'Black Sunday,' gave a proof of, though no measure of, the enormous force which had been exerted. Eighty miles to windward lies Barbadoes. All Saturday a heavy cannonading had been heard to the eastward. The English and French fleets were surely engaged. The soldiers were called out; the batteries manned: but the cannonade died away, and all went to bed in wonder. On the 1st of May the clocks struck six: but the sun did not, as usual in the tropics, answer to the call. The darkness was still intense, and grew more intense as the morning wore on. A slow and silent rain of impalpable dust was falling over the whole island. The Negroes rushed shrieking into the streets. Surely the last day was come. The white folk caught (and little blame to them) the panic; and some began to pray who had not prayed for years. The pious and the educated (and there were plenty of both in Barbadoes) were not proof against the infection. Old letters describe the scene in the churches that morning as hideous—prayers, sobs, and cries, in Stygian darkness, from trembling crowds. And still the darkness continued, and the dust fell.

I have a letter, written by one long since dead, who had at least powers of description of no common order, telling how, when he tried to go out of his house upon the east coast, he could not find the trees on his own lawn, save by feeling for their stems. He stood amazed not only in utter darkness, but in utter silence. For the trade-wind had fallen dead; the everlasting roar of the surf was gone; and the only noise was the crashing of branches, snapped by the weight of the clammy dust. He went in again, and waited. About one o'clock the veil began to lift; a lurid sunlight stared in from the horizon: but all was black overhead. Gradually the dust-cloud drifted away; the island saw the sun once more; and saw itself inches deep in black, and in this case fertilising, dust. The trade-wind blew suddenly once more out of the clear east, and the surf roared again along the shore.

Meanwhile, a heavy earthquake-wave had struck part at least of the shores of Barbadoes. The gentleman on the east coast, going out, found traces of the sea, and boats and logs washed up, some 10 to 20 feet above high-tide mark: a convulsion which seems to have gone unmarked during the general dismay.

One man at least, an old friend of John Hunter, Sir Joseph Banks, and others their compeers, was above the dismay, and the superstitious panic which accompanied it. Finding it still dark when he rose to dress, he opened (so the story used to run) his window; found it stick, and felt upon the sill a coat of soft powder. 'The volcano in St. Vincent has broken out at last,' said the wise man, 'and this is the dust of it.' So he quieted his household and his Negroes, lighted his candles, and went to his scientific books, in that delight, mingled with an awe not the less deep because it is rational and self-possessed, with which he, like other men of science, looked at the wonders of this wondrous world.

Those who will recollect that Barbadoes is eighty miles to windward of St. Vincent, and that a strong breeze from E.N.E. is usually blowing from the former island to the latter, will be able to imagine, not to measure, the force of an explosion which must have blown this dust several miles into the air, above the region of the trade-wind, whether into a totally calm stratum, or into that still higher one in which the heated south-west wind is hurrying continually from the tropics toward the pole. As for the cessation of the trade-wind itself during the fall of the dust, I leave the fact to be explained by more learned men: the authority whom I have quoted leaves no doubt in my mind as to the fact.

On leaving St. Vincent, the track lies past the Grenadines. For sixty miles, long low islands of quaint forms and euphonious names—Becquia, Mustique, Canonau, Carriacou, Isle de Rhone —rise a few hundred feet out of the unfathomable sea, bare of wood, edged with cliffs and streaks of red and gray rock, resembling, says Dr. Davy, the Cyclades of the Grecian Archipelago: their number is counted at three hundred. The largest of them all is not 8000 acres in extent; the smallest about 600. A quiet prosperous race of little yeomen, beside a few planters, dwell there; the latter feeding and exporting much stock, the former much provisions, and both troubling themselves less than of yore with sugar and cotton. They build coasting vessels, and trade with them to the larger islands; and they might be, it is said, if they chose, much richer than they are,—if that be any good to them.

The steamer does not stop at any of these little sea-hermitages; so that we could only watch their shores: and they were worth watching. They had been, plainly, sea-gnawn for countless ages; and may, at some remote time, have been all joined in one long ragged chine of hills, the highest about 1000 feet. They seem to be for the most part made up of marls and limestones, with trap-dykes and other igneous matters here and there. And one could not help entertaining the fancy that they were a specimen of what the other islands were once, or at least would have been now, had not each of them had its volcanic vents, to pile up hard lavas thousands of feet aloft, above the marine strata, and so consolidate each ragged chine of submerged mountain into one solid conical island, like St. Vincent at their northern end, and at their southern end that beautiful Grenada to which we were fast approaching, and which we reached, on our outward voyage, at nightfall; running in toward a narrow gap of moonlit cliffs, beyond which we could discern the lights of a town. We did not enter the harbour: but lay close off its gateway in safe deep water; fired our gun, and waited for the swarm of negro boats, which began to splash out to us through the darkness, the jabbering of their crews heard long before the flash of their oars was seen.

Most weird and fantastic are these nightly visits to West Indian harbours. Above, the black mountain-depths, with their canopy of cloud, bright white against the purple night, hung with keen stars. The moon, it may be on her back in the west, sinking like a golden goblet behind some rock-fort, half shrouded in black trees. Below, a line of bright mist over a swamp, with the coco-palms standing up through it, dark, and yet glistering in the moon. A light here and there in a house: another here and there in a vessel, unseen in the dark. The echo of the gun from hill to hill. Wild voices from shore and sea. The snorting of the steamer, the rattling of the chain through the hawse-hole; and on deck, and under the quarter, strange gleams of red light amid pitchy darkness, from engines, galley fires, lanthorns; and black folk and white folk flitting restlessly across them.

The strangest show: 'like a thing in a play,' says every one when they see it for the first time. And when at the gun-fire one tumbles out of one's berth, and up on deck, to see the new island, one has need to rub one's eyes, and pinch oneself—as I was minded to do again and again during the next few weeks—to make sure that it is not all a dream. It is always worth the trouble, meanwhile, to tumble up on deck, not merely for the show, but for the episodes of West Indian life and manners, which, quaint enough by day, are sure to be even more quaint at night, in the confusion and bustle of the darkness. One such I witnessed in that same harbour of Grenada, not easily to be forgotten.

A tall and very handsome middle-aged brown woman, in a limp print gown and a gorgeous turban, stood at the gangway in a glare of light, which made her look like some splendid witch by a Walpurgis night-fire. 'Tell your boatman to go round to the other side,' quoth the officer in charge.

'Fanqua! (François) You go round oder side of de ship!'

Fanqua, who seemed to be her son, being sleepy, tipsy, stupid, or lazy, did not stir.

'Fanqua! You hear what de officer say? You go round.'

No move.

'Fanqua! You not ashamed of youself? You not hear de officer say he turn a steam-pipe over you?'
No move.
'Fanqua!' (authoritative).
'Fanqua!' (indignant).
'Fanqua!' (argumentative).
'Fanqua!' (astonished).
'Fanqua!' (majestic).
'Fanqua!' (confidentially alluring).
'Fanqua!' (regretful).
And so on, through every conceivable tone of expression.

But Fanqua did not move; and the officer and bystanders laughed.

She summoned all her talents, and uttered one last 'Fanqua!' which was a triumph of art.

Shame and surprise were blended in her voice with tenderness and pity, and they again with meek despair. To have been betrayed, disgraced, and so unexpectedly, by one whom she loved, and must love still, in spite of this, his fearful fall!—It was more than heart could bear. Breathing his name but that once more, she stood a moment, like a queen of tragedy, one long arm drawing her garments round her, the other outstretched, as if to cast off—had she the heart to do it—the rebel; and then stalked away into the darkness of the paddle-boxes—for ever and a day to brood speechless over her great sorrow? Not in the least. To begin chattering away to her acquaintances, as if no Fanqua existed in the world.

It was a piece of admirable play-acting; and was meant to be. She had been conscious all the while that she was an object of attention—possibly of admiration—to a group of men; and she knew what was right to be done and said under the circumstances, and did it perfectly, even to the smallest change of voice. She was doubtless quite sincere the whole time, and felt everything which her voice expressed: but she felt it, because it was proper to feel it; and deceived herself probably more than she deceived any one about her.

A curious phase of human nature is that same play-acting, effect-studying, temperament, which ends, if indulged in too much, in hopeless self-deception, and 'the hypocrisy which,' as Mr. Carlyle says, 'is honestly indignant that you should think it hypocritical.' It is common enough among Negresses, and among coloured people too: but is it so very uncommon among whites? Is it not the bane of too many Irish? of too many modern French? of certain English, for that matter, whom I have known, who probably had no drop of French or Irish blood in their veins? But it is all the more baneful the higher the organisation is; because, the more brilliant the intellect, the more noble the instincts, the more able its victim is to say—
'See: I feel what I ought, I say what I ought, I do what I

ought: and what more would you have? Why do you Philistines persist in regarding me with distrust and ridicule? What is this common honesty, and what is this "single eye," which you suspect me of not possessing?'

Very beautiful was that harbour of George Town, seen by day. In the centre an entrance some two hundred yards across: on the right, a cliff of volcanic sand, interspersed with large boulders hurled from some volcano now silent, where black women, with baskets on their heads, were filling a barge with gravel. On the left, rocks of hard lava, surmounted by a well-lined old fort, strong enough in the days of 32-pounders. Beyond it, still on the left, the little city, scrambling up the hillside, with its red roofs and church spires, among coco-nut and bread-fruit trees, looking just like a German toy town. In front, at the bottom of the harbour, villa over villa, garden over garden, up to the large and handsome Government House, one of the most delectable spots of all this delectable land; and piled above it, green hill upon green hill, which, the eye soon discovers, are the Sommas of old craters, one inside the other towards the central peak of Mount Maitland, 1700 feet high. On the right bow, low sharp cliff-points of volcanic ash; and on the right again, a circular lake a quarter of a mile across and 40 feet in depth, with a coral reef, almost awash, stretching from it to the ash-cliff on the south side of the harbour mouth. A glance shows that this is none other than an old crater, like that inside English Harbour in Antigua, probably that which has hurled out the boulders and the ash; and one whose temper is still uncertain, and to be watched anxiously in earthquake times. The Etang du Vieux Bourg is its name; for, so tradition tells, in the beginning of the seventeenth century the old French town stood where the white coral-reef gleams under water; in fact, upon the northern lip of the crater. One day, however, the Enceladus below turned over in his sleep, and the whole town was swallowed up, or washed away. The sole survivor was a certain blacksmith, who thereupon was made— or as sole survivor made himself—Governor of the island of Grenada. So runs the tale; and so it seemed likely to run again, during the late earthquake at St. Thomas's. For on the very same day, and before any earthquake-wave from St. Thomas's had reached Grenada—if any ever reached it, which I could not clearly ascertain—this Etang du Vieux Bourg boiled up suddenly, hurling masses of water into the lower part of the town, washing away a stage, and doing much damage. The people were, and with good reason, in much anxiety for some hours after: but the little fit of ill-temper went off, having vented itself, as is well known, in the sea between St. Thomas's and Santa Cruz, many miles away.

The bottom of the crater, I was assured, was not permanently altered: but the same informant—an eye-witness on whom I can fully depend—shared the popular opinion that it had opened, sucked in sea-water, and spouted it out again. If so, the good folks of George Town are quite right in holding that they had a very narrow escape of utter destruction.

An animated and picturesque spot, as the steamer runs alongside, is the wooden wharf where passengers are to land and the ship to coal. The coaling Negroes and Negresses, dressed or undressed, in their dingiest rags, contrast with the country Negresses, in gaudy prints and gaudier turbans, who carry on their heads baskets of fruit even more gaudy than their dresses. Both country and town Negroes, meanwhile, look—as they are said to be—comfortable and prosperous; and I can well believe the story that beggars are unknown in the island. The coalers, indeed, are only too well off, for they earn enough, by one day of violent and degrading toil, to live in reckless shiftless comfort, and, I am assured, something very like debauchery, till the next steamer comes in.

No sooner is the plank down, than a struggling line getting on board meets a struggling line getting on shore; and it is well if the passenger, on landing, is not besmirched with coal-dust, after a narrow escape of being shoved into the sea off the stage. But, after all, civility pays in Grenada, as in the rest of the world; and the Negro, like the Frenchman, though surly and rude enough if treated with the least haughtiness, will generally, like the Frenchman, melt at once at a touch of the hat, and an appeal to 'Laissez passer Mademoiselle.' On shore we got, through be-coaled Negroes, men and women, safe and not very much be-coaled ourselves; and were driven up steep streets of black porous lava, between lava houses and walls, and past lava gardens, in which jutted up everywhere, amid the loveliest vegetation, black knots and lumps scorched by the nether fires.

The situation of the house—the principal one of the island—to which we drove, is beautiful beyond description. It stands on a knoll some 300 feet in height, commanded only by a slight rise to the north; and the wind of the eastern mountains sweeps fresh and cool through a wide hall and lofty rooms. Outside, a pleasure-ground and garden, with the same flowers as we plant out in summer at home; and behind, tier on tier of green wooded hill, with cottages and farms in the hollows, might have made us fancy ourselves for a moment in some charming country-house in Wales. But opposite the drawing-room window rose a *Candelabra Cereus*, thirty feet high. On the lawn in front great shrubs of red Frangipani carried rose-coloured flowers which filled the air with fragrance, at the end of thick and all but leafless branches. Trees hung over them with smooth greasy stems of bright copper—which has gained them the name of 'Indian skin,' at least in Trinidad, where we often saw them wild; another glance showed us that every tree and shrub around was different from those at home: and we recollected where we were; and recollected, too, as we looked at the wealth of flower and fruit and verdure, that it was sharp winter at home. We admired this and that: especially a most lovely Convolvulus—I know not whether we have it in our hothouses[1] —with purple maroon flowers; and an old hog-plum[2]—Mombin of the French—a huge tree, which was striking, not so much from its size as from its shape. Growing among blocks of lava, it had assumed the exact shape of an English oak in a poor soil and exposed situation; globular-headed, gnarled, stunted, and most unlike to its giant brethren of the primeval woods, which range upward 60 or 80 feet without a branch. We walked up to see the old fort, commanding the harbour from a height of 800 feet. We sat and rested by the roadside under a great cotton-wood tree, and looked down on gorges of richest green, on negro gardens, and groo-groo palms, and here and there a cabbage-palm, or a huge tree at whose name we could not guess; then turned through an arch cut in the rock into the interior of the fort, which now holds neither guns nor soldiers, to see at our feet the triple harbour, the steep town, and a very paradise of garden and orchard; and then down again, with the regretful thought, which haunted me throughout the islands—What might the West Indies not have been by now, had it not been for slavery, rum, and sugar?

We got down to the steamer again, just in time, happily, not to see a great fight in the water between two Negroes; to watch which all the women had stopped their work, and cheered the combatants with savage shouts and laughter. At last the coaling and the cursing were over; and we steamed out again to sea.

I have antedated this little episode—delightful for more reasons than I set down here—because I do not wish to trouble my readers with two descriptions of the same island—and those mere passing glimpses.

There are two craters, I should say, in Grenada, beside the harbour. One, the Grand Etang, lies high in the central group of mountains, which rise to 3700 feet, and is itself about 1740 feet above the sea. Dr. Davy describes it as a lake of great beauty, surrounded by bamboos and tree-ferns. The other crater-lake lies on the north-east coast, and nearer to the sea-level: and I more than suspect that more would be recognised, up and down the island, by the eye of a practised geologist.

The southern end of Grenada—of whatsoever rock it may be composed—shows evidence of the same wave-destruction as do the Grenadines. Arches and stacks, and low horizontal strata laid bare along the cliff, in some places white with guano, prove that the sea has been at work for ages, which must be many and long, considering that the surf, on that leeward side of the island, is little or none the whole year round. With these low cliffs, in strongest contrast to the stately and precipitous southern point of St. Lucia, the southern point of Grenada slides into the sea, the last of the true Antilles. For Tobago, Robinson Crusoe's island, which lies away unseen to windward, is seem-

---

[1] *Ipomœa Horsfallii.* [2] *Spondias lutea.*

THE MOXOS BOCA.

ingly a fragment of South America, like the island of Trinidad, to which the steamer now ran dead south for seventy miles.

It was on the shortest day of the year—St. Thomas's Day—at seven in the morning (half-past eleven of English time, just as the old women at Eversley would have been going round the parish for their 'goodying'), that we became aware of the blue mountains of North Trinidad ahead of us; to the west of them the island of the Dragon's Mouth; and westward again, a cloud among the clouds, the last spur of the Cordilleras of the Spanish Main. There was South America at last; and as a witness that this, too, was no dream, the blue water of the Windward Islands changed suddenly into foul bottle-green. The waters of the Orinoco, waters from the peaks of the Andes far away, were staining the sea around us. With thoughts full of three great names, connected, as long as civilised man shall remain, with those waters —Columbus, Raleigh, Humboldt—we steamed on, to see hills, not standing out, like those of the isles which we had passed, in intense clearness of green and yellow, purple and blue, but all shrouded in haze, like those of the Hebrides or the West of Ireland. Onward through a narrow channel in the mountain-wall, not a rifle-shot across, which goes by the name of the Ape's Mouth, banked by high cliffs of dark Silurian rock—not bare, though, as in Britain, but furred with timber, festooned with lianas, down to the very spray of the gnawing surf. One little stack of rocks, not thirty feet high, and as many broad, stood almost in the midst of the channel, and in the very northern mouth of it, exposed to the full cut of surf and trade-wind. But the plants on it, even seen through the glasses, told us where we were. One huge low tree covered the top with shining foliage, like that of a Portugal laurel; all around it upright Cerei reared their gray candelabra, and below them, hanging down the rock to the very surf, deep green night-blowing Cereus twined and waved, looking just like a curtain of gigantic stag's-horn moss. We ran through the channel; then amid more low wooded islands, it may be for a mile, before a strong back current rushing in from the sea; and then saw before us a vast plain of muddy water. No shore was visible to the westward; to the eastward the northern hills of Trinidad, forest clad, sank to the water; to the south lay a long line of coast, generally level with the water's edge, and green with mangroves, or dotted with coco-palms. That was the Gulf of Paria, and Trinidad beyond.

Shipping at anchor, and buildings along the flat shore, marked Port of Spain, destined hereafter to stand, not on the seaside, but, like Lynn in Norfolk, and other fen-land towns, in the midst of some of the richest reclaimed alluvial in the world.

As the steamer stopped at last, her screw whirled up from the bottom clouds of yellow mud, the mingled deposits of the Caroni and the Orinoco. In half an hour more we were on shore, amid Negroes, Coolies, Chinese, French, Spaniards, short-legged Guaraon dogs, and black vultures.

CHAPTER III

TRINIDAD

It may be worth while to spend a few pages in telling something of the history of this lovely island since the 31st of July 1499, when Columbus, on his third voyage, sighted the three hills in the south-eastern part. He had determined, it is said, to name the first land which he should see after the Blessed Trinity; the triple peaks seemed to him a heaven-sent confirmation of his intent, and he named the island Trinidad: but the Indians called it Iere.

He ran from Punta Galera, at the north-eastern extremity—so named from the likeness of a certain rock to a galley under sail—along the east and south of the island; turned eastward at Punta Galeota; and then northward, round Punta Icacque, through the Boca Sierpe, or serpent's mouth, into the Gulf of Paria, which he named 'Golfo de Balena,' the Gulf of the Whale, and 'Golfo Triste,' the Sad Gulf; and went out by the northern passage of the Boca Drago. The names which he gave to the island and its surroundings remain, with few alterations, to this day.

He was surprised, says Washington Irving, at the verdure and fertility of the country, having expected to find it more parched and sterile as he approached the equator; whereas he beheld groves of palm-trees, and luxuriant forests sweeping down to the seaside, with fountains and running streams beneath the shade. The shore was low and uninhabited: but the country rose in the interior, and was cultivated in many places, and enlivened by hamlets and scattered habitations. In a word, the softness and purity of the climate, and the verdure, freshness, and sweetness of the country, appeared to equal the delights of early spring in the beautiful province of Valencia in Spain.

He found the island peopled by a race of Indians with fairer complexions than any he had hitherto seen; 'people all of good stature, well made, and of very graceful bearing, with much and smooth hair.' They wore, the chiefs at least, tunics of coloured cotton, and on their heads beautiful worked handkerchiefs, which looked in the distance as if they were made of silk. The women, meanwhile, according to the report of Columbus's son, seem, some of them at least, to have gone utterly without clothing.

They carried square bucklers, the first Columbus had seen in the New World; and bows and arrows, with which they made feeble efforts to drive off the Spaniards who landed at Punta Arenal, near Icacque, and who, finding no streams, sank holes in the sand, and so filled their casks with fresh water, as may be done, it is said, at the same spot even now.

And there—the source of endless misery to these happy harmless creatures—a certain Cacique, so goes the tale, took off Columbus's cap of crimson velvet, and replaced it with a circle of gold which he wore.

Alas for them! That fatal present of gold brought down on them enemies far more ruthless than the Caribs of the northern islands, who had a habit of coming down in their canoes and carrying off the gentle Arrawaks to eat them at their leisure, after the fashion which Defoe, always accurate, has immortalised in *Robinson Crusoe*. Crusoe's island is, almost certainly, meant for Tobago; Man Friday had been stolen in Trinidad.

Columbus came no more to Trinidad. But the Spaniards had got into their wicked heads that there must be gold somewhere in the island; and they came again and again. Gold they could not get; for it does not exist in Trinidad. But slaves they could get; and the history of the Indians of Trinidad for the next century is the same as that of the rest of the West Indies: a history of mere rapine and cruelty. The Arrawaks, to do them justice, defended themselves more valiantly than the still gentler people of Hayti, Cuba, Jamaica, Porto Rico, and the Lucayas: but not so valiantly as the fierce cannibal Caribs of the Lesser Antilles, whom the Spaniards were never able to subdue.

It was in 1595, nearly a century after Columbus discovered the island, that 'Sir Robert Duddeley in the *Bear*, with Captain Munck, in the *Beare's Whelpe*, with two small pinnesses, called the *Frisking* and the *Earwig*,' ran across from Cape Blanco in Africa, straight for Trinidad, and anchored in Cedros Bay, which he calls Curiapan, inside Punta Icacque and Los Gallos—a bay which was then, as now, 'very full of pelicans.' The existence of the island was known to the English: but I am not aware that any Englishman had explored it. Two years before, an English ship, whose exploits are written in Hakluyt by one Henry May, had run in, probably to San Fernando, 'to get refreshing; but could not, by reason the Spaniards had taken it. So that for want of victuals the company would have forsaken the ship.' How different might have been the history of Trinidad, if at that early period, while the Indians were still powerful, a little colony of English had joined them, and intermarried with them. But it was not to be. The ship got away through the Boca Drago. The year after, seemingly, Captain Whiddon, Raleigh's faithful follower, lost eight men in the island in a Spanish ambush. But Duddeley was the first Englishman, as far as I am aware, who marched, 'for his experience and pleasure, four long marches through the island; the last fifty miles going and coming through a most monstrous thicke wood, for so is most part of the island; and lodging myself in Indian townes.' Poor Sir Robert—'larding the lean earth as he stalked along'—in ruff and trunk hose, possibly too in burning steel breastplate, most probably along the old Indian path from San Fernando past Savannah Grande, and down the Ortoire to Mayaro on the east coast. How hot he must have been. How often, we will hope, he must have bathed on the journey in those crystal brooks, beneath the balisiers and the bamboos. He found 'a fine-shaped and a gentle people, all naked and painted red' (with roucou), 'their commanders wearing crowns of feathers,' and a country 'fertile and full of fruits, strange beasts and fowls, whereof munkeis, babions, and parats were in great abundance.' His 'munkeis' were, of course, the little Sapajous; his 'babions' no true Baboons; for America disdains that degraded and dog-like form; but the great red Howlers. He was much delighted with the island; and 'inskonced himself'—$i.e.$ built a fort: but he found the Spanish governor, Berreo, not well pleased at his presence; 'and no gold in the island save Marcasite' (iron pyrites); considered that Berreo and his three hundred Spaniards were 'both poore and strong, and so he had no reason to assault them.' He had but fifty men himself, and, moreover, was tired of waiting in vain for Sir Walter Raleigh. So he sailed away northward, on the 12th of March, to plunder Spanish ships, with his brains full of stories of El Dorado, and the wonders of the Orinoco—among them 'four golden half-moons weighing a noble each, and two bracelets of silver,' which a boat's crew of his had picked up from the Indians on the other side of the Gulf of Paria.

He left somewhat too soon. For on the 22d of March Raleigh sailed into Cedros Bay, and then went up to La Brea and the Pitch Lake. There he noted, as Columbus had done before him, oysters growing on the mangrove roots; and noted, too, 'that abundance of stone pitch, that all the ships of the world might be therewith laden from thence; and we made trial of it in trimming our shippes, to be most excellent good, and melteth not with the sun as the pitch of Norway.' From thence he ran up the west coast to 'the mountain of Annaparima' (St. Fernando hill), and passing the mouth of the Caroni, anchored at what was then the village of Port of Spain.

There some Spaniards boarded him, to buy linen and other things, all which he 'entertained kindly, and feasted after our manner, by means whereof I learned as much of the estate of

Guiana as I could, or as they knew, for those poore souldiers having been many years without wine, a few draughts made them merrie, in which mood they vaunted of Guiana and the riches thereof,'—much which it had been better for Raleigh had he never heard.

Meanwhile the Indians came to him every night with lamentable complaints of Berreo's cruelty. 'He had divided the island and given to every soldier a part. He made the ancient Caciques that were lords of the court, to be their slaves. He kept them in chains; he dropped their naked bodies with burning bacon, and such other torments, which' (continues Raleigh) 'I found afterward to be true. For in the city' (San Josef), 'when I entered it, there were five lords, or little kings, in one chain, almost dead of famine, and wasted with torments.' Considering which; considering Berreo's treachery to Whiddon's men; and considering also that as Berreo himself, like Raleigh, was just about to cross the gulf to Guiana in search of El Dorado, and expected supplies from Spain; 'to leave a garrison in my back, interested in the same enterprise, I should have savoured very much of the asse.' So Raleigh fell upon the 'Corps du Guard' in the evening, put them to the sword, sent Captain Caulfield with sixty soldiers onward, following himself with forty more, up the Caroni river, which was then navigable by boats; and took the little town of San Josef.

It is not clear whether the Corps du Guard which he attacked was at Port of Spain itself, or at the little mud fort at the confluence of the Caroni and San Josef rivers, which was to be seen, with some old pieces of artillery in it, in the memory of old men now living. But that he came up past that fort, through the then primeval forest, tradition reports; and tells, too, how the prickly climbing palm,[1] the Croc-chien, or Hook-dog, pest of the forests, got its present name upon that memorable day. For, as the Spanish soldiers ran from the English, one of them was caught in the innumerable hooks of the Croc-chien, and never looking behind him in his terror, began shouting, 'Suelta mi, Ingles!' (Let me go, Englishman!)—or, as others have it, 'Valga mi, Ingles!' (Take ransom for me, Englishman!)—which name the palm bears unto this day.

So Raleigh, having, as one historian of Trinidad says, 'acted like a tiger, lest he should savour of the ass,' went his way to find El Dorado, and be filled with the fruit of his own devices: and may God have mercy on him; and on all who, like him, spoil the noblest instincts, and the noblest plans, for want of the 'single eye.'

But before he went, he 'called all the Caciques who were enemies to the Spaniard, for there were some that Berreo had brought out of other countreys and planted there, to eat out

---

[1] *Desmoncus.*

and waste those that were natural of the place; and, by his Indian interpreter that he had brought out of England, made them understand that he was the servant of a Queene, who was the great Cacique of the North, and a virgin, and had more Caciques under her than there were trees in that island; and that she was an enemy to the Castellani in respect of their tyranny and oppression, and that she delivered all such nations about her as were by them oppressed, and, having freed all the northern world from their servitude, had sent me to free them also, and withal to defend the country of Guiana from their invasion and conquest. I showed them her Majesty's picture' (doubtless in ruff, farthingale, and stomacher laden with jewels), 'which they so admired and honoured, as it had been easy to make them idolatrous thereof.'

And so Raleigh, with Berreo as prisoner, 'hasted away toward his proposed discovery,' leaving the poor Indians of Trinidad to be eaten up by fresh inroads of the Spaniards.

There were, in his time, he says, five nations of Indians in the island,—'Jaios,' 'Arwacas,' 'Salvayos' (Salivas?), 'Nepoios,' and round San Josef 'Carinepagotes'; and there were others, he confesses, which he does not name. Evil times were come upon them. Two years after, the Indians at Punta Galera (the north-east point of the island) told poor Keymis that they intended to escape to Tobago when they could no longer keep Trinidad, though the Caribs of Dominica were 'such evil neighbours to it' that it was quite uninhabited. Their only fear was lest the Spaniards, worse neighbours than even the Caribs, should follow them thither.

But as Raleigh and such as he went their way, Berreo and such as he seem to have gone their way also. The 'Conquistadores,' the offscourings not only of Spain but of South Germany, and indeed of every Roman Catholic country in Europe, met the same fate as befell, if monk chroniclers are to be trusted, the great majority of the Normans who fought at Hastings. 'The bloodthirsty and deceitful men did not live out half their days.' By their own passions, and by no miraculous Nemesis, they civilised themselves off the face of the earth; and to them succeeded, as to the conquerors at Hastings, a nobler and gentler type of invaders. During the first half of the seventeenth century, Spaniards of ancient blood and high civilisation came to Trinidad, and re-settled the island: especially the family of Farfan—'Farfan de los Godos,' once famous in mediæval chivalry —if they will allow me the pleasure of for once breaking a rule of mine, and mentioning a name—who seem to have inherited for some centuries the old blessings of Psalm xxxvii.—

'Put thou thy trust in the Lord, and be doing good; dwell in the land, and verily thou shalt be fed.

'The Lord knoweth the days of the godly: and their inheritance shall endure for ever.

'They shall not be confounded in perilous times; and in the days of dearth they shall have enough.'

Toward the end of the seventeenth century the Indians summoned up courage to revolt, after a foolish ineffectual fashion. According to tradition, and an old 'romance muy doloroso,' which might have been heard sung within the last hundred years, the governor, the Cabildo, and the clergy went to witness an annual feast of the Indians at Arena, a sandy spot (as its name signifies) near the central mountain of Tamana. In the middle of one of their warlike dances, the Indians, at a given signal, discharged a flight of arrows, which killed the governor, all the priests, and almost all the rest of the whites. Only a Farfan escaped, not without suspicion of forewarning by the rebels. He may have been a merciful man and just; while considering the gentle nature of the Indians, it is possible that some at least of their victims deserved their fate, and that the poor savages had wrongs to avenge which had become intolerable. As for the murder of the priests, we must remember always that the Inquisition was then in strength throughout Spanish America; and could be, if it chose, aggressive and ruthless enough.

By the end of the seventeenth century there were but fifteen pueblos, or Indian towns, in the island; and the smallpox had made fearful ravages among them. Though they were not forced to work as slaves, a heavy capitation tax, amounting, over most of the island, to two dollars a head, was laid on them almost to the end of the last century. There seems to have been no reason in the nature of things why they should not have kept up their numbers; for the island was still, nineteen-twentieths of it, rich primeval forest. It may have been that they could not endure the confined life in the pueblos, or villages, to which they were restricted by law. But, from some cause or other, they died out, and that before far inferior numbers of invaders. In 1783, when the numbers of the whites were only 126, of the free coloured 295, and of the slaves 310, the Indians numbered only 2032. In 1798, after the great immigration from the French West Indies, there were but 1082 Indians in the island. It is true that the white population had increased meanwhile to 2151, the free coloured to 4476, and the slaves to 10,000. But there was still room in plenty for 2000 Indians. Probably many of them had been absorbed by intermarriage with the invaders. At present, there is hardly an Indian of certainly pure blood in the island, and that only in the northern mountains.

Trinidad ought to have been, at least for those who were not Indians, a happy place from the seventeenth almost to the nineteenth century, if it be true that happy is the people who have no history. Certain Dutchmen, whether men of war or pirates is not known, attacked it some time toward the end of the seventeenth century, and, trying to imitate Raleigh, were well beaten in the jungles between the Caroni and San Josef. The Indians, it is said, joined the Spaniards in the battle; and the little town of San Josef was rewarded for its valour by being raised to the rank of a city by the King of Spain.

The next important event which I find recorded is after the treaty of 27th August 1701, between 'His Most Christian' and 'His Most Catholic Majesty,' by which the Royal Company of Guinea, established in France, was allowed to supply the Spanish colonies with 4800 Negroes per annum for ten years; of whom Trinidad took some share, and used them in planting cacao. So much the worse for it.

Next Captain Teach, better known as 'Blackbeard,' made his appearance about 1716, off Port of Spain; plundered and burnt a brig laden with cacao; and when a Spanish frigate came in, and cautiously cannonaded him at a distance, sailed leisurely out of the Boca Grande. Little would any Spanish Guarda Costa trouble the soul of the valiant Captain Teach, with his six pistols slung in bandoliers down his breast, lighted matches stuck underneath the brim of his hat, and his famous black beard, the terror of all merchant captains from Trinidad to Guinea River, twisted into tails, and tied up with ribbons behind his ears. How he behaved himself for some years as a 'ferocious human pig,' like Ignatius Loyola before his conversion, with the one virtue of courage; how he would blow out the candle in the cabin, and fire at random into his crew, on the ground 'that if he did not kill one of them now and then they would forget who he was'; how he would shut down the hatches, and fill the ship with the smoke of brimstone and what not, to see how long he and his could endure a certain place,—to which they are, some of them, but too probably gone; how he has buried his money, or said that he had, 'where none but he and Satan could find it, and the longest liver should take all'; how, out of some such tradition, Edgar Poe built up the wonderful tale of the *Gold Bug;* how the planters of certain Southern States, and even the Governor of North Carolina, paid him blackmail, and received blackmail from him likewise; and lastly, how he met a man as brave as he, but with a clear conscience and a clear sense of duty, in the person of Mr. Robert Maynard, first lieutenant of the *Pearl,* who found him after endless difficulties, and fought him hand-to-hand in Oberecock River, in Virginia, 'the lieutenant and twelve men against Blackbeard and fourteen, till the sea was tinctured with blood around the vessel'; and how Maynard sailed into Bathtown with the gory head, black beard and all, hung at his jibboom end; all this is written—in the books in which it is written; which need not be read now, however sensational, by the British public.

The next important event which I find recorded in the annals of Trinidad is, that in 1725 the cacao crop failed. Some perhaps would have attributed the phenomenon to a comet, like that Sir William Beeston who, writing in 1664, says—'About this time appeared first the comet, which was the forerunner of the blasting of the cacao-trees, when they generally failed in Jamaica, Cuba, and Hispaniola.' But no comet seems to have appeared in 1725 whereon to lay the blame; and therefore Father Gumilla, the Jesuit, may have been excused for saying that the failure of the trees was owing to the planters not paying their tithes; and for fortifying his statement by the fact that one planter alone, named Rabelo, who paid his tithes duly, saved his trees and his crop.

The wicked (according to Dauxion Lavaysse, a Frenchman inoculated somewhat with scientific and revolutionary notions, who wrote a very clever book, unfortunately very rare now) said that the Trinidad cacao was then, as now, very excellent; that therefore it was sold before it was gathered; and that thus the planters were able to evade the payment of tithes. But Señor Rabelo had planted another variety, called Forestero, from the Brazils, which was at once of hardier habit, inferior quality, and slower ripening. Hence his trees withstood the blight: but, *en revanche*, hence also, merchants would not buy his crop before it was picked: thus his duty became his necessity, and he could not help paying his tithes.

Be that as it may, the good folk of Trinidad (and, to judge from their descendants, there must have been good folk among them) grew, from the failure of the cacao plantations, exceeding poor; so that in 1733 they had to call a meeting at San Josef, in order to tax the inhabitants, according to their means, toward thatching the Cabildo hall with palm-leaves. Nay, so poor did they become, that in 1740, the year after the smallpox had again devastated the island and the very monkeys had died of it,—as the hapless creatures died of cholera in hundreds a few years since, and of yellow fever the year before last, sensibly diminishing their numbers near the towns—let the conceit of human nature wince under the fact as it will, it cannot wince from under the fact,—in 1740, I say, the war between Spain and England—that about Jenkins's ear—forced them to send a curious petition to his Majesty of Spain; and to ask—Would he be pleased to commiserate their situation? The failure of the cacao had reduced them to such a state of destitution that they could not go to Mass save once a year, to fulfil their 'annual precepts'; when they appeared in clothes borrowed from each other.

Nay, it is said by those who should know best, that in those days the whole august body of the Cabildo had but one pair of small-clothes, which did duty among all the members.

Let no one be shocked. The small-clothes desiderated would have been of black satin, probably embroidered; and fit, though somewhat threadbare, for the thigh of a magistrate and gentleman of Spain. But he would not have gone on ordinary days in a sansculottic state. He would have worn that most comfortable of loose nether garments, which may be seen on sailors in prints of the great war, and which came in again a while among the cunningest Highland sportsmen, namely, slops. Let no one laugh, either, at least in contempt, as the average British Philistine will think himself bound to do, at the fact that these men had not only no balance at their bankers, but no bankers with whom to have a balance. No men are more capable of supporting poverty with content and dignity than the Spaniards of the old school. For none are more perfect gentlemen, or more free from the base modern belief that money makes the man; and I doubt not that a member of the old Cabildo of San Josef in slops was far better company than an average British Philistine in trousers.

So slumbered on, only awakening to an occasional gentle revolt against their priests, or the governor sent to them from the Spanish Court, the good Spaniards of Trinidad; till the peace of 1783 woke them up, and they found themselves suddenly in a new, and an unpleasantly lively, world.

Rodney's victories had crippled Spain utterly; and crippled, too, the French West Indian islands, though not France itself: but the shrewd eye of a M. Rome de St. Laurent had already seen in Trinidad a mine of wealth, which might set up again, not the Spanish West Indians merely, but those of the French West Indians who had exhausted, as they fancied, by bad cultivation, the soils of Guadaloupe, Martinique, and St. Lucia. He laid before the Intendant at Caraccas, on whom Trinidad then depended, a scheme of colonisation, which was accepted, and carried out in 1783, by a man who, as far as I can discover, possessed in a pre-eminent degree that instinct of ruling justly, wisely, gently, and firmly, which is just as rare in this age as it was under the *ancien régime*. Don Josef Maria Chacon was his name,—a man, it would seem, like poor Kaiser Joseph of Austria, born before his time. Among his many honourable deeds, let this one at least be remembered; that he turned out of Trinidad the last Inquisitor who ever entered it.

Foreigners, who must be Roman Catholics (though on this point Chacon was as liberal as public opinion allowed him to be), were invited to settle on grants of Crown land. Each white person of either sex was to have some thirty-two acres, and half that quantity for every slave that he should bring. Free people of colour were to have half the quantity; and a long list of conditions was annexed, which, considering that they were tainted with the original sin of slave-holding, seem wise and just enough. Two articles especially prevented, as far as possible, absenteeism. Settlers who retired from the island might take away their property; but they must pay ten per cent on all which they had accumulated; and their lands reverted to the Crown. Similarly, if the heirs of a deceased settler should not reside in the colony, fifteen per cent was to be levied on the inheritance. Well had it been for every West Indian island, British or other, if similar laws had been in force in them for the last hundred years.

So into Trinidad poured, for good and evil, a mixed population, principally French, to the number of some 12,000; till within a year or two the island was Spanish only in name. The old Spaniards, who held, many of them, large sheets of the forests which they had never cleared, had to give them up, with grumblings and heart-burnings, to the newcomers. The boundaries of these lands were uncertain. The island had never been surveyed: and no wonder. The survey has been only completed during the last few years; and it is a mystery, to the non-scientific eye, how it has ever got done. One can well believe the story of the northern engineer who, when brought over to plan out a railroad, shook his head at the first sight of the 'high woods.' 'At home,' quoth he, 'one works outside one's work: here one works inside it.' Considering the density of the forests, one may as easily take a general sketch of a room from underneath the carpet as of Trinidad from the ground. However, thanks to the energy of a few gentlemen, who found occasional holes in the carpet through which they could peep, the survey of Trinidad is now about complete.

But in those days ignorance of the island, as well as the battle between old and new interests, brought lawsuits, and all but civil war. Many of the French settlers were no better than they should be; many had debts in other islands; many of the Negroes had been sent thither because they were too great ruffians to be allowed at home; and, what was worse, the premium of sixteen acres of land for every slave imported called up a system of stealing slaves, and sometimes even free coloured people, from other islands, especially from Grenada, by means of 'artful Negroes and mulatto slaves,' who were sent over as crimps. I shall not record the words in which certain old Spaniards describe the new population of Trinidad ninety years ago. They, of course, saw everything in the blackest light; and the colony has long since weeded and settled itself under a course of good government. But poor Don Josef Maria Chacon must have had a hard time of it while he tried to break into something like order such a motley crew.

He never broke them in, poor man. For just as matters were beginning to right themselves, the French Revolution broke out; and every French West Indian island burst into flame,—physical, alas! as well as moral. Then hurried into Trinidad, to make confusion worse confounded, French Royalist families, escaping from the horrors in Hayti; and brought with them, it is said, many still faithful house-slaves born on their estates. But the Republican French, being nearly ten to one, were practical masters of the island; and Don Chacon, whenever he did anything unpopular, had to submit to 'manifestations,' with tricolour flag, *Marseillaise*, and *Ça Ira*, about the streets of Port of Spain; and to be privately informed by Admiral Artizabal that a guillotine was getting ready to cut off the heads of all loyal Spaniards, French, and British. This may have been an exaggeration: but wild deeds were possible enough in those wild days. Artizabal, the story goes, threatened to hang a certain ringleader (name not given) at his yard-arm. Chacon begged the man's life, and the fellow was 'spared to become the persecutor of his preserver, even to banishment, and death from a broken heart.'[1]

At last the explosion came. The English sloop *Zebra* was sent down into the Gulf of Paria to clear it of French privateers, manned by the defeated maroons and brigands of the French islands, who were paying respect to no flag, but pirating indiscriminately. Chacon confessed himself glad enough to have them exterminated. He himself could not protect his own trade. But the neutrality of the island must be respected. Skinner, the *Zebra's* captain, sailed away towards the Boca, and found, to his grim delight, that the privateers had mistaken him for a certain English merchantman whom they had blockaded in Port of Spain, and were giving him chase. He let them come up and try to board; and what followed may be easily guessed. In three-quarters of an hour they were all burnt, sunk, or driven on shore; the remnant of their crews escaped to Port of Spain, to join the French Republicans and vow vengeance.

Then, in a hapless hour, Captain Vaughan came into Port of Spain in the *Alarm* frigate. His intention was, of course, to protect the British and Spanish. They received him with open arms. But the privateers' men attacked a boat's crew of the *Alarm*, were beaten, raised a riot, and attacked a Welsh lady's house where English officers were at a party; after which, with pistol shots and climbing over back walls, the English, by help of a few Spanish gentlemen, escaped, leaving behind them their surgeon severely wounded.

Next morning, at sunrise, almost the whole of the frigate's crew landed in Port of Spain, fully armed, with Captain Vaughan at their head; the hot Welsh blood boiling in him. He unfurled the British flag, and marched into the town to take vengeance on the mob. A Spanish officer, with two or three men, came forward. What did a British captain mean by violating the law of nations? Vaughan would chastise the rascally French who had attacked his men. Then he must either kill the Spaniard or take him prisoner: and the officer tendered his sword.

'I will not accept the arms of a brave man who is doing his

[1] M. Joseph, *History of Trinidad*, from which most of these facts are taken.

duty,' quoth poor over-valiant Vaughan, and put him aside. The hot Welsh blood was nevertheless the blood of a gentleman. They struck up 'Britons, Strike Home,' and marched on. The British and Spanish came out to entreat him. If a fight began, they would be all massacred. Still he marched on. The French, with three or four thousand slaves, armed, and mounting the tricolour cockade, were awaiting them, seemingly on the Savannah north of the town. Chacon was at his wits' end. He had but eighty soldiers, who said openly they would not fire on the English, but on the French. But the English were but 240, and the French twelve times that number. By deft cutting through cross streets Chacon got between the two bodies of madmen, and pleaded the indignity to Spain and the violation of neutral ground. The English must fight him before they fought the French. They would beat him: but as soon as the first shot was fired, the French would attack them likewise, and both parties alike would be massacred in the streets.

The hot Welsh blood cooled down before reason and courage. Vaughan saluted Chacon; and marched back, hooted by the Republicans, who nevertheless kept at a safe distance. The French hunted every English and Irish person out of the town, some escaping barely with their lives. Only one man, however, was killed; and he, poor faithful slave, was an English Negro.

Vaughan saw that he had done wrong; that he had possibly provoked a war; and made for his error the most terrible reparation which man can make.

His fears were not without foundation. His conduct formed the principal count in the list of petty complaints against England, on the strength of which, five months after, in October 1796, Spain declared war against England, and, in conjunction with France and Holland, determined once more to dispute the empire of the seas.

The moment was well chosen. England looked, to those who did not know her pluck, to have sunk very low. France was rising fast; and Buonaparte had just begun his Italian victories. So the Spanish Court—or at least Godoy, 'Prince of Peace'—sought to make profit out of the French Republic. About the first profit which it made was the battle of St. Vincent; about the second, the loss of Trinidad.

On February 14, while Jervis and Nelson were fighting off Cape St. Vincent, Harvey and Abercrombie came into Carriacou in the Grenadines with a gallant armada; seven ships of the line, thirteen other men-of-war, and nigh 8000 men, including 1500 German jägers, on board.

On the 16th they were struggling with currents of the Bocas, piloted by a Mandingo Negro, Alfred Sharper, who died in 1836, 105 years of age. The line-of-battle ships anchored in the magnificent landlocked harbour of Chaguaramas, just inside the

Boca de Monos. The frigates and transports went up within five miles of Port of Spain.

Poor Chacon had, to oppose this great armament, 5000 Spanish troops, 300 of them just recovering from yellow fever; a few old Spanish militia, who loved the English better than the French; and what Republican volunteers he could get together. They of course clamoured for arms, and demanded to be led against the enemy, as to this day; forgetting, as to this day, that all the fiery valour of Frenchmen is of no avail without officers, and without respect for those officers. Beside them, there lay under a little fort on Gaspar Grande island, in Chaguaramas harbour—ah, what a Paradise to be defiled by war—four Spanish line-of-battle ships and a frigate. Their admiral, Apodaca, was a foolish old devotee. Their crews numbered 1600 men, 400 of whom were in hospital with yellow fever, and many only convalescent. The terrible Victor Hugues, it is said, offered a band of Republican sympathisers from Guadaloupe: but Chacon had no mind to take that Trojan horse within his fortress. 'We have too many lawless Republicans here already. Should the King send me aid, I will do my duty to preserve his colony for the crown: if not, it must fall into the hands of the English, whom I believe to be generous enemies, and more to be trusted than treacherous friends.'

What was to be done? Perhaps only that which was done. Apodaca set fire to his ships, either in honest despair, or by orders from the Prince of Peace. At least, he would not let them fall into English hands. At three in the morning Port of Spain woke up, all aglare with the blaze six miles away to the north-west. Negroes ran and shrieked, carrying this and that up and down upon their heads. Spaniards looked out, aghast. Frenchmen cried, 'Aux armes!' and sang the *Marseillaise*. And still, over the Five Islands, rose the glare. But the night was calm; the ships burnt slowly; and the *San Damaso* was saved by English sailors. So goes the tale; which, if it be, as I believe, correct, ought to be known to those adventurous Yankees who have talked, more than once, of setting up a company to recover the Spanish ships and treasure sunk in Chaguaramas. For the ships burned before they sunk; and Apodaca, being a prudent man, landed, or is said to have landed, all the treasure on the Spanish Main opposite.

He met Chacon in Port of Spain at daybreak. The good governor, they say, wept, but did not reproach. The admiral crossed himself; and, when Chacon said 'All is lost,' answered (or did not answer, for the story, like most good stories, is said not to be quite true), 'Not all; I saved the image of St. Jago de Compostella, my patron and my ship's.' His ship's patron, however, says M. Joseph, was St. Vincent. Why tell the rest of the story? It may well be guessed. The English landed in force. The French Republicans (how does history repeat itself!) broke open the arsenal, overpowering the Spanish guard, seized some 3000 to 5000 stand of arms, and then never used them, but retired into the woods. They had, many of them, fought like tigers in other islands; some, it may be, under Victor Hugues himself. But here they had no leaders. The Spanish, overpowered by numbers, fell back across the Dry River to the east of the town, and got on a height. The German jägers climbed the beautiful Laventille hills, and commanded the Spanish and the two paltry mud forts on the slopes: and all was over, happily with almost no loss of life.

Chacon was received by Abercrombie and Harvey with every courtesy; a capitulation was signed which secured the honours of war to the military, and law and safety to the civil inhabitants; and Chacon was sent home to Spain to be tried by a court-martial; honourably acquitted; and then, by French Republican intrigues, calumniated, memorialised against, subscribed against, and hunted (Buonaparte having, with his usual meanness, a hand in the persecution) into exile and penury in Portugal. At last his case was heard a second time, and tardy justice done, not by popular clamour, but by fair and deliberate law. His nephew set out to bring the good man home in triumph. He found him dying in a wretched Portuguese inn. Chacon heard that his honour was cleared at last, and so gave up the ghost.

Thus ended—as Earth's best men have too often ended—the good Don Alonzo Chacon. His only monument in the island is one, after all, 'ære perennius;' namely, that most beautiful flowering shrub which bears his name; *Warsewiczia*, some call it; others, *Calycophyllum*: but the botanists of the island continue loyally the name of *Chaconia* to those blazing crimson spikes which every Christmas-tide renew throughout the wild forests, of which he would have made a civilised garden, the memory of the last and best of the Spanish Governors.

So Trinidad became English; and Picton ruled it, for a while, with a rod of iron.

I shall not be foolish enough to enter here into the merits or demerits of the Picton case, which once made such a noise in England. His enemies' side of the story will be found in M'Callum's *Travels in Trinidad;* his friends' side in Robinson's *Life of Picton*, two books, each of which will seem, I think, to him who will read them alternately, rather less wise than the other. But those who may choose to read the two books must remember that questions of this sort have not two sides merely, but more; being not superficies, but solids; and that the most important side is that on which the question stands, namely, its bottom; which is just the side which neither party liked to be turned up, because under it (at least in the West Indies) all the beetles and cockroaches, centipedes and scorpions, are nestled away out of sight: and there, as long since decayed, they, or their exuviæ and dead bodies, may remain. The good people of Trinidad have long since agreed to let bygones be bygones; and it speaks well for the common-sense and good feeling of the islanders, as well as for the mildness and justice of British rule, that in two generations such a community as that of modern Trinidad should have formed itself out of materials so discordant. That British rule has been a solid blessing to Trinidad, all honest folk know well. Even in Picton's time, the population increased, in six years, from 17,700 to 28,400; in 1851 it was 69,600; and it is now far larger.

But Trinidad has gained, by becoming English, more than mere numbers. Had it continued Spanish, it would probably now be, like Cuba, a slave-holding and slave-trading island, wealthy, luxurious, profligate; and Port of Spain would be such another wen upon the face of God's earth as that magnificent abomination, the city of Havanna. Or, as an almost more ugly alternative, it might have played its part in that great triumph of Bliss by Act of Parliament, which set mankind to rights for ever, when Mr. Canning did the universe the honour of 'calling the new world into existence to redress the balance of the old.' It might have been—probably would have been—conquered by a band of 'sympathisers' from the neighbouring Republic of Venezuela, and have been 'called into existence' by the massacre of the respectable folk, the expulsion of capital, and the establishment (with a pronunciamento and a revolution every few years) of a Republic such as those of Spanish America, combining every vice of civilisation with every vice of savagery. From that fate, as every honest man in Trinidad knows well, England has saved the island; and therefore every honest man in Trinidad is loyal (with occasional grumblings, of course, as is the right of free-born Britons, at home and abroad) to the British flag.

CHAPTER IV

PORT OF SPAIN

THE first thing notable, on landing in Port of Spain at the low quay which has been just reclaimed from the mud of the gulf, is the multitude of people who are doing nothing. It is not that they have taken an hour's holiday to see the packet come in. You will find them, or their brown duplicates, in the same places to-morrow and next day. They stand idle in the market-place, not because they have not been hired, but because they do not want to be hired; being able to live like the Lazzaroni of Naples, on 'Midshipman's half-pay—nothing a day, and find yourself.' You are told that there are 8000 human beings in Port of Spain alone without visible means of subsistence, and you congratulate Port of Spain on being such an Elysium that people can live there—not without eating, for every child and most women you pass are eating something or other all day long —but without working. The fact is, that though they will eat as much and more than a European, if they can get it, they can do well without food; and feed, as do the Lazzaroni, on mere heat and light. The best substitute for a dinner is a sleep under a south wall in the blazing sun; and there are plenty of south walls in Port of Spain. In the French islands, I am told, such Lazzaroni are caught up and set to Government work, as 'strong rogues and masterless men,' after the ancient English fashion. But is such a course fair? If a poor man neither steals, begs, nor rebels (and these people do not do the two latter), has he not as much right to be idle as a rich man? To say that neither has a right to be idle is, of course, sheer socialism, and a heresy not to be tolerated.

Next, the stranger will remark, here as at Grenada, that every one he passes looks strong, healthy, and well-fed. One meets few or none of those figures and faces, small, scrofulous, squinny, and haggard, which disgrace the so-called civilisation of a British city. Nowhere in Port of Spain will you see such human beings as in certain streets of London, Liverpool, or Glasgow. Every one, plainly, can live and thrive if they choose; and very pleasant it is to know that.

The road leads on past the Custom-house; and past, I am sorry to say, evil smells, which are too common still in Port of Spain, though fresh water is laid on from the mountains. I have no wish to complain, especially on first landing, of these kind and hospitable citizens. But as long as Port of Spain—the suburbs especially—smells as it does after sundown every evening, so long will an occasional outbreak of cholera or yellow fever hint that there are laws of cleanliness and decency which are both able and ready to avenge themselves. You cross the pretty 'Marine Square,' with its fountain and flowering trees, and beyond them on the right the Roman Catholic Cathedral, a stately building, with Palmistes standing as tall sentries round; soon you go up a straight street, with a glimpse of a large English church, which must have been still more handsome than now before its tall steeple was shaken down by an earthquake. The then authorities, I have been told, applied to the Colonial Office for money to rebuild it: but the request was refused; on the ground, it may be presumed, that whatever ills Downing Street might have inflicted on the West Indies, it had not, as yet, gone so far as to play the part of Poseidon Ennosigæus.

Next comes a glimpse, too, of large—even too large—Government buildings, brick-built, pretentious, without beauty of form. But, however ugly in itself a building may be in Trinidad, it is certain, at least after a few years, to look beautiful, because embowered among noble flowering timber trees, like those that fill 'Brunswick Square,' and surround the great church on its south side.

Under cool porticoes and through tall doorways are seen dark 'stores,' filled with all manner of good things from Britain or from the United States. These older-fashioned houses, built, I presume, on the Spanish model, are not without a certain stateliness, from the depth and breadth of their chiaroscuro. Their doors and windows reach almost to the ceiling, and ought to be plain proofs, in the eyes of certain discoverers of the 'giant cities of Bashan,' that the old Spanish and French colonists were nine or ten feet high apiece. On the doorsteps sit Negresses in gaudy print dresses, with stiff turbans (which are, according to this year's fashion, of chocolate and yellow silk plaid, painted with thick yellow paint, and cost in all some four dollars), all aiding in the general work of doing nothing: save where here and there a hugely fat Negress, possibly with her 'head tied across' in a white turban (sign of mourning), sells, or tries to sell, abominable sweetmeats, strange fruits, and junks of sugar-cane, to be gnawed by the dawdlers in mid-street, while they carry on their heads everything and anything, from half a barrow-load of yams to a saucer or a beer-bottle. We never, however, saw, as Tom Cringle did, a Negro carrying a burden on his chin.

I fear that a stranger would feel a shock—and that not a

slight one—at the first sight of the average negro women of Port of Spain, especially the younger. Their masculine figures, their ungainly gestures, their loud and sudden laughter, even when walking alone, and their general coarseness, shocks, and must shock. It must be remembered that this is a seaport town; and one in which the licence usual in such places on both sides of the Atlantic is aggravated by the superabundant animal vigour and the perfect independence of the younger women. It is a painful subject. I shall touch it in these pages as seldom and as lightly as I can. There is, I verily believe, a large class of Negresses in Port of Spain and in the country, both Catholic and Protestant, who try their best to be respectable, after their standard: but unfortunately, here, as elsewhere over the world, the scum rises naturally to the top, and intrudes itself on the eye. The men are civil fellows enough, if you will, as in duty bound, be civil to them. If you are not, ugly capacities will flash out fast enough, and too fast. If any one says of the Negro, as of the Russian, 'He is but a savage polished over: you have only to scratch him, and the barbarian shows underneath:' the only answer to be made is—Then do not scratch him. It will be better for you, and for him.

When you have ceased looking—even staring—at the black women and their ways, you become aware of the strange variety of races which people the city. Here passes an old Coolie Hindoo, with nothing on but his lungee round his loins, and a scarf over his head; a white-bearded, delicate-featured old gentleman, with probably some caste-mark of red paint on his forehead; his thin limbs, and small hands and feet, contrasting strangely with the brawny Negroes round. There comes a bright-eyed young lady, probably his daughter-in-law, hung all over with bangles, in a white muslin petticoat, crimson cotton-velvet jacket, and green gauze veil, with her naked brown baby astride on her hip; a clever, smiling, delicate little woman, who is quite aware of the brightness of her own eyes. And who are these three boys in dark blue coatees and trousers, one of whom carries, hanging at one end of a long bamboo, a couple of sweet potatoes; at the other, possibly, a pebble to balance them? As they approach, their doleful visage betrays them. Chinese they are, without a doubt: but whether old or young, men or women, you cannot tell, till the initiated point out that the women have chignons and no hats, the men hats with their pigtails coiled up under them. Beyond this distinction, I know none visible. Certainly none in those sad visages—'Offas, non facies,' as old Ammianus Marcellinus has it.

But why do Chinese never smile? Why do they look as if some one had sat upon their noses as soon as they were born, and they had been weeping bitterly over the calamity ever since? They, too, must have their moments of relaxation: but when? Once, and once only, in Port of Spain, we saw a Chinese woman, nursing her baby, burst into an audible laugh : and we looked at each other, as much astonished as if our horses had begun to talk.

There again is a group of coloured men of all ranks, talking eagerly, business, or even politics ; some of them as well dressed as if they were fresh from Europe ; some of them, too, six feet high, and broad in proportion ; as fine a race, physically, as one would wish to look upon ; and with no want of shrewdness either, or determination, in their faces : a race who ought, if

CHINESE MAN AND WOMAN.

they will be wise and virtuous, to have before them a great future. Here come home from the convent school two coloured young ladies, probably pretty, possibly lovely, certainly gentle, modest, and well-dressed according to the fashions of Paris or New York ; and here comes the unmistakable Englishman, tall, fair, close-shaven, arm-in-arm with another man, whose more delicate features, more sallow complexion, and little moustache mark him as some Frenchman or Spaniard of old family. Both are dressed as if they were going to walk up Pall Mall or the Rue de Rivoli ; for 'go-to-meeting clothes' are somewhat too much *de rigueur* here ; a shooting-jacket and wide-awake betrays the newly-landed Englishman. Both take off their hats

with a grand air to a lady in a carriage; for they are very fine
gentlemen indeed, and intend to remain such: and well that is
for the civilisation of the island; for it is from such men as
these, and from their families, that the good manners for which
West Indians are, or ought to be, famous, have permeated down,
slowly but surely, through all classes of society save the very
lowest.

The straight and level street, swarming with dogs, vultures,
chickens, and goats, passes now out of the old into the newer
part of the city; and the type of the houses changes at once.
Some are mere wooden sheds of one or two rooms, comfortable
enough in that climate, where a sleeping-place is all that is
needed—if the occupiers would but keep them clean. Other
houses, wooden too, belong to well-to-do folk. Over high walls
you catch sight of jalousies and verandahs, inside which must
be most delightful darkness and coolness. Indeed, one cannot
fancy more pleasant nests than some of the little gaily-painted
wooden houses, standing on stilts to let the air under the floors,
and all embowered in trees and flowers, which line the roads in
the suburbs; and which are inhabited, we are told, by people
engaged in business.

But what would—or at least ought to—strike the newcomer's
eye with most pleasurable surprise, and make him realise into
what a new world he has been suddenly translated—even more
than the Negroes, and the black vultures sitting on roof-ridges,
or stalking about in mid-street—are the flowers which show
over the walls on each side of the street. In that little garden,
not thirty feet broad, what treasures there are! A tall palm—
whether Palmiste or Oil-palm—has its smooth trunk hung all
over with orchids, tied on with wire. Close to it stands a
purple Dracæna, such as are put on English dinner-tables in
pots: but this one is twenty feet high; and next to it is that
strange tree the Clavija, of which the Creoles are justly fond.
A single straight stem, fifteen feet high, carries huge oblong
leaves atop, and beneath them, growing out of the stem itself,
delicate panicles of little white flowers, fragrant exceedingly.
A double blue pea[1] and a purple Bignonia are scrambling over
shrubs and walls. And what is this which hangs over into the
road, some fifteen feet in height—long, bare, curving sticks,
carrying each at its end a flat blaze of scarlet? What but the
Poinsettia, paltry scions of which, like the Dracæna, adorn our
hothouses and dinner-tables. The street is on fire with it all
the way up, now in mid-winter; while at the street end opens
out a green park, fringed with noble trees all in full leaf; underneath them more pleasant little suburban villas; and behind
all, again, a background of steep wooded mountain a thousand
feet in height. That is the Savannah, the public park and race-
ground; such as neither London nor Paris can boast.

[1] *Clitoria Ternatea;* which should be in all our hothouses.

One may be allowed to regret that the exuberant loyalty of the citizens of Port of Spain has somewhat defaced one end at least of their Savannah; for in expectation of a visit from the Duke of Edinburgh, they erected for his reception a pile of brick, of which the best that can be said is that it holds a really large and stately ballroom, and the best that can be hoped is that the authorities will hide it as quickly as possible with a ring of Palmistes, Casuarinas, Sandboxes, and every quick-growing tree. Meanwhile, as His Royal Highness did not come, the citizens wisely thought that they might as well enjoy their new building themselves. So there, on set high days, the Governor and the Lady of the Governor hold their court. There, when the squadron comes in, officers in uniform dance at desperate sailors' pace with delicate Creoles; some of them, coloured as well as white, so beautiful in face and figure that one could almost pardon the jolly tars if they enacted a second Mutiny of the *Bounty*, and refused one and all to leave the island and the fair dames thereof. And all the while the warm night wind rushes in through the high open windows; and the fire-flies flicker up and down, in and out, and you slip away on to the balcony to enjoy—for after all it is very hot—the purple star-spangled night; and see aloft the saw of the mountain ridges against the black-blue sky; and below—what a contrast! —the crowd of white eyeballs and white teeth—Negroes, Coolies, Chinese—all grinning and peeping upward against the railing, in the hope of seeing—through the walls—the 'buccra quality' enjoy themselves.

An even pleasanter sight we saw once in that large room, a sort of agricultural and horticultural show, which augured well for the future of the colony. The flowers were not remarkable, save for the taste shown in their arrangement, till one recollected that they were not brought from hothouses, but grown in mid-winter in the open air. The roses, of which West Indians are very fond, as they are of all 'home,' *i.e.* European, flowers, were not as good as those of Europe. The rose in Trinidad, though it flowers three times a year, yet, from the great heat and moisture, runs too much to wood. But the roots, especially the different varieties of yam, were very curious; and their size proved the wonderful food-producing powers of the land when properly cultivated. The poultry, too, were worthy of an English show. Indeed, the fowl seems to take to tropical America as the horse has to Australia, as to a second native-land; and Trinidad alone might send an endless supply to the fowl-market of the Northern States, even if that should not be quite true which some one said, that you might turn an old cock loose in the bush, and he, without further help, would lay more eggs, and bring up more chickens, than you could either eat or sell.

But the most interesting element of that exhibition was the

coco-nut fibre products of Messrs. Uhrich and Gerold, of which more in another place. In them lies a source of further wealth to the colony, which may stand her in good stead when Port of Spain becomes, as it must become, one of the great emporiums of the West.

Since our visit the great ballroom has seen—even now is seeing—strange vicissitudes. For the new Royal College, having as yet no buildings of its own, now keeps school, it is said, therein—alas for the inkstains on that beautiful floor! And by last advices, a 'troupe of artistes' from Martinique, there being no theatre in Port of Spain, have been doing their play-acting in it; and Terpsichore and Thalia (Melpomene, I fear, haunts not the stage of Martinique) have been hustling all the other Muses downstairs at sunset, and joining their jinglings to the chorus of tom-toms and chac-chacs which resounds across the Savannah, at least till 10 P.M., from all the suburbs.

The road—and all the roads round Port of Spain, thanks to Sir Ralph Woodford, are as good as English roads—runs between the Savannah and the mountain spurs, and past the Botanic Gardens, which are a credit, in more senses than one, to the Governors of the island. For in them, amid trees from every quarter of the globe, and gardens kept up in the English fashion, with fountains, too, so necessary in this tropical clime, stood a large 'Government House.' This house was some years ago destroyed; and the then Governor took refuge in a cottage just outside the garden. A sum of money was voted to rebuild the big house: but the Governors, to their honour, have preferred living in the cottage, adding to it from time to time what was necessary for mere comfort; and have given the old gardens to the city, as a public pleasure-ground, kept up at Government expense.

This Paradise—for such it is—is somewhat too far from the city; and one passes in it few people, save an occasional brown nurse. But when Port of Spain becomes, as it surely will, a great commercial city, and the slopes of Laventille, Belmont, and St. Ann's, just above the gardens, are studded, as they surely will be, with the villas of rich merchants, then will the generous gift of English Governors be appreciated and used; and the Botanic Gardens will become a Tropic Garden of the Tuileries, alive, at five o'clock every evening, with human flowers of every hue.

CHAPTER V

A LETTER FROM A WEST INDIAN COTTAGE ORNÉE

30th December 1869.

MY DEAR ——, We are actually settled in a West Indian country-house, amid a multitude of sights and sounds so utterly new and strange, that the mind is stupefied by the continual effort to take in, or (to confess the truth) to gorge without hope of digestion, food of every conceivable variety. The whole day long new objects and their new names have jostled each other in the brain, in dreams as well as in waking thoughts. Amid such a confusion, to describe this place as a whole is as yet impossible. It must suffice if you find in this letter a sketch or two—not worthy to be called a study—of particular spots which seem typical, beginning with my bathroom window, as the scene which first proved to me, at least, that we were verily in the Tropics.

You look out—would that you did look in fact!—over the low sill. The gravel outside, at least, is an old friend; it consists of broken bits of gray Silurian rock, and white quartz among it; and one touch of Siluria makes the whole world kin. But there the kindred ends. A few green weeds, looking just like English ones, peep up through the gravel. Weeds, all over the world, are mostly like each other; poor, thin, pale in leaf, small and meagre in stem and flower: meaner forms which fill up for good, and sometimes, too, for harm, the gaps left by Nature's aristocracy of grander and, in these Tropics, more tyrannous and destroying forms. So like home weeds they look: but pick one, and you find it unlike anything at home. That one happens to be, as you may see by its little green mouse-tails, a pepper-weed,[1] first cousin to the great black pepper-bush in the gardens near by, with the berries of which you may burn your mouth gratis.

So it is, you would find, with every weed in the little cleared dell, some fifteen feet deep, beyond the gravel. You could not

[1] *Peperomia.*

—I certainly cannot—guess at the name, seldom at the family, of a single plant. But I am going on too fast. What are those sticks of wood which keep the gravel bank up? Veritable bamboos; and a bamboo-pipe, too, is carrying the trickling cool water into the bath close by. Surely we are in the Tropics. You hear a sudden rattle, as of boards and brown paper, overhead, and find that it is the clashing of the huge leaves of a young fan palm,[1] growing not ten feet from the window. It has no stem as yet; and the lower leaves have to be trimmed off or they would close up the path, so that only the great forked green butts of them are left, bound to each other by natural matting: but overhead they range out nobly in leafstalks ten feet long, and fans full twelve feet broad; and this is but a baby, a three years' old thing. Surely, again, we are in the Tropics. Ten feet farther, thrust all awry by the huge palm leaves, grows a young tree, unknown to me, looking like a walnut. Next to it an orange, covered with long prickles and small green fruit, its roots propped up by a semi-cylindrical balk of timber, furry inside, which would puzzle a Hampshire woodsman; for it is, plainly, a groo-groo or a coco-palm, split down the middle. Surely, again, we are in the Tropics. Beyond it, again, blaze great orange and yellow flowers, with long stamens, and pistil curving upwards out of them. They belong to a twining, scrambling bush, with finely-pinnated mimosa leaves. That is the 'Flower-fence,'[2] so often heard of in past years; and round it hurries to and fro a great orange butterfly, larger seemingly than any English kind. Next to it is a row of Hibiscus shrubs, with broad crimson flowers; then a row of young Screw-pines,[3] from the East Indian Islands, like spiral pine-apple plants twenty feet high standing on stilts. Yes: surely we are in the Tropics. Over the low roof (for the cottage is all of one storey) of purple and brown and white shingles, baking in the sun, rises a tall tree, which looks (as so many do here) like a walnut, but is not one. It is the 'Poui' of the Indians,[4] and will be covered shortly with brilliant saffron flowers.

I turn my chair and look into the weedy dell. The ground on the opposite slope (slopes are, you must remember, here as steep as house-roofs, the last spurs of true mountains) is covered with a grass like tall rye-grass, but growing in tufts. That is the famous Guinea-grass[5] which, introduced from Africa, has spread over the whole West Indies. Dark lithe coolie prisoners, one a gentle young fellow, with soft beseeching eyes, and 'Felon' printed on the back of his shirt, are cutting it for the horses, under the guard of a mulatto turnkey, a tall, steadfast, dignified man; and between us and them are growing along the edge of the gutter, veritable pine-apples in the open air, and a low green

[1] *Sabal.* [2] *Poinziana.* [3] *Pandanus.*
[4] *Tecoma (serratifolia ?).* [5] *Panicum jumentorum.*

tree just like an apple, which is a Guava ; and a tall stick, thirty
feet high, with a flat top of gigantic curly horse-chestnut leaves,
which is a Trumpet-tree.[1] There are hundreds of them in the
mountains round : but most of them dead, from the intense
drought and fires of last year. Beyond it, again, is a round-
headed tree, looking like a huge Portugal laurel, covered with
racemes of purple buds. That is an 'Angelim';[2] when full-
grown, one of the finest timbers in the world. And what are
those at the top of the brow, rising out of the rich green scrub?
Verily, again, we are in the Tropics. They are palms, doubtless, some thirty feet high each, with here and there a young
one springing up like a gigantic crown of male-fern. The old
ones have straight gray stems, often prickly enough, and thick-
ened in the middle ; gray last year's leaves hanging down ; and
feathering round the top, a circular plume of pale green leaves,
like those of a coco-nut. But these are not cocos. The last
year's leaves of the coco are rich yellow, and its stem is curved.
These are groo-groos ;[3] they stand as fresh proofs that we are
indeed in the Tropics, and as 'a thing of beauty and a joy for
ever.'

For it is a joy for ever, a sight never to be forgotten, to have
once seen palms, breaking through and, as it were, defying the
soft rounded forms of the broad-leaved vegetation by the stern
grace of their simple lines ; the immovable pillar-stem looking
the more immovable beneath the toss and lash and flicker of
the long leaves, as they awake out of their sunlit sleep, and rage
impatiently for a while before the mountain gusts, and fall
asleep again. Like a Greek statue in a luxurious drawing-room,
sharp cut, cold, virginal ; shaming, by the grandeur of mere
form, the voluptuousness of mere colour, however rich and
harmonious ; so stands the palm in the forest ; to be worshipped
rather than to be loved. Look at the drawings of the Oreodoxa-
avenue at Rio, in M. Agassiz's charming book. Would that you
could see actually such avenues, even from the sea, as we have
seen them in St. Vincent and Guadaloupe : but look at the
mere pictures of them in that book, and you will sympathise,
surely, with our new palm-worship.

And lastly, what is that giant tree which almost fills the
centre of the glen, towering with upright but branching limbs,
and huge crown, thinly leaved, double the height of all the trees
around? An ash? Something like an ash in growth ; but
when you look at it through the glasses (indispensable in the
tropic forest), you see that the foliage is more like that of the
yellow horse-chestnut. And no British ash, not even the Altyre
giants, ever reached to half that bulk. It is a Silk-cotton tree ;
a Ceiba[4]—say, rather, the Ceiba of the glen ; for these glens

---

[1] *Cecropia.*
[2] *Andira inermis.*
[3] *Acrocomia sclerocarpa.*
[4] *Eriodendron anfractuosum.*

have a habit of holding each one great Ceiba, which has taken its stand at the upper end, just where the mountain-spurs run together in an amphitheatre; and being favoured (it may be supposed) by the special richness of the down-washed soil at that spot, grows to one of those vast air-gardens of creepers and parasites of which we have so often read and dreamed. Such a one is this: but we will not go up to it now. This

GROO-GROOS.

sketch shall be completed by the background of green and gray, fading aloft into tender cobalt: the background of mountain, ribbed and gullied into sharpest slopes by the tropic rains, yet showing, even where steepest, never a face of rock, or a crag peeping through the trees. Up to the sky-line, a thousand feet aloft, all is green; and that, instead of being, as in Europe, stone or moor, is jagged and feathered with gigantic trees. How rich! you would say. Yet these West Indians only mourn over its desolation and disfigurement; and point to the sheets of gray stems, which hang like mist along the upper slopes. They look to us, on this 30th of December, only as April signs that the woodlands have not quite burst into full leaf. But to the inhabitants they are tokens of those fearful fires which raged over the island during the long drought of this summer; when the forests were burning for a whole month, and this house scarcely saved; when whole cane-fields, mills, dwelling-houses, went up as tinder and flame in a moment, and the smoky haze from the burning island spread far out to sea. And yet, where the fire passed six months ago, all is now a fresh impenetrable undergrowth of green; creepers covering the land, climbing up and shrouding the charred stumps; young palms, like Prince of Wales's feathers, breaking up, six or eight feet high, among a wilderness of sensitive plants, scarlet-flowered dwarf Balisiers,[1] climbing fern,[2] convolvuluses of every hue, and an endless variety of outlandish leaves, over which flutter troops of butterflies. How the seeds of the plants and the eggs of the insects have been preserved, who can tell? But there their children are, in myriads; and ere a generation has passed, every dead gray stem will have disappeared before the ants and beetles and great wood-boring bees who rumble round in blue-black armour; the young plants will have grown into great trees beneath the immeasurable vital force which pours all the year round from the blazing sun above, and all be as it was once more. In verity we are in the Tropics, where the so-called 'powers of nature' are in perpetual health and strength, and as much stronger and swifter, for good and evil, than in our chilly clime, as is the young man in the heat of youth compared with the old man shivering to his grave. Think over that last simile. If you think of it in the light which physiology gives, you will find that it is not merely a simile, but a true analogy; another manifestation of a great physical law.

Thus much for the view at the back—a chance scene, without the least pretensions to what average people would call beauty of landscape. But oh that we could show you the view in front! The lawn with its flowering shrubs, tiny specimens of which we admire in hothouses at home; the grass as green (for it is now the end of the rainy season) as that of England in May, winding away into the cool shade of strange evergreens; the yellow coco-nut palms on the nearest spur of hill throwing back the tender blue of the higher mountains; the huge central group of trees —Saman,[3] Sandbox,[4] and Fig, with the bright ostrich plumes of a climbing palm towering through the mimosa-like foliage of the Saman; and Erythrinas[5] (Bois immortelles, as they call them here), their all but leafless boughs now blazing against the blue sky with vermilion flowers, trees of red coral sixty feet in height. Ah that we could show you the avenue on the right, composed of palms from every quarter of the Tropics—palms with smooth stems, or with prickly ones, with fan leaves, feather

[1] *Heliconia Caribæa.* [2] *Lygodium venustum.*
[3] *Inga Saman;* 'Caraccas tree.' [4] *Hura crepitans.*
[5] *Erythrina umbrosa.*

leaves, leaves (as in the wine-palm[1]) like Venus's hair fern; some, again, like the Cocorite,[2] almost stemless, rising in a huge ostrich plume which tosses in the land breeze, till the long stiff leaflets seem to whirl like the spokes of a green glass wheel. Ah that we could wander with you through the Botanic Garden beyond, amid fruits and flowers brought together from all the lands of the perpetual summer; or even give you, through the great arches of the bamboo clumps, as they creak and rattle sadly in the wind, and the Bauhinias, like tall and ancient white-thorns, which shade the road, one glance of the flat green

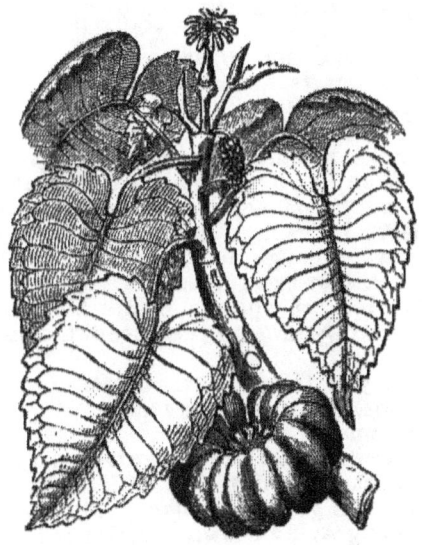

SANDBOX.

Savannah, with its herds of kine, beyond which lies, buried in flowering trees, and backed by mountain woods, the city of Port of Spain. One glance, too, under the boughs of the great Cotton-tree at the gate, at the still sleeping sea, with one tall coolie ship at anchor, seen above green cane-fields and coolie gardens, gay with yellow Croton and purple Dracæna, and crimson Poinsettia, and the grand leaves of the grandest of all plants, the Banana, food of paradise. Or, again, far away to the extreme right, between the flat tops of the great Saman-avenue at the barracks and the wooded mountain-spurs which rush down into the sea, the islands of the Bocas floating in the shining water; and beyond them, a cloud among the clouds,

[1] *Caryota.* [2] *Maximiliana.*

the peak of a mighty mountain, with one white tuft of mist upon its top. Ah that we could show you but that, and tell you that you were looking at the 'Spanish Main'; at South America itself, at the last point of the Venezuelan Cordillera, and the hills where jaguars lie. If you could but see what we see daily; if you could see with us the strange combination of rich and luscious beauty, with vastness and repose, you would understand, and excuse, the tendency to somewhat grandiose language which tempts perpetually those who try to describe the Tropics, and know well that they can only fail.

In presence of such forms and such colouring as this, one becomes painfully sensible of the poverty of words, and the futility, therefore, of all word-painting; of the inability, too, of the senses to discern and define objects of such vast variety; of our æsthetic barbarism, in fact, which has no choice of epithets save between such as 'great,' and 'vast,' and 'gigantic'; between such as 'beautiful,' and 'lovely,' and 'exquisite,' and so forth; which are, after all, intellectually only one stage higher than the half-brute Wah! wah! with which the savage grunts his astonishment—call it not admiration; epithets which are not, perhaps, intellectually as high as the 'God is great' of the Mussulman, who is wise enough not to attempt any analysis either of Nature or of his feelings about her; and wise enough also (not having the fear of Spinoza before his eyes) to 'in omni ignoto confugere ad Deum'—in presence of the unknown to take refuge in God.

To describe to you, therefore, the Botanic Garden (in which the cottage stands) would take a week's work of words, which would convey no images to your mind. Let it be enough to say, that our favourite haunt in all the gardens is a little dry valley, beneath the loftiest group of trees. At its entrance rises a great Tamarind, and a still greater Saman; both have leaves like a Mimosa—as the engraving shows. Up its trunk a Cereus has reared itself, for some thirty feet at least; a climbing Seguine [1] twines up it with leaves like 'lords and ladies'; but the glory of the tree is that climbing palm, the feathers of which we saw crowning it from a distance. Up into the highest branches and down again, and up again into the lower branches, and rolling along the ground in curves as that of a Boa bedecked with huge ferns and prickly spikes, six feet and more long each, the Rattan [2] hangs in mid-air, one hardly sees how, beautiful and wonderful, beyond what clumsy words can tell. Beneath the great trees (for here great trees grow freely beneath greater trees, and beneath greater trees again, delighting in the shade) is a group of young Mangosteens,[3] looking, to describe the unknown by the known, like walnuts with leaflets eight inches

---

[1] *Philodendron.*   [2] *Calamus Rotangi*, from the East Indies.
[3] *Garcinia Mangostana*, from Malacca. The really luscious and famous variety has not yet fruited in Trinidad.

long, their boughs clustered with yellow and green sour fruit; and beyond them stretches up the lawn a dense grove of nutmegs, like Portugal laurels, hung about with olive-yellow apples. Here and there a nutmeg-apple has split, and shows within the delicate crimson caul of mace; or the nutmegs, the mace still clinging round them, lie scattered on the grass. Under the perpetual shade of the evergreens haunt Heliconias and other

TAMARIND.

delicate butterflies, who seem to dread the blaze outside, and flutter gently from leaf to leaf, their colouring—which is usually black with markings of orange, crimson, or blue—coming into strongest contrast with the uniform green of leaf and grass. This is our favourite spot for entomologising, when the sun outside altogether forbids the least exertion. Turn with us—alas! only in fancy—out of the grove into a neighbouring path, between tea-shrubs, looking like privets with large myrtle flowers, and young clove-trees, covered with the groups of green buds which are the cloves of commerce; and among fruit-trees from every part of the Tropics, with the names of which I will not burden you. Glance at that beautiful and most poisonous shrub, which we found wild at St. Thomas's.[1] Glance, too—but,

[1] *Thevetia nerriifolia.*

again, why burden you with names which you will not recollect, much more with descriptions which do not describe? Look, though, down that Allspice avenue, at the clear warm light which is reflected off the smooth yellow ever-peeling stems; and then, if you can fix your eye steadily on any object, where all are equally new and strange, look at this stately tree. A bough has been broken off high up, and from the wounded spot two plants are already contending. One is a parasitic Orchis; the other a parasite of a more dangerous family. It looks like a straggling Magnolia, some two feet high. In fifty years it will be a stately tree. Look at the single long straight air-root which it is letting down by the side of the tree bole. That root, if left, will be the destroyer of the whole tree. It will touch the earth, take root below, send out side-fibres above, call down younger roots to help it, till the whole bole, clasped and stifled in their embraces, dies and rots out, and the Matapalo (or Scotch attorney,[1] as it is rudely called here) stands alone on stilted roots, and board walls of young wood, slowly coalescing into one great trunk; master of the soil once owned by the patron on whose vitals he has fed: a treacherous tyrant; and yet, like many another treacherous tyrant, beautiful to see, with his shining evergreen foliage, and grand labyrinth of smooth roots, standing high in air, or dangling from the boughs in search of soil below; and last, but not least, his Magnolia-like flowers, rosy or snowy-white, and green egg-shaped fruits.

Now turn homewards, past the Rosa del monte[2] bush (bushes, you must recollect, are twenty feet high here), covered with crimson roses, full of long silky crimson stamens: and then try —as we do daily in vain—to recollect and arrange one-tenth of the things which you have seen.

One look round at the smaller wild animals and flowers. Butterflies swarm round us, of every hue. Beetles, you may remark, are few; they do not run in swarms about these arid paths as they do at home. But the wasps and bees, black and brown, are innumerable. That huge bee in steel-blue armour, booming straight at you—whom some one compared to the Lord Mayor's man in armour turned into a cherub, and broken loose —(get out of his way, for he is absorbed in business)—is probably a wood-borer,[3] of whose work you may read in Mr. Wood's *Homes without Hands*. That long black wasp, commonly called a Jack Spaniard, builds pensile paper nests under every roof and shed. Watch, now, this more delicate brown wasp, probably one of the *Pelopœi* of whom we have read in Mr. Gosse's *Naturalist in Jamaica* and Mr. Bates's *Travels on the Amazons*. She has made under a shelf a mud nest of three long cells, and filled them one by one with small spiders, and the precious egg which, when hatched, is to feed on them. One

---

[1] *Clusia.*   [2] *Brownea.*   [3] *Xylocopa.*

hundred and eight spiders we have counted in a single nest like this; and the wasp, much of the same shape as the Jack Spaniard, but smaller, works, unlike him, alone, or at least only with her husband's help. The long mud nest is built upright, often in the angle of a doorpost or panel; and always added to, and entered from, below. With a joyful hum she flies back to it all day long with her pellets of mud, and spreads them out with her mouth into pointed arches, one laid on the other, making one side of the arch out of each pellet, and singing low but cheerily over her work. As she works downward, she parts off the tube of the nest with horizontal floors of a finer and harder mud, and inside each storey places some five spiders, and among them the precious egg, or eggs, which is to feed on them when hatched. If we open the uppermost chamber, we shall find every vestige of the spiders gone, and the cavity filled (and, strange to say, exactly filled) by a brown-coated wasp-pupa, enveloped in a fine silken shroud. In the chamber below, perhaps, we shall find the grub full-grown, and finishing his last spider; and so on, down six or eight storeys, till the lowest holds nothing but spiders, packed close, but not yet sealed up. These spiders, be it remembered, are not dead. By some strange craft, the wasp knows exactly where to pierce them with her sting, so as to stupefy, but not to kill, just as the sand-wasps of our banks at home stupefy the large weevils which they store in their burrows as food for their grubs.

There are wasps too, here, who make pretty little jar-shaped nests, round, with a neatly lined round lip. Paper-nests, too, more like those of our tree-wasps at home, hang from the trees in the woods. Ants' nests, too, hang sometimes from the stronger boughs, looking like huge hard lumps of clay. And, once at least, we have found silken nests of butterflies or moths, containing many chrysalids each. Meanwhile, dismiss from your mind the stories of insect plagues. If good care is taken to close the mosquito curtains at night, the flies about the house are not nearly as troublesome as we have often found the midges in Scotland. As for snakes, we have seen none; centipedes are, certainly, apt to get into the bath, but can be fished out dead, and thrown to the chickens. The wasps and bees do not sting, or in any wise interfere with our comfort, save by building on the books. The only ants who come into the house are the minute, harmless, and most useful 'crazy ants,' who run up and down wildly all day, till they find some eatable thing, an atom of bread or a disabled cockroach, of which last, by the by, we have seen hardly any here. They then prove themselves in their sound senses by uniting to carry off their prey, some pulling, some pushing, with a steady combination of effort which puts to shame an average negro crew. And these are all we have to fear, unless it be now and then a huge spider, which it is not the fashion here to kill, as they feed on flies. So comfort yourself with the thought that, as regards insect pests, we are quite as comfortable as in an English country-house, and infinitely more comfortable than in a Scotch shooting lodge, let alone an Alpine châlet.

Lizards run about the walks in plenty, about the same size as the green lizard of the South of Europe, but of more sober colours. The parasol ants—of whom I could tell you much, save that you will read far more than I can tell you in half a dozen books at home—walk in triumphal processions, each with a bit of green leaf borne over its head, and probably, when you look closely, with a little ant or two riding on it, and getting a lift home after work on their stronger sister's back—and these are all the monsters which you are likely to meet.

Would that there were more birds to be seen and heard! But of late years the free Negro, like the French peasant during the first half of this century, has held it to be one of the indefeasible rights of a free man to carry a rusty gun, and to shoot every winged thing. He has been tempted, too, by orders from London shops for gaudy birds—humming-birds especially. And when a single house, it is said, advertises for 20,000 bird-skins at a time, no wonder if birds grow scarce; and no wonder, too, if the wholesale destruction of these insect-killers should avenge itself by a plague of vermin, caterpillars, and grubs innumerable. Already the turf of the Savannah or public park, close by, is being destroyed by hordes of mole-crickets, strange to say, almost exactly like those of our old English meadows; and unless something is done to save the birds, the cane and other crops will surely suffer in their turn. A gun-licence would be, it seems, both unpopular and easily evaded in a wild forest country. A heavy export tax on bird-skins has been proposed. May it soon be laid on, and the vegetable wealth of the island saved, at the expense of a little less useless finery in young ladies' hats.

So we shall see and hear but few birds round Port of Spain, save the black vultures[1]—Corbeaux, as they call them here; and the black 'tick birds,'[2] a little larger than our English blackbird, with a long tail and a thick-hooked bill, who perform for the cattle here the same friendly office as is performed by starlings at home. Privileged creatures, they cluster about on rails and shrubs within ten feet of the passer, while overhead in the tree-tops the 'Qu'est ce qu'il dit,'[3] a brown and yellow bird, who seems almost equally privileged and insolent, inquires perpetually what you say. Besides these, swallows of various kinds, little wrens,[4] almost exactly like our English ones, and night-hawking goat-suckers, few birds are seen. But, unseen, in the depths of every wood, a songster breaks out ever and anon in notes equal for purity and liveliness to those of our

[1] *Cathartes Urubu.*
[2] *Crotophaga Ani.*
[3] *Lanius Pitanga.*
[4] *Troglodytes Eudon.*

English thrush, and belies the vulgar calumny that tropic birds, lest they should grow too proud of their gay feathers, are denied the gift of song.

One look, lastly, at the animals which live, either in cages or at liberty, about the house. The queen of all the pets is a black and gray spider monkey[1] from Guiana—consisting of a tail which has developed, at one end, a body about twice as big as a hare's; four arms (call them not legs), of which the front ones have no thumbs, nor rudiments of thumbs; and a head of black hair, brushed forward over the foolish, kindly, greedy, sad face, with its wide, suspicious, beseeching eyes, and mouth which, as in all these American monkeys, as far as we have seen, can have no expression, not even that of sensuality, because it has no lips. Others have described the spider monkey as four legs and a tail, tied in a knot in the middle: but the tail is, without doubt, the most important of the five limbs. Wherever the monkey goes, whatever she does, the tail is the standing-point, or rather hanging-point. It takes one turn at least round something or other, provisionally, and in case it should be wanted; often, as she swings, every other limb hangs in the most ridiculous repose, and the tail alone supports. Sometimes it carries, by way of ornament, a bunch of flowers or a live kitten. Sometimes it is curled round the neck, or carried over the head in the hands, out of harm's way; or when she comes silently up behind you, puts her cold hand in yours, and walks by your side like a child, she steadies herself by taking a half-turn of her tail round your wrist. Her relative Jack, of whom hereafter, walks about carrying his chain, to ease his neck, in a loop of his tail. The spider monkey's easiest attitude in walking, and in running also, is, strangely, upright, like a human being: but as for her antics, nothing could represent them to you, save a series of photographs, and those instantaneous ones; for they change, every moment, not by starts, but with a deliberate ease which would be grace in anything less horribly ugly, into postures such as Callot or Breughel never fancied for the ugliest imps who ever tormented St. Anthony. All absurd efforts of agility which you ever saw at a *séance* of the Hylobates Lar Club at Cambridge are quiet and clumsy compared to the rope-dancing which goes on in the boughs of the Poui tree, or, to their great detriment, of the Bougainvillea and the Gardenia on the lawn. But with all this, Spider is the gentlest, most obedient, and most domestic of beasts. Her creed is, that yellow bananas are the *summum bonum;* and that she must not come into the dining-room, or even into the verandah; whither, nevertheless, she slips, in fear and trembling, every morning, to steal the little green parrot's breakfast out of his cage, or the baby's milk, or fruit off the side-board;

---

[1] *Ateles* (undescribed species).

in which case she makes her appearance suddenly and silently, sitting on the threshold like a distorted fiend; and begins scratching herself, looking at everything except the fruit, and pretending total absence of mind, till the proper moment comes for unwinding her lengthy ugliness, and making a snatch at the table. Poor weak-headed thing, full of foolish cunning; always doing wrong, and knowing that it is wrong, but quite unable to resist temptation; and then profuse in futile explanations, gesticulations, mouthings of an 'Oh!—oh!—oh!' so pitiably human, that you can only punish her by laughing at her, which she does not at all like. One cannot resist the fancy, while watching her, either that she was once a human being, or that she is trying to become one. But, at present, she has more than one habit to learn, or to recollect, ere she become as fit for human society as the dog or the cat.[1] Her friends are, every human being who will take notice of her, and a beautiful little Guazupita, or native deer, a little larger than a roe, with great black melting eyes, and a heart as soft as its eyes, who comes to lick one's hand; believes in bananas as firmly as the monkey; and when she can get no hand to lick, licks the hairy monkey for mere love's sake, and lets it ride on her back, and kicks it off, and lets it get on again and take a half-turn of its tail round her neck, and throttle her with its arms, and pull her nose out of the way when a banana is coming: and all out of pure love; for the two have never been introduced to each other by man; and the intimacy between them, like that famous one between the horse and the hen, is of Nature's own making up.

Very different from the spider monkey in temper is her cousin Jack, who sits, sullen and unrepentant, at the end of a long chain, having an ugly liking for the calves of passers-by, and ugly teeth to employ on them. Sad at heart he is, and testifies his sadness sometimes by standing bolt upright, with his long arms in postures oratoric, almost prophetic, or, when duly pitied and moaned to, lying down on his side, covering his hairy eyes with one hairy arm, and weeping and sobbing bitterly. He seems, speaking scientifically, to be some sort of Mycetes or Howler, from the flat globular throat, which indicates the great development of the hyoid bone; but, happily for the sleep of the neighbourhood, he never utters in captivity any sound beyond a chuckle; and he is supposed, by some here, from his burly thick-set figure, vast breadth between the ears, short neck, and general cast of countenance, to have been, in a prior state of existence, a man and a brother—and that by no means of negro blood—who has gained, in this his purgatorial stage of existence, nothing save a well-earned tail. At

---

[1] Alas for Spider! She came to the Zoological Gardens last summer, only to die pitifully.

all events, more than one of us was impressed, at the first sight, with the conviction that we had seen him before.

Poor Jack! and it is come to this: and all from the indulgence of his five senses, plus 'the sixth sense of vanity.' His only recreation save eating is being led about by the mulatto turnkey, the one human being with whom he, dimly understanding what is fit for him, will at all consort; and having wild pines thrown down to him from the Poui tree above by the spider monkey, whose gambols he watches with pardonable envy. Like the great Mr. Barry Lyndon (the acutest sketch of human nature dear Thackeray ever made), he cannot understand why the world is so unjust and foolish as to have taken a prejudice against him. After all, he is nothing but a strong nasty brute; and his only reason for being here is that he is a new and undescribed species, never seen before, and, it is to be hoped, never to be seen again.

In a cage near by (for there is quite a little menagerie here) are three small Sapajous,[1] two of which belong to the island; as abject and selfish as monkeys usually are, and as uninteresting; save for the plain signs which they give of being actuated by more than instinct,—by a 'reasoning' power exactly like in kind, though not equal in degree, to that of man. If, as people are now too much induced to believe, the brain makes the man, and not some higher Reason connected intimately with the Moral Sense, which will endure after the brain has turned to dust; if to foresee consequences from experience, and to adapt means to ends, be the highest efforts of the intellect: then who can deny that the Sapajou proves himself a man and a brother, plus a tail, when he puts out a lighted cigar-end before he chews it, by dipping it into the water-pan; and that he may, therefore, by long and steady calculations about the conveniences of virtue and inconveniences of vice, gradually cure himself and his children of those evil passions which are defined as 'the works of the flesh,' and rise to the supremest heights of justice, benevolence, and purity? We, who have been brought up in an older, and as we were taught to think, a more rational creed, may not be able yet to allow our imaginations so daringly hopeful a range: but the world travels fast, and seems travelling on into some such theory just now; leaving behind, as antiquated bigots, those who dare still to believe in the eternal and immutable essence of Goodness, and in the divine origin of man, created in the likeness of God, that he might be perfect even as his Father in heaven is perfect.

But to return to the animals. The cage next to the monkeys holds a more pleasant beast; a Toucan out of the primeval forest, as gorgeous in colour as he is ridiculous in shape. His general plumage is black, set off by a snow-white gorget fringed

[1] *Cebus.*

with crimson; crimson and green tail coverts, and a crimson and green beak, with blue cere about his face and throat. His enormous and weak bill seems made for the purpose of swallowing bananas whole; how he feeds himself with it in the forest it is difficult to guess: and when he hops up and down on his great clattering feet—two toes turned forward, and two back—twisting head and beak right and left (for he cannot see well straight before him) to see whence the bananas are coming; or when again, after gorging a couple, he sits gulping and winking, digesting them in serene satisfaction, he is as good a specimen as can be seen of the ludicrous—dare I say the intentionally ludicrous?—element in nature.

Next to him is a Kinkajou;[1] a beautiful little furry bear—or racoon—who has found it necessary for his welfare in this world of trees to grow a long prehensile tail, as the monkeys of the New World have done. He sleeps by day; save when woke up to eat a banana, or to scoop the inside out of an egg with his long lithe tongue: but by night he remembers his forest-life, and performs strange dances by the hour together, availing himself not only of his tail, which he uses just as the spider monkey does, but of his hind feet, which he can turn completely round at will, till the claws point forward like those of a bat. But with him, too, the tail is the sheet-anchor, by which he can hold on, and bring all his four feet to bear on his food. So it is with the little Ant-eater,[2] who must needs climb here to feed on the tree ants. So it is, too, with the Tree Porcupine,[3] or Coendou, who (in strange contrast to the well-known classic Porcupine of the rocks of Southern Europe) climbs trees after leaves, and swings about like the monkeys. For the life of animals in the primeval forest is, as one glance would show you, principally arboreal. The flowers, the birds, the insects, are all a hundred feet over your head as you walk along in the all but lifeless shade; and half an hour therein would make you feel how true was Mr. Wallace's simile—that a walk in the tropic forest was like one in an empty cathedral while the service was being celebrated upon the roof.

In the next two cages, however, are animals who need no prehensile tails; for they are cats, furnished with those far more useful and potent engines, retractile claws; a form of beast at which the thoughtful man will never look without wonder; so unique, so strange, and yet as perfect, that it suits every circumstance of every clime; as does that equally unique form the dragon-fly. We found the dragon-flies here, to our surprise,

[1] *Cercoleptes.*

[2] *Myrmecophaga Didactyla.* I owe to the pencil of a gifted lady this sketch of the animal in repose, which is as perfect as it is, I believe, unique.

[3] *Synetheres.*

exactly similar to, and as abundant as, the dragon-flies at home, and remembering that there were dragon-flies of exactly the same type ages and ages ago, in the days of the Œningen and Solenhofen slates, said—Here is indeed a perfect work of God, which, as far as man can see, has needed no improvement (if

THE LITTLE ANT-EATER

such an expression be allowable) throughout epochs in which the whole shape of continents and seas, and the whole climate of the planet, has changed again and again. The cats are: an ocelot, a beautiful spotted and striped fiend, who hisses like a snake; a young jaguar, a clumsy, happy kitten, about as big as a pug dog, with a puny kitten's tail, who plays with the spider monkey, and only shows by the fast-increasing bulk of his square lumbering head, that in six months he will be ready to eat the monkey, and in twelve to eat the keeper.

There are strange birds, too. One, whom you may see in the Zoological Gardens, like a plover with a straight beak and bittern's plumage, from 'The Main,' whose business is to walk about the table at meals uttering sad metallic noises and catching flies. His name is Sun-bird,[1] 'Sun-fowlo' of the Surinam Negroes, according to dear old Stedman, 'because, when it extends its wings, which it often does, there appears on the interior part of each wing a most beautiful representation of the sun. This bird,' he continues very truly, 'might be styled the perpetual motion, its body making a continual movement, and its tail keeping time like the pendulum of a clock.'[2] A game-bird, olive, with a bare red throat, also from The Main, called a Chacaracha,[3] who is impudently brave, and considers the house his own; and a great black Curassow,[4] also from The Main, who patronises the turkeys and guinea-fowl; stalks in dignity before them; and when they do not obey, enforces his authority by pecking them to death. There is thus plenty of amusement here, and instruction too, for those to whom the ways of dumb animals during life are more interesting than their stuffed skins after death.

But there is the signal-gun, announcing the arrival of the Mail from home. And till it departs again there will be no time to add to this hasty, but not unfaithful, sketch of first impressions in a tropic island.

[1] *Helias Eurypyga.*
[2] Stedman's *Surinam*, vol. i. p. 118. What a genius was Stedman. What an eye and what a pen he had for all natural objects. His denunciations of the brutalities of old Dutch slavery are full of genuine eloquence and of sound sense likewise; and the loves of Stedman and his brown Joanna are one of the sweetest idylls in the English tongue.
[3] *Penelope* (?).   [4] *Crax.*

CHAPTER VI

MONOS

EARLY in January, I started with my host and his little suite on an expedition to the islands of the Bocas. Our object was twofold: to see tropical coast scenery, and to get, if possible, some Guacharo birds (pronounced Huáchăro), of whom more hereafter. Our chance of getting them depended on the sea being calm outside the Bocas, as well as inside. The calm inside was no proof of the calm out. Port of Spain is under the lee of the mountains; and the surf might be thundering along the northern shore, tearing out stone after stone from the soft cliffs, and shrouding all the distant points in salt haze, though the gulf along which we were rowing was perfectly smooth, and the shipping and the mangrove scrub and the coco-palms hung double, reflected as in a mirror, not of glass but of mud; and on the swamps of the Caroni the malarious fog hung motionless in long straight lines, waiting for the first blaze of sunrise to sublime it and its invisible poisons into the upper air, where it would be swept off, harmless, by the trade-wind which rushed along half a mile above our heads.

So away we rowed, or rather were rowed by four stalwart Negroes, along the northern shore of the gulf, while the sun leapt up straight astern, and made the awning, or rather the curtains of the awning, needful enough. For the perpendicular rays of the sun in the Tropics are not so much dreaded as the horizontal ones, which strike on the forehead, or, still more dangerous, on the back of the head; and in the West Indies, as in the United States, the early morning and the latter part of the afternoon are the times for sunstrokes. Some sort of shade for the back of the head is necessary for an European, unless (which is not altogether to be recommended) he adopts the La Platan fashion of wearing the natural, and therefore surest, sunshade of his own hair hanging down to his shoulders after the manner of our old cavaliers.

The first islands which we made—The Five Islands, as they are called—are curious enough. Isolated remnants of limestone, the biggest perhaps one hundred yards long by one hundred feet high, channelled and honeycombed into strange shapes by rain and waves, they are covered—that at least on which we landed—almost exclusively by Matapalos, which seem to have strangled the original trees and established themselves in every cranny of the rocks, sending out arms, legs, fingers, ropes, pillars, and what not, of live holdfasts over every rock and over each other, till little but the ubiquitous Seguine[1] and Pinguins[2] find room or sustenance among them. The island on which we landed is used, from time to time, as a depôt for coolie immigrants when first landed. There they remain to rest after the voyage, till they can be apportioned by the Government officers to the estates which need them. Of this admirable system of satisfying the great need of the West Indies, free labourers, I may be allowed to say a little here.

'Immigrants' are brought over from Hindostan at the expense of the colony. The Indian Government jealously watches the emigration, and through agents of its own rigidly tests the *bona-fide* 'voluntary' character of the engagement. That they are well treated on the voyage is sufficiently proved, that on 2264 souls imported last year the death-rate during the voyage was only 2·7 per cent, although cholera attacked the crew of one of the ships before it left the Hooghly. During the last three years ships with over 300 emigrants have arrived several times in Trinidad without a single death. On their arrival in Trinidad, those who are sick are sent at once to the hospital; those unfit for immediate labour are sent to the depôt. The healthy are 'indentured'—in plain English, apprenticed—for five years, and distributed among the estates which have applied for them. Husbands and wives are not allowed to be separated, nor are children under fifteen parted from their parents or natural protectors. They are expected by the law to work for 280 days in the year, nine hours a day; and receive the same wages as the free labourers: but for this system task-work is by consent universally substituted; and (as in the case of an English apprentice) the law, by various provisions, at once punishes them for wilful idleness, and protects them from tyranny or fraud on the part of their employers. Till the last two years the newcomers received their wages entirely in money. But it was found better to give them for the first year (and now for the two first years) part payment in daily rations: a pound of rice, four ounces of dholl (a kind of pea), an ounce of coco-nut oil or ghee, and two ounces of sugar to each adult; and half the same to each child between five and ten years old.

This plan has been found necessary, in order to protect the Coolies both from themselves and from each other. They themselves prefer receiving the whole of their wages in cash. With that fondness for mere hard money which marks a half-

---

[1] *Philodendron.*   [2] *Bromelia.*

educated Oriental, they will, as a rule, hoard their wages; and stint themselves of food, injuring their powers of work, and even endangering their own lives; as is proved by the broad fact that the death-rate among them has much decreased, especially during the first year of residence, since the plan of giving them rations has been at work. The newcomers need, too, protection from their own countrymen. Old Coolies who have served their time and saved money find it convenient to turn rice-sellers or money-lenders. They have powerful connections on many estates; they first advance money or luxuries to a newcomer, and when he is once entrapped, they sell him the necessaries of life at famine prices. Thus the practical effect of rations has been to lessen the number of those little roadside shops, which were a curse to Trinidad, and are still a curse to the English workman. Moreover—for all men are not perfect, even in Trinidad—the Coolie required protection, in certain cases, against a covetous and short-sighted employer, who might fancy it to be his interest to let the man idle during his first year, while weak, and so save up an arrear of 'lost days' to be added at the end of the five years, when he was a strong skilled labourer. An employer will have, of course, far less temptation to do this, while, as now, he is bound to feed the Coolie for the first two years. Meanwhile, be it remembered, the very fact that such a policy was tempting, goes to prove that the average Coolie grew, during his five years' apprenticeship, a stronger, and not a weaker, man.

There is thorough provision—as far as the law can provide—for the Coolies in case of sickness. No estate is allowed to employ indentured Coolies, which has not a duly 'certified' hospital, capable of holding one-tenth at least of the Coolies on the estate, with an allowance of 800 cubic feet to each person; and these hospitals are under the care of district medical visitors, appointed by the Governor, and under the inspection (as are the labour-books, indeed every document and arrangement connected with the Coolies) of the Agent-General of Immigrants or his deputies. One of these officers, the Inspector, is always on the move, and daily visits, without warning, one or more estates, reporting every week to the Agent-General. The Governor may at any time, without assigning any cause, cancel the indenture of any immigrant, or remove any part or the whole of the indentured immigrant labourers from any estate; and this has been done ere now.

I know but too well that, whether in Europe or in the Indies, no mere laws, however wisely devised, will fully protect the employed from the employer; or, again, the employer from the employed. What is needed is a moral bond between them; a bond above, or rather beneath, that of mere wages, however fairly paid, for work, however fairly done. The patriarchal system had such a bond; so had the feudal: but they are both dead and gone, having done, I presume, all that it was in them to do, and done it, like all human institutions, not over well. And meanwhile, that nobler bond, after which Socialists so-called have sought, and after which I trust they will go on seeking still—a bond which shall combine all that was best in patriarchism and feudalism, with that freedom of the employed which those forms of society failed to give—has not been found as yet; and, for a generation or two to come, 'cash-payment seems likely to be the only nexus between man and man.' Because that is the meanest and weakest of all bonds, it must be watched jealously and severely by any Government worthy of the name; for to leave it to be taken care of by the mere

COOLIES A-FIELD.

brute tendencies of supply and demand, and the so-called necessities of the labour market, is simply to leave the poor man who cannot wait to be blockaded and starved out by the rich who can. Therefore all Colonial Governments are but doing their plain duty in keeping a clear eye and a strong hand on this whole immigration movement; and in fencing it round, as in Trinidad, with such regulations as shall make it most difficult for a Coolie to be seriously or permanently wronged without direct infraction of the law, and connivance of Government officers; which last supposition is, in the case of Trinidad, absurd, as long as Dr. Mitchell, whom I am proud to call my friend, holds a post for which he is equally fitted by his talents and his virtues.

I am well aware that some benevolent persons, to whom humanity owes much, regard Coolie immigration to the West Indies with some jealousy, fearing, and not unnaturally, that it may degenerate into a sort of slave-trade. I think that if they will study the last immigration ordinance enacted by the Governor of Trinidad, June 24, 1870, and the report of the Agent-General of Immigrants for the year ending September 30, 1869, their fears will be set at rest as far as this colony is concerned. Of other colonies I say nothing, simply because I know nothing: save that, if there are defects and abuses elsewhere, the remedy is simple: namely, to adopt the system of Trinidad, and work it as it is worked there.

After he has served his five years' apprenticeship, the Coolie has two courses before him. Either he can re-indenture himself to an employer, for not more than twelve months, which as a rule he does; or he can seek employment where he likes. At the end of a continuous residence of ten years in all, and at any period after that, he is entitled to a free passage back to Hindostan; or he may exchange his right to a free passage for a Government grant of ten acres of land. He has meanwhile, if he has been thrifty, grown rich. His wife walks about, at least on high-days, bedizened with jewels: nay, you may see her, even on work-days, hoeing in the cane-piece with heavy silver bangles hanging down over her little brown feet: and what wealth she does not carry on her arms, ankles, neck, and nostril, her husband has in the savings' bank. The ship *Arima*, as an instance, took back 320 Coolies last year, of whom seven died on the voyage. These people carried with them 65,585 dollars; and one man, Heerah, handed over 6000 dollars for transmission through the Treasury, and was known to have about him 4000 more. This man, originally allotted to an estate, had, after serving out his industrial contract, resided in the neighbouring village of Savannah Grande as a shopkeeper and money-lender for the last ten years. Most of this money, doubtless, had been squeezed out of other Coolies by means not unknown to Europeans, as well as to Hindoos: but it must have been there to be squeezed out. And the new 'feeding ordinance' will, it is to be hoped, pare the claws of Hindoo and Chinese usurers.

The newly offered grant of Government land has, as yet, been accepted only in a few cases. 'It was not to be expected,' says the report, 'that the Indian, whose habits have been fixed in special grooves for tens of centuries, should hurriedly embrace an offer which must strike at all his prejudices of country, and creed, and kin.' Still, about sixty had settled in 1869 near the estates in Savonetta, where I saw them, and at Point à Pierre; other settlements have been made since, of which more hereafter. And, as a significant fact, many Coolies who have returned to India are now coming back a second time to Trinidad, bringing their kinsfolk and fellow-villagers with them, to a land where violence is unknown, and famine impossible. Moreover, numerous Coolies from the French Islands are now immigrating, and buying land. These are chiefly Madrassees, who are, it is said, stronger and healthier than the Calcutta Coolies. In any case, there seems good hope that a race of Hindoo peasant-proprietors will spring up in the colony, whose voluntary labour will be available at crop-time ; and who will teach the Negro thrift and industry, not only by their example, but by competing against him in the till lately understocked labour-market.

Very interesting was the first glimpse of Hindoos ; and still more of Hindoos in the West Indies—the surplus of one of the oldest civilisations of the old world, come hither to replenish the new ; novel was the sight of the dusky limbs swarming up and down among the rocks beneath the Matapalo shade ; the group in the water as we landed, bathing and dressing themselves at the same time, after the modest and graceful Hindoo fashion ; the visit to the wooden barracks, where a row of men was ranged on one side of the room, with their women and children on the other, having their name, caste, native village, and so forth, taken down before they were sent off to the estates to which they were indentured. Three things were noteworthy ; first, the healthy cheerful look of all, speaking well for the care and good feeding which they had had on board ship ; next, the great variety in their faces and complexions. Almost all of them were low-caste people. Indeed few high-caste Hindoos, except some Sepoys who found it prudent to emigrate after the rebellion, have condescended, or dared, to cross the 'dark water'; and only a very few of those who come west are Mussulmans. But among the multitude of inferior castes who do come there is a greater variety of feature and shape of skull than in an average multitude, as far as I have seen, of any European nation. Caste, the physiognomist soon sees, began in a natural fact. It meant difference, not of rank, but of tribe and language ; and India is not, as we are apt to fancy, a nation : it is a world. One must therefore regard this emigration of the Coolies, like anything else which tends to break down caste, as a probable step forward in their civilisation. For it must tend to undermine in them, and still more in their children, the petty superstitions of old tribal distinctions ; and must force them to take their stand on wider and sounder ground, and see that 'a man's a man for a' that.'

The third thing noteworthy in the crowd which cooked, chatted, lounged, sauntered idly to and fro under the Matapalos—the pillared air-roots of which must have put them in mind of their own Banyans at home—was their good manners. One saw in a moment that one was among gentlemen and ladies. The dress of many of the men was nought but a scarf wrapped round the loins ; that of most of the women nought but the longer scarf which the Hindoo woman contrives to arrange in a most graceful, as well as a perfectly modest covering, even for her feet and head. These garments, and perhaps a brass pot, were probably all the worldly goods of most of them just then. But every attitude, gesture, tone, was full of grace; of ease, courtesy, self-restraint, dignity—of that 'sweetness and light,' at least in externals, which Mr. Matthew Arnold desiderates. I am well aware that these people are not perfect; that, like most heathen folk and some Christian, their morals are by no means spotless, their passions by no means trampled out. But

COOLIES COOKING.

they have acquired—let Hindoo scholars tell how and where— a civilisation which shows in them all day long; which draws the European to them and them to the European, whenever the latter is worthy of the name of a civilised man, instinctively, and by the mere interchange of glances; a civilisation which must make it easy for the Englishman, if he will but do his duty, not only to make use of these people, but to purify and ennoble them.

Another thing was noteworthy about the Coolies, at the very first glance, and all we saw afterwards proved that that first glance was correct; I mean their fondness for children. If you took notice of a child, not only the mother smiled thanks and delight, but the men around likewise, as if a compliment had been paid to their whole company. We saw afterwards almost daily proofs of the Coolie men's fondness for their children ; of their fondness also—an excellent sign that the morale is not destroyed at the root—for dumb animals. A Coolie cow or donkey is petted, led about tenderly, tempted with tit-bits. Pet animals, where they can be got, are the Coolie's delight, as they are the delight of the wild Indian. I wish I could say the same of the Negro. His treatment of his children and of his beasts of burden is, but too often, as exactly opposed to that of the Coolie as are his manners. No wonder that the two races do not, and it is to be feared never will, amalgamate ; that the Coolie, shocked by the unfortunate awkwardness of gesture and vulgarity of manners of the average Negro, and still more of the Negress, looks on them as savages; while the Negro, in his turn, hates the Coolie as a hard-working interloper, and despises him as a heathen ; or that heavy fights between the two races arise now and then, in which the Coolie, in spite of his slender limbs, has generally the advantage over the burly Negro, by dint of his greater courage, and the terrible quickness with which he wields his beloved weapon, the long hardwood quarterstaff.

But to return : we rowed away with a hundred confused, but most pleasant new impressions, amid innumerable salaams to the Governor by these kindly courteous people, and then passed between the larger limestone islands into the roadstead of Chaguaramas, which ought to be, and some day may be, the harbour for the British West India fleet ; and for the shipping, too, of that commerce which, as Humboldt prophesied, must some day spring up between Europe and the boundless wealth of the Upper Orinoco, as yet lying waste. Already gold discoveries in the Sierra de Parima (of which more hereafter) are indicating the honesty of poor murdered Raleigh. Already the good President of Ciudad Bolivar (Angostura) has disbanded the ruffian army, which is the usual curse of a Spanish American republic, and has inaugurated, it is to be hoped, a reign of peace and commerce. Already an American line of steamers runs as far as Nutrias, some eight hundred miles up the Orinoco and Apure ; while a second will soon run up the Meta, almost to Santa Fé de Bogotá, and bring down the Orinoco the wealth, not only of Southern Venezuela, but of central New Grenada ; and then a day may come when the admirable harbour of Chaguaramas may be one of the entrepôts of the world ; if a certain swamp to windward, which now makes the place pestilential, could but be drained. The usual method of so doing now is to lay the swamp as dry as possible by open ditches, and then plant it with coco-nuts, whose roots have some mysterious power both of drying and purifying the soil ; but were Chaguaramas ever needed as an entrepôt, it would not be worth while to wait for coco-nuts to grow. A dyke across the mouth, and a steam-pump on it, as in the fens of Norfolk and of Guiana, to throw the landwater over into the sea, would probably expel the evil spirit of malaria at once and for ever.

We rowed on past the Boca de Monos, by which we had entered the gulf at first, and looked out eagerly enough for sharks, which are said to swarm at Chaguaramas. But no warning fin appeared above the ripple; only, more than once, close to the stern of the boat, a heavy fish broke water with a sharp splash and swirl, which was said to be a Barracouta, following us up in mere bold curiosity, but perfectly ready to have attacked any one who fell overboard. These Barracoutas—Sphyrænas as the learned, or 'pike' as the sailors, call them, though they are no kin to our pike at home—are, when large, nearly as dangerous as a shark. In some parts of the West Indies folk dare not bathe for fear of them; for they lie close inshore, amid the heaviest surf; and woe to any living thing which they come across. Moreover, they have this somewhat mean advantage over you, that while, if they eat you, you will agree with them perfectly, you cannot eat them, at least at certain or uncertain seasons of the year, without their disagreeing with you, without sickness, trembling pains in all joints, falling off of nails and hair for years to come, and possible death. Those who may wish to know more of the poisonous fishes of the West Indies may profitably consult a paper in the *Proceedings* of the Scientific Association of Trinidad by that admirable naturalist, and—let me say of him (though I have not the honour of knowing him) what has long been said by all who have that honour—admirable man, the Hon. Richard Hill of Jamaica. He mentions some thirteen species which are more or less poisonous, at all events at times: but on the cause of their unwholesomeness he throws little light; and still less on the extraordinary but undoubted fact that the same species may be poisonous in one island and harmless in another; and that of two species so close as to be often considered as the same, one may be poisonous, the other harmless. The yellowbilled sprat,[1] for instance, is usually so poisonous that 'death has occurred from eating it in many cases immediately, and in some recorded instances even before the fish was swallowed.' Yet a species caught with this, and only differing from it (if indeed it be distinct) by having a yellow spot instead of a black one on the gill-cover, is harmless. Mr. Hill attributes the poisonous quality, in many cases, to the foul food which the fish get from coral reefs, such as the Formigas bank, midway between Cuba, Hayti, and Jamaica, where, as you 'approach it from the east, you find the cheering blandness of the sea-breeze

[1] *Alosa Bishopi.*

suddenly changing to the nauseating smell of a fish-market.' There, as off similar reefs in the Bahamas and round Anegada, as well as at one end of St. Kitts, the fish are said to be all poisonous. If this theory be correct, the absence of coral reefs round Trinidad may help to account for the fact stated by Mr. Joseph, that poisonous fish are unknown in that island. The statement, however, is somewhat too broadly made; for the Chouf-chouf,[1] a prickly fish which blows itself out like a bladder, and which may be seen hanging in many a sailor's cottage in England, is as evil-disposed in Trinidad as elsewhere. The very vultures will not eat it; and while I was in the island a family of Coolies, in spite of warning, contrived to kill themselves with the nasty vermin: the only one who had wit enough to refuse it being an idiot boy.

These islands of the Bocas, three in number, are some two miles long each, and some eight hundred to one thousand feet in height; at least, so say the surveyors. To the eye, as is usual in the Tropics, they look much lower. One is inclined here to estimate hills at half, or less than half, their actual height; and that from causes simple enough. Not only does the intense clearness of the atmosphere make the summits appear much nearer than in England; but the trees on the summit increase the deception. The mind, from home association, supposes them to be of the same height as average English trees on a hill-top—say fifty feet—and estimates, rapidly and unconsciously, the height of the mountain by that standard. The trees are actually nearer a hundred and fifty than fifty feet high; and the mountain is two or three times as big as it looks.

But it is not their height, nor the beauty of their outline, nor the size of the trunks which still linger on them here and there, which gives these islands their special charm. It is their exquisite little land-locked southern coves—places to live and die in—

'The world forgetting, by the world forgot.'

Take as an example that into which we rowed that day in Monos, as the old Spaniards named it, from monkeys long since extinct; a curved shingle beach some fifty yards across, shut in right and left by steep rocks wooded down almost to the sea, and worn into black caves and crannies, festooned with the night-blowing Cereus, which crawls about with hairy green legs, like a tangle of giant spiders. Among it, in the cracks, upright Cerei, like candelabra twenty and thirty feet high, thrust themselves aloft into the brushwood. An Aroid[2] rides parasitic on roots and stems, sending downward long air-roots, and upward brown rat-tails of flower, and broad leaves, four feet by two, which wither into whity-brown paper, and are used, being tough and fibrous, to wrap round the rowlocks of the oars.

[1] *Tetraodon.*
[2] *Anthurium Huegelii?*—Grisebach, *Flora of the West Indies.*

Tufts of Karatas, too, spread their long prickly leaves among the bush of 'rastrajo,' or second growth after the primeval forest has been cleared, which dips suddenly right and left to the beach. It, and the little strip of flat ground behind it, hold a three-roomed cottage—of course on stilts; a shed which serves as a kitchen; a third ruined building, which is tenanted mostly by lizards and creeping flowers; some twenty or thirty coco-nut trees; and on the very edge of the sea an almond-tree, its roots built up to seaward with great stones, its trunk hung with fishing lines; and around it, scattered on the shingle, strange shells, bits of coral, coco-nuts and their fragments; almonds from the tree; the round scaly fruit of the Mauritia palm, which has probably floated across the gulf from the forests of the Orinoco or the Caroni; and the long seeds of the mangrove, in shape like a roach-fisher's float, and already germinating, their leaves showing at the upper end, a tiny root at the lower. In that shingle they will not take root: but they are quite ready to go to sea again next tide, and wander on for weeks, and for hundreds of miles, till they run ashore at last on a congenial bed of mud, throw out spider legs right and left, and hide the foul mire with their gay green leaves.

The almond-tree,[1] with its flat stages of large smooth leaves, and oily eatable seeds in an almond-like husk, is not an almond at all, or any kin thereto. It has been named, as so many West Indian plants have, after some known plant to which it bore a likeness, and introduced hither, and indeed to all shores from Cuba to Guiana, from the East Indies, through Arabia and tropical Africa, having begun its westward journey, probably, in the pocket of some Portuguese follower of Vasco de Gama.

We beached the boat close to the almond-tree, and were welcomed on shore by the lord of the cove, a gallant red-bearded Scotsman, with a head and a heart; a handsome Creole wife, and lovely brownish children, with no more clothes on than they could help. An old sailor, and much-wandering Ulysses, he is now coastguardman, water-bailiff, policeman, practical warden, and indeed practical viceroy of the island, and an easy life of it he must have.

The sea gives him fish enough for his family, and for a brawny brown servant. His coco-nut palms yield him a little revenue; he has poultry, kids, and goats' milk more than he needs; his patch of provision-ground in the place gives him corn and roots, sweet potatoes, yam, tania, cassava, and fruit too, all the year round. He needs nothing, owes nothing, fears nothing. News and politics are to him like the distant murmur of the surf at the back of the island; a noise which is nought to him. His Bible, his almanac, and three or four old books on

[1] *Terminalia Catappa.*

a shelf, are his whole library. He has all that man needs, more than man deserves, and is far too wise to wish to better himself.

I sat down on the beach beneath the amber shade of the palms; and watched my white friends rushing into the clear sea, and disporting themselves there like so many otters, while the policeman's little boy launched a log canoe, not much longer than himself, and paddled out into the midst of them, and then jumped upright in it, a little naked brown Cupidon; whereon he and his canoe were of course upset, and pushed under water, and scrambled over, and the whole cove rang with shouts and splashing, enough to scare away the boldest shark, had one been on watch off the point. I looked at the natural beauty and repose; at the human vigour and happiness: and I said to myself, and said it often afterwards in the West Indies: Why do not other people copy this wise Scot? Why should not many a young couple, who have education, refinement, resources in themselves, but are, happily or unhappily for them, unable to keep a brougham and go to London balls, retreat to some such paradise as this (and there are hundreds like it to be found in the West Indies), leaving behind them false civilisation, and vain desires, and useless show; and there live in simplicity and content 'The Gentle Life'? It is not true that the climate is too enervating. It is not true that nature is here too strong for man. I have seen enough in Trinidad, I saw enough even in little Monos, to be able to deny that; and to say that in the West Indies, as elsewhere, a young man can be pure, able, high-minded, industrious, athletic: and I see no reason why a woman should not be likewise all that she need be.

A cultivated man and wife, with a few hundreds a year—just enough, in fact, to enable them to keep a Coolie servant or two, might be really wealthy in all which constitutes true wealth; and might be useful also in their place; for each such couple would be a little centre of civilisation for the Negro, the Coolie; and it may be for certain young adventurers who, coming out merely to make money and return as soon as possible, are but too apt to lose, under the double temptations of gain and of drink, what elements of the 'Gentle Life' they have gained from their mothers at home.

The following morning early we rowed away again, full of longing, but not of hope, of reaching one or other of the Guacharo caves. Keeping along under the lee of the island, we crossed the 'Umbrella Mouth,' between it and Huevos, or Egg Island. On our right were the islands; on our left the shoreless gulf; and ahead the great mountain of the mainland, with a wreath of white fleece near its summit, and the shadows of clouds moving in dark patches up its sides. As we crossed, the tumbling swell which came in from the outer sea, and the columns of white spray which rose right and left against the two door-posts of that mighty gateway, augured ill for our chances of entering a cave. But on we went, with a warning not to be upset if we could avoid it, in the shape of a shark's back fin above the oily swell; and under Huevos, and round into a lonely cove, with high crumbling cliffs bedecked with Cereus and Aloes in flower, their tall spikes of green flowers standing out against the sky, twenty or thirty feet in height, and beds of short wild pine-apples,[1] like amber-yellow fur, and here and there hanging leaves trailing down to the water; and on into a nook, the sight of which made us give up all hopes of the cave, but which in itself was worth coming from Europe to see. The work of ages of trade-surf had cut the island clean through, with a rocky gully between soft rocks some hundred feet in width. It was just passable at high tide; and through it we were to have rowed, and turned to the left to the cave in the windward cliffs. But ere we reached it the war outside said 'No' in a voice which would take no denial, and when we beached the boat behind a high rock, and scrambled up to look out, we saw a sight, one half of which was not unworthy of the cliffs of Hartland or Bude. On the farther side of the knife-edge of rock, crumbling fast into the sea, a waste of breakers rolled through the chasm, though there was scarcely any wind to drive them, leaping, spouting, crashing, hammering down the soft cliffs, which seemed to crumble, and did doubtless crumble, at every blow; and beyond that the open blue sea, without a rock or a sail, hazy, in spite of the blazing sunlight, beneath the clouds of spray. But there ceased the likeness to a rock scene on the Cornish coast; for at the other foot of the rock, not twenty yards from that wild uproar, the land-locked cove up which we had come lay still as glass, and the rocks were richer with foliage than an English orchard. Everywhere down into the very sea, the Matapalos held and hung; their air-roots dangled into the very water; many of them had fallen into it, but grew on still, and blossomed with great white fragrant flowers, somewhat like those of a Magnolia, each with a shining cake of amber wax as big as a shilling in the centre; and over the Matapalos, tree on tree, liane on liane, up to a negro garden, with its strange huge-leaved vegetables and glossy fruit-trees, and its black owner standing on the cliff, and peering down out of his little nest with grinning teeth and white wondering eyes, at the white men who were gathering, off a few yards of beach, among the great fallen leaves of the Matapalos, such shells as delighted our childhood in the West India cabinet at home.

We lingered long, filling our eyes with beauty: and then rowed away. What more was to be done? Through that very chasm we were to have passed out to the cave. And yet the

[1] *Pitcairnia?*

sight of this delicious nook repaid us—so more than one of the party thought—for our disappointment. There was another Guacharo cave in the Monos channel, more under the lee. We would try that to-morrow.

As the sun sank that evening, we sat ourselves upon the eastern rocks, and gazed away into the pale, sad, boundless west; while Venus hung high, not a point, as here, but a broad disc of light, throwing a long gleam over the sea. Fish skipped over the clear calm water; and above, pelicans—the younger brown, the older gray—wheeled round and round in lordly flight, paused, gave a sudden half-turn, then fell into the water with widespread wings, and after a splash, rose with another skipjack in their pouch. As it grew dark, dark things came trooping over the sea, by twos and threes, then twenty at a time, all past us toward a cave near by. Birds we fancied them at first, of the colour and size of starlings; but they proved to be bats, and bats, too, which have the reputation of catching fish. So goes the tale, believed by some who see them continually, and have a keen eye for nature; and who say that the bat sweeps the fish up off the top of the water with the scoop-like membrane of his hind-legs and tail. For this last fact I will not vouch. But I am assured that fish scales were found, after I left the island, in the stomachs of these bats; and that of the fact of their picking up small fish there can be no doubt. 'You could not,' says a friend, 'be out at night in a boat, and hear their continual swish, swish, in the water, without believing it.' If so, the habit is a quaint change of nature in them; for they belong, I am assured by my friend Professor Newton, not to the insect-eating, but to the fruit-eating family of bats, who, in the West as in the East Indies, may be seen at night hovering round the Mango-trees, and destroying much more fruit than they eat.

So we sat watching the little dark things flit by, like the gibbering ghosts of the suitors in the *Odyssey*, into the darkness of the cave; and then turned to long talk of things concerning which it is best nowadays not to write; till it was time to feel our way indoors, by such light as Venus gave, over the slippery rocks, and then, cautiously enough, past the Manchineel[1] bush, a broken sprig of which would have raised an instant blister on the face or hand.

Our night, as often happens in the Tropics, was not altogether undisturbed; for, shortly after I had become unconscious of the chorus of toads and cicadas, my hammock came down by the head. Then I was woke by a sudden bark close outside, exactly like that of a clicketting fox; but as the dogs did not reply or give chase, I presumed it to be the cry of a bird, possibly a little owl. Next there rushed down the mountain a

---

[1] *Hippomane Mancinella.*

MONOS.

storm of wind and rain, which made the coco-leaves flap and creak, and rattle against the gable of the house; and set every door and window banging, till they were caught and brought to reason. And between the howls of the wind I became aware of a strange noise from seaward—a booming, or rather humming, most like that which a locomotive sometimes makes when blowing off steam. It was faint and distant, but deep and strong enough to set one guessing its cause. The sea beating into caves seemed, at first, the simplest answer. But the water was so still on our side of the island, that I could barely hear the lap of the ripple on the shingle twenty yards off; and the nearest surf was a mile or two away, over a mountain a thousand feet high. So puzzling vainly, I fell asleep, to awake, in the gray dawn, to the prettiest idyllic picture, through the half-open door, of two kids dancing on a stone at the foot of a coco-nut tree, with a background of sea and dark rocks.

As we went to bathe we heard again, in perfect calm, the same mysterious booming sound, and were assured by those who ought to have known, that it came from under the water, and was most probably made by none other than the famous musical or drum fish; of whom one had heard, and hardly believed, much in past years.

Mr. Joseph, author of the *History of Trinidad* from which I have so often quoted, reports that the first time he heard this singular fish was on board a schooner, at anchor off Chaguaramas.

'Immediately under the vessel I heard a deep and not unpleasant sound, similar to those one might imagine to proceed from a thousand Æolian harps; this ceased, and deep twanging notes succeeded; these gradually swelled into an uninterrupted stream of singular sounds like the booming of a number of Chinese gongs under the water; to these succeeded notes that had a faint resemblance to a wild chorus of a hundred human voices singing out of tune in deep bass.'

'In White's *Voyage to Cochin China*,' adds Mr. Joseph, 'there is as good a description of this, or a similar submarine concert, as mere words can convey: this the voyager heard in the Eastern seas. He was told the singers were a flat kind of fish; he, however, did not see them.'

'Might not this fish,' he asks, 'or one resembling it in vocal qualities, have given rise to the fable of the Sirens?'

It might, certainly, if the fact be true. Moreover, Mr. Joseph does not seem to be aware that the old Spanish Conquistadores had a myth that music was to be heard in this very Gulf of Paria, and that at certain seasons the Nymphs and Tritons assembled therein, and with ravishing strains sang their watery loves. The story of the music has been usually treated as a sailor's fable, and the Sirens and Tritons supposed to be mere stupid manatis, or sea-cows, coming in as they do still now and then to browse on mangrove shoots and turtle-grass : [1] but if the story of the music be true, the myth may have had a double root.

Meanwhile I see Hardwicke's *Science Gossip* for March gives an extract from a letter of M. O. de Thoron, communicated by him to the Académie des Sciences, December 1861, which confirms Mr. Joseph's story. He asserts that in the Bay of Pailon, in Esmeraldos, Ecuador, *i.e.* on the Pacific Coast, and also up more than one of the rivers, he has heard a similar sound, attributed by the natives to a fish which they call 'The Siren,' or 'Musico.' At first, he says, he thought it was produced by a fly, or hornet of extraordinary size; but afterwards, having advanced a little farther, he heard a multitude of different voices, which harmonised together, imitating a church organ to great perfection. The good people of Trinidad believe that the fish which makes this noise is the trumpet-fish, or Fistularia—a beast strange enough in shape to be credited with strange actions: but ichthyologists say positively no: that the noise (at least along the coast of the United States) is made by a Pogonias, a fish somewhat like a great bearded perch, and cousin of the Maigre of the Mediterranean, which is accused of making a similar purring or grunting noise, which can be heard from a depth of one hundred and twenty feet, and guides the fishermen to their whereabouts.

How the noise is made is a question. Cuvier was of opinion that it was made by the air-bladder, though he could not explain how : but the truth, if truth it be, seems stranger still. These fish, it seems, have strong bony palates and throat-teeth for crushing shells and crabs, and make this wonderful noise simply by grinding their teeth together.

I vouch for nothing, save that I heard this strange humming more than once. As for the cause of it, I can only say, as was said of yore, that 'I hold it for rashness to determine aught amid such fertility of Nature's wonders.'

One afternoon we made an attempt on the other Guacharo cave, which lies in the cliff on the landward side of the Monos Boca. But, alas! the wind had chopped a little to the northward ; a swell was rolling in through the Boca ; and when we got within twenty yards of the low-browed arch our crew lay on their oars and held a consultation, of which there could but be one result. They being white gentlemen, and not Negroes, could trust themselves and each other, and were ready, as I know well, to 'dare all that became a man.' But every now and then a swell rolled in high enough to have cracked our sculls against the top, and out again deep enough to have staved the boat against the rocks. If we went to wreck, the current was setting strongly out to sea ; and the Boca was haunted by sharks, and (according to the late Colonel Hamilton Smith) by

---

[1] *Thalassia testudinum.*

a worse monster still, namely, the giant ray,[1] which goes by the name of devil-fish on the Carolina shores. He saw, he says, one of these monsters rise in this very Boca, at a sailor who had fallen overboard, cover him with one of his broad wings, and sweep him down into the depths. And, on the whole, if Guacharos are precious, so is life. So, like Gyges of old, we 'elected to survive,' and rowed away with wistful eyes, determining to get Guacharos—a determination which was never carried out—from one of the limestone caverns of the northern mountains.

And now it may be asked, and reasonably enough, what Guacharos[2] are; and why five English gentlemen and a canny Scots coastguardman should think it worth while to imperil their lives to obtain them.

I cannot answer better than by giving Humboldt's account of the Cave of Caripe, on the Spanish main hard by, where he discovered them, or rather described them to civilised Europe, for the first time :—

'The Cueva del Guacharo is pierced in the vertical profile of a rock. The entrance is towards the south, and forms a vault eighty feet broad and seventy-two feet high. This elevation is but a fifth less than the colonnade of the Louvre. The rock that surmounts the grotto is covered with trees of gigantic height. The Mammee-tree and the Genipa, with large and shining leaves, raise their branches vertically towards the sky; while those of the Courbaril and the Erythrina form, as they extend themselves, a thick vault of verdure. Plants of the family of Pothos with succulent stems, Oxalises, and Orchideæ of a singular construction, rise in the driest clefts of the rocks; while creeping plants waving in the winds are interwoven in festoons before the opening of the cavern. We distinguished in these festoons a Bignonia of a violet blue, the purple Dolichos, and, for the first time, that magnificent Solandra, the orange flower of which has a fleshy tube more than four inches long. The entrances of grottoes, like the view of cascades, derive their principal charm from the situation, more or less majestic, in which they are placed, and which in some sort determines the character of the landscape. What a contrast between the Cueva of Caripe and those caverns of the north crowned with oaks and gloomy larch-trees!

'But this luxury of vegetation embellishes not only the outside of the vault, it appears even in the vestibule of the grotto. We saw with astonishment plantain-leaved Heliconias, eighteen feet high, the Praga palm-trees, and arborescent Arums follow the banks of the river, even to those subterranean places. The vegetation continues in the Cave of Caripe, as in the deep crevices of the Andes, half excluded from the light of day; and

---

[1] *Cephaloptera.*   [2] *Steatornis Caripensis.*

does not disappear till, advancing in the interior, we reach thirty or forty paces from the entrance. . . .

'The Guacharo quits the cavern at nightfall, especially when the moon shines. It is almost the only frugivorous nocturnal bird that is yet known; the conformation of its feet sufficiently shows that it does not hunt like our owls. It feeds on very hard fruits, as the Nutcracker and the Pyrrhocorax. The latter nestles also in clefts of rocks, and is known under the name of night-crow. The Indians assured us that the Guacharo does not pursue either the lamellicorn insects, or those phalænæ which serve as food to the goat-suckers. It is sufficient to compare the beaks of the Guacharo and goat-sucker to conjecture how much their manners must differ. It is difficult to form an idea of the horrible noise occasioned by thousands of these birds in the dark part of the cavern, and which can only be compared to the croaking of our crows, which in the pine forests of the north live in society, and construct their nests upon trees the tops of which touch each other. The shrill and piercing cries of the Guacharos strike upon the vaults of the rocks, and are repeated by the echo in the depth of the cavern. The Indians showed us the nests of these birds by fixing torches to the end of a long pole. These nests were fifty or sixty feet high above our heads, in holes in the shape of funnels, with which the roof of the grotto is pierced like a sieve. The noise increased as we advanced, and the birds were affrighted by the light of the torches of copal. When this noise ceased a few minutes around us we heard at a distance the plaintive cries of the birds roosting in other ramifications of the cavern. It seemed as if these bands answered each other alternately.

'The Indians enter into the Cueva del Guacharo once a year, near midsummer, armed with poles, by means of which they destroy the greater part of the nests. At this season several thousands of birds are killed; and the old ones, as if to defend their brood, hover over the heads of the Indians, uttering terrible cries. The young, which fall to the ground, are opened on the spot. Their peritoneum is extremely loaded with fat, and a layer of fat reaches from the abdomen to the anus, forming a kind of cushion between the legs of the bird. This quantity of fat in frugivorous animals, not exposed to the light, and exerting very little muscular motion, reminds us of what has been long since observed in the fattening of geese and oxen. It is well known how favourable darkness and repose are to this process. The nocturnal birds of Europe are lean, because, instead of feeding on fruits, like the Guacharo, they live on the scanty produce of their prey. At the period which is commonly called at Caripe the "oil harvest," the Indians build huts with palm-leaves near the entrance, and even in the porch of the cavern. Of these we still saw some remains. There, with a fire of brushwood, they melt in pots of clay the fat of the young birds just killed. This fat is known by the name of butter or oil (*manteca* or *aceite*) of the Guacharo. It is half liquid, transparent, without smell, and so pure that it may be kept above a year without becoming rancid. At the convent of Caripe no other oil is used in the kitchen of the monks but that of the cavern; and we never observed that it gave the aliments a disagreeable taste or smell.

'Young Guacharos have been sent to the port of Cumana, and lived there several days without taking any nourishment, the seeds offered to them not suiting their taste. When the crops and gizzards of the young birds are opened in the cavern, they are found to contain all sorts of hard and dry fruits, which furnish, under the singular name of Guacharo seed (*semilla del Guacharo*), a very celebrated remedy against intermittent fevers. The old birds carry these seeds to their young. They are carefully collected and sent to the sick at Cariaco, and other places of the low regions, where fevers are prevalent...

'The natives connect mystic ideas with this cave, inhabited by nocturnal birds; they believe that the souls of their ancestors sojourn in the deep recesses of the cavern. "Man," say they, "should avoid places which are enlightened neither by the sun" (*Zis*) "nor by the moon" (*Nuna*). To go and join the Guacharos is to rejoin their fathers, is to die. The magicians (*piaches*) and the poisoners (*imorons*) perform their nocturnal tricks at the entrance of the cavern, to conjure the chief of the evil spirits (*ivorokiamo*). Thus in every climate the first fictions of nations resemble each other, those especially which relate to two principles governing the world, the abode of souls after death, the happiness of the virtuous, and the punishment of the guilty. The most different and barbarous languages present a certain number of images which are the same, because they have their source in the nature of our intellect and our sensations. Darkness is everywhere connected with the idea of death. The Grotto of Caripe is the Tartarus of the Greeks; and the Guacharos, which hover over the rivulet, uttering plaintive cries, remind us of the Stygian birds....

'The missionaries, with all their authority, could not prevail on the Indians to penetrate farther into the cavern. As the vault grew lower, the cries of the Guacharos became more shrill We were obliged to yield to the pusillanimity of our guides, and trace back our steps. The appearance of the cavern was indeed very uniform. We find that a bishop of St. Thomas of Guiana had gone farther than ourselves. He had measured nearly two thousand five hundred feet from the mouth to the spot where he stopped, though the cavern reached farther. The remembrance of this fact was preserved in the convent of Caripe, without the exact period being noted. The bishop had provided himself with great torches of white wax of Castille. We had torches composed only of the bark of trees and native resin. The thick smoke which issues from these torches, in a narrow subterranean passage, hurts the eyes and obstructs the respiration.

'We followed the course of the torrent to go out of the cavern. Before our eyes were dazzled by the light of day, we saw, without the grotto, the water of the river sparkling amid the foliage of the trees that concealed it. It was like a picture placed in the distance, and to which the mouth of the cavern served as a frame. Having at length reached the entrance, and seated ourselves on the banks of the rivulet, we rested after our fatigue. We were glad to be beyond the hoarse cries of the birds, and to leave a place where darkness does not offer even the charm of silence and tranquillity. We could scarcely persuade ourselves that the name of the Grotto of Caripe had hitherto remained unknown in Europe. The Guacharos alone would have been sufficient to render it celebrated. These nocturnal birds have been nowhere yet discovered except in the mountains of Caripe and Cumanacoa.'

So much from the great master, who was not aware (never having visited Trinidad) that the Guacharo was well known there under the name of Diablotin. But his account of Caripe was fully corroborated by my host, who had gone there last year, and, by the help of the magnesium light, had penetrated farther into the cave than either the bishop or Humboldt. He had brought home also several Guacharos from the Trinidad caves, all of which died on the passage, for want, seemingly, of the oily nuts on which they feed. A live Guacharo has, as yet, never been seen in Europe; and to get one safe to the Zoological Gardens, as well as to get one or two corpses for the Cambridge Museum, was our hope—a hope still, alas! unfulfilled. A nest, however, of the Guacharo has been brought to England by my host since my departure; a round lump of mud, of the size and shape of a large cheese, with a shallow depression on the top, in which the eggs are laid. A list of the seeds found in the stomachs of Guacharos by my friend Mr. Prestoe of the Botanical Gardens, Port of Spain, will be found in an Appendix.

We rowed away, toward our island paradise. But instead of going straight home, we turned into a deep cove called Ance Maurice—all coves in the French islands are called Ances—where was something to be seen, and not to be forgotten again. We grated in, over a shallow bottom of pebbles interspersed with gray lumps of coral pulp, and of Botrylli, azure, crimson, and all the hues of the flower-garden; and landed on the bank of a mangrove swamp, bored everywhere with the holes of land-crabs. One glance showed how these swamps are formed: by that want of tide which is the curse of the West Indies.

At every valley mouth the beating of the waves tends all the year round to throw up a bank of sand and shingle, damming the land-water back to form a lagoon. This might indeed empty itself during the floods of the rainy season; but during the dry season it must remain a stagnant pond, filling gradually with festering vegetable matter from the hills, beer-coloured, and as hideous to look at as it is to smell. Were there a tide, as in England, of from ten to twenty feet, that swamp would be drained twice a day to nearly that depth; and healthy vegetation, as in England, establish itself down to the very beach. A tide of a foot or eighteen inches only, as is too common in the West Indies, will only drain the swamp to that depth; and probably, if there be any strong pebble-bearing surf outside, not at all. So there it all lies, festering in the sun, and cooking poison day and night; while the mangroves and graceful white roseaux[1] (tall canes) kindly do their best to lessen the mischief, by rooting in the slush, and absorbing the poison with their leaves. A white man, sleeping one night on the edge of that pestilential little triangle, half an acre in size, would be in danger of catching a fever and ague, which would make a weaker man of him for the rest of his life. And yet so thoroughly fitted for the climate is the Negro, that not ten yards from the edge of the mud stood a comfortable negro-house, with stout healthy folk therein, evidently well to do in the world, to judge from the poultry, and the fruit-trees and provision-ground which stretched up the glen.

Through the provision-ground we struggled up, among weeds as high as our shoulders; so that it was difficult, as usual, to distinguish garden from forest. But no matter to the black owner. The weeds were probably of only six weeks' growth; and when they got so high that he actually could not find his tanias[2] among them, he would take cutlass and hoe, and make a lazy raid upon them, or rather upon a quarter of them, certain of two facts; that in six weeks more they would be all as high as ever; and that if they were, it did not matter; for so fertile is the soil, so genial the climate, that he would get in spite of them more crop off the ground than he needed. 'Pity the poor weeds. Is there not room enough in the world for them and for us?' seems the Negro's motto. But he knows his own business well enough, and can exert himself when he really needs to do so; and if the weeds harmed him seriously he would make short work with them. Still this soil, and this climate, put a premium on bad farming, as they do on much else that is bad.

Up we pushed along the narrow path, past curious spiral flags[3] just throwing out their heads of delicate white or purple flower, and under the shade of great Balisiers or wild plantains,[4] with leaves six or eight feet long; and many another curious plant unknown to me; and then through a little copse, of which we had to beware, for it was all black Roseau[5]—a sort of dwarf palm some fifteen feet high, whose stems are covered with black

---

[1] *Gynerium saccharoides.*
[2] *Xanthosoma;* a huge plant like our Arums, with an edible root.
[3] *Costus.* [4] *Heliconia.* [5] *Bactris.*

steel needles, which, on being touched, run right through your finger, or your hand, if you press hard enough, and then break off; on which you cut them out if you can. If you cannot, they are apt, like needles, to make voyages about among the muscles, and reappear at some unexpected spot, causing serious harm. Of all the vegetable pests of the forest, none, not even the crocchien, is so ugly a neighbour as certain varieties of black Roseau.

All this while—I fear I may be prolix: but one must write as one walked, stopping every moment to seize something new, and longing for as many pairs of eyes as a spider—all this while, I say, we heard the roar of the trade-surf growing louder and louder in front; and pushing cautiously through the Roseau, found ourselves on a cliff thirty feet high, and on the other side of the island.

Now it was plain how the Bocas had been made; for here was one making.

Before us seethed a shallow horse-shoe bay, almost a lake, some two hundred yards across inside, but far narrower at the mouth. Into it, between two lofty points of hard rock, worn into caves and pillars and natural arches, the trade-surf came raging in from the north, hurling columns of foam right and left, and then whirling round and round beneath us upon a narrow shore of black sand with such fury that one seemed to see the land torn away by each wave. The cliffs, some thirty feet high where we stood, rose to some hundred at the mouth, in intense black and copper and olive shadows, with one bright green tree in front of a cave's mouth, on which, it seemed, the sun had never shone; while a thousand feet overhead were glimpses of the wooded mountain-tops, with tender slanting lights, for the sun was growing low, through blue-gray mist on copse and lawn high above. A huge dark-headed Balata,[1] like a storm-torn Scotch pine, crowned the left-hand cliff; two or three young Fan-palms,[2] just ready to topple headlong, the right-hand one; and beyond all, through the great gateway gleamed, as elsewhere, the foam-flecked hazy blue of the Caribbean Sea.

We stood spellbound for a minute at the sudden change of scene and of feeling. From the still choking blazing steam of the leeward glen, we had stepped in a moment into coolness and darkness, pervaded by the delicious rush of the northeastern wind; into a hidden sanctuary of Nature where one would have liked to build, and live and die: had not a second glance warned us that to die was the easiest of the three. For the whole cliff was falling daily into the sea, and it was hardly safe to venture to the beach for fear of falling stones and earth.

[1] *Mimusops Balata.*
[2] Probably *Thrinax radiata* (Grisebach, p. 515).

Down, however, we went, by a natural ladder of Matapalo roots, and saw at once how the cove was being formed. The rocks are probably Silurian; and if so, of quite immeasurable antiquity. But instead of being hard, as Silurian rocks are wont to be, they are mere loose beds of dark sand and shale, yellow with sulphur, or black with carbonaceous matter, amid which strange flakes and nodules of white quartz lie loose, ready to drop out at the blow of every wave. The strata, too, sloped upward and outward toward the sea, which is therefore able to undermine them perpetually; and thus the searching surge, having once formed an entrance in the cliff-face, between what are now the two outer points, has had nought to do but to gnaw inward; and will gnaw, till the Isle of Monos is cut sheer in two, and the 'Ance Biscayen,' as the wonderful little bay is called, will join itself to the Ance Maurice and the Gulf of Paria. In two or three generations hence the little palm-wood will have fallen into the sea. In two or three more the negro house and garden and the mangrove swamp will be gone likewise: and in their place the trade-surf will be battering into the Gulf of Paria from the Northern Sea, through just such a mountain chasm as we saw at Huevos; and a new Boca will have been opened.

But not, understand, a deep and navigable one, as long as the land retains its present level. To make that, there must be a general subsidence of the land and sea bottom around. For surf, when eating into land, gnaws to little deeper than low-water mark: no deeper, probably, than the bottoms of the troughs between the waves. Its tendency is—as one may see along the Ramsgate cliffs—to pare the land away into a flat plain, just covered by a shallow sea. No surf or currents could have carved out the smaller Bocas to a depth of between twenty and eighty fathoms; much less the great Boca of the Dragon's Mouth, between Chacachacarra and the Spanish Main, to a depth of more than seventy fathoms. They are sunken mountain passes, whose sides have been since carved into upright cliffs by the gnawing of the sea; and, as Mr. Wall well observes,[1] 'the situation of the Bocas is in a depression of the range, perhaps of the highest antiquity.'

We wandered along the beach, looking up at a cliff clothed, wherever it was not actually falling away, with richest verdure down to the water's edge; but in general utterly bare, falling away too fast to give root-hold to any plant. We lay down on the black sand, and gazed, and gazed, and picked up quartz crystals fallen from above, and wondered how the cove had got its name. Had some old Biscayan whaler, from Biarritz or St. Jean de Luz, wandered into these seas in search of fish, when, in the beginning of the seventeenth century, he and his fellows

---

[1] *Geological Survey of Trinidad.*

had killed out all the Right Whales of the Bay of Biscay? And had he, missing the Bocas, been wrecked and perished, as he may well have done, against those awful walls? At last we turned to re-ascend—for the tide was rising—after our leader had congratulated us on being, perhaps, the only white men who had ever seen Ance Biscayen—a congratulation which was premature; for, as we went to climb up the Matapalo-root ladder, we were stopped by several pairs of legs coming down it, which belonged, it seemed, to a bathing party of pleasant French people, 'marooning' (as picnicking is called here) on the island; and after them descended the yellow frock of a Dominican monk, who, when landed, was discovered to be an old friend, now working hard among the Roman Catholic Negroes of Port of Spain.

On the way back to our island paradise we found along the shore two plants worth notice—one, a low tree, with leaves somewhat like box, but obovate (larger at the tip than at the stalk), and racemes of little white flowers of a delicious honey-scent.[1] It ought to be, if it be not yet, introduced into England, as a charming addition to the winter hothouse. As for the other plant, would that it could be introduced likewise, or rather that, if introduced, it would flower in a house; for it is a glorious climber, second only to that which poor Dr. Krueger calls 'the wonderful Norantea,' which shall be described in its place. You see a tree blazing with dark gold, passing into orange, and that to red; and on nearing it find it tiled all over with the flowers of a creeper,[2] arranged in flat rows of spreading brushes, some foot or two long, and holding each hundreds of flowers, growing on one side only of the twig, and turning their multitudinous golden and orange stamens upright to the sun. There —I cannot describe it. It must be seen first afar off, and then close, to understand the vagaries of splendour in which Nature indulges here. And yet the Norantea, common in the high woods, is even more splendid, and, in a botanist's eyes, a stranger vagary still.

On past the whaling quay. It was deserted; for the whales had not yet come in, and there was no chance of seeing a night scene which is described as horribly beautiful—the sharks around a whale while flensing is going on, each monster bathed in phosphorescent light, which makes his whole outline, and every fin, even his evil eyes and teeth, visible far under water, as the glittering fiend comes up from below, snaps his lump out of the whale's side, and is shouldered out of the way by his fellows. We were unlucky indeed, in the matter of sharks; for, with the exception of a problematical back-fin or two, we saw none in the West Indies, though they were swarming round us.

The next day the boat's head was turned homewards. And

---

[1] *Jacquinia armillaris.* [2] *Combretum (laxifolium ?).*

what had been learnt at the little bay of Ance Biscayen suggested, as we went on, a fresh geological question. How the outer islands of the Bocas had been formed, or were being formed, was clear enough. But what about the inner islands? Gaspar Grande, and Diego, and the Five Islands, and the peninsula—or island—of Punta Grande? How were these isolated lumps of limestone hewn out into high points, with steep cliffs, not to the windward, but to the leeward? What made the steep cliff at the south end of Punta Grande, on which a mangrove swamp now abuts? No trade-surf, no current capable of doing that work, has disturbed the dull waters of the 'Golfo Triste,' as the Spaniards named the Gulf of Paria, since the land was of anything like its present shape. And gradually we began to dream of a time when the Bocas did not exist; when the Spanish Main was joined to the northern mountains of the island by dry land, now submerged or eaten away by the trade-surf; when the northern currents of the Orinoco, instead of escaping through the Bocas as now, were turned eastward, past these very islands, and along the foot of the northern mountains, over what is now the great lowland of Trinidad, depositing those rich semi-alluvial strata which have been since upheaved, and sawing down along the southern slope of the mountains those vast beds of shingle and quartz boulders which now form as it were a gigantic ancient sea-beach right across the island. A dream it may be: but one which seemed reasonable enough to more than one in the boat, and which subsequent observations tended to verify.

CHAPTER VII

THE HIGH WOODS

I HAVE seen them at last. I have been at last in the High Woods, as the primeval forest is called here ; and they are not less, but more, wonderful than I had imagined them. But they must wait awhile ; for in reaching them, though they were only ten miles off, I passed through scenes so various, and so characteristic of the Tropics, that I cannot do better than sketch them one by one.

I drove out in the darkness of the dawn, under the bamboos, and Bauhinias, and palms which shade the road between the Botanic Gardens and the savannah, toward Port of Spain. The frogs and cicalas had nearly finished their nightly music. The fire-flies had been in bed since midnight. The air was heavy with the fragrance of the Bauhinias, and after I passed the great Australian Blue-gum which overhangs the road, and the Wallaba-tree,[1] with its thin curved pods dangling from innumerable bootlaces six feet long, almost too heavy with the fragrance of the 'white Ixora.'[2] A flush of rose was rising above the eastern mountains, and it was just light enough to see overhead the great flowers of the 'Bois chataigne,'[3] among its horse-chestnut-like leaves; red flowers as big as a child's two hands, with petals as long as its fingers. Children of Mylitta the moon goddess, they cannot abide the day ; and will fall, brown and shrivelled, before the sun grows high, after one night of beauty and life, and probably of enjoyment. Even more swiftly fades an even more delicate child of the moon, the *Ipomœa Bona-nox*, whose snow-white patines, as broad as the hand, open at nightfall on every hedge, and shrivel up with the first rays of dawn.

On through the long silent street of Port of Spain, where the air was heavy with everything but the fragrance of Ixoras, and the dogs and vultures sat about the streets, and were all but driven over every few yards, till I picked up a guide—will he let me say a friend ?—an Aberdeenshire Scot, who hurried out

---

[1] *Eperua falcata.*   [2] *Posoqueria.*   [3] *Carolinea.*

fresh from his bath, his trusty cutlass on his hip, and in heavy shooting-boots and gaiters; for no clothing, be it remembered, is too strong for the bush; and those who enter it in the white calico garments in which West-India planters figure on the stage, are like to leave in it, not only their clothes, but their skin besides.

In five minutes more we were on board the gig, and rowing away south over the muddy mirror; and in ten minutes more the sun was up, and blazing so fiercely that we were glad to cool ourselves in fancy, by talking over salmon-fishings in Scotland and New Brunswick, and wadings in icy streams beneath the black pine-woods.

Behind us were the blue mountains, streaked with broad lights and shades by the level sun. On our left the interminable low line of bright green mangrove danced and quivered in the mirage, and loomed up in front, miles away, till single trees seemed to hang in air far out at sea. On our right, hot mists wandered over the water, blotting out the horizon, till the coasting craft, with distorted sails and masts, seemed afloat in smoke. One might have fancied oneself in the Wash off Sandringham on a burning summer's noon.

Soon logs and stumps, standing out of the water, marked the mouth of the Caroni; and we had to take a sweep out seaward to avoid its mud-banks. Over that very spot, now unnavigable, Raleigh and his men sailed in to conquer Trinidad.

On one log a huge black and white heron moped all alone, looking in the mist as tall as a man; and would not move for all our shouts. Schools of fish dimpled the water; and brown pelicans fell upon them, dashing up fountains of silver. The trade-breeze, as it rose, brought off the swamps a sickly smell, suggestive of the need of coffee, quinine, Angostura bitters, or some other febrifuge. In spite of the glorious sunshine, the whole scene was sad, desolate, almost depressing, from its monotony, vastness, silence; and we were glad, when we neared the high tree which marks the entrance of the Chaguanas Creek, and turned at last into a recess in the mangrove bushes; a desolate pool, round which the mangrove roots formed an impenetrable net. As far as the eye could pierce into the tangled thicket, the roots interlaced with each other, and arched down into the water in innumerable curves, by no means devoid of grace, but hideous just because they were impenetrable. Who could get over those roots, or through the scrub which stood stilted on them, letting down at every yard or two fresh air-roots from off its boughs, to add fresh tangle, as they struck into the mud, to the horrible imbroglio? If one had got in among them, I fancied, one would never have got out again. Struggling over and under endless trap-work, without footing on it or on the mud below, one must have sunk exhausted in an hour or two, to die of fatigue and heat, or chill and fever.

Let the mangrove foliage be as gay and green as it may—and it is gay and green—a mangrove swamp is a sad, ugly, evil place; and so I felt that one to be that day.

The only moving things were some large fish, who were leaping high out of water close to the bushes, glittering in the sun. They stopped as we came up: and then all was still, till a slate-blue heron[1] rose lazily off a dead bough, flapped fifty yards up the creek, and then sat down again. The only sound beside the rattle of our oars was the metallic note of a pigeon in the high tree, which I mistook then and afterwards for the sound of a horn.

On we rowed, looking out sharply right and left for an alligator basking on the mud among the mangrove roots. But none appeared, though more than one, probably, was watching us, with nothing of him above water but his horny eyes. The heron flapped on ahead, and settled once more, as if leading us on up the ugly creek, which grew narrower and fouler, till the oars touched the bank on each side, and drove out of the water shoals of four-eyed fish, ridiculous little things about as long as your hand, who, instead of diving to the bottom like reasonable fish, seemed possessed with the fancy that they could succeed better in the air, or on land; and accordingly jumped over each other's backs, scrambled out upon the mud, swam about with their goggle-eyes projecting above the surface of the water, and, in fact, did anything but behave like fish.

This little creature (Star-gazer,[2] as some call him) is, you must understand, one of the curiosities of Trinidad and of the Guiana Coast. He looks, on the whole, like a gray mullet, with a large blunt head, out of which stand, almost like horns, the eyes, from which he takes his name. You may see, in Wood's *Illustrated Natural History*, a drawing of him, which is—I am sorry to say—one of the very few bad ones in the book; and read how, 'at a first glance, the fish appears to possess four distinct eyes, each of these organs being divided across the middle, and apparently separated into two distinct portions. In fact an opaque band runs transversely across the corner of the eye, and the iris, or coloured portion, sends out two processes, which meet each other under the transverse band of the cornea, so that the fish appears to possess even a double pupil. Still, on closer investigation, the connection between the divisions of the pupil are apparent, and can readily be seen in the young fish. The lens is shaped something like a jargonelle pear, and so arranged that its broad extremity is placed under the large segment of the cornea.'

These strangely specialised eyes—so folks believe here—the fish uses by halves. With the lower halves he sees through the water, with the upper halves through the air; and, elevated by

---

[1] *Ardea leucogaster.* [2] *Anableps tetropthalmus.*

this quaint privilege, he aspires to be a terrestrial animal, emulating, I presume, the alligators around, and tries to take his walks upon the mud. You may see, as you go down to bathe on the east coast, a group of black dots, in pairs, peering up out of the sand, at the very highest verge of the surf-line. As you approach them, they leap up, and prove themselves to belong to a party of four-eyes, who run—there is no other word—down the beach, dash into the roaring surf, and the moment they see you safe in the sea run back again on the next wave, and begin staring at the sky once more. He who sees four-eyes for the first time without laughing must be much wiser, or much stupider, than any man has a right to be.

Suddenly the mangroves opened, and the creek ended in a wharf, with barges alongside. Baulks of strange timbers lay on shore. Sheds were full of empty sugar-casks, ready for the approaching crop-time. A truck was waiting for us on a tramway; and we scrambled on shore on a bed of rich black mud, to be received, of course, in true West Indian fashion, with all sorts of courtesies and kindnesses.

And here let me say, that those travellers who complain of discourtesy in the West Indies can have only themselves to thank for it. The West Indian has self-respect, and will not endure people who give themselves airs. He has prudence too, and will not endure people whom he expects to betray his hospitality by insulting him afterwards in print. But he delights in pleasing, in giving, in showing his lovely islands to all who will come and see them; Creole, immigrant, coloured or white man, Spaniard, Frenchman, Englishman, or Scotchman, each and all, will prove themselves thoughtful hosts and agreeable companions, if they be only treated as gentlemen usually expect to be treated elsewhere. On board a certain steamer, it was once proposed that the Royal Mail Steam Packet Company should issue cheap six-month season tickets to the West Indies, available for those who wished to spend the winter in wandering from island to island. The want of hotels was objected, naturally enough, by an Englishman present. But he was answered at once, that one or two good introductions to a single island would ensure hospitality throughout the whole archipelago.

A long-legged mule, after gibbing enough to satisfy his own self-respect, condescended to trot off with us up the tramway, which lay along a green drove strangely like one in the Cambridgeshire fens. But in the ditches grew a pea with large yellow flower-spikes, which reminded us that we were not in England; and beyond the ditches rose on either side, not wheat and beans, but sugar-cane ten and twelve feet high. And a noble grass it is, with its stems as thick as one's wrist, tillering out below in bold curves over the well-hoed dark soil, and its broad bright leaves falling and folding above in curves as bold as those of the stems: handsome enough thus, but more handsome still, I am told, when the 'arrow,' as the flower is called, spreads over the cane-piece a purple haze, which flickers in long shining waves before the breeze. One only fault it has; that, from the luxuriance of its growth, no wind can pass through it; and that therefore the heat of a cane-field trace is utterly stifling. Here and there we passed a still uncultivated spot; a desolate reedy swamp, with pools, and stunted alder-like trees, reminding us again of the Deep Fens, while the tall chimneys of the sugar-works, and the high woods beyond, completed the illusion. One might have been looking over Holm Fen toward Caistor Hanglands; or over Deeping toward the remnants of the ancient Bruneswald.

Soon, however, we had a broad hint that we were not in the Fens, but in a Tropic island. A window in heaven above was suddenly opened; out of it, without the warning cry of Gardyloo—well known in Edinburgh of old—a bucket of warm water, happily clean, was emptied on each of our heads; and the next moment all was bright again. A thunder-shower, without a warning thunder-clap, was to me a new phenomenon, which was repeated several times that day. The suddenness and the heaviness of the tropic showers at this season is as amusing as it is trying. The umbrella or the waterproof must be always ready, or you will get wet through. And getting wet here is a much more serious matter than in a temperate climate, where you may ride or walk all day in wet clothes and take no harm; for the rapid radiation, produced by the intense sunshine, causes a chill which may beget, only too easily, fever and ague not to be as easily shaken off.

The cause of these rapid and heavy showers is simple enough. The trade-wind, at this season of the year, is saturated with steam from the ocean which it has crossed; and the least disturbance in its temperature, from ascending hot air or descending cold, precipitates the steam in a sudden splash of water, out of a cloud, if there happens to be one near; if not, out of the clear air. Therefore it is that these showers, when they occur in the daytime, are most common about noon; simply because then the streams of hot air rise most frequently and rapidly, to struggle with the cooler layers aloft. There is thunder, of course, in the West Indies, continuous and terrible. But it occurs after midsummer, at the breaking up of the dry season and coming on of the wet.

At last the truck stopped at a manager's house with a Palmiste,[1] or cabbage-palm, on each side of the garden gate, a pair of columns which any prince would have longed for as ornaments for his lawn. It is the fashion here, and a good fashion it is, to leave the Palmistes, a few at least, when the

---

[1] *Oreodoxa oleracea.*

land is cleared; or to plant them near the house, merely on account of their wonderful beauty. One Palmiste was pointed out to me, in a field near the road, which had been measured by its shadow at noon, and found to be one hundred and fifty-three feet in height. For more than a hundred feet the stem rose straight, smooth, and gray. Then three or four spathes of flowers, four or five feet long each, jutted out and upward like; while from below them, as usual, one dead leaf, twenty feet long or more, dangled head downwards in the breeze. Above them rose, as always, the green portion of the stem for some twenty feet; and then the flat crown of feathers, as dark as yew, spread out against the blue sky, looking small enough up there, though forty feet at least in breadth. No wonder if the man who possessed such a glorious object dared not destroy it, though he spared it for a different reason from that for which the Negroes spare, whenever they can, the gigantic Ceibas, or silk cotton trees. These latter are useless as timber; and their roots are, of course, hurtful to the canes. But the Negro is shy of felling the Ceiba. It is a magic tree, haunted by spirits. There are 'too much jumbies in him,' the Negro says; and of those who dare to cut him down some one will die, or come to harm, within the year. In Jamaica, says my friend Mr. Gosse, 'they believe that if a person throws a stone at the trunk, he will be visited with sickness, or other misfortune. When they intend to cut one down, they first pour rum at the root as a propitiatory offering.' The Jamaica Negro, however, fells them for canoes, the wood being soft, and easily hollowed. But here, as in Demerara, the trees are left standing about in cane-pieces and pastures to decay into awful and fantastic shapes, with prickly spurs and board-walls of roots, high enough to make a house among them simply by roofing them in; and a flat crown of boughs, some seventy or eighty feet above the ground, each bough as big as an average English tree, from which dangles a whole world of lianes, matapalos, orchids, wild pines with long air-roots or gray beards; and last, but not least, that strange and lovely parasite, the *Rhipsalis cassytha*, which you mistake first for a plume of green seaweed, or a tress of Mermaid's hair which has got up there by mischance, and then for some delicate kind of pendent mistletoe; till you are told, to your astonishment, that it is an abnormal form of Cactus—a family which it resembles, save in its tiny flowers and fruit, no more than it resembles the Ceiba-tree on which it grows; and told, too, that, strangely enough, it has been discovered in Angola—the only species of the Cactus tribe in the Old World.

And now we set ourselves to walk up to the Depôt, where the Government timber was being felled, and the real 'High Woods' to be seen at last. Our path lay, along the half-finished tramway, through the first Cacao plantation I had ever seen, though, I am happy to say, not the last by many a one.

Imagine an orchard of nut-trees, with very large long leaves. Each tree is trained to a single stem. Among them, especially near the path, grow plants of the common hothouse Datura, its long white flowers perfuming all the air. They have been planted as landmarks, to prevent the young Cacao-trees being cut over when the weeds are cleared. Among them, too, at some twenty yards apart, are the stems of a tree looking much like an ash, save that it is inclined to throw out broad spurs, like a Ceiba. You look up, and see that they are Bois immortelles,[1] fifty or sixty feet high, one blaze of vermilion against the blue sky. Those who have stood under a Lombardy poplar in early spring, and looked up at its buds and twigs, showing like pink coral against the blue sky, and have felt the beauty of the sight, can imagine faintly—but only

CACAO.

faintly—the beauty of these *Madres de Cacao* (Cacao-mothers), as they call them here, because their shade is supposed to shelter the Cacao-trees, while the dew collected by their leaves keeps the ground below always damp.

I turned my dazzled eyes down again, and looked into the delicious darkness under the bushes. The ground was brown with fallen leaves, or green with ferns; and here and there a slant ray of sunlight pierced through the shade, and flashed on the brown leaves, and on a gray stem, and on a crimson jewel which hung on the stem—and there, again, on a bright orange one; and as my eye became accustomed to the darkness, I saw that the stems and larger boughs, far away into the wood, were dotted with pods, crimson or yellow or green, of the size and shape of a small hand closed with the fingers straight out. They were the Cacao-pods, full of what are called at home coco-

---

[1] *Erythrina umbrosa.*

nibs. And there lay a heap of them, looking like a heap of gay flowers; and by them sat their brown owner, picking them to pieces and laying the seeds to dry on a cloth. I went up and told him that I came from England, and never saw Cacao before, though I had been eating and drinking it all my life; at which news he grinned amusement till his white teeth and eyeballs made a light in that dark place, and offered me a fresh broken pod, that I might taste the pink sour-sweet pulp in which the rows of nibs lie packed, a pulp which I found very pleasant and refreshing.

He dries his Cacao-nibs in the sun, and, if he be a well-to-do and careful man, on a stage with wheels, which can be run into a little shed on the slightest shower of rain; picks them over and over, separating the better quality from the worse; and at last sends them down on mule-back to the sea, to be sold in London as Trinidad cocoa, or perhaps sold in Paris to the chocolate makers, who convert them into chocolate, *Menier* or other, by mixing them with sugar and vanilla, both, possibly, from this very island. This latter fact once inspired an adventurous German with the thought that he could make chocolate in Trinidad just as well as in Paris. And (so goes the story) he succeeded. But the fair Creoles would not buy it. It could not be good; it could not be the real article, unless it had crossed the Atlantic twice to and from that centre of fashion, Paris. So the manufacture, which might have added greatly to the wealth of Trinidad, was given up, and the ladies of the island eat nought but French chocolate, costing, it is said, nearly four times as much as home-made chocolate need cost.

As we walked on through the trace (for the tramway here was still unfinished) one of my kind companions pointed out a little plant, which bears in the island the ominous name of the Brinvilliers.[1] It is one of those deadly poisons too common in the bush, and too well known to the negro Obi-men and Obi-women. And as I looked at the insignificant weed I wondered how the name of that wretched woman should have spread to this remote island, and have become famous enough to be applied to a plant. French Negroes may have brought the name with them: but then arose another wonder. How were the terrible properties of the plant discovered? How eager and ingenious must the human mind be about the devil's work, and what long practice—considering its usual slowness and dulness—must it have had at the said work, ever to have picked out this paltry thing among the thousand weeds of the forest as a tool for its jealousy and revenge. It may have taken ages to discover the Brinvilliers, and ages more to make its poison generally known. Why not? As the Spaniards say, 'The devil knows many things, because he is old.' Surely this is one of the many facts which

---

[1] *Spigelia anthelmia.*

point toward some immensely ancient civilisation in the Tropics, and a civilisation which may have had its ugly vices, and have been destroyed thereby.

Now we left the Cacao grove: and I was aware, on each side of the trace, of a wall of green, such as I had never seen before on earth, not even in my dreams; strange colossal shapes towering up, a hundred feet and more in height, which, alas! it was impossible to reach; for on either side of the trace were fifty yards of half-cleared ground, fallen logs, withes, huge stumps ten feet high, charred and crumbling; and among them and over them a wilderness of creepers and shrubs, and all the luxuriant young growth of the 'rastrajo,' which springs up at once whenever the primeval forest is cleared—all utterly impassable. These rastrajo forms, of course, were all new to me. I might have spent weeks in botanising merely at them: but all I could remark, or cared to remark, there as in other places, was the tendency in the rastrajo toward growing enormous rounded leaves. How to get at the giants behind was the only question to one who for forty years had been longing for one peep at Flora's fairy palace, and saw its portals open at last. There was a deep gully before us, where a gang of convicts was working at a wooden bridge for the tramway, amid the usual abysmal mud of the tropic wet season. And on the other side of it there was no rastrajo right and left of the trace. I hurried down it like any schoolboy, dashing through mud and water, hopping from log to log, regardless of warnings and offers of help from good-natured Negroes, who expected the respectable elderly 'buccra' to come to grief; struggled perspiring up the other side of the gully; and then dashed away to the left, and stopped short, breathless with awe, in the primeval forest at last.

In the primeval forest; looking upon that upon which my teachers and masters, Humboldt, Spix, Martius, Schomburgk, Waterton, Bates, Wallace, Gosse, and the rest, had looked already, with far wiser eyes than mine, comprehending somewhat at least of its wonders, while I could only stare in ignorance. There was actually, then, such a sight to be seen on earth; and it was not less, but far more wonderful than they had said.

My first feeling on entering the high woods was helplessness, confusion, awe, all but terror. One is afraid at first to venture in fifty yards. Without a compass or the landmark of some opening to or from which he can look, a man must be lost in the first ten minutes, such a sameness is there in the infinite variety. That sameness and variety make it impossible to give any general sketch of a forest. Once inside, 'you cannot see the wood for the trees.' You can only wander on as far as you dare, letting each object impress itself on your mind as it may, and carrying away a confused recollection of innumerable perpendicular lines, all straining upwards, in fierce competition, towards the light-food far above ; and next of a green cloud, or rather mist, which hovers round your head, and rises, thickening and thickening to an unknown height. The upward lines are of every possible thickness, and of almost every possible hue; what leaves they bear, being for the most part on the tips of the twigs, give a scattered, mist-like appearance to the underfoliage. For the first moment, therefore, the forest seems more open than an English wood. But try to walk through it, and ten steps undeceive you. Around your knees are probably Mamures,[1] with creeping stems and fan-shaped leaves, something like those of a young coco-nut palm. You try to brush through them, and are caught up instantly by a string or wire belonging to some other plant. You look up and round: and then you find that the air is full of wires—that you are hung up in a network of fine branches belonging to half a dozen different sorts of young trees, and intertwined with as many different species of slender creepers. You thought at your first glance among the tree-stems that you were looking through open air ; you find that you are looking through a labyrinth of wire-rigging, and must use the cutlass right and left at every five steps. You push on into a bed of strong sedge-like Sclerias, with cutting edges to their leaves. It is well for you if they are only three, and not six feet high. In the midst of them you run against a horizontal stick, triangular, rounded, smooth, green. You take a glance along it right and left, and see no end to it either way, but gradually discover that it is the leaf-stalk of a young Cocorite palm.[2] The leaf is five-and-twenty feet long, and springs from a huge ostrich plume, which is sprawling out of the ground and up above your head a few yards off. You cut the leaf-stalk through right and left, and walk on, to be stopped suddenly (for you get so confused by the multitude of objects that you never see anything till you run against it) by a gray lichen-covered bar, as thick as your ankle. You follow it up with your eye, and find it entwine itself with three or four other bars, and roll over with them in great knots and festoons and loops twenty feet high, and then go up with them into the green cloud over your head, and vanish, as if a giant had thrown a ship's cables into the tree-tops. One of them, so grand that its form strikes even the Negro and the Indian, is a Liantasse.[3] You see that at once by the form of its cable—six or eight inches across in one direction, and three or four in another, furbelowed all down the middle into regular knots, and looking like a chain cable between two flexible iron bars. At another of the loops, about as thick as your arm, your companion, if you have a forester with you, will spring joyfully. With a few blows of his cutlass he will sever it as high up as he can reach, and again below,

[1] *Carludovica.*   [2] *Maximiliana Caribœa.*   [3] *Schnella excisa.*

K   AT L.

THE HIGH WOODS.

some three feet down; and, while you are wondering at this seemingly wanton destruction, he lifts the bar on high, throws his head back, and pours down his thirsty throat a pint or more of pure cold water. This hidden treasure is, strange as it may seem, the ascending sap, or rather the ascending pure rain-water which has been taken up by the roots, and is hurrying aloft, to be elaborated into sap, and leaf, and flower, and fruit, and fresh tissue for the very stem up which it originally climbed; and therefore it is that the woodman cuts the Water-vine through first at the top of the piece which he wants, and not at the bottom; for so rapid is the ascent of the sap that if he cut the stem below, the water would have all fled upwards before he could cut it off above. Meanwhile, the old story of Jack and the Bean-stalk comes into your mind. In such a forest was the old dame's hut; and up such a bean-stalk Jack climbed, to find a giant and a castle high above. Why not? What may not be up there? You look up into the green cloud, and long for a moment to be a monkey. There may be monkeys up there over your head, burly red Howler,[1] or tiny peevish Sapajou,[2] peering down at you; but you cannot peer up at them. The monkeys, and the parrots, and the humming-birds, and the flowers, and all the beauty, are upstairs—up above the green cloud. You are in 'the empty nave of the cathedral,' and 'the service is being celebrated aloft in the blazing roof.'

We will hope that, as you look up, you have not been careless enough to walk on; for if you have you will be tripped up at once: nor to put your hand out incautiously to rest it against a tree, or what not, for fear of sharp thorns, ants, and wasps' nests. If you are all safe, your next steps, probably, as you struggle through the bush between tree-trunks of every possible size, will bring you face to face with huge upright walls of seeming boards, whose rounded edges slope upward till, as your eye follows them, you find them enter an enormous stem, perhaps round, like one of the Norman pillars of Durham nave, and just as huge; perhaps fluted, like one of William of Wykeham's columns at Winchester. There is the stem: but where is the tree? Above the green cloud. You struggle up to it, between two of the board walls, but find it not so easy to reach. Between you and it are half a dozen tough strings which you had not noticed at first—the eye cannot focus itself rapidly enough in this confusion of distances—which have to be cut through ere you can pass. Some of them are rooted in the ground, straight and tense; some of them dangle and wave in the wind at every height. What are they? Air-roots of wild Pines,[3] or of Matapalos, or of Figs, or of Seguines,[4] or of some other parasite? Probably: but you cannot see. All you can

---

[1] *Mycetes.* [2] *Cebus.* [3] *Tillandsia.*
[4] *Philodendron, Anthurium,* etc.

see is, as you put your chin close against the trunk of the tree and look up, as if you were looking up against the side of a great ship set on end, that some sixty or eighty feet up in the green cloud, arms as big as English forest trees branch off; and that out of their forks a whole green garden of vegetation has tumbled down twenty or thirty feet, and half climbed up again. You scramble round the tree to find whence this aerial garden has sprung: you cannot tell. The tree-trunk is smooth and free from climbers; and that mass of verdure may belong possibly to the very cables which you met ascending into the green cloud twenty or thirty yards back, or to that impenetrable tangle, a dozen yards on, which has climbed a small tree, and then a taller one again, and then a taller still, till it has climbed out of sight and possibly into the lower branches of the big tree. And what are their species? what are their families? Who knows? Not even the most experienced woodman or botanist can tell you the names of plants of which he only sees the stems. The leaves, the flowers, the fruit, can only be examined by felling the tree; and not even always then, for sometimes the tree when cut refuses to fall, linked as it is by chains of liane to all the trees around. Even that wonderful water-vine which we cut through just now may be one of three or even four different plants.[1]

Soon you will be struck by the variety of the vegetation, and will recollect what you have often heard, that social plants are rare in the tropic forests. Certainly they are rare in Trinidad; where the only instances of social trees are the Moras (which I have never seen growing wild) and the Moriche palms. In Europe, a forest is usually made up of one dominant plant— of firs or of pines, of oaks or of beeches, of birch or of heather. Here no two plants seem alike. There are more species on an acre here than in all the New Forest, Savernake, or Sherwood. Stems rough, smooth, prickly, round, fluted, stilted, upright, sloping, branched, arched, jointed, opposite-leaved, alternate-leaved, leafless, or covered with leaves of every conceivable pattern, are jumbled together, till the eye and brain are tired of continually asking 'What next?' The stems are of every colour—copper, pink, gray, green, brown, black as if burnt, marbled with lichens, many of them silvery white, gleaming afar in the bush, furred with mosses and delicate creeping film-ferns, or laced with the air-roots of some parasite aloft. Up

---

[1] It may be a true vine, *Vitis Caribœa*, or *Cissus Sicyoides* (I owe the names of these water-vines, as I do numberless facts and courtesies, to my friend Mr. Prestoe, of the Botanic Gardens, Port of Spain); or, again, a Cinchonaceous plant, allied to the Quinine trees, *Uncaria Guianensis*; or possibly something else; for the botanic treasures of these forests are yet unexhausted, in spite of the labours of Krueger, Lockhart, Purdie, and De Schach.

this stem scrambles a climbing Seguine[1] with entire leaves; up the next another quite different, with deeply-cut leaves;[2] up the next the Ceriman[3] spreads its huge leaves, latticed and forked again and again. So fast do they grow, that they have not time to fill up the spaces between their nerves, and are consequently full of oval holes; and so fast does its spadix of flowers expand, that (as indeed do some other Aroids) an actual genial heat and fire of passion, which may be tested by the thermometer, or even by the hand, is given off during fructification. Beware of breaking it, or the Seguines. They will probably give off an evil smell, and as probably a blistering milk. Look on at the next stem. Up it, and down again, a climbing fern[4] which is often seen in hothouses has tangled its finely-cut fronds. Up the next, a quite different fern is crawling, by pressing tightly to the rough bark its creeping root-stalks, furred like a hare's leg. Up the next, the prim little Griffechatte[5] plant has walked, by numberless clusters of small cats'-claws, which lay hold of the bark. And what is this delicious scent about the air? Vanille? Of course it is; and up that stem zigzags the green fleshy chain of the Vanille Orchis. The scented pod is far above, out of your reach; but not out of the reach of the next parrot, or monkey, or negro hunter, who winds the treasure. And the stems themselves: to what trees do they belong? It would be absurd for one to try to tell you who cannot tell one-twentieth of them himself.[6] Suffice it to say, that over your head are perhaps a dozen kinds of admirable timber, which might be turned to a hundred uses in Europe, were it possible to get them thither: your guide (who here will be a second hospitable and cultivated Scot) will point with pride to one column after another, straight as those of a cathedral, and sixty to eighty feet without branch or knob. That, he will say, is Fiddlewood;[7] that a Carapo,[8] that a Cedar,[9] that a Roble[10] (oak); that, larger than all you have seen yet, a Locust;[11] that a Poui;[12] that a Guatecare,[13] that an Olivier,[14] woods which, he will tell you, are all but incorruptible, defying weather and insects. He will show you, as curiosities, the smaller but intensely hard Letter wood[15], Lignum vitæ,[16] and

---

[1] *Philodendron.*   [2] *Philodendron lacerum.* A noble plant.
[3] *Monstera pertusa;* a still nobler one: which may be seen, with *Philodendrons*, in great beauty at Kew.
[4] *Lygodium.*   [5] (———?).
[6] To know more of them, the reader should consult Dr. Krueger's list of woods sent from Trinidad to the Exhibition of 1862; or look at the collection itself (now at Kew), which was made by that excellent forester —if he will allow me to name him—Sylvester Devenish, Esquire, Crown Surveyor.
[7] *Vitex.*   [8] *Carapa Guianensis.*   [9] *Cedrela.*   [10] *Machærium.*
[11] *Hymenæa Courbaril.*   [12] *Tecoma serratifolia.*   [13] *Lecythis.*
[14] *Bucida.*   [15] *Brosimum Aubletii.*   [16] *Guaiacum.*

Purple heart.[1] He will pass by as useless weeds, Ceibas[2] and Sandbox-trees,[3] whose bulk appals you. He will look up, with something like a malediction, at the Matapalos, which, every fifty yards, have seized on mighty trees, and are enjoying, I presume, every different stage of the strangling art, from the baby Matapalo, who, like the one which you saw in the Botanic Garden, has let down his first air-root along his victim's stem, to the old sinner whose dark crown of leaves is supported, eighty feet in air, on innumerable branching columns of every size, cross-clasped to each other by transverse bars. The giant tree on which his seed first fell has rotted away utterly, and he stands in its place, prospering in his wickedness, like certain folk whom David knew too well. Your guide walks on with a sneer. But he stops with a smile of satisfaction as he sees lying on the ground dark green glossy leaves, which are fading into a bright crimson; for overhead somewhere there must be a Balata,[4] the king of the forest; and there, close by, is his stem —a madder-brown column, whose head may be a hundred and fifty feet or more aloft. The forester pats the sides of his favourite tree, as a breeder might that of his favourite race-horse. He goes on to evince his affection, in the fashion of West Indians, by giving it a chop with his cutlass; but not in wantonness. He wishes to show you the hidden virtues of this (in his eyes) noblest of trees—how there issues out swiftly from the wound a flow of thick white milk, which will congeal, in an hour's time, into a gum intermediate in its properties between caoutchouc and gutta-percha. He talks of a time when the English gutta-percha market shall be supplied from the Balatas of the northern hills, which cannot be shipped away as timber. He tells you how the tree is a tree of a generous, virtuous, and elaborate race—'a tree of God, which is full of sap,' as one said of old of such—and what could he say better, less or more? For it is a Sapota, cousin to the Sapodilla, and other excellent fruit-trees, itself most excellent even in its fruit-bearing power; for every five years it is covered with such a crop of delicious plums, that the lazy Negro thinks it worth his while to spend days of hard work, besides incurring the penalty of the law (for the trees are Government property), in cutting it down for the sake of its fruit. But this tree your guide will cut himself. There is no gully between it and the Government station; and he can carry it away; and it is worth his while to do so; for it will square, he thinks, into a log more than three feet in diameter, and eighty, ninety—he hopes almost a hundred—feet in length of hard, heavy wood, incorruptible, save in salt water; better than oak, as good as teak, and only surpassed in this island by the Poui. He will make a stage round it, some eight

[1] *Copaifera.*
[2] *Eriodendron.*
[3] *Hura crepitans.*
[4] *Mimusops Balata.*

feet high, and cut it above the spurs. It will take his convict gang (for convicts are turned to some real use in Trinidad) several days to get it down, and many more days to square it with the axe. A trace must be made to it through the wood, clearing away vegetation for which an European millionaire, could he keep it in his park, would gladly pay a hundred pounds a yard. The cleared stems, especially those of the palms, must be cut into rollers; and the dragging of the huge log over them will be a work of weeks, especially in the wet season. But it can be done, and it shall be; so he leaves a significant mark on his new-found treasure, and leads you on through the bush, hewing his way with light strokes right and left, so carelessly that you are inclined to beg him to hold his hand, and not destroy in a moment things so beautiful, so curious, things which would be invaluable in an English hothouse.

And where are the famous Orchids? They perch on every bough and stem: but they are not, with three or four exceptions, in flower in the winter; and if they were, I know nothing about them—at least, I know enough to know how little I know. Whosoever has read Darwin's *Fertilisation of Orchids*, and finds in his own reason that the book is true, had best say nothing about the beautiful monsters till he has seen with his own eyes more than his master.

And yet even the three or four that are in flower are worth going many a mile to see. In the hothouse they seem almost artificial from their strangeness: but to see them 'natural,' on natural boughs, gives a sense of their reality, which no unnatural situation can give. Even to look up at them perched on bough and stem, as one rides by; and to guess what exquisite and fantastic form may issue, in a few months or weeks, out of those fleshy, often unsightly, leaves, is a strange pleasure; a spur to the fancy which is surely wholesome, if we will but believe that all these things were invented by A Fancy, which desires to call out in us, by contemplating them, such small fancy as we possess; and to make us poets, each according to his power, by showing a world in which, if rightly looked at, all is poetry.

Another fact will soon force itself on your attention, unless you wish to tumble down and get wet up to your knees. The soil is furrowed everywhere by holes; by graves, some two or three feet wide and deep, and of uncertain length and shape, often wandering about for thirty or forty feet, and running confusedly into each other. They are not the work of man, nor of an animal; for no earth seems to have been thrown out of them. In the bottom of the dry graves you sometimes see a decaying root: but most of them just now are full of water, and of tiny fish also, who burrow in the mud and sleep during the dry season, to come out and swim during the wet. These graves are, some of them, plainly quite new. Some, again, are very old; for trees of all sizes are growing in them and over them.

What makes them? A question not easily answered. But the shrewdest foresters say that they have held the roots of trees now dead. Either the tree has fallen and torn its roots out of the ground, or the roots and stumps have rotted in their place, and the soil above them has fallen in.

But they must decay very quickly, these roots, to leave their quite fresh graves thus empty: and—now one thinks of it—how few fallen trees, or even dead sticks, there are about. An English wood, if left to itself, would be cumbered with fallen timber; and one has heard of forests in North America, through which it is all but impossible to make way, so high are piled up, among the still-growing trees, dead logs in every stage of decay. Such a sight may be seen in Europe, among the high Silver-fir forests of the Pyrenees. How is it not so here? How indeed? And how comes it—if you will look again—that there are few or no fallen leaves, and actually no leaf-mould? In an English wood there would be a foot—perhaps two feet—of black soil, renewed by every autumn leaf fall. Two feet? One has heard often enough of bison-hunting in Himalayan forests among Deodaras one hundred and fifty feet high, and scarlet Rhododendrons thirty feet high, growing in fifteen or twenty feet of leaf-and-timber mould. And here, in a forest equally ancient, every plant is growing out of the bare yellow loam, as it might in a well-hoed garden bed. Is it not strange?

Most strange; till you remember where you are—in one of Nature's hottest and dampest laboratories. Nearly eighty inches of yearly rain and more than eighty degrees of perpetual heat make swift work with vegetable fibre, which, in our cold and sluggard clime, would curdle into leaf-mould, perhaps into peat. Far to the north, in poor old Ireland, and far to the south, in Patagonia, begin the zones of peat, where dead vegetable fibre, its treasures of light and heat locked up, lies all but useless age after age. But this is the zone of illimitable sun-force, which destroys as swiftly as it generates, and generates again as swiftly as it destroys. Here, when the forest giant falls, as some tell me that they have heard him fall, on silent nights, when the cracking of the roots below and the lianes aloft rattles like musketry through the woods, till the great trunk comes down, with a boom as of a heavy gun, re-echoing on from mountain-side to mountain-side; then—

> 'Nothing in him that doth fade,
> But doth suffer an *air*-change
> Into something rich and strange.'

Under the genial rain and genial heat the timber tree itself, all its tangled ruin of lianes and parasites, and the boughs and leaves snapped off not only by the blow, but by the very wind, of the falling tree—all melt away swiftly and peacefully in a few months—say almost a few days—into the water, and carbonic acid, and sunlight, out of which they were created at first, to be absorbed instantly by the green leaves around, and, transmuted into fresh forms of beauty, leave not a wrack behind. Explained thus—and this I believe to be the true explanation—the absence of leaf-mould is one of the grandest, as it is one of the most startling, phenomena of the forest.

Look here at a fresh wonder. Away in front of us a smooth gray pillar glistens on high. You can see neither the top nor the bottom of it. But its colour, and its perfectly cylindrical shape, tell you what it is—a glorious Palmiste; one of those queens of the forest which you saw standing in the fields; with its capital buried in the green cloud and its base buried in that bank of green velvet plumes, which you must skirt carefully round, for they are a prickly dwarf palm, called here black Roseau.[1] Close to it rises another pillar, as straight and smooth, but one-fourth of the diameter—a giant's walking-cane. Its head, too, is in the green cloud. But near are two or three younger ones only forty or fifty feet high, and you see their delicate feather heads, and are told that they are Manacques;[2] the slender nymphs which attend upon the forest queen, as beautiful, though not as grand, as she.

The land slopes down fast now. You are tramping through stiff mud, and those Roseaux are a sign of water. There is a stream or gully near: and now for the first time you can see clear sunshine through the stems; and see, too, something of the bank of foliage on the other side of the brook. You catch sight, it may be, of the head of a tree aloft, blazing with golden trumpet flowers, which is a Poui; and of another lower one covered with hoar-frost, perhaps a Croton;[3] and of another, a giant covered with purple tassels. That is an Angelim. Another giant overtops even him. His dark glossy leaves toss off sheets of silver light as they flicker in the breeze; for it blows hard aloft outside while you are in stifling calm. That is a Balata. And what is that on high?—Twenty or thirty square yards of rich crimson a hundred feet above the ground. The flowers may belong to the tree itself. It may be a Mountain-mangrove,[4] which I have never seen in flower: but take the glasses and decide. No. The flowers belong to a liane. The 'wonderful' Prince of Wales's Feather[5] has taken possession of the head of a huge Mombin,[6] and tiled it all over with crimson combs which crawl out to the ends of the branches, and dangle twenty or thirty feet down, waving and leaping in the breeze. And over all blazes the cloudless blue.

You gaze astounded. Ten steps downward, and the vision is

---

[1] *Bactris.* [2] *Euterpe oleracea.* [3] *Croton gossypifolium.*
[4] *Moronobea coccinea.* [5] *Norantea.* [6] *Spondias lutea* (Hog-plum).

gone. The green cloud has closed again over your head, and you are stumbling in the darkness of the bush, half blinded by the sudden change from the blaze to the shade. Beware. 'Take care of the Croc-chien!' shouts your companion : and you are aware of, not a foot from your face, a long, green, curved whip, armed with pairs of barbs some four inches apart ; and are aware also, at the same moment, that another has seized you by the arm, another by the knees, and that you must back out, unless you are willing to part with your clothes first, and your flesh afterwards. You back out, and find that you have walked into the tips—luckily only into the tips—of the fern-like fronds of a trailing and climbing palm such as you see in the Botanic Gardens. That came from the East, and furnishes the rattan-canes. This[1] furnishes the gri-gri-canes, and is rather worse to meet, if possible, than the rattan. Your companion, while he helps you to pick the barbs out, calls the palm laughingly by another name, 'Suelta-mi-Ingles'; and tells you the old story of the Spanish soldier at San Josef. You are near the water now ; for here is a thicket of Balisiers.[2] Push through, under their great plantain-like leaves. Slip down the muddy bank to that patch of gravel. See first, though, that it is not tenanted already by a deadly Mapepire, or rattlesnake, which has not the grace, as his cousin in North America has, to use his rattle.

The brooklet, muddy with last night's rain, is dammed and bridged by winding roots, in shape like the jointed wooden snakes which we used to play with as children. They belong probably to a fig, whose trunk is somewhere up in the green cloud. Sit down on one, and look, around and aloft. From the soil to the sky, which peeps through here and there, the air is packed with green leaves of every imaginable hue and shape. Round our feet are Arums,[3] with snow-white spadixes and hoods, one instance among many here of brilliant colour developing itself in deep shade. But is the darkness of the forest actually as great as it seems? Or are our eyes, accustomed to the blaze outside, unable to expand rapidly enough, and so liable to mistake for darkness air really full of light reflected downward, again and again, at every angle, from the glossy surfaces of a million leaves? At least we may be excused ; for a bat has made the same mistake, and flits past us at noonday. And there is another—No ; as it turns, a blaze of metallic azure off the upper side of the wings proves this one to be no bat, but a Morpho—a moth as big as a bat. And what was that second larger flash of golden green, which dashed at the moth, and back to yonder branch not ten feet off? A Jacamar[4]—kingfisher, as they miscall her here, sitting fearless of man, with the moth in her long beak. Her throat is snowy white, her under-

---

[1] *Desmoncus.*   [2] *Heliconia.*
[3] *Spathiphyllum canufolium.*   [4] *Galbula.*

parts rich red brown. Her breast, and all her upper plumage and long tail, glitter with golden green. There is light enough in this darkness, it seems. But now a look again at the plants. Among the white-flowered Arums are other Arums, stalked and spotted, of which beware; for they are the poisonous Seguine-diable,[1] the dumb-cane, of which evil tales were told in the days of slavery. A few drops of its milk, put into the mouth of a refractory slave, or again into the food of a cruel master, could cause swelling, choking, and burning agony for many hours.

Over our heads bend the great arrow leaves and purple leaf-stalks of the Tanias;[2] and mingled with them, leaves often larger still: oval, glossy, bright, ribbed, reflecting from their underside a silver light. They belong to Arumas;[3] and from their ribs are woven the Indian baskets and packs. Above these, again, the Balisiers bend their long leaves, eight or ten feet long apiece; and under the shade of the leaves their gay flower-spikes, like double rows of orange and black birds' beaks upside down. Above them, and among them, rise stiff upright shrubs, with pairs of pointed leaves, a foot long some of them, pale green above, and yellow or fawn-coloured beneath. You may see, by the three longitudinal nerves in each leaf, that they are Melastomas of different kinds—a sure token they that you are in the Tropics—a probable token that you are in Tropical America.

And over them, and among them, what a strange variety of foliage: look at the contrast between the Balisiers and that branch which has thrust itself among them, which you take for a dark copper-coloured fern, so finely divided are its glossy leaves. It is really a Mimosa—Bois Mulâtre,[4] as they call it here. What a contrast again, the huge feathery fronds of the Cocorite palms which stretch right away hither over our heads, twenty and thirty feet in length. And what is that spot of crimson flame hanging in the darkest spot of all from an under-bough of that low weeping tree? A flower-head of the Rosa del Monte.[5] And what that bright straw-coloured fox's brush above it, with a brown hood like that of an Arum, brush and hood nigh three feet long each? Look—for you require to look more than once, sometimes more than twice—here, up the stem of that Cocorite, or as much of it as you can see in the thicket. It is all jagged with the brown butts of its old fallen leaves; and among the butts perch broad-leaved ferns, and fleshy Orchids, and above them, just below the plume of mighty fronds, the yellow fox's brush, which is its spathe of flower.

What next? Above the Cocorites dangle, amid a dozen different kinds of leaves, festoons of a liane, or of two, for one

---

[1] *Dieffenbachia*, of which varieties are not now uncommon in hothouses.
[2] *Xanthosoma*.   [3] *Calathea*.
[4] *Pentaclethra filamentosa*.   [5] *Brownea*.

has purple flowers, the other yellow—Bignonias, Bauhinias—what not? And through them a Carat[1] palm has thrust its thin bending stem, and spread out its flat head of fan-shaped leaves twenty feet long each: while over it, I verily believe, hangs eighty feet aloft the head of the very tree upon whose roots we are sitting. For amid the green cloud you may see sprigs of leaf somewhat like that of a weeping willow;[2] and there, probably, is the trunk to which they belong, or rather what will be a trunk at last. At present it is like a number of round-edged boards of every size, set on end, and slowly coalescing at their edges. There is a slit down the middle of the trunk, twenty or thirty feet long. You may see the green light of the forest shining through it. Yes. That is probably the fig; or, if not, then something else. For who am I, that I should know the hundredth part of the forms on which we look?—And above all you catch a glimpse of that crimson mass of Norantea which we admired just now; and, black as yew against the blue sky and white cloud, the plumes of one Palmiste, who has climbed toward the light, it may be for centuries, through the green cloud; and now, weary and yet triumphant, rests her dark head among the bright foliage of a Ceiba, and feeds unhindered on the sun.

There, take your tired eyes down again; and turn them right, or left, or where you will, to see the same scene, and yet never the same. New forms, new combinations; a wealth of creative Genius—let us use the wise old word in its true sense—incomprehensible by the human intellect or the human eye, even as He is who makes it all, Whose garment, or rather Whose speech, it is. The eye is not filled with seeing, or the ear with hearing; and never would be, did you roam these forests for a hundred years. How many years would you need merely to examine and discriminate the different species? And when you had done that, how many more to learn their action and reaction on each other? How many more to learn their virtues, properties, uses? How many more to answer the perhaps ever unanswerable question—How they exist and grow at all? By what miracle they are compacted out of light, air, and water, each after its kind? How, again, those kinds began to be, and what they were like at first? Whether those crowded, struggling, competing shapes are stable or variable? Whether or not they are varying still? Whether even now, as we sit here, the great God may not be creating, slowly but surely, new forms of beauty round us? Why not? If He chose to do it, could He not do it? And even had you answered that question, which would require whole centuries of observation as patient and accurate as that which Mr. Darwin employed on Orchids and climbing plants, how much nearer would you be to

---

[1] *Sabal.* [2] *Ficus salicifolia?*

the deepest question of all—Do these things exist, or only appear? Are they solid realities, or a mere phantasmagoria, orderly indeed, and law-ruled, but a phantasmagoria still; a picture-book by which God speaks to rational essences, created in His own likeness? And even had you solved that old problem, and decided for Berkeley or against him, you would still have to learn from these forests a knowledge which enters into man, not through the head, but through the heart; which (let some modern philosophers say what they will) defies all analysis, and can be no more defined or explained by words than a mother's love. I mean, the causes and the effects of their beauty; that 'Æsthetic of plants,' of which Schleiden has spoken so well in that charming book of his, *The Plant*, which all should read who wish to know somewhat of 'The Open Secret.'

But when they read it, let them read with open hearts. For that same 'Open Secret' is, I suspect, one of those which God may hide from the wise and prudent, and yet reveal to babes.

At least, so it seemed to me, the first day that I went, awe-struck, into the High Woods; and so it seemed to me, the last day that I came, even more awe-struck, out of them.

CEIBA.

CHAPTER VIII

LA BREA

WE were, of course, desirous to visit that famous Lake of Pitch, which our old nursery literature described as one of the 'Wonders of the World.' It is not that; it is merely a very odd, quaint, unexpected, and only half-explained phenomenon: but no wonder. That epithet should be kept for such matters as the growth of a crystal, the formation of a cell, the germination of a seed, the coming true of a plant, whether from a fruit or from a cutting: in a word, for any and all those hourly and momentary miracles which were attributed of old to some *Vis Formatrix* of nature; and are now attributed to some other abstract formula, as they will be to some fresh one, and to a dozen more, before the century is out; because the more accurately and deeply they are investigated, the more inexplicable they will be found.

So it is; but the 'public' are not inclined to believe that so it is, and will not see, till their minds get somewhat of a truly scientific training.

If any average educated person were asked—Which seemed to him more wonderful, that a hen's egg should always produce a chicken, or that it should now and then produce a sparrow or a duckling?—can it be doubted what answer he would give? or that it would be the wrong answer? What answer, again, would he make to the question—Which is more wonderful, that dwarfs and giants (*i.e.* people under four feet six or over six feet six) should be exceedingly rare, or that the human race is not of all possible heights from three inches to thirty feet? Can it be doubted that in this case, as in the last, the wrong answer would be given? He would defend himself, probably, if he had a smattering of science, by saying that experience teaches us that Nature works by 'invariable laws'; by which he would mean, usually unbroken customs; and that he has, therefore, a right to be astonished if they are broken. But he would be wrong. The just cause of astonishment is, that the laws are, on the whole, invariable; that the customs are so seldom broken; that sun and moon, plants and animals, grains of dust and vesicles of vapour, are not perpetually committing some vagary or other, and making as great fools of themselves as human beings are wont to do. Happily for the existence of the universe, they do not. But how, and still more why, things in general behave so respectably and loyally, is a wonder which is either utterly inexplicable, or explicable, I hold, only on the old theory that they obey Some One—whom we obey to a very limited extent indeed. Not that this latter theory gets rid of the perpetual and omnipresent element of wondrousness. If matter alone exists, it is a wonder and a mystery how it obeys itself. If A Spirit exists, it is a wonder and a mystery how He makes matter obey Him. All that the scientific man can do is, to confess the presence of mystery all day long; and to live in that wholesome and calm attitude of wonder which we call awe and reverence; that so he may be delivered from the unwholesome and passionate fits of wonder which we call astonishment, the child of ignorance and fear, and the parent of rashness and superstition. So will he keep his mind in the attitude most fit for seizing new facts, whenever they are presented to him. So he will be able, when he doubts of a new fact, to examine himself whether he doubts it on just grounds; whether his doubt may not proceed from mere self-conceit, because the fact does not suit his preconceived theories; whether it may not proceed from an even lower passion, which he shares (being human) with the most uneducated; namely, from dread of the two great bogies, Novelty and Size—novelty, which makes it hard to convince the country fellow that in the Tropics great flowers grow on tall trees, as they do here on herbs; size, which makes it hard to convince him that in far lands trees are often two and three hundred feet high, simply because he has never seen one here a hundred feet high. It is not surprising, but saddening, to watch what power these two phantoms have over the minds of those who would be angry if they were supposed to be uneducated. How often has one heard the existence of the sea-serpent declared impossible and absurd, on these very grounds, by people who thought they were arguing scientifically: the sea-serpent could not exist, firstly because—because it was so odd, strange, new, in a word, and unlike anything that they had ever seen or fancied; and, secondly, because it was so big. The first argument would apply to a thousand new facts, which physical science is daily proving to be true; and the second, when the reputed size of the sea-serpent is compared with the known size of the ocean, rather more silly than the assertion that a ten-pound pike could not live in a half-acre pond, because it was too small to hold him. The true arguments against the existence of a sea-serpent, namely, that no Ophidian could live long under water, and that therefore the sea-serpent, if he existed, would be seen continually at the surface; and again, that the appearance taken for a sea-serpent has been proved, again and again, to be merely a long line of rolling porpoises—these really sound arguments would be nothing to such people, or only be accepted as supplementing and corroborating their dislike to believe in anything new, or anything a little bigger than usual.

But so works the average, *i.e.* the uneducated and barbaric intellect, afraid of the New and the Big, whether in space or in time. How the fear of those two phantoms has hindered our knowledge of this planet, the geologist knows only too well.

It was excusable, therefore, that this Pitch Lake should be counted among the wonders of the world; for it is, certainly, tolerably big. It covers ninety-nine acres, and contains millions of tons of so-called pitch.

Its first discoverers, of course, were not bound to see that a pitch lake of ninety-nine acres was no more wonderful than any of the little pitch wells—'spues' or 'galls,' as we should call them in Hampshire—a yard across; or any one of the tiny veins and lumps of pitch which abound in the surrounding forests; and no less wonderful than if it had covered ninety-nine thousand acres instead of ninety-nine. Moreover, it was a novelty. People were not aware of the vast quantity of similar deposits which exist up and down the hotter regions of the globe. And being new and big too, its genesis demanded, for the comfort of the barbaric intellect, a cataclysm, and a convulsion, and some sort of prodigious birth, which was till lately referred, like many another strange object, to volcanic action. The explanation savoured somewhat of a 'bull'; for what a volcano could do to pitch, save to burn it up into coke and gases, it is difficult to see.

It now turns out that the Pitch Lake, like most other things, owes its appearance on the surface to no convulsion or vagary at all, but to a most slow, orderly, and respectable process of nature, by which buried vegetable matter, which would have become peat, and finally brown coal, in a temperate climate, becomes, under the hot tropic soil, asphalt and oil, continually oozing up beneath the pressure of the strata above it. Such, at least, is the opinion of Messrs. Wall and Sawkins, the geological surveyors of Trinidad, and of several chemists whom they quote; and I am bound to say, that all I saw at the lake and elsewhere, during two separate visits, can be easily explained on their hypothesis, and that no other possible cause suggests itself as yet. The same cause, it may be, has produced the submarine spring of petroleum, off the shore near Point Rouge, where men can at times skim the floating oil off the surface of the sea; the petroleum and asphalt of the Windward Islands and of Cuba, especially the well-known Barbadoes tar; and the petroleum springs of the mainland, described by Humboldt, at Truxillo, in the Gulf of Cumana; and 'the inexhaustible deposits of mineral pitch in the provinces of Merida and Coro, and, above all, in that of Maracaybo. In the latter it is employed for caulking the ships which navigate the lake.'[1] But the reader shall hear what the famous lake is like, and judge for himself. Why not? He may not be 'scientific,' but, as Professor Huxley well says, what is scientific thought but common sense well regulated?

Running down, then, by steamer, some thirty-six miles south from Port of Spain, along a flat mangrove shore, broken only at one spot by the conical hill of San Fernando, we arrived off a peninsula, whose flat top is somewhat higher than the lowland right and left. The uplands are rich with primeval forest, and perhaps always have been. The lower land, right and left, was, I believe, cultivated for sugar, till the disastrous epoch of 1846: but it is now furred over with rastrajo woods.

We ran, on our first visit, past the pitch point of La Brea, south-westward to Trois, where an industrial farm for convicts had been established by my host the Governor. We were lifted on shore through a tumbling surf; and welcomed by an intelligent and courteous German gentleman, who showed us all that was to be seen; and what we saw was satisfactory enough. The estate was paying, though this was only its third year. An average number of 77 convicts had already cleared 195 acres, of which 182 were under cultivation. Part of this had just been reclaimed from pestilential swamp: a permanent benefit to the health of the island. In spite of the exceptional drought of the year before, and the subsequent plague of caterpillars, 83,000 pounds of rice had been grown; and the success of the rice crop, it must be remembered, will become more and more important to the island, as the increase of Coolie labourers increases the demand for the grain. More than half the plantains put in (22,000) were growing, and other vegetables in abundance. But, above all, there were more than 7000 young coco-palms doing well, and promising a perpetual source of wealth for the future. For as the trees grow, and the crops raised between them diminish, the coco-palms will require little or no care, but yield fruit the whole year round without further expense; and the establishment can then be removed elsewhere, to reclaim a fresh sheet of land.

Altogether, the place was a satisfactory specimen of what can be effected in a tropical country by a Government which will govern. Since then, another source of profitable employment for West Indian convicts has been suggested to me. Bamboo, it is now found, will supply an admirable material for paper; and I have been assured by paper-makers that those who will plant the West Indian wet lands with bamboo for their use, may realise enormous profits.

[1] Quoted from Codazzi, by Messrs. Wall and Sawkins, in an Appendix on Asphalt Deposits, an excellent monograph which first pointed out, as far as I am aware, the fact that asphalt, at least at the surface, is found almost exclusively in the warmer parts of the globe.

We scrambled back into the boat—had, of course, a heap of fruit, bananas, oranges, pine-apples, tossed in after us—and ran back again in the steamer to the famous La Brea.

As we neared the shore, we perceived that the beach was black as pitch; and the breeze being off the land, the asphalt smell (not unpleasant) came off to welcome us. We rowed in, and saw in front of a little row of wooden houses a tall mulatto, in blue policeman's dress, gesticulating and shouting to us. He was the ward-policeman, and I found him (as I did all the coloured police) able and courteous, shrewd and trusty. These police are excellent specimens of what can be made of the Negro, or half-Negro, if he be but first drilled, and then given a responsibility which calls out his self-respect. He was warning our crew not to run aground on one or other of the pitch reefs, which here take the place of rocks. A large one, a hundred yards off on the left, has been almost all dug away, and carried to New York or to Paris to make asphalt pavement.

The boat was run ashore, under his directions, on a spit of sand between the pitch; and when she ceased bumping up and down in the muddy surf, we scrambled out into a world exactly the hue of its inhabitants—of every shade, from jet-black to copper-brown. The pebbles on the shore were pitch. A tide-pool close by was enclosed in pitch: a four-eyes was swimming about in it, staring up at us; and when we hunted him, tried to escape, not by diving, but by jumping on shore on the pitch, and scrambling off between our legs. While the policeman, after profoundest courtesies, was gone to get a mule-cart to take us up to the lake, and planks to bridge its water-channels, we took a look round at this oddest of corners of the earth.

In front of us was the unit of civilisation—the police-station, wooden, on wooden stilts (as all well-built houses are here), to ensure a draught of air beneath them. We were, of course, asked to come in and sit down, but preferred looking about, under our umbrellas; for the heat was intense. The soil is half pitch, half brown earth, among which the pitch sweals in and out, as tallow sweals from a candle. It is always in slow motion under the heat of the tropic sun: and no wonder if some of the cottages have sunk right and left in such a treacherous foundation. A stone or brick house could not stand here: but wood and palm-thatch are both light and tough enough to be safe, let the ground give way as it will.

The soil, however, is very rich. The pitch certainly does not injure vegetation, though plants will not grow actually in it. The first plants which caught our eyes were pine-apples; for which La Brea is famous. The heat of the soil, as well as of the air, brings them to special perfection. They grow about anywhere, unprotected by hedge or fence; for the Negroes here seem honest enough, at least towards each other. And at the corner of the house was a bush worth looking at, for we had heard of it for many a year. It bore prickly, heart-shaped pods an inch long, filled with seeds coated with a red waxy pulp.

This was a famous plant—*Bixa Orellana*, Roucou; and that pulp was the well-known Arnotta dye of commerce. In England and Holland it is used merely, I believe, to colour cheeses; but in the Spanish Main, to colour human beings. The Indian of the Orinoco prefers paint to clothes; and when he has 'roucoued' himself from head to foot, considers himself in full dress, whether for war or dancing. Doubtless he knows his own business best from long experience. Indeed, as we stood broiling on the shore, we began somewhat to regret that European manners and customs prevented our adopting the Guaraon and Arawak fashion.

The mule-cart arrived; the lady of the party was put into it on a chair, and slowly bumped and rattled past the corner of Dundonald Street—so named after the old sea-hero, who was, in his lifetime, full of projects for utilising this same pitch—and up a pitch road, with a pitch gutter on each side.

The pitch in the road has been, most of it, laid down by hand, and is slowly working down the slight incline, leaving pools and ruts full of water, often invisible, because covered with a film of brown pitch-dust, and so letting in the unwary walker over his shoes. The pitch in the gutter-bank is in its native place, and as it spues slowly out of the soil into the ditch in odd wreaths and lumps, we could watch, in little, the process which has produced the whole deposit —probably the whole lake itself.

CASHEW NUT.

A bullock-cart, laden with pitch, came jolting down past us; and we observed that the lumps, when the fracture is fresh, have all a drawn-out look; that the very air-bubbles in them, which are often very numerous, are all drawn out likewise, long and oval, like the air-bubbles in some ductile lavas.

On our left, as we went on, the bush was low, all of yellow Cassia and white Hibiscus, and tangled with lovely convolvulus-like creepers, Ipomœa and Echites, with white, purple, or yellow flowers. On the right were negro huts and gardens, fewer and fewer as we went on—all rich with fruit-trees, especially with oranges, hung with fruit of every hue; and beneath them, of course, the pine-apples of La Brea. Everywhere along the road grew, seemingly wild here, that pretty low tree, the Cashew, with rounded yellow-veined leaves and little green flowers, followed by a quaint pink and red-striped pear, from which hangs, at the larger and lower end, a kidney-shaped bean, which bold folk eat when roasted: but woe to those who try it when raw, for the acrid oil blisters the lips; and even while the beans are roasting, the fumes of the oil will blister the cook's face if she holds it too near the fire.

As we went onward up the gentle slope (the rise is one hundred and thirty-eight feet in rather more than a mile), the ground became more and more full of pitch, and the vegetation poorer and more rushy, till it resembled, on the whole, that of an English fen. An Ipomœa or two, and a scarlet-flowered dwarf Heliconia, kept up the tropic type, as does a stiff brittle fern about two feet high.[1] We picked the weeds, which looked like English mint or basil, and found that most of them had three longitudinal nerves in each leaf, and were really Melastomas, though dwarfed into a far meaner habit than that of the noble forms we saw at Chaguanas, and again on the other side of the lake. On the right, too, in a hollow, was a whole wood of Groo-groo palms, gray stemmed, gray leaved; and here and there a patch of white or black Roseau rose gracefully eight or ten feet high among the reeds.

The plateau of pitch now widened out, and the whole ground looked like an asphalt pavement, half overgrown with marsh-loving weeds, whose roots feed in the sloppy water which overlies the pitch. But, as yet, there was no sign of the lake. The incline, though gentle, shuts off the view of what is beyond. This last lip of the lake has surely overflowed, and is overflowing still, though very slowly. Its furrows all curve downward; and it is, in fact, as one of our party said, 'a black glacier.' The pitch, expanding under the burning sun of day, must needs expand most towards the line of least resistance, that is, downhill; and when it contracts again under the coolness of night, it contracts, surely from the same cause, more downhill than it does uphill; and so each particle never returns to the spot whence it started, but rather drags the particles above it downward toward itself. At least, so it seemed to us. Thus may be explained the common mistake which is noticed by Messrs. Wall and Sawkins[2] in their admirable description of the lake.

'All previous descriptions refer the bituminous matter scattered over the La Brea district, and especially that between the village and the lake, to streams which have issued at some former epoch from the lake, and extended into the sea. This supposition is totally incorrect, as solidification would have probably ensued before it had proceeded one-tenth of the distance; and such of the asphalt as has undoubtedly escaped from the lake has not advanced more than a few yards, and

---

[1] *Blechnum serrulatum.*
[2] *Geological Survey of Trinidad;* Appendix G, on Asphaltic Deposits.

always presents the curved surfaces already described, and never appears as an extended sheet.'

Agreeing with this statement as a whole, I nevertheless cannot but think it probable that a great deal of the asphalt, whether it be in large masses or in scattered veins, may be moving very slowly downhill, from the lake to the sea, by the process of expansion by day, and contraction by night; and may be likened to a caterpillar, or rather caterpillars innumerable, progressing by expanding and contracting their rings, having strength enough to crawl downhill, but not strength enough to back uphill again.

At last we surmounted the last rise, and before us lay the famous lake—not at the bottom of a depression, as we expected, but at the top of a rise, whence the ground slopes away from it on two sides, and rises from it very slightly on the two others. The black pool glared and glittered in the sun. A group of islands, some twenty yards wide, were scattered about the middle of it. Beyond it rose a noble forest of Moriche fan-palms;[1] and to the right of them high wood with giant Mombins and undergrowth of Cocorite—a paradise on the other side of the Stygian pool.

We walked, with some misgivings, on to the asphalt, and found it perfectly hard. In a few yards we were stopped by a channel of clear water, with tiny fish and water-beetles in it; and, looking round, saw that the whole lake was intersected with channels, so unlike anything which can be seen elsewhere, that it is not easy to describe them.

Conceive a crowd of mushrooms, of all shapes, from ten to fifty feet across, close together side by side, their tops being kept at exactly the same level, their rounded rims squeezed tight against each other; then conceive water poured on them so as to fill the parting seams, and in the wet season, during which we visited it, to overflow the tops somewhat. Thus would each mushroom represent, tolerably well, one of the innumerable flat asphalt bosses, which seem to have sprung up each from a separate centre, while the parting seams would be of much the same shape as those in the asphalt, broad and shallow atop, and rolling downward in a smooth curve, till they are at bottom mere cracks, from two to ten feet deep. Whether these cracks actually close up below, and the two contiguous masses of pitch become one, cannot be seen. As far as the eye goes down, they are two, though pressed close to each other. Messrs. Wall and Sawkins explain the odd fact clearly and simply. The oil, they say, which the asphalt contains when it rises first, evaporates in the sun, of course most on the outside of the heap, leaving a tough coat of asphalt, which has, generally, no power to unite with the corresponding coat of the next mass.

[1] *Mauritia flexuosa.*

Meanwhile, Mr. Manross, an American gentleman, who has written a very clever and interesting account of the lake,[1] seems to have been so far deceived by the curved and squeezed edges of these masses, that he attributes to each of them a revolving motion, and supposes that the material is continually passing from the centre to the edges, when it 'rolls under,' and rises again in the middle. Certainly the strange stuff looks, at the first glance, as if it were behaving in this way; and certainly, also, his theory would explain the appearance of sticks and logs in the pitch. But Messrs. Wall and Sawkins say that they observed no such motion; nor did we: and I agree with them, that it is not very obvious to what force, or what influence, it could be attributable. We must, therefore, seek for some other way of accounting for the sticks—which utterly puzzled us, and which Mr. Manross well describes as 'numerous pieces of wood which, being involved in the pitch, are constantly coming to the surface. They are often several feet in length, and five or six inches in diameter. On reaching the surface they generally assume an upright position, one end being detained in the pitch, while the other is elevated by the lifting of the middle. They may be seen at frequent intervals over the lake, standing up to the height of two or even three feet. They look like stumps of trees protruding through the pitch; but their parvenu character is curiously betrayed by a ragged cap of pitch which invariably covers the top, and hangs down like hounds' ears on either side.'

Whence do they come? Have they been blown on to the lake, or left behind by man? or are they fossil trees, integral parts of the vegetable stratum below which is continually rolling upward? or are they of both kinds? I do not know. Only this is certain, as Messrs. Wall and Sawkins have pointed out, that not only 'the purer varieties of asphalt, such as approach or are identical with asphalt glance, have been observed' (though not, I think, in the lake itself) 'in isolated masses, where there was little doubt of their proceeding from ligneous substances of larger dimensions, such as roots and pieces of trunks and branches;' but moreover, that 'it is also necessary to admit a species of conversion by contact; since pieces of wood included accidentally in the asphalt, for example, by dropping from overhanging vegetation, are often found partially transformed into the material.' This is a statement which we verified again and again; as we did the one which follows, namely, that the hollow bubbles which abound on the surface of the pitch 'generally contain traces of the lighter portions of vegetation,' and 'are manifestly derived from leaves, etc., which are blown about the lake by the wind, and are covered with asphalt, and as they become asphalt themselves, give off gases, which form bubbles round them.'

[1] *American Journal of Science*, Sept. 1855.

THE PITCH LAKE.

But how is it that those logs stand up out of the asphalt, with asphalt caps and hounds' ears (as Mr. Manross well phrases it) on the tops of them?

We pushed on across the lake, over the planks which the Negroes laid down from island to island. Some, meanwhile, preferred a steeple-chase with water-jumps, after the fashion of the midshipmen on a certain second visit to the lake. How the Negroes grinned delight and surprise at the vagaries of English lads—a species of animal altogether new to them. And how they grinned still more when certain staid and portly dignitaries caught the infection, and proved, by more than one good leap, that they too had been English schoolboys—alas! long, long ago.

So, whether by bridging, leaping, or wading, we arrived at last at the little islands, and found them covered with a thick, low scrub; deep sedge, and among them Pinguins, like huge pine-apples without the apple; gray wild Pines—parasites on Matapalos, which of course have established themselves, like robbers and vagrants as they are, everywhere; a true Holly, with box-like leaves; and a rare Cocoa-plum,[1] very like the holly in habit, which seems to be all but confined to these little patches of red earth, afloat on the pitch. Out of the scrub, when we were there, flew off two or three night-jars, very like our English species, save that they had white in the wings; and on the second visit, one of the midshipmen, true to the English boy's birds'-nesting instinct, found one of their eggs, white-spotted, in a grass nest.

Passing these little islands, which are said (I know not how truly) to change their places and number, we came to the very fountains of Styx, to that part of the lake where the asphalt is still oozing up.

As the wind set toward us, we soon became aware of an evil smell—petroleum and sulphuretted hydrogen at once—which gave some of us a headache. The pitch here is yellow and white with sulphur foam; so are the water-channels; and out of both water and pitch innumerable bubbles of gas arise, loathsome to the smell. We became aware also that the pitch was soft under our feet. We left the impression of our boots; and if we had stood still awhile, we should soon have been ankle-deep. No doubt there are spots where, if a man stayed long enough, he would be slowly and horribly engulfed. 'But,' as Mr. Manross says truly, 'in no place is it possible to form those bowl-like depressions round the observer described by former travellers.' What we did see is, that the fresh pitch oozes out at the lines of least resistance, namely, in the channels between the older and more hardened masses, usually at the upper ends of them; so that one may stand on pitch compara-

---

[1] *Chrysobalanus Pellocarpus.*

tively hard, and put one's hand into pitch quite liquid, which is flowing softly out, like some ugly fungoid growth, such as may be seen in old wine-cellars, into the water. One such pitch-fungus had grown several yards in length in the three weeks between our first and second visit; and on another, some of our party performed exactly the same feat as Mr. Manross—

'In one of the star-shaped pools of water, some five feet deep, a column of pitch had been forced perpendicularly up from the bottom. On reaching the surface of the water it had formed a sort of centre table, about four feet in diameter, but without touching the sides of the pool. The stem was about a foot in diameter. I leaped out on this table, and found that it not only sustained my weight, but that the elasticity of the stem enabled me to rock it from side to side. Pieces torn from the edges of this table sank readily, showing that it had been raised by pressure, and not by its buoyancy.'

True, though strange: but stranger still did it seem to us, when we did at last what the Negroes asked us, and dipped our hands into the liquid pitch, to find that it did not soil the fingers. The old proverb, that one cannot touch pitch without being defiled, happily does not stand true here, or the place would be intolerably loathsome. It can be scraped up, moulded into any shape you will; wound in a string (as was done by one of the midshipmen) round a stick, and carried off: but nothing is left on the hand save clean gray mud and water. It may be kneaded for an hour before the mud be sufficiently driven out of it to make it sticky. This very abundance of earthy matter it is which, while it keeps the pitch from soiling, makes it far less valuable than it would be were it pure.

It is easy to understand whence this earthy matter (twenty or thirty per cent) comes. Throughout the neighbourhood the ground is full, to the depth of hundreds of feet, of coaly and asphaltic matter. Layers of sandstone or of shale containing this decayed vegetable, alternate with layers which contain none. And if, as seems probable, the coaly matter is continually changing into asphalt and oil, and then working its way upward through every crack and pore, to escape from the enormous pressure of the superincumbent soil, it must needs carry up with it innumerable particles of the soils through which it passes.

In five minutes we had seen, handled, and smelt enough to satisfy us with this very odd and very nasty vagary of tropic nature; and as we did not wish to become faint and ill, between the sulphuretted hydrogen and the blaze of the sun reflected off the hot black pitch, we hurried on over the water-furrows, and through the sedge-beds to the farther shore—to find ourselves in a single step out of an Inferno into a Paradiso.

We looked back at the foul place, and agreed that it is well for the human mind that the Pitch Lake was still unknown when Dante wrote that hideous poem of his—the opprobrium (as I hold) of the Middle Age. For if such were the dreams of its noblest and purest genius, what must have been the dreams of the ignoble and impure multitude? But had he seen this lake, how easy, how tempting too, it would have been to him to embody in imagery the surmise of a certain 'Father,' and heighten the torments of the lost beings, sinking slowly into that black Bolge beneath the baking rays of the tropic sun, by the sight of the saved, walking where we walked, beneath cool fragrant shade, among the pillars of a temple to which the Parthenon is mean and small.

Sixty feet and more aloft, the short smooth columns of the Moriches[1] towered around us, till, as we looked through the 'pillared shade,' the eye was lost in the green abysses of the forest. Overhead, their great fan-leaves form a groined roof, compared with which that of St. Mary Redcliff, or even of King's College, is as clumsy as all man's works are beside the works of God; and beyond the Moriche wood, ostrich plumes packed close round madder-brown stems, formed a wall to our temple, which bore such tracery, carving, painting, as would have stricken dumb with awe and delight him who ornamented the Loggie of the Vatican. True, all is 'still-life' here: no human forms, hardly even that of a bird, is mixed with the vegetable arabesques. A higher state of civilisation, ages after we are dead, may introduce them, and complete the scene by peopling it with a race worthy of it. But the Creator, at least, has done His part toward producing perfect beauty, all the more beautiful from its contrast with the ugliness outside. For the want of human beings fit for all that beauty, man is alone to blame; and when we saw approach us, as the only priest of such a temple, a wild brown man, who feeds his hogs on Moriche fruit and Mombin plums, and whose only object was to sell us an ant-eater's skin, we thought to ourselves—knowing the sad history of the West Indies—what might this place have become, during the three hundred and fifty years which have elapsed since Columbus first sailed round it, had men—calling themselves Christian, calling themselves civilised—possessed any tincture of real Christianity, of real civilisation? What a race, of mingled Spaniard and Indian, might have grown up throughout the West Indies. What a life, what a society, what an art, what a science it might have developed ere now, equalling, even surpassing, that of Ionia, Athens, and Sicily, till the famed isles and coasts of Greece should have been almost forgotten in the new fame of the isles and coasts of the Caribbean Sea.

What might not have happened, had men but tried to copy their Father in heaven? What has happened is but too well known, since, in July 1498, Columbus, coming hither, fancied

[1] *Mauritia flexuosa.*

(and not so wrongly) that he had come to the 'base of the Earthly Paradise.'

What might not have been made, with something of justice and mercy, common sense and humanity, of these gentle Arawaks and Guaraons. What was made of them, almost ere Columbus was dead, may be judged from this one story, taken from Las Casas :—[1]

'There was a certain man named Juan Bono, who was employed by the members of the Audiencia of St. Domingo to go and obtain Indians. He and his men, to the number of fifty or sixty, landed on the Island of Trinidad. Now the Indians of Trinidad were a mild, loving, credulous race, the enemies of the Caribs, who ate human flesh. On Juan Bono's landing, the Indians, armed with bows and arrows, went to meet the Spaniards, and to ask them who they were, and what they wanted. Juan Bono replied, that his crew were good and peaceful people, who had come to live with the Indians; upon which, as the commencement of good fellowship, the natives offered to build houses for the Spaniards. The Spanish captain expressed a wish to have one large house built. The accommodating Indians set about building it. It was to be in the form of a bell, and to be large enough for a hundred persons to live in. On any great occasion it would hold many more. Every day, while this house was being built, the Spaniards were fed with fish, bread, and fruit by their good-natured hosts. Juan Bono was very anxious to see the roof on, and the Indians continued to work at the building with alacrity. At last it was completed, being two storeys high, and so constructed that those within could not see those without. Upon a certain day, Juan Bono collected the Indians together—men, women, and children —in the building, "to see," as he told them, "what was to be done."

'Whether they thought they were coming to some festival, or that they were to do something more for the great house, does not appear. However, there they all were, four hundred of them, looking with much delight at their own handiwork. Meanwhile, Juan Bono brought his men round the building, with drawn swords in their hands; then, having thoroughly entrapped his Indian friends, he entered with a party of armed men, and bade the Indians keep still, or he would kill them. They did not listen to him, but rushed to the door. A horrible massacre ensued. Some of the Indians forced their way out; but many of them, stupefied at what they saw, and losing heart, were captured and bound. A hundred, however, escaped, and snatching up their arms, assembled in one of their own houses, and prepared to defend themselves. Juan Bono summoned them to surrender: they would not hear of it; and then, as Las

---

[1] See Mr. Helps' *Spanish Conquest in America*, vol. ii. p. 10.

Casas says, "he resolved to pay them completely for the hospitality and kind treatment he had received," and so, setting fire to the house, the whole hundred men, together with some women and children, were burnt alive. The Spanish captain and his men retired to the ships with their captives; and his vessel happening to touch at Porto Rico, when the Jeronimite Fathers were there, gave occasion to Las Casas to complain of this proceeding to the Fathers, who, however, did nothing in the way of remedy or punishment. The reader will be surprised to hear the Clerigo's authority for this deplorable narrative. It is Juan Bono himself. "From his own mouth I heard that which I write." Juan Bono acknowledged that never in his life had he met with the kindness of father or mother but in the island of Trinidad. "Well, then, man of perdition, why did you reward them with such ungrateful wickedness and cruelty?"—"On my faith, padre, because they (he meant the Auditors) gave me for destruction (he meant instruction) to take them in peace, if I could not by war."

Such was the fate of the poor gentle folk who for unknown ages had swung their hammocks to the stems of these Moriches, spinning the skin of the young leaves into twine, and making sago from the pith, and thin wine from the sap and fruit, while they warned their children not to touch the nests of the humming-birds, which even till lately swarmed around the lake. For—so the Indian story ran—once on a time a tribe of Chaymas built their palm-leaf ajoupas upon the very spot where the lake now lies, and lived a merry life. The sea swarmed with shell-fish and turtle, and the land with pine-apples; the springs were haunted by countless flocks of flamingoes and horned screamers, pajuis and blue ramiers; and, above all, by humming-birds. But the foolish Chaymas were blind to the mystery and the beauty of the humming-birds, and would not understand how they were no other than the souls of dead Indians, translated into living jewels; and so they killed them in wantonness, and angered 'The Good Spirit.' But one morning, when the Guaraons came by, the Chayma village had sunk deep into the earth, and in its place had risen this lake of pitch. So runs the tale, told some forty years since to M. Joseph, author of a clever little history of Trinidad, by an old half-caste Indian, Señor Trinidada by name, who was said then to be nigh one hundred years of age.

Surely the people among whom such a myth could spring up, were worthy of a nobler fate. Surely there were in them elements of 'sweetness and light,' which might have been cultivated to some fine fruit, had there been anything like sweetness and light in their first conquerors—the offscourings, not of Spain and Portugal only, but of Germany, Italy, and, indeed, almost every country in Europe. The present Spanish landowners of Trinidad, be it remembered always, do not derive from those old ruffians, but from noble and ancient families, who settled in the island during the seventeenth century, bringing with them a Spanish grace, Spanish simplicity, and Spanish hospitality, which their descendants have certainly not lost. Were it my habit to 'put people into books,' I would gladly tell in these pages of charming days spent in the company of Spanish ladies and gentlemen. But I shall only hint here at the special affection and respect with which they—and, indeed, the French Creoles likewise—are regarded by Negro and by Indian.

For there are a few Indians remaining in the northern mountains, and specially at Arima—simple hamlet-folk, whom you can distinguish, at a glance, from mulattoes or quadroons, by the tawny complexion, and by a shape of eye, and length between the eye and the mouth, difficult to draw, impossible to describe, but discerned instantly by any one accustomed to observe human features. Many of them, doubtless, have some touch of Negro blood, and are the offspring of 'Cimarons'—'Maroons,' as they are still called in Jamaica. These Cimarons were Negroes who, even in the latter half of the sixteenth century (as may be read in the tragical tale of John Oxenham, given in Hakluyt's *Voyages*), had begun to flee from their cruel masters into the forests, both in the Islands and in the Main. There they took to themselves Indian wives, who preferred them, it is said, to men of their own race, and lived a jolly hunter's life, slaying with tortures every Spaniard who fell into their hands. Such, doubtless, haunted the northern Cerros of Tocuche, Aripo, and Oropuche, and left some trace of themselves among the Guaraons. Spanish blood, too, runs notoriously in the veins of some of the Indians of the island; and the pure race here is all but vanished. But out of these three elements has arisen a race of cacao-growing mountaineers as simple and gentle, as loyal and peaceable, as any in Her Majesty's dominions. Dignified, courteous, hospitable, according to their little means, they salute the white Señor without defiance and without servility, and are delighted if he will sit in their clay and palm ajoupas, and eat oranges and Malacca apples[1] from their own trees, on their own freehold land.

They preserve, too, the old Guaraon arts of weaving baskets and other utensils, pretty enough, from the strips of the Aruma leaves. From them the Negro, who will not, or cannot, equal them in handicraft, buys the pack in which wares are carried on the back, and the curious strainer in which the Cassava is deprived of its poisonous juice. So cleverly are the fibres twisted, that when the strainer is hung up, with a stone weight at the lower end, the diameter of the strainer decreases as its length increases, and the juice is squeezed out through the pores to drip into a calabash, and, nowadays, to be thrown carefully

[1] *Jambosa Malaccensis.*

away, lest children or goats should drink it. Of old, it was kept with care and dried down to a gum, and used to poison arrows, as it is still used, I believe, on the Orinoco; now, its poisonous properties are expelled by boiling it down into Cassaripe, which has a singular power of preserving meat, and is the foundation of the 'pepperpot' of the colonists.

And this is all that remains of the once beautiful, deft, and happy Indians of Trinidad, unless, indeed, some of them, warned by the fate of the Indians of San Josef and the Northern Mountains, fled from such tyrants as Juan Bono and Berreo across the Gulf of Paria, and, rejoining their kinsmen on the mainland, gladly forgot the sight of that Cross which was to them the emblem, not of salvation, but of destruction.

For once a year till of late—I know not whether the thing may be seen still—a strange phantom used to appear at San Fernando, twenty miles to the north. Canoes of Indians came mysteriously across the Gulf of Paria from the vast swamps of the Orinoco; and the naked folk landed, and went up through the town, after the Naparima ladies (so runs the tale) had sent down to the shore garments for the women, which were worn only through the streets, and laid by again as soon as they entered the forest. Silent, modest, dejected, the gentle savages used to vanish into the woods by paths known to their kinsfolk centuries ago—paths which run, wherever possible, along the vantage-ground of the topmost chines and ridges of the hills. The smoke of their fires rose out of lonely glens, as they collected the fruit of trees known only to themselves. In a few weeks their wild harvest was over; they came back through San Fernando; made, almost in silence, their little purchases in the town, and paddled away across the gulf towards the unknown wildernesses from whence they came.

And now—as if sent to drive away sad thoughts and vain regrets—before our feet lay a jest of Nature's, almost as absurd as a 'four-eyed fish,' or 'calling-crab.' A rough stick, of the size of your little finger, lay on the pitch. We watched it a moment, and saw that it was crawling—that it was a huge Caddis, like those in English ponds and streams, though of a very different family. They are the larvæ of Phryganeas—this of a true moth.[1] The male of this moth will come out, as a moth should, and fly about on four handsome wings. The female will never develop her wings, but remain to her life's end a crawling grub, like the female of our own Vapourer moth, and that of our English Glow-worm. But more, she will never (at least, in some species of this family) leave her silk and bark case, but live and die, an anchoritess in narrow cell, leaving behind her more than one puzzle for physiologists. The case is fitted close to the body of the caterpillar, save at the mouth,

---

[1] *Oiketicus.*

where it hangs loose in two ragged silken curtains. We all looked at the creature, and it looked at us, with its last two or three joints and its head thrust out of its house. Suddenly, disgusted at our importunity, it laid hold of its curtains with two hands, right and left, like a human being, folded them modestly over its head, held them tight together, and so retired to bed, amid the inextinguishable laughter of the whole party.

The noble Moriche palm delights in wet, at least in Trinidad and on the lower Orinoco: but Schomburgk describes forests of them—if, indeed, it be the same species—as growing in the mountains of Guiana up to an altitude of four thousand feet. The soil in which they grow here is half pitch pavement, half loose brown earth, and over both, shallow pools of water, which will become much deeper in the wet season; and all about float or lie their pretty fruit, the size of an apple, and scaled like a fir-cone. They are last year's, empty and decayed. The ripe fruit contains first a rich pulpy nut, and at last a hard cone, something like that of the vegetable ivory palm,[1] which grows in the mainland, but not here. Delicious they are, and precious, to monkeys and parrots, as well as to the Orinoco Indians, among whom the Tamanacs, according to Humboldt, say, that when a man and woman survived that great deluge, which the Mexicans call the age of water, they cast behind them, over their heads, the fruits of the Moriche palm, as Deucalion and Pyrrha cast stones, and saw the seeds in them produce men and women, who repeopled the earth. No wonder, indeed, that certain tribes look on this tree as sacred, or that the missionaries should have named it the tree of life.

'In the season of inundations these clumps of Mauritia, with their leaves in the form of a fan, have the appearance of a forest rising from the bosom of the waters. The navigator in proceeding along the channels of the delta of the Oroonoco at night, sees with surprise the summit of the palm-trees illumined by large fires. These are the habitations of the Guaraons (Tivitivas and Waraweties of Raleigh), which are suspended from the trunks of the trees. These tribes hang up mats in the air, which they fill with earth, and kindle on a layer of moist clay the fire necessary for their household wants. They have owed their liberty and their political independence for ages to the quaking and swampy soil, which they pass over in the time of drought, and on which they alone know how to walk in security to their solitude in the delta of the Oroonoco, to their abode on the trees, where religious enthusiasm will probably never lead any American Stylites. . . . The Mauritia palm-tree, the *tree of life* of the missionaries, not only affords the Guaraons a safe dwelling during the risings of the Oroonoco, but its shelly fruit, its farinaceous pith, its juice, abounding in saccharine matter, and the fibres of its

---

[1] *Phytelephas macrocarpa.*

petioles, furnish them with food, wine, and thread proper for making cords and weaving hammocks. These customs of the Indians of the delta of the Oroonoco were found formerly in the Gulf of Darien (Uraba), and in the greater part of the inundated lands between the Guerapiche and the mouths of the Amazon. It is curious to observe in the lowest degree of human civilisation the existence of a whole tribe depending on one single species of palm-tree, similar to those insects which feed on one and the same flower, or on one and the same part of a plant.'[1]

In a hundred yards more we were on dry ground, and the vegetation changed at once. The Mauritias stopped short at the edge of the swamp; and around us towered the smooth stems of giant Mombins, which the English West Indians call hog-plums, according to the unfortunate habit of the early settlers of discarding the sonorous and graceful Indian and Spanish names of plants, and replacing them by names English, or corruptions of the original, always ugly, and often silly and vulgar. So the English call yon noble tree a hog-plum; the botanist (who must, of course, use his world-wide Latin designation), *Spondias lutea;* I shall, with the reader's leave, call it a Mombin, by which name it is, happily, known here, as it was in the French West Indies in the days of good Père Labat. Under the Mombins the undergrowth is, for the most part, huge fans of Cocorite palm, thirty or forty feet high, their short rugged trunks, as usual, loaded with creepers, orchids, birds'-nests, and huge round black lumps, which are the nests of ants; all lodged among the butts of old leaves and the spathes of old flowers. Here, as at Chaguanas, grand Ceримans and Seguines scrambled twenty feet up the Cocorite trunks, delighting us by the luscious life in the fat stem and fat leaves, and the brilliant, yet tender green, which literally shone in the darkness of the Cocorite bower; and all, it may be, the growth of the last six months; for, as was plain from the charred stems of many Cocorites and Moriches, the fire had swept through the wood last summer, destroying all that would burn. And at the foot of the Cocorites, weltering up among and over their roots, was pitch again; and here and there along the side of the path were pitch springs, round bosses a yard or two across and a foot or two high, each with a crater atop a few inches across, filled either with water or with liquid and oozing pitch; and yet not interfering, as far as could be seen, with the health of the vegetation which springs out of it.

We followed the trace which led downhill, to the shore of the peninsula farthest from the village. As we proceeded we entered forest still unburnt, and a tangle of beauty such as we saw at Chaguanas. There rose, once more, the tall cane-like

[1] Humboldt, *Personal Narrative,* vol. v. pp. 728, 729, of Helen Maria Williams's Translation.

Manacque palms, which we christened the forest nymphs. The path was lined, as there, with the great leaves of the Melastomas, throwing russet and golden light down from their undersides. Here, as there, Mimosa leaflets, as fine as fern or seaweed, shiver in the breeze. A species of Balisier, which we did not see there, carried crimson and black parrot beaks with blue seed-vessels; a Canne de Rivière,[1] with a stem eight feet high, wreathed round with pale green leaves in spiral twists, unfolded hooded flowers of thinnest transparent white wax, with each a blush of pink inside. Bunches of bright yellow Cassia blossoms dangled close to our heads; white Ipomœas scrambled over them again; and broad-leaved sedges, five feet high, carrying on bright brown flower-heads, like those of our Wood-rush, blue, black, and white shot for seeds.[2] Overhead, sprawled and dangled the common Vine-bamboo,[3] ugly and unsatisfactory in form, because it has not yet, seemingly, made up its mind whether it will become an arborescent or a climbing grass; and, meanwhile, tries to stand upright on stems quite unable to support it, and tumbles helplessly into the neighbouring copsewood, taking every one's arm without asking leave. A few ages hence, its ablest descendants will probably have made their choice, if they have constitution enough to survive in the battle of life—which, from the commonness of the plant, they seem likely to have. And what their choice will be, there is little doubt. There are trees here of a truly noble nature, whose ancestors have conquered ages since; it may be by selfish and questionable means. But their descendants, secure in their own power, can afford to be generous, and allow a whole world of lesser plants to nestle in their branches, another world to fatten round their feet. There are humble and modest plants, too, here—and those some of the loveliest—which have long since cast away all ambition, and are content to crouch or perch anywhere, if only they may be allowed a chance ray of light, and a chance drop of water wherewith to perfect their flowers and seed. But, throughout the great republic of the forest, the motto of the majority is—as it is, and always has been, with human beings—'Every one for himself, and the devil take the hindmost.' Selfish competition, overreaching tyranny, the temper which fawns and clings as long as it is down, and when it has risen, kicks over the stool by which it climbed—these and the other 'works of the flesh' are the works of the average plant, as far as it can practise them. So by the time the Bamboo-vine makes up its mind, it will have discovered, by the experience of many generations, the value of the proverb, 'Never do for yourself what you can get another to do for you,' and will have developed into a true high climber, selfish and insolent, choking and strangling, like yonder beautiful green pest, of which beware; namely, a

---

[1] *Costus.*   *Scleria latifolia.*   [3] *Panicum divaricatum.*

tangle of Razor-grass.[1] The brother, in old times, of that broad-leaved sedge which carries the shot-seeds, it has long since found it more profitable to lean on others than to stand on its own legs, and has developed itself accordingly: It has climbed up the shrubs some fifteen feet, and is now tumbling down again in masses of the purest deep green, which are always softly rounded, because each slender leaf is sabre-shaped, and always curves inward and downward into the mass, presenting to the paper thousands of minute saw-edges, hard enough and sharp enough to cut clothes, skin, and flesh to ribands, if it is brushed in the direction of the leaves. For shape and colour, few plants would look more lovely in a hothouse; but it would soon need to be confined in a den by itself, like a jaguar or an alligator.

Here, too, we saw a beautiful object, which was seen again more than once about the high woods; a large flower,[2] spreading its five flat orange-scarlet lobes round yellow bells. It grows in little bunches, in the axils of pairs of fleshy leaves, on a climbing vine. When plucked, a milky sap exudes from it. It is a cousin of our periwinkles, and cousin, too, of the Thevetia, which we saw at St. Thomas's, and of the yellow Allamandas which ornament hothouses at home, as this, and others of its family, especially the yellow Odontadenia, surely ought to do. There are many species of the family about, and all beautiful.

We passed too, in the path, an object curious enough, if not beautiful. Up a smooth stem ran a little rib, seemingly of earth and dead wood, almost straight, and about half an inch across, leading to a great brown lump among the branches, as big as a bushel basket. We broke it open, and found it a covered gallery, swarming with life. Brown ant-like creatures, white maggot-like creatures, of several shapes and sizes, were hurrying up and down, as busy as human beings in Cheapside. They were Termites, 'white ants'—of which of the many species I know not—and the lump above was their nest. But why they should find it wisest to perch their nest aloft is as difficult to guess, as to guess why they take the trouble to build this gallery up to it, instead of walking up the stem in the open air. It may be that they are afraid of birds. It may be, too, that they actually dislike the light. At all events, the majority of them —the workers and soldiers, I believe, without exception—are blind, and do all their work by an intensely developed sense of touch, and it may be of smell and hearing also. Be that as it may, we should have seen them, had we had time to wait, repair the breach in their gallery, with as much discipline and division of labour as average human workers in a manufactory, before the business of food-getting was resumed.

We hurried on along the trace, which now sloped rapidly

---

[1] *Seleria flagellum.*   [2] *Echites symphytocarpa* (?).

downhill. Suddenly, a loathsome smell defiled the air. Was there a gas-house in the wilderness? Or had the pales of Paradise been just smeared with bad coal-tar? Not exactly: but across the path crept, festering in the sun, a black runnel of petroleum and water; and twenty yards to our left stood, under a fast-crumbling trunk, what was a year or two ago a little engine-house. Now roof, beams, machinery, were all tumbled and tangled in hideous and somewhat dangerous ruin, over a shaft, in the midst of which a rusty pump-cylinder gurgled, and clicked, and bubbled, and spued, with black oil and nasty gas; a foul ulcer in Dame Nature's side, which happily was healing fast beneath the tropic rain and sun. The creepers were climbing over it, the earth crumbling into it, and in a few years more the whole would be engulfed in forest, and the oil-spring, it is to be hoped, choked up with mud.

This is the remnant of one of the many rash speculations connected with the Pitch Lake. At a depth of some two hundred and fifty feet 'oil was struck,' as the American saying is. But (so we were told) it would not rise in the boring, and had to be pumped up. It could not, therefore, compete in price with the Pennsylvanian oil, which, when tapped, springs out of the ground of itself, to a height sometimes of many feet, under the pressure of the superincumbent rocks, yielding enormous profits, and turning needy adventurers into millionaires, though full half of the oil is sometimes wasted for the want of means to secure it.

We passed the doleful spot with a double regret—for the nook of Paradise which had been defiled, and for the good money which had been wasted: but with a hearty hope, too, that, whatever natural beauty may be spoilt thereby, the wealth of these asphalt deposits may at last be utilised. Whether it be good that a few dozen men should 'make their fortunes' thereby, depends on what use the said men make of the said 'fortunes'; and certainly it will not be good for them if they believe, as too many do, that their dollars, and not their characters, constitute their fortunes. But it is good, and must be, that these treasures of heat and light should not remain for ever locked up and idle in the wilderness; and we wished all success to the enterprising American who had just completed a bargain with the Government for a large supply of asphalt, which he hoped by his chemical knowledge to turn to some profitable use.

Another turn brought us into a fresh nook of Paradise; and this time to one still undefiled. We hurried down a narrow grass path, the Cannes de Rivière and the Balisiers brushing our heads as we passed; while round us danced brilliant butterflies, bright orange, sulphur-yellow, black and crimson, black and lilac, and half a dozen hues more, till we stopped, surprised and delighted. For beneath us lay the sea, seen through a narrow gap of richest verdure.

On the left, low palms feathered over the path, and over the cliff. On the right—when shall we see it again?—rose a young 'Bois flot,'[1] of which boys make their fishing floats, with long, straight, upright shoots, and huge crumpled, rounded leaves, pale rusty underneath—a noble rastrajo plant, already, in its six months' growth, some twenty feet high. Its broad pale sulphur flowers were yet unopened; but, instead, an ivy-leaved Ipomœa had climbed up it, and shrouded it from head to foot with hundreds of white convolvulus-flowers; while underneath it grew a tuft of that delicate silver-backed fern, which is admired so much in hothouses at home. Between it and the palms we saw the still, shining sea; muddy inshore, and a few hundred yards out changing suddenly to bright green; and the point of the cove, which seemed built up of bright red brick, fast crumbling into the sea, with all its palms and cactuses, lianes and trees. Red stacks and skerries stood isolated and ready to fall at the end of the point, showing that the land has, even lately, extended far out to sea; and that Point Rouge, like Point Courbaril and Point Galba—so named, one from some great Locust-tree, the other from some great Galba—must have once stood there as landmarks. Indeed all the points of the peninsula are but remnants of a far larger sheet of land, which has been slowly eaten up by the surges of the gulf; which has perhaps actually sunk bodily beneath them, even as the remnant, I suspect, is sinking now. We scrambled twenty feet down to the beach, and lay down, tired, under a low cliff, feathered with richest vegetation. The pebbles on which we sat were some of pitch, some of hard sandstone, but most of them of brick; pale, dark, yellow, lavender, spotted, clouded, and half a dozen more delicate hues; some coarse, some fine as Samian ware; the rocks themselves were composed of an almost glassy substance, strangely jumbled, even intercalated now and then with soft sand. This, we were told, is a bit of the porcellanite formation of Trinidad, curious to geologists, which reappears at several points in Erin, Trois, and Cedros, in the extreme south-western horn of the island.

How was it formed, and when? That it was formed by the action of fire, any child would agree who had ever seen a brick-kiln. It is simply clay and sand baked, and often almost vitrified into porcelain-jasper. The stratification is gone; the porcellanite has run together into irregular masses, or fallen into them by the burning away of strata beneath; and the cracks in it are often lined with bubbled slag.

But whence came the fire? We must be wary about calling in the *Deus e machina* of a volcano. There is no volcanic rock

[1] *Ochroma*.

in the neighbourhood, nor anywhere in the island; and the porcellanite, says Mr. Wall, 'is identically the same with the substances produced immediately above or below seams of coal, which have taken fire, and burnt for a length of time.' There is lignite and other coaly matter enough in the rocks to have burnt like coal, if it had once been ignited; and the cause of ignition may be, as Mr. Wall suggests, the decomposition of pyrites, of which also there is enough around. That the heat did not come from below, as volcanic heat would have done, is proved by the fact that the lignite beds underneath the porcellanite are unburnt. We found asphalt under the porcellanite. We found even one bit of red porcellanite with unburnt asphalt included in it.

May not this strange formation of natural brick and chinaware be of immense age—humanly, not geologically, speaking? May it not be far older than the Pitch Lake above—older, possibly, than the formation of any asphalt at all? And may not the asphalt mingled with it have been squeezed into it and round it, as it is being squeezed into and through the unburnt strata at so many points in Guapo, La Brea, Oropuche, and San Fernando? At least, so it seemed to us, as we sat on the shore, waiting for the boat to take us round to La Brea, and drank in dreamily with our eyes the beauty of that strange lonely place. The only living things, save ourselves, which were visible were a few pelicans sleeping on a skerry, and a shoal of dolphins rolling silently in threes—husband, wife, and little child—as they fished their way along the tide mark between the yellow water and the green. The sky blazed overhead, the sea below; the red rocks and green forests blazed around; and we sat enjoying the genial silence, not of darkness, but of light, not of death, but of life, as the noble heat permeated every nerve, and made us feel young, and strong, and blithe once more.

COOLIE AND NEGRO

CHAPTER IX

SAN JOSEF

THE road to the ancient capital of the island is pleasant enough, and characteristic of the West Indies. Not, indeed, as to its breadth, make, and material, for they, contrary to the wont of West India roads, are as good as they would be in England, but on account of the quaint travellers along it, and the quaint sights which are to be seen over every hedge. You pass all the races of the island going to and from town or field-work, or washing clothes in some clear brook, beside which a solemn Chinaman sits catching for his dinner strange fishes, known to my learned friend, Dr. Günther, and perhaps to one or two other men in Europe; but certainly not to me. Always somebody or something new and strange is to be seen, for eight most pleasant miles.

The road runs at first along a low cliff foot, with an ugly Mangrove swamp, looking just like an alder-bed at home, between you and the sea; a swamp which it would be worth while to drain by a steam-pump, and then plant with coco-nuts or bamboos; for its miasma makes the southern corner of Port of Spain utterly pestilential. You cross a railroad, the only one in the island, which goes to a limestone quarry, and so out along a wide straight road, with negro cottages right and left, embowered in fruit and flowers. They grow fewer and finer as you ride on; and soon you are in open country, principally of large paddocks. These paddocks, like all West Indian ones, are apt to be ragged with weeds and scrub. But the coarse broad-leaved grasses seem to keep the mules in good condition enough, at least in the rainy season. Most of these paddocks have, I believe, been under cane cultivation at some time or other; and have been thrown into grass during the period of depression dating from 1845. It has not been worth while, as yet, to break them up again, though the profits of sugar-farming are now, or at least ought to be, very large. But the soil along this line is originally poor and sandy; and it is far more profitable to break up the rich vegas, or low alluvial lands, even at the trouble of clearing them of forest. So these paddocks are left, often with noble trees standing about in them, putting one in mind—if it were not for the Palmistes and Bamboos and the crowd of black vultures over an occasional dead animal—of English parks.

But few English parks have such backgrounds. To the right, the vast southern flat, with its smoking engine-house chimneys and bright green cane-pieces, and, beyond all, the black wall of the primeval forest; and to the left, some half mile off, the steep slopes of the green northern mountains blazing in the sun, and sending down, every two or three miles, out of some charming glen, a clear pebbly brook, each winding through its narrow strip of vega. The vega is usually a highly cultivated cane-piece, where great lizards sit in the mouths of their burrows, and watch the passer-by with intense interest. Coolies and Negroes are at work in it: but only a few; for the strength of the hands is away at the engine-house, making sugar day and night. There is a piece of cane in act of being cut. The men are hewing down the giant grass with cutlasses; the women stripping off the leaves, and then piling the cane in carts drawn by mules, the leaders of which draw by rope traces two or three times as long as themselves. You wonder why such a seeming waste of power is allowed, till you see one of the carts stick fast in a mud-hole, and discover that even in the West Indies there is a good reason for everything, and that the Creoles know their own business best. For the wheelers, being in the slough with the cart, are powerless; but the leaders, who have scrambled through, are safe on dry land at the end of their long traces, and haul out their brethren, cart and all, amid the yells, and I am sorry to say blows, of the black gentlemen in attendance. But cane-cutting is altogether a busy, happy scene. The heat is awful, and all limbs rain perspiration: yet no one seems to mind the heat; all look fat and jolly; and they have cause to do so, for all, at every spare moment, are sucking sugar-cane.

You pull up, and take off your hat to the party. The Negroes shout, 'Marnin', sa!' The Coolies salaam gracefully, hand to forehead. You return the salaam, hand to heart, which is considered the correct thing on the part of a superior in rank; whereat the Coolies look exceedingly pleased; and then the whole party, without visible reason, burst into shouts of laughter.

The manager rides up, probably under an umbrella, as you are, and a pleasant and instructive chat follows, wound up, usually, if the house be not far off, by an invitation to come in and have a light drink; an invitation which, considering the state of the thermometer, you will be tempted to accept, especially as you know that the claret and water will be excellent. And so you dawdle on, looking at this and that new and odd sight, but most of all feasting your eyes on the beauty of the northern mountains, till you reach the gentle rise on which stands, eight miles from Port of Spain, the little city of San Josef. We should call it, here in England, a village: still, it is not every village in England which has fought the Dutch, and earned its right to be called a city by beating some of the bravest sailors of the seventeenth century. True, there is not a single shop in it with plate-glass windows: but what matters that, if its citizens have all that civilised people need, and more, and will heap what they have on the stranger so hospitably that they almost pain him by the trouble which they take? True, no carriages and pairs, with powdered footmen, roll about the streets; and the most splendid vehicles you are likely to meet are American buggies—four-wheeled gigs with heads, and aprons through which the reins can be passed in wet weather. But what matters that, as long as the buggies keep out sun and rain effectually, and as long as those who sit in them be real gentlemen, and those who wait for them at home, whether in the city, or the estates around, be real ladies? As for the rest—peace, plenty, perpetual summer, time to think and read—(for there are no daily papers in San Josef)—and what can man want more on earth? So I thought more than once, as I looked at San Josef nestling at the mouth of its noble glen, and said to myself,—If the telegraph cable were but laid down the islands, as it will be in another year or two, and one could hear a little more swiftly and loudly the beating of the Great Mother's heart at home, then would San Josef be about the most delectable spot which I have ever seen for a cultivated and civilised man to live, and work, and think, and die in.

San Josef has had, nevertheless, its troubles and excitements

A MANGROVE SWAMP.

more than once since it defeated the Dutch. Even as late as 1837, it was, for a few hours, in utter terror and danger from a mutiny of free black recruits. No one in the island, civil or military, seems to have been to blame for the mishap. It was altogether owing to the unwisdom of military authorities at home, who seem to have fancied that they could transform, by a magical spurt of the pen, heathen savages into British soldiers.

The whole tragedy—for tragedy it was—is so curious, and so illustrative of the negro character, and of the effects of the slave trade, that I shall give it at length, as it stands in that clever little *History of Trinidad*, by M. Thomas, which I have quoted more than once:—

'Donald Stewart, or rather Dâaga,[1] was the adopted son of Madershee, the old and childless king of the tribe called Paupaus, a race that inhabit a tract of country bordering on that of the Yarrabas. These races are constantly at war with each other.

'Dâaga was just the man whom a savage, warlike, and depredatory tribe would select for their chieftain, as the African Negroes choose their leaders with reference to their personal prowess. Dâaga stood six feet six inches without shoes. Although scarcely muscular in proportion, yet his frame indicated in a singular degree the union of irresistible strength and activity. His head was large; his features had all the peculiar traits which distinguish the Negro in a remarkable degree; his jaw was long, eyes large and protruded, high cheek-bones, and flat nose; his teeth were large and regular. He had a singular cast in his eyes, not quite amounting to that obliquity of the visual organs denominated a squint, but sufficient to give his features a peculiarly forbidding appearance;—his forehead, however, although small in proportion to his enormous head, was remarkably compact and well formed. The whole head was disproportioned, having the greater part of the brain behind the ears; but the greatest peculiarity of this singular being was his voice. In the course of my life I never heard such sounds uttered by human organs as those formed by Dâaga. In ordinary conversation he appeared to me to endeavour to soften his voice—it was a deep tenor; but when a little excited by any passion (and this savage was the child of passion) his voice sounded like the low growl of a lion, but when much excited it could be compared to nothing so aptly as the notes of a gigantic brazen trumpet.

'I repeatedly questioned this man respecting the religion of his tribe. The result of his answers led me to infer that the Paupaus believed in the existence of a future state; that they have a confused notion of several powers, good and evil, but these are ruled by one supreme being called Holloloo. This account of the religion of Dâaga was confirmed by the military

---

[1] Pronounced like the Spanish noun Daga.

chaplain who attended him in his last moments. He also informed me that he believed in predestination;—at least he said that Holloloo, he knew, had ordained that he should come to white man's country and be shot.

'Dâaga, having made a successful predatory expedition into the country of the Yarrabas, returned with a number of prisoners of that nation. These he, as usual, took, bound and guarded, towards the coast to sell to the Portuguese. The interpreter, his countryman, called these Portuguese WHITE GENTLEMEN. The white gentlemen proved themselves more than a match for the black gentlemen; and the whole transaction between the Portuguese and Paupaus does credit to all concerned in this gentlemanly traffic in human flesh.

'Dâaga sold his prisoners; and under pretence of paying him, he and his Paupau guards were enticed on board a Portuguese vessel;—they were treacherously overpowered by the Christians, who bound them beside their late prisoners, and the vessel sailed over "the great salt water."

'This transaction caused in the breast of the savage a deep hatred against all white men—a hatred so intense that he frequently, during and subsequent to the mutiny, declared he would eat the first white man he killed; yet this cannibal was made to swear allegiance to our Sovereign on the Holy Evangelists, and was then called a British soldier.

'On the voyage the vessel on board which Dâaga had been entrapped was captured by the British. He could not comprehend that his new captors liberated him: he had been overreached and trepanned by one set of white men, and he naturally looked on his second captors as more successful rivals in the human, or rather inhuman, Guinea trade; therefore this event lessened not his hatred for white men in the abstract.

'I was informed by several of the Africans who came with him that when, during the voyage, they upbraided Dâaga with being the cause of their capture, he pacified them by promising that when they should arrive in white man's country, he would repay their perfidy by attacking them in the night. He further promised that if the Paupaus and the Yarrabas would follow him, he would fight his way back to Guinea. This account was fully corroborated by many of the mutineers, especially those who were shot with Dâaga: they all said the revolt never would have happened but for Donald Stewart, as he was called by the officers; but Africans who were not of his tribe called him Longa-longa, on account of his height.

'Such was this extraordinary man, who led the mutiny I am about to relate.

'A quantity of captured Africans having been brought hither from the islands of Grenada and Dominica, they were most imprudently induced to enlist as recruits in the 1st West India Regiment. True it is, we have been told they did this voluntarily:

but, it may be asked, if they had any will in the matter, how could they understand the duties to be imposed on them by becoming soldiers, or how comprehend the nature of an oath of allegiance? without which they could not, legally speaking, be considered as soldiers. I attended the whole of the trials of these men, and well know how difficult it was to make them comprehend any idea which was at all new to them by means of the best interpreters procurable.

'It has been said that by making those captured Negroes soldiers, a service was rendered them: this I doubt. Formerly it was most true that a soldier in a black regiment was better off than a slave; but certainly a free African in the West Indies now is infinitely in a better situation than a soldier, not only in a pecuniary point of view, but in almost every other respect.

'To the African savage, while being drilled into the duties of a soldier, many things seem absolute tyranny which would appear to a civilised man a mere necessary restraint. To keep the restless body of an African Negro in a position to which he has not been accustomed—to cramp his splay-feet, with his great toes standing out, into European shoes made for feet of a different form—to place a collar round his neck, which is called a stock, and which to him is cruel torture—above all, to confine him every night to his barracks—are almost insupportable. One unacquainted with the habits of the Negro cannot conceive with what abhorrence he looks on having his disposition to nocturnal rambles checked by barrack regulations.[1]

'Formerly the "King's man," as the black soldier loved to call himself, looked (not without reason) contemptuously on the planter's slave, although he himself was after all but a slave to the State: but these recruits were enlisted shortly after a number of their recently imported countrymen were wandering freely over the country, working either as free labourers, or settling, to use an apt American phrase, as squatters; and to assert that the recruit, while under military probation, is better off than the free Trinidad labourer, who goes where he lists and earns as much in one day as will keep him for three days, is an absurdity. Accordingly we find that Lieutenant-Colonel Bush, who commanded the 1st West India Regiment, thought that the mutiny was mainly owing to the ill advice of their civil, or, we should rather say, unmilitary countrymen. This, to a certain degree, was the fact: but, by the declaration of Dâaga and many of his countrymen, it is evident the seeds of mutiny were sown on the passage from Africa.

'It has been asserted that the recruits were driven to mutiny by hard treatment of their commanding officers. There seems not the slightest truth in this assertion; they were treated with

[1] See Bryan Edwards on the character of the African Negroes; also Chanvelon's *Histoire de la Martinique*.

fully as much kindness as their situation would admit of, and their chief was peculiarly a favourite of Colonel Bush and the officers, notwithstanding Dâaga's violent and ferocious temper often caused complaints to be brought against him.

'A correspondent of the *Naval and Military Gazette* was under an apprehension that the mutineers would be joined by the prædial apprentices of the circumjacent estates: not the slightest foundation existed for this apprehension. Some months previous to this Dâaga had planned a mutiny, but this was interrupted by sending a part of the Paupau and Yarraba recruits to St. Lucia. The object of all those conspiracies was to get back to Guinea, which they thought they could accomplish by marching to eastward.

'On the night of the 17th of June 1837, the people of San Josef were kept awake by the recruits, about 280 in number, singing the war-song of the Paupaus. This wild song consisted of a short air and chorus. The tone was, although wild, not inharmonious, and the words rather euphonious. As near as our alphabet can convey them, they ran thus:—

> "Dangkarrée
> Au fey,
> Olun werrei,
> Au lay,"

which may be rendered almost literally by the following couplet:—

> Air by the chief: "Come to plunder, come to slay;"
> Chorus of followers: "We are ready to obey."

'About three o'clock in the morning their war-song (highly characteristic of a predatory tribe) became very loud, and they commenced uttering their war-cry. This is different from what we conceive the Indian war-whoop to be: it seems to be a kind of imitation of the growl of wild beasts, and has a most thrilling effect.

'Fire now was set to a quantity of huts built for the accommodation of African soldiers to the northward of the barracks, as well as to the house of a poor black woman called Dalrymple. These burnt briskly, throwing a dismal glare over the barracks and picturesque town of San Josef, and overpowering the light of the full moon, which illumined a cloudless sky. The mutineers made a rush at the barrack-room, and seized on the muskets and fusees in the racks. Their leader, Dâaga, and a daring Yarraba named Ogston instantly charged their pieces; the former of these had a quantity of ball-cartridges, loose powder, and ounce and pistol-balls, in a kind of gray worsted cap. He must have provided himself with these before the mutiny. How he became possessed of them, especially the pistol-balls, I never could learn; probably he was supplied by his unmilitary countrymen : pistol-balls are never given to infantry. Previous to this Dâaga and three others made a rush at the regimental store-room, in which was deposited a quantity of powder. An old African soldier, named Charles Dickson, interfered to stop them, on which Maurice Ogston, the Yarraba chief, who had armed himself with a sergeant's sword, cut down the faithful African. When down Dâaga said, in English, "Ah, you old soldier, you knock down." Dixon was not Dâaga's countryman, hence he could not speak to him in his own language. The Paupau then levelled his musket and shot the fallen soldier, who groaned and died. The war-yells, or rather growls, of the Paupaus and Yarrabas now became awfully thrilling, as they helped themselves to cartridges : most of them were fortunately blank, or without ball. Never was a premeditated mutiny so wild and ill planned. Their chief, Dâaga, and Ogston seemed to have had little command of the subordinates, and the whole acted more like a set of wild beasts who had broken their cages than men resolved on war.

'At this period, had a rush been made at the officers' quarters by one half (they were more than 200 in number), and the other half surrounded the building, not one could have escaped. Instead of this they continued to shout their war-song, and howl their war-notes; they loaded their pieces with ball-cartridge, or blank cartridge and small stones, and commenced firing at the long range of white buildings in which Colonel Bush and his officers slept. They wasted so much ammunition on this useless display of fury that the buildings were completely riddled. A few of the old soldiers opposed them, and were wounded; but it fortunately happened that they were, to an inconceivable degree, ignorant of the right use of firearms—holding their muskets in their hands when they discharged them, without allowing the butt-end to rest against their shoulders or any part of their bodies. This fact accounts for the comparatively little mischief they did in proportion to the quantity of ammunition thrown away.

'The officers and sergeant-major escaped at the back of the building, while Colonel Bush and Adjutant Bentley came down a little hill. The colonel commanded the mutineers to lay down their arms, and was answered by an irregular discharge of balls, which rattled amongst the leaves of a tree under which he and the adjutant were standing. On this Colonel Bush desired Mr. Bentley to make the best of his way to St. James's Barracks for all the disposable force of the 89th Regiment. The officers made good their retreat, and the adjutant got into the stable where his horse was. He saddled and bridled the animal while the shots were coming into the stable, without either man or beast getting injured. The officer mounted, but had to make his way through the mutineers before he could get into San Josef, the barracks standing on an eminence above the little town. On seeing the adjutant mounted, the mutineers set up a thrilling howl, and commenced firing at him. He discerned the gigantic figure of Dâaga (*alias* Donald Stewart), with his musket at the trail; he spurred his horse through the midst of them; they were grouped, but not in line. On looking back he saw Dâaga aiming at him; he stooped his head beside his horse's neck, and effectually sheltered himself from about fifty shots aimed at him. In this position he rode furiously down a steep hill leading from the barracks to the church, and was out of danger. His escape appears extraordinary: but he got safe to town, and thence to St. James's, and in a short time, considering it is eleven miles distant, brought out a strong detachment of European troops; these, however, did not arrive until the affair was over.

'In the meantime a part of the officers' quarters was bravely defended by two old African soldiers, Sergeant Merry and Corporal Plague. The latter stood in the gallery, near the room in which were the colours; he was ineffectually fired at by some hundreds, yet he kept his post, shot two of the mutineers, and, it is said, wounded a third. Such is the difference between a man acquainted with the use of firearms and those who handle them as mops are held.

'In the meantime Colonel Bush got to a police-station above the barracks, and got muskets and a few cartridges from a discharged African soldier who was in the police establishment. Being joined by the policemen, Corporal Craven[1] and Ensign Pogson, they concealed themselves on an eminence above, and as the mutineers (about 100 in number) approached, the fire of muskets opened on them from the little ambush. The little party fired separately, loading as fast as they discharged their pieces; they succeeded in making the mutineers change their route.

'It is wonderful what little courage the savages in general showed against the colonel and his little party; who absolutely beat them, although but a twenty-fifth of their number, and at their own tactics, *i.e.* bush fighting.

'A body of the mutineers now made towards the road to Maraccas, when the colonel and his three assistants contrived to get behind a silk-cotton tree, and recommenced firing on them. The Africans hesitated and set forward, when the little party continued to fire on them; they set up a yell, and retreated down the hill.

'A part of the mutineers now concealed themselves in the bushes about San Josef barracks. These men, after the affair was over, joined Colonel Bush, and with a mixture of cunning and effrontery smiled as though nothing had happened, and as

---

[1] This man, who was a friend of Dâaga's, owed his life to a solitary act of humanity on the part of the chief of this wild tragedy. A musket was levelled at him, when Dâaga pushed it aside, and said, 'Not this man.'

though they were glad to see him; although, in general, they each had several shirts and pairs of trousers on preparatory for a start to Guinea, by way of Band de l'Est.[1]

'In the meantime the San Josef militia were assembled, to the number of forty. Major Giuseppi, and Captain and Adjutant Rousseau, of the second division of militia forces, took command of them. They were in want of flints, powder, and balls—to obtain these they were obliged to break open a merchant's store; however, the adjutant so judiciously distributed his little force as to hinder the mutineers from entering the town, or obtaining access to the militia arsenal, wherein there was a quantity of arms. Major Chadds and several old African soldiers joined the militia, and were by them supplied with arms.

'A good deal of skirmishing occurred between the militia and detached parties of the mutineers, which uniformly ended in the defeat of the latter. At length Dâaga appeared to the right of a party of six, at the entrance of the town; they were challenged by the militia, and the mutineers fired on them, but without effect. Only two of the militia returned the fire, when all but Dâaga fled. He was deliberately reloading his piece, when a militiaman, named Edmond Luce, leaped on the gigantic chief, who would have easily beat him off, although the former was a strong young man of colour: but Dâaga would not let go his gun; and, in common with all the mutineers, he seemed to have no idea of the use of the bayonet. Dâaga was dragging the militiaman away, when Adjutant Rousseau came to his assistance, and placed a sword to Dâaga's breast. Doctor Tardy and several others rushed on the tall Negro, who was soon, by the united efforts of several, thrown down and secured. It was at this period that he repeatedly exclaimed, while he bit his own shoulder, "The first white man I catch after this I will eat him."[2]

'Meanwhile about sixteen of the mutineers, led by the daring Ogston, took the road to Arima; in order, as they said, to commence their march to Guinea: but fortunately the militia of that village, composed principally of Spaniards, Indians, and Sambos, assembled. A few of these met them and stopped their march. A kind of parley (if intercourse carried on by signs could be so called) was carried on between the parties. The mutineers made signs that they wished to go forward, while the few militiamen endeavoured to detain them, expecting a reinforcement momently. After a time the militia agreed to allow them to approach the town; as they were

[1] People will smile at the simplicity of those savages; but it should be recollected that civilised convicts were lately in the constant habit of attempting to escape from New South Wales in order to walk to China.
[2] I had this anecdote from one of his countrymen, an old Paupau soldier, who said he did not join the mutiny.

advancing they were met by the commandant, Martin Sorzano, Esq., with sixteen more militiamen. The commandant judged it imprudent to allow the Africans to enter the town with their muskets full cocked and poised ready to fire. An interpreter was now procured, and the mutineers were told that if they would retire to their barracks the gentlemen present would intercede for their pardon. The Negroes refused to accede to these terms, and while the interpreter was addressing some, the rest tried to push forward. Some of the militia opposed them by holding their muskets in a horizontal position, on which one of the mutineers fired, and the militia returned the fire. A *mêlée* commenced, in which fourteen mutineers were killed and wounded. The fire of the Africans produced little effect: they soon took to flight amid the woods which flanked the road. Twenty-eight of them were taken, amongst whom was the Yarraba chief, Ogston. Six had been killed, and six committed suicide by strangling and hanging themselves in the woods. Only one man was wounded amongst the militia, and he but slightly, from a small stone fired from a musket of one of the Yarrabas.

'The quantity of ammunition expended by the mutineers, and the comparatively little mischief done by them, was truly astonishing. It shows how little they understood the use of firearms. Dixon was killed, and several of the old African soldiers were wounded, but not one of the officers was in the slightest degree hurt.

'I have never been able to get a correct account of the number of lives this wild mutiny cost, but believe it was not less than forty, including those slain by the militia at Arima; those shot at San Josef; those who died of their wounds (and most of the wounded men died); the six who committed suicide; the three that were shot by sentence of the court-martial, and one who was shot while endeavouring to escape (Satchell).

'A good-looking young man, named Torrens, was brought as prisoner to the presence of Colonel Bush. The colonel wished to speak to him, and desired his guards to liberate him; on which the young savage shook his sleeve, in which was concealed a razor, made a rush at the colonel, and nearly succeeded in cutting his throat. He slashed the razor in all directions until he made an opening: he rushed through this; and, notwithstanding he was fired at, and I believe wounded, he effected his escape, was subsequently re-taken, and again made his escape with Satchell, who after this was shot by a policeman.

'Torrens was re-taken, tried, and recommended to mercy. Of this man's fate I am unable to speak, not knowing how far the recommendation to mercy was attended to. In appearance he seemed the mildest and best-looking of the mutineers, but his conduct was the most ferocious of any. The whole of the mutineers were captured within one week of the mutiny, save this man, who was taken a month after.

'On the 19th of July, Donald Stewart, otherwise Dâaga, was brought to a court-martial. On the 21st William Satchell was tried. On the 22d a court-martial was held on Edward Coffin; and on the 24th one was held on the Yarraba chief, Maurice Ogston, whose country name was, I believe, Mawee. Torrens was tried on the 29th.

'The sentences of these courts-martial were unknown until the 14th of August, having been sent to Barbadoes in order to be submitted to the Commander-in-Chief, Lieutenant-General Whittingham, who approved of the decision of the courts, which was that Donald Stewart (Dâaga), Maurice Ogston, and Edward Coffin should suffer death by being shot, and that William Satchell should be transported beyond seas during the term of his natural life. I am unacquainted with the sentence of Torrens.

'Donald Stewart, Maurice Ogston, and Edward Coffin were executed on the 16th of August 1837, at San Josef Barracks. Nothing seemed to have been neglected which could render the execution solemn and impressive; the scenery and the weather gave additional awe to the melancholy proceedings. Fronting the little eminence where the prisoners were shot was the scene where their ill-concerted mutiny commenced. To the right stood the long range of building on which they had expended much of their ammunition for the purpose of destroying their officers. The rest of the panorama was made up of an immense view of forest below them, and upright masses of mountains above them. Over those, heavy bodies of mist were slowly sailing, giving a sombre appearance to the primeval woods which, in general, covered both mountains and plains. The atmosphere indicated an inter-tropical morning during the rainy season, and the sun shone resplendently between dense columns of clouds.

'At half-past seven o'clock the condemned men asked to be allowed to eat a hearty meal, as they said persons about to be executed in Guinea were always indulged with a good repast. It is remarkable that these unhappy creatures ate most voraciously, even while they were being brought out of their cell for execution.

'A little before the mournful procession commenced, the condemned men were dressed from head to foot in white habiliments trimmed with black; their arms were bound with cords. This is not usual in military executions, but was deemed necessary on the present occasion. An attempt to escape, on the part of the condemned, would have been productive of much confusion, and was properly guarded against.

'The condemned men displayed no unmanly fear. On the

contrary, they steadily kept step to the Dead March which the band played; yet the certainty of death threw a cadaverous and ghastly hue over their black features, while their singular and appropriate costume, and the three coffins being borne before them, altogether rendered it a frightful picture: hence it was not to be wondered at that two of the European soldiers fainted.

'The mutineers marched abreast. The tall form and horrid looks of Dâaga were almost appalling. The looks of Ogston were sullen, calm, and determined; those of Coffin seemed to indicate resignation.

'At eight o'clock they arrived at the spot where three graves were dug; here their coffins were deposited. The condemned men were made to face to westward; three sides of a hollow square were formed, flanked on one side by a detachment of the 89th Regiment and a party of artillery, while the recruits, many of whom shared the guilt of the culprits, were appropriately placed in the line opposite them. The firing-party were a little in advance of the recruits.

'The sentence of the courts-martial, and other necessary documents, having been read by the fort adjutant, Mr. Meehan, the chaplain of the forces, read some prayers appropriated for these melancholy occasions. The clergyman then shook hands with the three men about to be sent into another state of existence. Dâaga and Ogston coolly gave their hands: Coffin wrung the chaplain's hand affectionately, saying, in tolerable English, "I am now done with the world."

'The arms of the condemned men, as has been before stated, were bound, but in such a manner as to allow them to bring their hands to their heads. Their night-caps were drawn over their eyes. Coffin allowed his to remain, but Ogston and Dâaga pushed theirs up again. The former did this calmly; the latter showed great wrath, seeming to think himself insulted; and his deep metallic voice sounded in anger above that of the provost-marshal,[1] as the latter gave the words "Ready! present!" But at this instant his vociferous daring forsook him. As the men levelled their muskets at him, with inconceivable rapidity he sprang bodily round, still preserving his squatting posture, and received the fire from behind; while the less noisy, but more brave, Ogston looked the firing-party full in the face as they discharged their fatal volley.

'In one instant all three fell dead, almost all the balls of the firing-party having taken effect. The savage appearance and manner of Dâaga excited awe. Admiration was felt for the calm bravery of Ogston, while Edward Coffin's fate excited commiseration.

[1] One of his countrymen explained to me what Dâaga said on this occasion—viz., 'The curse of Holloloo on white men. Do they think that Dâaga fears to fix his eyeballs on death?'

'There were many spectators of this dreadful scene, and amongst others a great concourse of Negroes. Most of these expressed their hopes that after this terrible example the recruits would make good soldiers.'

Ah, stupid savages. Yes: but also—ah, stupid civilised people.

CHAPTER X

NAPARIMA AND MONTSERRAT

I HAD a few days of pleasant wandering in the centre of the island, about the districts which bear the names of Naparima and Montserrat; a country of such extraordinary fertility, as well as beauty, that it must surely hereafter become the seat of a high civilisation. The soil seems inexhaustibly rich. I say inexhaustibly; for as fast as the upper layer is impoverished, it will be swept over by the tropic rains, to mingle with the vegas, or alluvial flats below, and thus enriched again, while a fresh layer of virgin soil is exposed above. I have seen, cresting the highest ridges of Montserrat, ten feet at least of fat earth, falling clod by clod right and left upon the gardens below. There are, doubtless, comparatively barren tracts of gravel toward the northern mountains; there are poor sandy lands, likewise, at the southern part of the island, which are said, nevertheless, to be specially fitted for the growth of cotton: but from San Fernando on the west coast to Manzanilla on the east, stretches a band of soil which seems to be capable of yielding any conceivable return to labour and capital, not omitting common sense.

How long it has taken to prepare this natural garden for man is one of those questions of geological time which have been well called of late 'appalling.' How long was it since the 'older Parian' rocks (said to belong to the Neocomian, or greensand, era) of Point à Pierre were laid down at the bottom of the sea? How long since a still unknown thickness of tertiary strata in the Nariva district laid down on them? How long since not less than six thousand feet of still later tertiary strata laid down on them again? What vast, though probably slow, processes changed that sea-bottom from one salt enough to carry corals and limestones, to one brackish enough to carry abundant remains of plants, deposited probably by the Orinoco, or by some river which then did duty for it? Three such periods of disturbance have been distinguished, the net result of which is, that the strata (comparatively recent in geological time) have been fractured, tilted, even set upright on end, over the whole lowland. Trinidad seems to have had its full share of those later disturbances of the earth-crust, which carried tertiary strata up along the shoulders of the Alps; which upheaved the chalk of the Isle of Wight, setting the tertiary beds of Alum Bay upright against it; which even, after the Age of Ice, thrust up the Isle of Moen in Denmark and the Isle of Ely in Cambridgeshire, entangling the boulder clay among the chalk—how long ago? Long enough ago, in Trinidad at least, to allow water—probably the estuary waters of the Orinoco—to saw all the upheaved layers off at the top into one flat sea-bottom once more, leaving as projections certain harder knots of rock, such as the limestones of Mount Tamana; and, it may be, the curious knoll of hard clay rock under which nestles the town of San Fernando. Long enough ago, also, to allow that whole sea-bottom to be lifted up once more, to the height, in one spot, of a thousand feet, as the lowland which occupies six-sevenths of the Isle of Trinidad. Long enough ago, again, to allow that lowland to be sawn out into hills and valleys, ridges and gulleys, which are due to the action of Colonel George Greenwood's geologic panacea, 'Rain and Rivers,' and to nothing else. Long enough ago, once more, for a period of subsidence, as I suspect, to follow the period of upheaval; a period at the commencement of which Trinidad was perhaps several times as large as it is now, and has gradually been eaten away by the surf, as fresh pieces of the soft cliffs have been brought, by the sinking of the land, face to face with its slow but sure destroyer.

And how long ago began the epoch—the very latest which this globe has seen, which has been long enough for all this? The human imagination can no more grasp that time than it can grasp the space between us and the nearest star.

Such thoughts were forced upon me as the steamer stopped off San Fernando; and I saw, some quarter of a mile out at sea, a single stack of rock, which is said to have been joined to the mainland in the memory of the fathers of this generation; and on shore, composed, I am told, of the same rock, that hill of San Fernando which forms a beacon by sea and land for many a mile around. An isolated boss of the older Parian, composed of hardened clay which has escaped destruction, it rises, though not a mile long and a third of a mile broad, steeply to a height of nearly six hundred feet, carrying on its cliffs the remains of a once magnificent vegetation. Now its sides are quarried for the only road-stone met with for miles around; cultivated for pasture, in which the round-headed mango-trees grow about like oaks at home; or terraced for villas and gardens, the charm of which cannot be told in words. All round it, rich sugar estates spread out, with the noble Palmistes left standing here and there along the roads and terraces; and everywhere is activity and high cultivation, under the superintendence of gentlemen who are prospering, because they deserve to prosper.

Between the cliff and the shore nestles the gay and growing little town, which was, when we took the island in 1795, only a group of huts. In it I noted only one thing which looked unpleasant. The negro houses, however roomy and comfortable, and however rich the gardens which surrounded them, were mostly patched together out of the most heterogeneous and wretched scraps of wood; and on inquiry I found that the materials were, in most cases, stolen; that when a Negro wanted to build a house, instead of buying the materials, he pilfered a board here, a stick there, a nail somewhere else, a lock or a clamp in a fourth place, about the sugar-estates, regardless of the serious injury which he caused to working buildings; and when he had gathered a sufficient pile, hidden safely away behind his neighbour's house, the new hut rose as if by magic. This continual pilfering, I was assured, was a serious tax on the cultivation of the estates around. But I was told, too, frankly enough, by the very gentleman who complained, that this habit was simply an heirloom from the bad days of slavery, when the pilfering of the slaves from other estates was connived at by their own masters, on the ground that if A's Negroes robbed B, B's Negroes robbed C, and so all round the alphabet; one more evil instance of the demoralising effect of a state of things which, wrong in itself, was sure to be the parent of a hundred other wrongs.

Being, happily for me, in the Governor's suite, I had opportunities of seeing the interior of the island which an average traveller could not have; and I looked forward with interest to visiting new settlements in the forests of the interior, which very few inhabitants of the island, and certainly no strangers, had as yet seen. Our journey began by landing on a good new jetty, and being transferred at once to the tramway which adjoined it. A truck, with chairs on it, as usual here, carried us off at a good mule-trot; and we ran in the fast-fading light through a rolling hummocky country, very like the lowlands of Aberdeenshire, or the neighbourhood of Waterloo, save that, as night came on, the fireflies flickered everywhere among the canes, and here and there the palms and Ceibas stood up, black and gaunt, against the sky. At last we escaped from our truck, and found horses waiting, on which we floundered, through mud and moonlight, to a certain hospitable house, and found a hungry party, who had been long waiting for a dinner worth the waiting.

It was not till next morning that I found into what a charming place I had entered overnight. Around were books, pictures, china, vases of flowers, works of art, and all appliances of European taste, even luxury; but in a house utterly un-European. The living rooms, all on the first floor, opened into each other by doorless doorways, and the walls were of cedar and other valuable woods, which good taste had left still unpapered. Windowless bay windows, like great port-holes, opened from each of them into a gallery which ran round the house, sheltered by broad sloping eaves. The deep shade of the eaves contrasted brilliantly with the bright light outside ; and contrasted too with the wooden pillars which held up the roof, and which seemed on their southern sides white-hot in the blazing sunshine.

What a field was there for native art ; for richest ornamentation of these pillars and those beams. Surely Trinidad, and the whole of northern South America, ought to become some day the paradise of wood-carvers, who, copying even a few of the numberless vegetable and animal forms around, may far surpass the old wood-carving schools of Burmah and Hindostan. And I sat dreaming of the lianes which might be made to wreathe the pillars ; the flowers, fruits, birds, butterflies, monkeys, kinkajous, and what not, which might cluster about the capitals, or swing along the beams. Let men who have such materials, and such models, proscribe all tawdry and poor European art—most of it a bad imitation of bad Greek, or worse Renaissance—and trust to Nature and the facts which lie nearest them. But when will a time come for the West Indies when there will be wealth and civilisation enough to make such an art possible ? Soon, if all the employers of labour were like the gentleman at whose house we were that day, and like some others in the same island.

And through the windows and between the pillars of the gallery, what a blaze of colour and light. The ground-floor was hedged in, a few feet from the walls, with high shrubs, which would have caused unwholesome damp in England, but were needed here for shade. Foreign Crotons, Dracænas, Cereuses, and a dozen more curious shapes—among them a 'cup-tree,' with concave leaves, each of which would hold water. It was said to come from the East, and was unknown to me. Among them, and over the door, flowering creepers tangled and tossed, rich with flowers ; and beyond them a circular lawn (rare in the West Indies), just like an English one, save that the shrubs and trees which bounded it were hothouse plants. A few Carat-palms [1] spread their huge fan-leaves among the curious flowering trees ; other foreign palms, some of them very rare, beside them ; and on the lawn opposite my bedroom window stood a young Palmiste, which had been planted barely eight years, and was now thirty-eight feet in height, and more than six feet in girth at the butt. Over the roofs of the outhouses rose scarlet Bois immortelles, and tall clumps of Bamboo reflecting blue light from their leaves even under a cloud ; and beyond them and below them to the right, a park just like an English one carried stately trees scattered on the turf, and a sheet of artificial water. Coolies, in red or yellow waistcloths,

---

[1] *Sabal.*

and Coolie children, too, with nothing save a string round their stomachs (the smaller ones at least), were fishing in the shade. To the left, again, began at once the rich cultivation of the rolling cane-fields, among which the Squire had left standing, somewhat against the public opinion of his less tasteful neighbours, tall Carats, carrying their heads of fan-leaves on smooth stalks from fifty to eighty feet high, and Ceibas—some of them the hugest I had ever seen. Below in the valley were the sugar-works; and beyond this half-natural, half-artificial scene rose, some mile off, the lowering wall of the yet untouched forest.

It had taken only fifteen years, but fifteen years of hard work, to create this paradise. And only the summer before, all had been well-nigh swept away again. During the great drought the fire had raged about the woods. Estate after estate around had been reduced to ashes. And one day our host's turn came. The fire burst out of the woods at three different points. All worked with a will to stop it by cutting traces. But the wind was wild; burning masses from the tree-tops were hurled far among the canes, and all was lost. The canes burnt like shavings, exploding with a perpetual crackle at each joint. In a few hours the whole estate—works, coolie barracks, negro huts—was black ash; and the house only, by extreme exertion, saved. But the ground had scarcely cooled when replanting and rebuilding commenced; and now the canes were from ten to twelve feet high, the works nearly ready for the coming crop-time, and no sign of the fire was left, save a few leafless trees, which we found, on riding up to them, to be charred at the base.

And yet men say that the Englishman loses his energy in a tropic climate.

We had a charming Sunday there, amid charming society, down even to the dogs and cats; and not the least charming object among many was little Franky, the Coolie butler's child, who ran in and out with the dogs, gay in his little cotton shirt, and melon-shaped cap, and silver bracelets, and climbed on the Squire's knee, and nestled in his bosom, and played with his seals; and looked up trustingly into our faces with great soft eyes, like a little brown guazu-pita fawn out of the forest. A happy child, and in a happy place.

Then to church at Savanna Grande, riding of course; for the mud was abysmal, and it was often safer to ride in the ditch than on the road. The village, with a tramway through it, stood high and healthy. The best houses were those of Chinese. The poorer Chinese find peddling employments and trade about the villages, rather than hard work on the estates; while they cultivate on ridges, with minute care, their favourite sweet potato. Round San Fernando, a Chinese will rent from a sugar-planter a bit of land which seems hopelessly infested with weeds, even of the worst of all sorts—the creeping Para grass[1] —which was introduced a generation since, with some trouble, as food for cattle, and was supposed at first to be so great a boon that the gentleman who brought it in received public thanks and a valuable testimonial. The Chinaman will take the land for a single year, at a rent, I believe, as high as a pound an acre, grow on it his sweet potato crop, and return it to the owner, cleared, for the time being, of every weed. The richer shopkeepers have each a store: but they disdain to live at it. Near by each you see a comfortable low house, with verandahs, green jalousies, and often pretty flowers in pots; and catch glimpses inside of papered walls, prints, and smart moderator-lamps, which seem to be fashionable among the Celestials. But for one fashion of theirs, I confess, I was not prepared.

We went to church—a large, airy, clean, wooden one—which ought to have had a verandah round to keep off the intolerable sunlight, and which might, too, have had another pulpit. For in getting up to preach in a sort of pill-box on a long stalk, I found the said stalk surging and nodding so under my weight, that I had to assume an attitude of most dignified repose, and to beware of 'beating the drum ecclesiastic,' or 'danging the Bible to shreds,' for fear of toppling into the pews of the very smart, and really very attentive, brown ladies below. A crowded congregation it was, clean, gay, respectable and respectful, and spoke well both for the people and for their clergyman. But—happily not till the end of the sermon—I became aware, just in front of me, of a row of smartest Paris bonnets, net-lace shawls, brocades, and satins, fit for duchesses; and as the centre of each blaze of finery—'offam non faciem,' as old Ammianus Marcellinus has it—the unmistakable visage of a Chinese woman. Whether they understood one word; what they thought of it all; whether they were there for any purpose save to see and be seen, were questions to which I tried in vain, after service, to get an answer. All that could be told was, that the richer Chinese take delight in thus bedizening their wives on high days and holidays; not with tawdry cheap finery, but with things really expensive, and worth what they cost, especially the silks and brocades; and then in sending them, whether for fashion or for loyalty's sake, to an English church. Be that as it may, there they were, ladies from the ancient and incomprehensible Flowery Land, like fossil bones of an old world sticking out amid the vegetation of the new; and we will charitably hope that they were the better for being there.

After church we wandered about the estate to see huge trees. One Ceiba, left standing in a cane-piece, was very grand, from the multitude and mass of its parasites and its huge tresses of lianes; and grand also from its form. The prickly board-wall

---

[1] *Panicum sp.*

spurs were at least fifteen feet high, some of them, where they entered the trunk; and at the summit of the trunk, which could not have been less than seventy or eighty feet, one enormous limb (itself a tree) stuck out quite horizontally, and gave a marvellous notion of strength. It seemed as if its length must have snapped it off, years since, where it joined the trunk; or as if the leverage of its weight must have toppled the whole tree over. But the great vegetable had known its own business best, and had built itself up right cannily; and stood, and will stand for many a year, perhaps for many a century, if the Matapalos do not squeeze out its life. I found, by the by, in groping my way to that tree through canes twelve feet high, that one must be careful, at least with some varieties of cane, not to get cut. The leaf-edges are finely serrated; and more, the sheaths of the leaves are covered with prickly hairs, which give the Coolies sore shins if they work bare-legged. The soil here, as everywhere, was exceedingly rich, and sawn out into rolling mounds and steep gullies—sometimes almost too steep for cane-cultivation—by the tropic rains. If, as cannot be doubted, denudation by rain has gone on here, for thousands of years, at the same pace at which it goes on now, the amount of soil removed must be very great; so great, that the Naparimas may have been, when they were first uplifted out of the Gulf, hundreds of feet higher than they are now.

Another tree we went to see in the home park, of which I would have gladly obtained a photograph. A Poix doux,[1] some said it was; others that it was a Figuier.[2] I incline to the former belief, as the leaves seemed to me pinnated: but the doubt was pardonable enough. There was not a leaf on the tree which was not nigh one hundred feet over our heads. For size of spurs and wealth of parasites the tree was almost as remarkable as the Ceiba I mentioned just now. But the curiosity of the tree was a Carat-palm which had started between its very roots; had run its straight and slender stem up parallel with the bole of its companion, and had then pierced through the head of the tree, and all its wilderness of lianes, till it spread its huge flat crown of fans among the highest branches, more than a hundred feet aloft. The contrast between the two forms of vegetation, each so grand, but as utterly different in every line as they are in botanical affinities, and yet both living together in such close embrace, was very noteworthy; a good example of the rule, that while competition is most severe between forms most closely allied, forms extremely wide apart may not compete at all, because each needs something which the other does not.

On our return I was introduced to the 'Uncle Tom' of the neighbourhood, who had come down to spend Sunday at the

---

[1] *Inga.*   [2] *Ficus.*

Squire's house. He was a middle-sized Negro, in cast of features not above the average, and Isaac by name. He told me how he had been born in Baltimore, a slave to a Quaker master; how he and his wife Mary, during the second American war, ran away, and after hiding three days in the bush, got on board a British ship of war, and so became free. He then enlisted into one of the East Indian regiments, and served some years; as a reward for which he had given him his five acres of land in Trinidad, like others of his corps. These Negro yeomen-veterans, let it be said in passing, are among the ablest and steadiest of the coloured population. Military service has given them just enough of those habits of obedience of which slavery gives too much—if the obedience of a mere slave, depending not on the independent will, but on brute fear, is to be called obedience at all.

Would that in this respect, as in some others, the white subject of the British crown were as well off as the black one. Would that during the last fifty years we had followed the wise policy of the Romans and by settling our soldiers on our colonial frontiers, established there communities of loyal, able, and valiant citizens. Is it too late to begin now? Is there no colony left as yet not delivered over to a self-government which actually means, more and more—according to the statements of those who visit the colonies—government by an Irish faction; and which will offer a field for settling our soldiers when they have served their appointed time; so strengthening ourselves, while we reward a class of men who are far more respectable, and far more deserving, than most of those on whom we lavish our philanthropy?

Surely such men would prove as good subjects as old Isaac and his comrades. For fifty-three years, I was told, he had lived and worked in Trinidad, always independent; so independent, indeed, that the very last year, when all but starving, like many of the coloured people, from the long drought which lasted nearly eighteen months, he refused all charity, and came down to this very estate to work for three months in the stifling cane-fields, earning—or fancying that he earned—his own livelihood. A simple, kindly, brave Christian man he seemed, and all who knew him spoke of him as such. The most curious fact, however, which I gleaned from him was his recollection of his own 'conversion.' His Mary, of whom all spoke as a woman of a higher intellect than he, had 'been in the Gospel' several years before him, and used to read and talk to him; but, he said, without effect. At last he had a severe fever; and when he fancied himself dying, had a vision. He saw a grating in the floor, close by his bed, and through it the torments of the lost. Two souls he remembered specially; one 'like a singed hog,' the other 'all over black like a charcoal spade.' He looked in fear, and heard a voice cry, 'Behold your sins.' He prayed; promised, if he recovered, to try and do better; and felt himself forgiven at once.

This was his story, which I have set down word for word; and of which I can only say, that its imagery is no more gross, its confusion between the objective and subjective no more unphilosophical, than the speech on similar matters of many whom we are taught to call divines, theologians, and saints.

At all events, this crisis in his life produced, according to his own statement, not merely a religious, but a moral change. He became a better man henceforth. He had the reputation, among those who knew him well, of being altogether a good man. If so, it matters little what cause he assigned for the improvement. Wisdom is justified of all her children; and, I doubt not, of old black Isaac among the rest.

In 1864 he had a great sorrow. Old Mary, trying to smoke the mosquitoes out of her house with a charcoal-pan, set fire, in her shortsightedness, to the place; and everything was burned —the savings of years, the precious Bible among the rest. The Squire took her down to his house, and nursed her: but she died in two days of cold and fright; and Isaac had to begin life again alone. Kind folks built up his ajoupa, and started him afresh; and, to their astonishment, Isaac grew young again, and set to work for himself. He had depended too much for many years on his wife's superior intellect: now he had to act for himself; and he acted. But he spoke of her, like any knight of old, as of a guardian goddess—his guardian still in the other world, as she had been in this.

He was happy enough, he said: but I was told that he had to endure much vexation from the neighbouring Negroes, who were Baptists, narrow and conceited; and who—just as the Baptists of the lower class in England would be but too apt to do—tormented him by telling him that he was not sure of heaven, because he went to church instead of joining their body. But he, though he went to chapel in wet weather, clung to his own creed like an old soldier; and came down to Massa's house to spend the Sunday whenever there was a Communion, walking some five miles thither, and as much back again.

So much I learnt concerning old Isaac. And when in the afternoon he toddled away, and back into the forest, what wonder if I felt like Wordsworth after his talk with the old leech-gatherer?—

'And when he ended,
I could have laughed myself to scorn to find
In that decrepit man so firm a mind;
God, said I, be my help and stay secure,
I'll think of thee, leech-gatherer, on the lonely moor.'

On the Monday morning there was a great parade. All the Coolies were to come up to see the Governor; and after breakfast a long line of dark people arrived up the lawn, the women in their gaudiest muslins, and some of them in cotton velvet jackets of the richest colours. The Oriental instinct for harmonious hues, and those at once rich and sober, such as may be seen in Indian shawls, is very observable even in these Coolies, low-caste as most of them are. There were bangles and jewels among them in plenty; and as it was a high day and a holiday, the women had taken out the little gold or silver stoppers in their pierced nostrils, and put in their place the great gold ring which hangs down over the mouth, and is considered by them,

A COOLIE FAMILY.

as learned men tell us it was by Rebekah at the well, a special ornament. The men stood by themselves; the women by themselves; the children grouped in front; and a merrier, healthier, shrewder-looking party I have seldom seen. Complaints there were none. All seemed to look on the Squire as a father, and each face brightened when he spoke to them by name. But the great ceremony was the distributing by the Governor of red and yellow sweetmeats to the children out of a huge dish held up by the Hindoo butler, while Franky, in a long night-shirt of crimson cotton velvet, acted as aide-de-camp, and took his perquisites freely. Each of the little brown darlings got its share, the boys putting them into the flap of their waistcloths, the girls into the front of their veils; and some of the married women seemed ready enough to follow the children's example; some of them, indeed, were little more than children themselves. The pleasure of the men at the whole ceremony was very noticeable, and very pleasant. Well fed, well cared for, well taught (when they will allow themselves to be so), and with a local medical man appointed for their special benefit, Coolies under such a master ought to be, and are, prosperous and happy. Exceptions there are, and must be. Are there none among the workmen of English manufacturers and farmers? Abuses may spring up, and do. Do none spring up in London and elsewhere? But the Government has the power to interfere, and uses that power. These poor people are sufficiently protected by law from their white employers; what they need most is protection for the newcomers against the usury, or swindling, by people of their own race, especially Hindoos of the middle class, who are covetous and ill-disposed, and who use their experience of the island for their own selfish advantage. But that evil also Government is doing its best to put down. Already the Coolies have a far larger amount of money in the savings' banks of the island than the Negroes; and their prosperity can be safely trusted to wise and benevolent laws, enforced by men who can afford to stand above public opinion, as well as above private interest. I speak, of course, only of Trinidad, because only Trinidad I have seen. But what I say I know intimately to be true.

The parade over—and a pleasant sight it was, and one not easily to be forgotten—we were away to see the Salse, or 'mud-volcano,' near Monkey Town, in the forest to the south-east. The cross-roads were deep in mud, all the worse because it was beginning to dry on the surface, forming a tough crust above the hasty-pudding which, if broken through, held the horse's leg suspended as in a vice, and would have thrown him down, if it were possible to throw down a West-Indian horse. We passed in one place a quaint little relic of the older world; a small sugar-press, rather than mill, under a roof of palm-leaf, which was worked by hand, or a donkey, just as a Spanish settler would have worked it three hundred years ago. Then on through plenty of garden cultivation, with all the people at their doors as we passed, fat and grinning: then up to a good high-road, and a school for Coolies, kept by a Presbyterian clergyman, Mr. Morton—I must be allowed to mention his name —who, like a sensible man, wore a white coat instead of the absurd regulation black one, too much affected by all well-to-do folk, lay as well as clerical, in the West Indies. The school seemed good enough in all ways. A senior class of young men —including one who had had his head nearly cut off last year by misapplication of that formidable weapon the cutlass, which every coloured man and woman carries in the West Indies—could read pretty well ; and the smaller children—with as much clothing on as they could be persuaded to wear—were a sight pleasant to see. Among them, by the by, was a little lady who excited my astonishment. She was, I was told, twelve years old. She sat summing away on her slate, bedizened out in gauze petticoat, velvet jacket—between which and the petticoat, of course, the waist showed just as nature had made it—gauze veil, bangles, necklace, nose-jewel; for she was a married woman, and her Papa (Anglicè, husband) wished her to look her best on so important an occasion.

This over-early marriage among the Coolies is a very serious evil, but one which they have brought with them from their own land. The girls are practically sold by their fathers while yet children, often to wealthy men much older than they. Love is out of the question. But what if the poor child, as she grows up, sees some one, among that overplus of men, to whom she, for the first time in her life, takes a fancy? Then comes a scandal; and one which is often ended swiftly enough by the cutlass. Wife-murder is but too common among these Hindoos, and they cannot be made to see that it is wrong. 'I kill my own wife. Why not? I kill no other man's wife,' was said by as pretty, gentle, graceful a lad of two-and-twenty as one need see ; a convict performing, and perfectly, the office of housemaid in a friend's house. There is murder of wives, or quasi-wives now and then, among the baser sort of Coolies—murder because a poor girl will not give her ill-earned gains to the ruffian who considers her as his property. But there is also law in Trinidad, and such offences do not go unpunished.

Then on through Savanna Grande and village again, and past more sugar estates, and past beautiful bits of forest, left, like English woods, standing in the cultivated fields. One batch of a few acres on the side of a dell was very lovely. Huge Figuiers and Huras were mingled with palms and rich undergrowth, and lighted up here and there with purple creepers.

So we went on, and on, and into the thick forest, and what was, till Sir Ralph Woodford taught the islanders what an European road was like, one of the pattern royal roads of the island. Originally an Indian trace, it had been widened by the Spaniards, and transformed from a line of mud six feet broad to one of thirty. The only pleasant reminiscence which I have about it was the finding in flower a beautiful parasite, undescribed by Griesbach ;[1] a 'wild pine' with a branching spike of crimson flowers, purple tipped, which shone in the darkness of the bush like a great bunch of rosebuds growing among lily-leaves.

The present Governor, like Sir Ralph Woodford before him, has been fully aware of the old saying—which the Romans knew well, and which the English did not know, and only re-

---

[1] *Æchmæa Augusta.*

discovered some century since—that the 'first step in civilisation is to make roads; the second, to make more roads; and the third, to make more roads still.'

Through this very district (aided by men whose talents he had the talent to discover and employ) he has run wide, level, and sound roads, either already completed or in progress, through all parts of the island which I visited, save the precipitous glens of the northern shore.

Of such roads we saw more than one in the next few days. That day we had to commit ourselves, when we turned off the royal road, to one of the old Spanish-Indian jungle tracks. And here is a recipe for making one:—Take a railway embankment of average steepness, strew it freely with wreck, rigging and all, to imitate the fallen timber, roots, and lianes—a few flagstones and boulders here and there will be quite in place; plant the whole with the thickest pheasant-cover; set a field of huntsmen to find their way through it at the points of least resistance three times a week during a wet winter; and if you dare follow their footsteps, you will find a very accurate imitation of a forest-track in the wet season.

At one place we seemed to be fairly stopped. We plunged and slid down into a muddy brook, luckily with a gravel bar on which the horses could stand, at least one by one; and found opposite us a bank of smooth clay, bound with slippery roots, some ten feet high. We stood and looked at it, and the longer we looked—in hunting phrase—the less we liked it. But there was no alternative. Some one jumped off, and scrambled up on his hands and knees; his horse was driven up the bank to him —on its knees, likewise, more than once—and caught staggering among boughs and mud; and by the time the whole cavalcade was over, horses and men looked as if they had been brickmaking for a week.

But here again the cunning of these horses surprised me. On one very steep pitch, for instance, I saw before me two logs across the path, two feet and more in diameter, and what was worse, not two feet apart. How the brown cob meant to get over I could not guess; but as he seemed not to falter or turn tail, as an English horse would have done, I laid the reins on his neck and watched his legs. To my astonishment, he lifted a fore-leg out of the abyss of mud, put it between the logs, where I expected to hear it snap; clawed in front, and shuffled behind; put the other over the second log, the mud and water splashing into my face, and then brought the first freely out from between the logs, and—horrible to see—put a hind one in. Thus did he fairly walk through the whole; stopped a moment to get his breath; and then staggered and scrambled upward again, as if he had done nothing remarkable. Coming back, by the by, those two logs lay heavy on my heart for a mile ere I neared them. He might get up over them; but how would he get

down again? And I was not surprised to hear more than one
behind me say, 'I think I shall lead over.' But being in front,
if I fell, I could only fall into the mud, and not on the top of a
friend. So I let the brown cob do what he would, determined
to see how far a tropic horse's legs could keep him up; and, to
my great amusement, he quietly leapt the whole, descending
five or six feet into a pool of mud, which shot out over him and
me, half blinding us for the moment; then slid away on his
haunches downward; picked himself up; and went on as usual,
solemn, patient, and seemingly stupid as any donkey.

We had some difficulty in finding our quest, the Salse, or mud-
volcano. But at last, out of a hut half buried in verdure on the
edge of a little clearing, there tumbled the quaintest little old
black man, cutlass in hand, and, without being asked, went on
ahead as our guide. Crook-backed, round-shouldered, his only
dress a ragged shirt and ragged pair of drawers, he had evidently
thriven upon the forest life for many a year. He did not walk
nor run, but tumbled along in front of us, his bare feet plashing
from log to log and mud-heap to mud-heap, his gray woolly head
wagging right and left, and his cutlass brushing almost instinctively at every bough he passed, while he turned round every
moment to jabber something, usually in Creole French, which,
of course, I could not understand.

He led us well, up and down, and at last over a flat of rich
muddy ground, full of huge trees, and of their roots likewise,
where there was no path at all. The solitude was awful; so
was the darkness of the shade; so was the stifling heat; and
right glad we were when we saw an opening in the trees, and
the little man quickened his pace, and stopped with an air of
triumph not unmixed with awe on the edge of a circular pool of
mud and water some two or three acres in extent.

'Dere de debbil's woodyard,' said he, with somewhat bated
breath. And no wonder; for a more doleful, uncanny, half-
made spot I never saw. The sad forest ringed it round with
a green wall, feathered down to the ugly mud, on which, partly
perhaps from its saltness, partly from the changeableness of the
surface, no plant would grow, save a few herbs and creepers
which love the brackish water. Only here and there an Echites
had crawled out of the wood and lay along the ground, its long
shoots gay with large cream-coloured flowers and pairs of glossy
leaves; and on it, and on some dead brushwood, grew a lovely
little parasitic Orchis, an Oncidium, with tiny fans of leaves, and
flowers like swarms of yellow butterflies.

There was no track of man, not even a hunter's footprint;
but instead, tracks of beasts in plenty. Deer, quenco,[1] and
lapo,[2] with smaller animals, had been treading up and down,
probably attracted by the salt water. They were safe enough,

---

[1] *Dicoteles* (Peccary hog).   [2] *Cælogenys paca.*

the old man said. No hunter dare approach the spot. There were 'too much jumbies' here; and when one of the party expressed a wish to lie out there some night, in the hope of good shooting, the Negro shook his head. He would 'not do that for all the world. De debbil come out here at night, and walk about;' and he was much scandalised when the young gentleman rejoined that the chance of such a sight would be an additional reason for bivouacking there.

So we walked out upon the mud, which was mostly hard enough, past shallow pools of brackish water, smelling of asphalt, toward a group of little mud-volcanoes on the farther side. These curious openings into the nether-world are not permanent. They choke up after awhile, and fresh ones appear in another part of the area, thus keeping the whole clear of plants.

They are each some two or three feet high, of the very finest mud, which leaves no feeling of grit on the fingers or tongue, and dries, of course, rapidly in the sun. On the top, or near the top, of each is a round hole, a finger's breadth, polished to exceeding smoothness, and running down through the cone as far as we could dig. From each oozes perpetually, with a clicking noise of gas-bubbles, water and mud; and now and then, losing their temper, they spirt out their dirt to a considerable height; a feat which we did not see performed, but which is so common that we were in something like fear and trembling while we opened a cone with our cutlasses. For though we could hardly have been made dirtier than we were, an explosion in our faces of mud with 'a faint bituminous smell,' and impregnated with 'common salt, a notable proportion of iodine, and a trace of carbonate of soda and carbonate of lime,'[1] would have been both unpleasant and humiliating. But the most puzzling thing about the place is, that out of the mud comes up—not jumbies, but—a multitude of small stones, like no stones in the neighbourhood; we found concretions of iron sand, and scales which seemed to have peeled off them; and pebbles, quartzose, or jasper, or like in appearance to flint; but all evidently long rolled on a sea-beach. Messrs. Wall and Sawkins mention pyrites and gypsum as being found: but we saw none, as far as I recollect. All these must have been carried up from a considerable depth by the force of the same gases which make the little mud-volcanoes.

Now and then this 'Salse,' so quiet when we saw it, is said to be seized with a violent paroxysm. Explosions are heard, and large discharges of mud, and even flame, are said to appear. Some seventeen years ago (according to Messrs. Wall and Sawkins) such an explosion was heard six miles off; and next morning the surface was found quite altered, and trees had

---

[1] Dr. Davy (*West Indies*, art. 'Trinidad').

disappeared, or been thrown down. But—as they wisely say—
the reports of the inhabitants must be received with extreme
caution. In the autumn of last year, some such explosion is
said to have taken place at the Cedros Salse, a place so remote,
unfortunately, that I could not visit it. The Negroes and
Coolies, the story goes, came running to the overseer at the
noise, assuring him that something terrible had happened; and
when he, in defiance of their fears, went off to the Salse, he
found that many tons of mud—I was told thousands—had been
thrown out. How true this may be, I cannot say. But Messrs.
Wall and Sawkins saw with their own eyes, in 1856, about two
miles from this Cedros Salse, the results of an explosion which
had happened only two months before, and of which they give
a drawing. A surface two hundred feet round had been
upheaved fifteen feet, throwing the trees in every direction;
and the sham earthquake had shaken the ground for two
hundred or three hundred yards round, till the natives fancied
that their huts were going to fall.

There is a third Salse near Poole River, on the Upper Ortoire,
which is extinct, or at least quiescent; but this, also, I could
not visit. It is about seventeen miles from the sea, and about
two hundred feet above it. As for the causes of these Salses, I
fear the reader must be content, for the present, with a somewhat muddy explanation of the muddy mystery. Messrs. Wall
and Sawkins are inclined to connect it with asphalt springs
and pitch lakes. 'There is,' they say, 'easy gradation from the
smaller Salses to the ordinary naphtha or petroleum springs.'
It is certain that in the production of asphalt, carbonic acid,
carburetted hydrogen, and water are given off. 'May not,' they
ask, 'these orifices be the vents by which such gases escape?
And in forcing their way to the surface, is it not natural that
the liquid asphalt and slimy water should be drawn up and
expelled?' They point out the fact, that wherever such
volcanoes exist, asphalt or petroleum is found hard by. The
mud-volcanoes of Turbaco, in New Granada, famous from
Humboldt's description of them, lie in an asphaltic country.
They are much larger than those of Trinidad, the cones being,
some of them, twenty feet high. When Humboldt visited them
in 1801, they gave off hardly anything save nitrogen gas. But
in the year 1850, a 'bituminous odour' had begun to be diffused;
asphaltic oil swam on the surface of the small openings; and
the gas issuing from any of the cones could be ignited. Dr.
Daubeny found the mud-volcanoes of Macaluba giving out
bitumen, and bubbles of carbonic acid and carburetted
hydrogen. The mud-volcano of Saman, in the Western
Caucasus, gives off, with a continual stream of thick mud,
ignited gases, accompanied with mimic earthquakes like those
of the Trinidad Salses; and this out of a soil said to be full of
bituminous springs, and where (as in Trinidad) the tertiary

strata carry veins of asphalt, or are saturated with naphtha. At the famous sacred Fire wells of Baku, in the Eastern Caucasus, the ejections of mud and inflammable gas are so mixed with asphaltic products that Eichwald says 'they should be rather called naphtha-volcanoes than mud-volcanoes, as the eruptions always terminate in a large emission of naphtha.'

It is reasonable enough, then, to suppose a similar connection in Trinidad. But whence come, either in Trinidad or at Turbaco, the sea-salts and the iodine? Certainly not from the sea itself, which is distant, in the case of the Trinidad Salses, from two to seventeen miles. It must exist already in the strata below. And the ejected pebbles, which are evidently sea-worn, must form part of a tertiary sea-beach, covered by sands, and covering, perhaps, in its turn, vegetable *débris* which, as it is converted into asphalt, thrusts the pebbles up to the surface.

We had to hurry away from the strange place; for night was falling fast, or rather ready to fall, as always here, in a moment, without twilight, and we were scarce out of the forest before it was dark. The wild game were already moving, and a deer crossed our line of march, close before one of the horses. However, we were not benighted; for the sun was hardly down ere the moon rose, bright and full; and we floundered home through the mud, to start again next morning into mud again.

BANANA.

Through rich rolling land covered with cane; past large sugar-works, where crop-time and all its bustle was just beginning; along a tramway, which made an excellent horse-road, and then along one of the new roads, which are opening up the yet untouched riches of this island. In this district alone, thirty-six miles of good road and thirty bridges have been made, where formerly there were only two abominable bridle-paths. It was a solid pleasure to see good engineering round the hillsides; gullies, which but a year or two before were break-neck scrambles into fords often impassable after all, bridged with baulks of incorruptible timber, on piers sunk, to give a hold in that sea of hasty-pudding, sixteen feet below the river-bed; and side supports sunk as far into the banks; a solid pleasure to congratulate the warden (who had joined us) on his triumphs, and to hear how he had sought for miles around in the hasty-pudding sea, ere he could find either gravel or stone for road metal, and had found it after all ; or how in places, finding no stone at all, he had been forced to metal the way with burnt clay, which, as I can testify, is an excellent substitute ; or how again he had coaxed and patted the too-comfortable natives into being well paid for doing the very road-making which, if they had any notion of their own interests, they would combine to do for themselves. And so we rode on chatting,

> 'While all the land,
> Beneath a broad and equal-blowing breeze,
> Smelt of the coming summer ;'

for it was winter then, and only 80° in the shade, till the road entered the virgin forest, through which it has been driven, on the American principle of making land valuable by beginning with a road, and expecting settlers to follow it. Some such settlers we found, clearing right and left ; among them a most satisfactory sight ; namely, more than one Coolie family, who had served their apprenticeship, saved money, bought Government land, and set up as yeomen ; the foundation, it is to be hoped, of a class of intelligent and civilised peasant proprietors.

These men, as soon as they have cleared as much land as their wives and children, with their help, can keep in order, go off, usually, in gangs of ten to fifteen, to work, in many instances, on the estates from which they originally came. This fact practically refutes the opinion which was at first held by some attorneys and managers of sugar-estates, that the settling of free Indian immigrants would materially affect the labour supply of the colony. I must express an earnest hope that neither will any planters be short-sighted enough to urge such a theory on the present Governor, nor will the present Governor give ear to it. The colony at large must gain by the settlement of Crown lands by civilised people like the Hindoos, if it be only through the increased exports and imports ; while the sugar-estates will become more and more sure of a constant supply of labour, without the heavy expense of importing fresh immigrants. I am assured that the only expense to the colony is the fee for survey, amounting to eighteen dollars for a ten-acre allotment, as the Coolie prefers the thinly-wooded and comparatively poor lands, from the greater facility of clearing them ; and these lands are quite unsaleable to other customers. Therefore, for less than £4, an acclimatised Indian labourer with his family (and it must be remembered that, while the Negro families increase very slowly, the Coolies increase very rapidly, being more kind and careful parents) are permanently settled in the colony, the man to work five days a week on sugar-estates, the family to grow provisions for the market, instead of being shipped back to India at a cost, including gratuities and etceteras, of not less than £50.

One clearing we reached—were I five-and-twenty I should like to make just such another next to it—of a higher class still. A cultivated Scotchman, now no longer young, but hale and mighty, had taken up three hundred acres, and already cleared a hundred and fifty; and there he intended to pass the rest of a busy life, not under his own vine and fig-tree, but under his own castor-oil and cacao-tree. We were welcomed by as noble a Scot's face as I ever saw, and as keen a Scot's eye; and taken in and fed, horses and men, even too sumptuously, in a palm and timber house. Then we wandered out to see the site of his intended mansion, with the rich wooded hills of the Latagual to the north, and all around the unbroken forest, where, he told us, the howling monkeys shouted defiance morning and evening at him who did

'Invade their ancient solitary reign.'

Then we went down to see the Coolie barracks, where the folk seemed as happy and well cared for as they were certain to be under such a master; then down a rocky pool in the river, jammed with bare white logs (as in some North American forest), which had been stopped in flood by one enormous trunk across the stream; then back past the site of the ajoupa which had been our host's first shelter, and which had disappeared by a cause strange enough to English ears. An enormous silk-cotton near by was felled, in spite of the Negroes' fears. Its boughs, when it fell, did not reach the ajoupa by twenty feet or more; but the wind of its fall did, and blew the hut clean away. This may sound like a story out of Munchausen: but there was no doubt of the fact; and to us who saw the size of the tree which did the deed it seemed probable enough.

We rode away again, and into the 'Morichal,' the hills where Moriche palms are found; to see certain springs and a certain tree; and well worth seeing they were. Out of the base of a limestone hill, amid delicate ferns, under the shade of enormous trees, a clear pool bubbled up and ran away, a stream from its very birth, as is the wont of limestone springs. It was a spot fit for a Greek nymph; at least for an Indian damsel: but the nymph who came to draw water in a tin bucket, and stared stupidly and saucily at us, was anything but Greek, or even Indian, either in costume or manners. Be it so. White men are responsible for her being there; so white men must not complain. Then we went in search of the tree. We had passed, as we rode up, some Huras (Sandbox-trees) which would have been considered giants in England; and I had been laughed at more than once for asking, 'Is that the tree, or that?' I soon knew why. We scrambled up a steep bank of broken limestone, through ferns and Balisiers, for perhaps a hundred feet; and then were suddenly aware of a bole which justified the saying of one of our party—that, when surveying for a road he had come suddenly on it, he 'felt as if he had run against a church tower.' It was a Hura, seemingly healthy, undecayed, and growing vigorously. Its girth—we measured it carefully—was forty-four feet, six feet from the ground, and as I laid my face against it and looked up, I seemed to be looking up a ship's side. It was perfectly cylindrical, branchless, and smooth, save, of course, the tiny prickles which beset the bark, for a height at which we could not guess, but which we luckily had an opportunity of measuring. A wild pine grew in the lowest fork, and had kindly let down an air-root into the soil. We tightened the root, set it perpendicular, cut it off exactly where it touched the ground, and then pulled carefully till we brought the plant and half a dozen more strange vegetables down on our heads. The length of the air-root was just seventy-five feet. Some twenty feet or more above that first fork was a second fork; and then the tree began. Where its head was we could not see. We could only, by laying our faces against the bole and looking up, discern a wilderness of boughs carrying a green cloud of leaves, most of them too high for us to discern their shape without the glasses. We walked up the slope, and round about, in hopes of seeing the head of the tree clear enough to guess at its total height: but in vain. It was only when we had ridden some half mile up the hill that we could discern its masses rising, a bright green mound, above the darker foliage of the forest. It looked of any height, from one hundred and fifty to two hundred feet; less it could hardly be. 'It made,' says a note by one of our party, 'other huge trees look like shrubs.' I am not surprised that my friend Mr. St. Luce D'Abadie, who measured the tree since my departure, found it to be one hundred and ninety-two feet in height.

I was assured that there were still larger trees in the island. A certain Locust-tree and a Ceiba were mentioned. The Moras, too, of the southern hills, were said to be far taller. And I can well believe it; for if huge trees were as shrubs beside that Sandbox, it would be a shrub by the side of those Locusts figured by Spix and Martius, which fifteen Indians with outstretched arms could just embrace. At the bottom they were eighty-four feet round, and sixty where the boles became cylindrical. By counting the rings of such parts as could be reached, they arrived at the conclusion that they were of the age of Homer, and 332 years old in the days of Pythagoras. One estimate, indeed, reduced their antiquity to 2052 years old; while another (counting, I presume, two rings of fresh wood for every year) carried it up to 4104.

So we rode on and up the hills, by green and flowery paths, with here and there a cottage and a garden, and groups of enormous Palmistes towering over the tree-tops in every glen, talking over that wondrous weed, whose head we saw still far below. For weed it is, and nothing more. The wood is soft and almost useless, save for firing; and the tree itself, botanists tell us, is neither more nor less than a gigantic Spurge, the cousin-german of the milky garden weeds with which boys burn away their warts. But if the modern theory be true, that when we speak (as we are forced to speak) of the relationships of plants, we use no metaphor, but state an actual fact; that the groups into which we are forced to arrange them indicate not merely similarity of type, but community of descent—then how wonderful is the kindred between the Spurge and the Hura—indeed, between all the members of the Euphorbiaceous group, so fantastically various in outward form; so abundant, often huge, in the Tropics, while in our remote northern island their only representatives are a few weedy Spurges, two Dog's Mercuries —weeds likewise—and the Box. Wonderful it is if only these last have had the same parentage—still more if they have had the same parentage, too, with forms so utterly different from them as the prickly-stemmed scarlet-flowered Euphorbia common in our hothouses; as the huge succulent cactus-like Euphorbia of the Canary Islands; as the gale-like Phyllanthus; the many-formed Crotons, which in the West Indies alone comprise, according to Griesbach, at least twelve genera and thirty species; the hemp-like Maniocs, Physic-nuts, Castor-oils; the scarlet Poinsettia which adorns dinner-tables in winter; the pretty little pink and yellow Dalechampia, now common in hot-houses; the Manchineel, with its glossy poplar-like leaves; and this very Hura, with leaves still more like a poplar, and a fruit which differs from most of its family in having not three but many divisions, usually a multiple of three up to fifteen; a fruit which it is difficult to obtain, even where the tree is plentiful: for hanging at the end of long branches, it bursts when ripe with a crack like a pistol, scattering its seeds far and wide; from whence its name of *Hura crepitans.*

But what if all these forms are the descendants of one original form? Would that be one whit more wonderful, more inexplicable, than the theory that they were each and all, with their minute and often imaginary shades of difference, created separately and at once? But if it be—which I cannot allow—what can the theologian say, save that God's works are even more wonderful than we always believed them to be? As for the theory being impossible: who are we, that we should limit the power of God? 'Is anything too hard for the Lord?' asked the prophet of old; and we have a right to ask it as long as time shall last. If it be said that natural selection is too simple a cause to produce such fantastic variety: we always knew that God works by very simple, or seemingly simple, means; that the universe, as far as we could discern it, was one organisation of the most simple means; it was wonderful (or ought to have been) in our eyes, that a shower of rain should make the grass grow, and that the grass should become flesh, and the flesh food for the thinking brain of man; it was (or ought to have been) yet more wonderful in our eyes, that a child should resemble its parents, or even a butterfly resemble— if not always, still usually—its parents likewise. Ought God to appear less or more august in our eyes if we discover that His means are even simpler than we supposed? We held Him to be almighty and allwise. Are we to reverence Him less or more if we find that His might is greater, His wisdom deeper, than we had ever dreamed? We believed that His care was over all His works; that His providence watched perpetually over the universe. We were taught, some of us at least, by Holy Scripture, to believe that the whole history of the universe was made up of special providences: if, then, that should be true which Mr. Darwin says—'It may be metaphorically said that natural selection is daily and hourly scrutinising, throughout the world, every variation, even the slightest; rejecting that which is bad, preserving and adding up all that is good; silently and insensibly working, whenever and wherever opportunity offers, at the improvement of each organic being in relation to its organic and inorganic conditions of life,'—if this, I say, were proved to be true, ought God's care, God's providence, to seem less or more magnificent in our eyes? Of old it was said by Him without whom nothing is made—'My Father worketh hitherto, and I work.' Shall we quarrel with physical science, if she gives us evidence that these words are true? And if it should be proven that the gigantic Hura and the lowly Spurge sprang from one common ancestor, what would the orthodox theologian have to say to it, saving—'I always knew that God was great: and I am not surprised to find Him greater than I thought Him'?

So much for the giant weed of the Morichal, from which we rode on and up through rolling country growing lovelier at every step, and turned out of our way to see wild pine-apples in a sandy spot, or 'Arenal' in a valley beneath. The meeting of the stiff marl and the fine sand was abrupt, and well marked by the vegetation. On one side of the ravine the tall fan-leaved Carats marked the rich soil; on the other, the sand and gravel loving Cocorites appeared at once, crowding their ostrich plumes together. Most of them were the common species of the island[1] in which the pinnæ of the leaves grow in fours and fives, and at different angles from the leaf-stalk, giving the whole a brushy appearance, which takes off somewhat from the perfectness of its beauty. But among them we saw—for the first and last time in the forest—a few of a far more beautiful species,[2] common on the mainland. In it, the

---

[1] *Maximiliana Caribæa.* [2] *M. regia.*

pinnæ are set on all at the same distance apart, and all in the same plane, in opposite sides of the stalk, giving to the whole foliage a grand simplicity; and producing, when the curving leaf-points toss in the breeze, that curious appearance, which I mentioned in an earlier chapter, of green glass wheels with rapidly revolving spokes. At their feet grew the pine-apples, only in flower or unripe fruit, so that we could not quench our thirst with them, and only looked with curiosity at the small wild type of so famous a plant. But close by, and happily nearly ripe, we found a fair substitute for pine-apples in the fruit of the Karatas. This form of Bromelia, closely allied to the Pinguin of which hedges are made, bears a straggling plume of prickly leaves, six or eight feet long each, close to the ground. The forester looks for a plant in which the leaves droop outwards—a sign that the fruit is ripe. After beating it cautiously (for snakes are very fond of coiling under its shade) he opens the centre, and finds, close to the ground, a group of whitish fruits, nearly two inches long; peels carefully off the skin, which is beset with innumerable sharp hairs, and eats the sour-sweet refreshing pulp: but not too often, for there are always hairs enough left to make the tongue bleed if more than one or two are eaten.

With lips somewhat less parched, we rode away again to see the sight of the day; and a right pleasant sight it was. These Montserrat hills had been, within the last three years, almost the most lawless and neglected part of the island. Principally by the energy and tact of one man, the wild inhabitants had been conciliated, brought under law, and made to pay their light taxes, in return for a safety and comfort enjoyed perhaps by no other peasants on earth.

A few words on the excellent system, which bids fair to establish in this colony a thriving and loyal peasant proprietary. Up to 1847 Crown lands were seldom alienated. In that year a price was set upon them, and persons in illegal occupation ordered to petition for their holdings. Unfortunately, though a time was fixed for petitioning, no time was fixed for paying; and consequently the vast majority of petitioners never took any further steps in the matter. Unfortunately, too, the price fixed—£2 per acre—was too high; and squatting went on much as before.

It appeared to the late Governor that this evil would best be dealt with experimentally and locally; and he accordingly erected the chief squatting district, Montserrat, into a ward, giving the warden large discretionary powers as Commissioner of Crown lands. The price of Crown lands was reduced, in 1869, to £1 per acre; and the Montserrat system extended, as far as possible, to other wards; a movement which the results fully justified.

In 1867 there were in Montserrat 400 squatters, holding lands of from 3 to 120 acres, planted with cacao, coffee, or provisions. Some of the cacao plantations were valued at £1000. These people lived without paying taxes, and almost without law or religion. The Crown woods had been, of course, sadly plundered by squatters, and by others who should have known better. At every turn magnificent cedars might have been seen levelled by the axe, only a few feet of the trunk being used to make boards and shingles, while the greater part was left to rot or burn. These irregularities have been now almost stopped; and 266 persons, in Montserrat alone, have taken out grants of land, some of 400 acres. But this by no means represents the number of purchasers, as nearly an equal number have paid for their estates, though they have not yet received their grants, and nearly 500 more have made application. Two villages have been formed; one of which is that where we rested, containing the church. The other contains the warden's residence and office, the police-station, and a numerously attended school.

The squatters are of many races, and of many hues of black and brown. The half-breeds from the neighbouring coast of Venezuela, a mixture, probably, of Spanish, Negro, and Indian, are among the most industrious; and their cacao plantations, in some cases, hold 8000 to 10,000 trees. The south-west corner of Montserrat[1] is almost entirely settled by Africans of various tribes—Mandingos, Foulahs, Homas, Yarribas, Ashantees, and Congos. The last occupy the lowest position in the social scale. They lead, for the most part, a semi-barbarous life, dwelling in miserable huts, and subsisting on the produce of an acre or two of badly cultivated land, eked out with the pay of an occasional day's labour on some neighbouring estate. The social position of some of the Yarribas forms a marked contrast to that of the Congos. They inhabit houses of cedar, or other substantial materials. Their gardens are, for the most part, well stocked and kept. They raise crops of yam, cassava, Indian corn, etc.; and some of them subscribe to a fund on which they may draw in case of illness or misfortune. They are, however (as is to be expected from superior intellect while still uncivilised), more difficult to manage than the Congos, and highly impatient of control.

These Africans, Mr. Mitchell says, all belong nominally to some denomination of Christianity; but their lives are more influenced by their belief in Obeah. While the precepts of religion are little regarded, they stand in mortal dread of those who practise this mischievous imposture. Well might the

[1] I quote mostly from a report of my friend Mr. Robert Mitchell, who, almost alone, did this good work, and who has, since my departure, been sent to Demerara to assist at the investigation into the alleged ill-usage of the Coolie immigrants there. No more just or experienced public servant could have been employed on such an errand.

Commissioner say, in 1867, that several years must elapse before the chaos which reigned could be reduced to order. The wonder is, that in three years so much has been done. It was very difficult, at first, even to find the whereabouts of many of the squatters. The Commissioner had to work by compass through the pathless forest. Getting little or no food but cassava cakes and 'guango' of maize, and now and then a little coffee and salt fish, without time to hunt the game which passed him, and continually wet through, he stumbled in suddenly on one squatting after another, to the astonishment of its owner, who could not conceive how he had been found out, and had never before seen a white man alone in the forest. Sometimes he was in considerable danger of a rough reception from people who could not at first understand what they had to gain by getting legal titles, and buying the lands the fruit of which they had enjoyed either for nothing, or for payment of a small annual assessment for the cultivated portion. In another quarter — Toco — a notoriously lawless squatter had expressed his intention of shooting the Government official. The white gentleman walked straight up to the little forest fortress hidden in bush, and confronted the Negro, who had gun in hand.

'I could have shot you if I had liked, buccra.'

'No, you could not. I should have cut you down first: so don't play the fool,' answered the official quietly, hand on cutlass.

The wild man gave in; paid his rates; received the Crown title for his land; and became (as have all these sons of the forest) fast friends with one whom they have learnt at once to love and fear.

But among the Montserrat hills, the Governor had struck on a spot so fit for a new settlement, that he determined to found one forthwith. The quick-eyed Jesuits had founded a mission on the same spot many years before. But all had lapsed again into forest. A group of enormous Palmistes stands on a plateau, flat, and yet lofty and healthy. The soil is exceeding fertile. There are wells and brooks of pure water all around. The land slopes down for hundreds of feet in wooded gorges, full of cedar and other admirable timber, with Palmistes towering over them everywhere. Far away lies the lowland; and every breeze of heaven sweeps over the crests of the hills. So one peculiarly tall palm was chosen for a central landmark, an ornament to the town square such as no capital in Europe can boast. Traces were cut, streets laid out, lots of Crown lands put up for sale, and settlers invited in the name of the Government.

Scarcely eighteen months had passed since then, and already there Mitchell Street, Violin Street, Duboulay Street, Farfan Street, had each its new houses built of cedar and thatched with palm. Two Chinese shops had Celestials with pig-tails and thick-soled shoes grinning behind cedar counters, among stores of Bryant's safety matches, Huntley and Palmers' biscuits, and Allsopp's pale ale. A church had been built, the shell at least, and partly floored, with a very simple, but not tasteless, altar; the Abbé had a good house, with a gallery, jalousies, and white china handles to the doors. The mighty palm in the centre of Gordon Square had a neat railing round it, as befitted the Palladium of the village. Behind the houses, among the stumps of huge trees, maize and cassava, pigeon-peas and sweet potatoes, fattened in the sun, on ground which till then had been shrouded by vegetation a hundred feet thick; and as we sat at the head man's house, with French and English prints upon the walls, and drank beer from a Chinese shop, and looked out upon the loyal, thriving little settlement, I envied the two young men who could say, 'At least, we have not lived in vain; for we have made this out of the primeval forest.' Then on again. 'We mounted' (I quote now from the notes of one to whom the existence of the settlement was due) 'to the crest of the hills, and had a noble view southwards, looking over the rich mass of dark wood, flecked here and there with a scarlet stain of Bois Immortelle, to the great sea of bright green sugar cultivation in the Naparimas, studded by white works and villages, and backed far off by a hazy line of forest, out of which rose the peaks of the Moruga Mountains. More to the west lay San Fernando hill, the calm gulf, and the coast toward La Brea and Cedros melting into mist. M—— thought we should get a better view of the northern mountains by riding up to old Nicano's house; so we went thither, under the cacao rich with yellow and purple pods. The view was fine: but the northern range, though visible, was rather too indistinct, and the mainland was not to be seen at all.'

Nevertheless, the panorama from the top of Montserrat is at once the most vast, and the most lovely, which I have ever seen. And whosoever chooses to go and live there may buy any reasonable quantity of the richest soil at £1 per acre.

Then down off the ridge, toward the northern lowland, lay a headlong old Indian path, by which we travelled, at last, across a rocky brook, and into a fresh paradise.

I must be excused for using this word so often: but I use it in the original Persian sense, as a place in which natural beauty has been helped by art. An English park or garden would have been called of old a paradise; and the *enceinte* of a West Indian house, even in its present half-wild condition, well deserves the same title. That Art can help Nature there can be no doubt. 'The perfection of Nature' exists only in the minds of sentimentalists, and of certain well-meaning persons, who assert the perfection of Nature when they wish to controvert science, and deny it when they wish to prove this earth fallen and accursed. Mr. Nesfield can make landscapes, by obedience to certain laws which Nature is apt to disregard in the struggle for existence, more beautiful than they are already by Nature; and that without introducing foreign forms of vegetation. But if foreign forms, wisely chosen for their shapes and colours, be added, the beauty may be indefinitely increased. For the plants most capable of beautifying any given spot do not always grow therein, simply because they have not yet arrived there; as may be seen by comparing any wood planted with Rhododendrons and Azaleas with the neighbouring wood in its native state. Thus may be obtained somewhat of that variety and richness which is wanting everywhere, more or less, in the vegetation of our northern zone, only just recovering slowly from the destructive catastrophe of the glacial epoch; a richness which, small as it is, vanishes as we travel northward, till the drear landscape is sheeted more and more with monotonous multitudes of heather, grass, fir, or other social plants.

But even in the Tropics the virgin forest, beautiful as it is, is without doubt much less beautiful, both in form and colours, than it might be made. Without doubt, also, a mere clearing, after a few years, is a more beautiful place than the forest; because by it distance is given, and you are enabled to see the sky, and the forest itself beside; because new plants, and some of them very handsome ones, are introduced by cultivation, or spring up in the rastrajo; and lastly, but not least, because the forest on the edge of the clearing is able to feather down to the ground, and change what is at first a bare tangle of stems and boughs into a softly rounded bank of verdure and flowers. When, in some future civilisation, the art which has produced, not merely a Chatsworth or a Dropmore, but an average English shrubbery or park, is brought to bear on tropic vegetation, then Nature, always willing to obey when conquered by fair means, will produce such effects of form and colour around tropic estates and cities as we cannot fancy for ourselves.

Mr. Wallace laments (and rightly) the absence in the tropic forests of such grand masses of colour as are supplied by a heather moor, a furze or broom-croft, a field of yellow charlock, blue bugloss, or scarlet poppy. Tropic landscape gardening will supply that defect; and a hundred plants of yellow Allamanda, or purple Dolichos, or blue Clitoria, or crimson Norantea, set side by side, as we might use a hundred Calceolarias or Geraniums, will carry up the forest walls, and over the tree-tops, not square yards, but I had almost said square acres of richest positive colour. I can conceive no limit to the effects—always heightened by the intense sunlight and the peculiar tenderness of the distances—which landscape gardening will produce when once it is brought to bear on such material as it has never yet attempted to touch, at least in the West Indies, save in the Botanic Garden at Port of Spain.

TORTUGA.

And thus the little paradise at Tortuga to which we descended to sleep, though cleared out without any regard to art, was far more beautiful than the forest out of which it had been hewn three years before. The two first settlers regretted the days when the house was a mere palm-thatched hut, where they sat on stumps which would not balance, and ate potted meat with their pocket-knives. But it had grown now into a grand place, fit to receive ladies : such a house, or rather shed, as those South Sea Island ones which may be seen in Hodges' illustrations to *Cook's Voyages*, save that a couple of bedrooms have been boarded off at the back, a little office on one side, and a bulwark, like that of a ship, put round the gallery. And as we looked down through the purple gorges, and up at the mountain woods, over which the stars were flashing out bright and fast, and listened to the soft strange notes of the forest birds going to roost, again the thought came over me—Why should not gentlemen and ladies come to such spots as these to live 'the Gentle Life'?

We slept that night, some in beds, some in hammocks, some on the floor, with the rich warm night wind rushing down through all the house; and then were up once more in the darkness of the dawn, to go down and bathe at a little cascade, where a feeble stream dribbled under ferns and balisiers over soft square limestone rocks like the artificial rocks of the Serpentine, and those — copied probably from the rocks of Fontainebleau—which one sees in old French landscapes. But a bathe was hardly necessary. So drenched was the vegetation with night dew, that if one had taken off one's clothes at the house, and simply walked under the bananas, and through the tanias and maize which grew among them, one would have been well washed ere one reached the stream. As it was, the bathers came back with their clothes wet through. No matter. The sun was up, and half an hour would dry all again.

One object, on the edge of the forest, was worth noticing, and was watched long through the glasses ; namely, two or three large trees, from which dangled a multitude of the pendant nests of the Merles;[1] birds of the size of a jackdaw, brown and yellow, and mocking-birds, too, of no small ability. The pouches, two feet long and more, swayed in the breeze, fastened to the end of the boughs with a few threads. Each had, about half-way down, an opening into the round sac below, in and out of which the Merles crept and fluttered, talking all the while in twenty different notes. Most tropic birds hide their nests carefully in the bush: the Merles hang theirs fearlessly in the most exposed situations. They find, I presume, that they are protected enough from monkeys, wild cats, and gato-melaos (a sort of ferret) by being hung at the extremity of the bough. So thinks M. Léotaud, the accom-

---

[1] *Cassicus.*

plished describer of the birds of Trinidad. But he adds with good reason: 'I do not, however, understand how birds can protect their nestlings against ants; for so large is the number of these insects in our climes, that it would seem as if everything would become their prey.'

And so everything will, unless the bird-murder be stopped. Already the parasol-ants have formed a warren close to Port of Spain, in what was forty years ago highly cultivated ground, from which they devastate at night the northern gardens. The forests seem as empty of birds as the neighbourhood of the city; and a sad answer will soon have to be given to M. Léotaud's question:—

'The insectivorous tribes are the true representatives of our ornithology. There are so many which feed on insects and their larvæ, that it may be asked with much reason, What would become of our vegetation, of ourselves, should these insect destroyers disappear? Everywhere may be seen' (M. L. speaks, I presume, of five-and-twenty years ago: my experience would make me substitute for his words, 'Hardly anywhere can be seen') 'one of these insectivora in pursuit or seizure of its prey, either on the wing or on the trunks of trees, in the coverts of thickets or in the calices of flowers. Whenever called to witness one of those frequent migrations from one point to another, so often practised by ants, not only can the Dendrocolaptes (connected with our Creepers) be seen following the moving trail, and preying on the ants and the eggs themselves, but even the black Tanager abandons his usual fruits for this more tempting delicacy. Our frugivorous and baccivorous genera are also pretty numerous, and most of them are so fond of insect food that they unite, as occasion offers, with the insectivorous tribes.'

So it was once. Now a traveller, accustomed to the swarms of birds which, not counting the game, inhabit an average English cover, would be surprised and pained by the scarcity of birds in the forests of this island.

We rode down toward the northern lowland, along a broad new road of last year's making, terraced, with great labour, along the hill, and stopped to visit one of those excellent Government schools which do honour, first to that wise legislator, Lord Harris, and next to the late Governor. Here, in the depths of the forest, where never policeman or schoolmaster had been before, was a house of satin-wood and cedar not two years old, used at once as police-station and school, with a shrewd Spanish-speaking schoolmaster, and fifty-two decent little brown children on the school-books, and getting, when their lazy parents will send them, as good an education as they would get in England. I shall have more to say on the education system of Trinidad. All it seems to me to want, with its late modifications, is compulsory attendance.

Soon, turning down an old Indian path, we saw the Gulf once more, and between us and it the sheet of cane cultivation, of which one estate ran up to our feet, 'like a bright green bay entered by a narrow strait among the dark forest.' Just before we came to it we passed another pleasant sight: more Coolie settlers, who had had lands granted them in lieu of the return passage to which they were entitled, were all busily felling wood, putting up bamboo and palm-leaf cabins, and settling

COOLIE GROUP.

themselves down, each one his own master, yet near enough to the sugar-estates below to get remunerative work whenever needful.

Then on, over slow miles (you must not trot beneath the burning midday sun) of sandy stifling flat, between high canes, till we saw with joy, through long vistas of straight traces, the mangrove shrubbery which marked the sea. We turned into large sugar-works, to be cooled with sherry and ice by a hospitable manager, whose rooms were hung with good prints, and stored with good books and knick-knacks from Europe, showing the signs of a lady's hand. And here our party broke up. The rest carried their mud back to Port of Spain; I in the opposite direction back to San Fernando, down a little creek which served as a port to the estate.

Plastered up to the middle like the rest of the party, besides splashes over face and hat, I could get no dirtier than I was already. I got without compunction into a canoe some three feet wide; and was shoved by three Negroes down a long winding ditch of mingled mud, water, and mangrove-roots. To keep one's self and one's luggage from falling out during the journey was no easy matter; at one moment, indeed, it threatened to become impossible. For where the mangroves opened on the sea, the creek itself turned sharply northward along shore, leaving (as usual) a bed of mud between it and the sea some quarter of a mile broad; across which we had to pass as a short cut to the boat, which lay far out. The difficulty was, of course, to get the canoe out of the creek up the steep mud-bank. To that end she was turned on her side, with me on board. I could just manage, by jamming my luggage under my knees, and myself against the two gunwales, to keep in, holding on chiefly by my heels and the back of my neck. But it befell, that in the very agony of the steepest slope, when the Negroes (who worked like really good fellows) were nigh waist-deep in mud, my eye fell, for the first time in my life, on a party of Calling Crabs, who had been down to the water to fish, and were now scuttling up to their burrows among the mangrove-roots; and at the sight of the pairs of long-stalked eyes, standing upright like a pair of opera-glasses, and the long single arms which each brandished, with frightful menaces, as of infuriated Nelsons, I burst into such a fit of laughter that I nearly fell out into the mud. The Negroes thought for the instant that the 'buccra parson' had gone mad: but when I pointed with my head (I dare not move a finger) to the crabs, off they went in a true Negro guffaw, which, when once begun, goes on and on, like thunder echoing round the mountains, and can no more stop itself than a Blackcap's song. So all the way across the mud the jolly fellows, working meanwhile like horses, laughed for the mere pleasure of laughing; and when we got to the boat the Negro in charge of her saw us laughing, and laughed too for company, without waiting to hear the joke; and as two of them took the canoe home, we could hear them laughing still in the distance, till the lonely loathsome place rang again. I plead guilty to having given the men, as payment, not only for their work but for their jollity, just twice what they asked, which, after all, was very little.

But what are Calling Crabs? I must ask the reader to conceive a moderate-sized crab, the front of whose carapace is very broad and almost straight, with a channel along it, in which lie, right and left, his two eyes, each on a footstalk half as long as the breadth of his body; so that the crab, when at rest, carries his eyes as epaulettes, and peeps out at the joint of each shoulder.

But when business is to be done, the eye-stalks jump bolt upright side by side, like a pair of little lighthouses, and survey the field of battle in a fashion utterly ludicrous. Moreover, as if he were not ridiculous enough even thus, he is (as Mr. Wood well puts it) like a small man gifted with one arm of Hercules, and another of Tom Thumb. One of his claw arms, generally the left, has dwindled to a mere nothing, and is not seen ; while along the whole front of his shell lies folded one mighty right arm, on which he trusts; and with that arm, when danger appears, he beckons the enemy to come on, with such wild defiance, that he has gained therefrom the name of *Gelasimus Vocans* ('The Calling Laughable'); and it were well if all scientific names were as well fitted. He is, as might be guessed, a shrewd fighter, and uses the true old 'Bristol guard' in boxing, holding his long arm across his body, and fencing and biting therewith swiftly and sharply enough. Moreover, he is a respectable animal, and has a wife, and takes care of her ; and to see him in his glory, it is said, he should be watched sitting in the mouth of his burrow, his spouse packed safe behind him inside, while he beckons and brandishes, proclaiming to all passers-by the treasure which he protects, while he defies them to touch it.

Such is the 'Calling Crab,' of whom I must say, that if he was not made on purpose to be laughed at, then I should be induced to suspect that nothing was made for any purpose whatsoever.

After which sight, and weary of waiting, not without some fear that—as the Negroes would have put it—'If I tap da wan momant ma, I catch da confection,' while, of course, a bucket or two of hot water was emptied on us out of a passing cloud, I got on board the steamer, and away to San Fernando, to wash away dirt and forget fatigue, amid the hospitality of educated and high-minded men, and of even more charming women.

CHAPTER XI

THE NORTHERN MOUNTAINS

I HAD heard and read much of the beauty of mountain scenery in the Tropics. What I had heard and read is not exaggerated. I saw, it is true, in this little island no Andes, with such a scenery among them and below them as Humboldt alone can describe—a type of the great and varied tropical world as utterly different from that of Trinidad as it is from that of Kent—or Siberia. I had not even the chance of such a view as that from the Silla of Caraccas described by Humboldt, from which you look down at a height of nearly six thousand feet, through layer after layer of floating cloud, which increases the seeming distance to an awful depth, upon the blazing shores of the Northern Sea.

That view our host and his suite had seen themselves the year before; and they assured me that Humboldt had not overstated its grandeur. The mountains of Trinidad do not much exceed three thousand feet in height, and I could hope at most to see among them what my fancy had pictured among the serrated chines and green gorges of St. Vincent, Guadaloupe, and St. Lucia, hanging gardens compared with which those of Babylon of old must have been Cockney mounds. The rock among these mountains, as I have said already, is very seldom laid bare. Decomposed rapidly by the tropic rain and heat, it forms, even on the steepest slopes, a mass of soil many feet in depth, ever increasing, and ever sliding into the valleys, mingled with blocks and slabs of rock still undecomposed. The waste must be enormous now. Were the forests cleared, and the soil no longer protected by the leaves and bound together by the roots, it would increase at a pace of which we in this temperate zone can form no notion, and the whole mountain-range slide down in deluges of mud, as, even in the temperate zone, the Mont Ventoux and other hills in Provence are sliding now, since they have been rashly cleared of their primeval coat of woodland.

To this degrading influence of mere rain and air must be

attributed, I think, those vast deposits of boulder which encumber the mouths of all the southern glens, sometimes to a height of several hundred feet. Did one meet them in Scotland, one would pronounce them at once to be old glacier-moraines. But Messrs. Wall and Sawkins, in their geological survey of this island, have abstained from expressing any such opinion; and I think wisely. They are more simply explained as the mere leavings of the old sea-worn mountain wall, at a time when the Orinoco, or the sea, lay along their southern, as it now does along their northern, side. The terraces in which they rise mark successive periods of upheaval; and how long these periods were, no reasonable man dare guess. But as for traces of ice-action, none, as far as I can ascertain, have yet been met with. He would be a bold man who should deny that, during the abyss of ages, a cold epoch may have spread ice over part of that wide land which certainly once existed to the north of Trinidad and the Spanish Main: but if so, its traces are utterly obliterated. The commencement of the glacial epoch, as far as Trinidad is concerned, may be safely referred to the discovery of Wenham Lake ice, and the effects thereof sought solely in the human stomach and the increase of Messrs. Haley's well-earned profits. Is it owing to this absence of any ice-action that there are no lakes, not even a tarn, in the northern mountains? Far be it from me to thrust my somewhat empty head into the battle which has raged for some time past between those who attribute all lakes to the scooping action of glaciers and those who attribute them to original depressions in the earth's surface: but it was impossible not to contrast the lakeless mountains of Trinidad with the mountains of Kerry, resembling them so nearly in shape and size, but swarming with lakes and tarns. There are no lakes throughout the West Indies, save such as are extinct craters, or otherwise plainly attributable to volcanic action, as I presume are the lakes of tropical Mexico and Peru. Be that as it may, the want of water, or rather of visible water, takes away much from the beauty of these mountains, in which the eye grows tired toward the end of a day's journey with the monotonous surges of green woodland; and hails with relief, in going northward, the first glimpse of the sea horizon; in going south, the first glimpse of the hazy lowland, in which the very roofs and chimney-stalks of the sugar-estates are pleasant to the eye from the repose of their perpendicular and horizontal lines after the perpetual unrest of rolling hills and tangled vegetation.

We started, then (to begin my story), a little after five one morning, from a solid old mansion in the cane-fields, which bears the name of Paradise, and which has all the right to the name which beauty of situation and goodness of inhabitants can bestow.

As we got into our saddles the humming-birds were whirring round the tree-tops; the Qu'est-ce qu'il dits inquiring the subject of our talk. The black vultures sat about looking on in silence, hoping that something to their advantage might be dropped or left behind—possibly that one of our horses might die.

Ere the last farewell was given, one of our party pointed to a sight which I never saw before, and perhaps shall never see again. It was the Southern Cross. Just visible in that winter season on the extreme southern horizon in early morning, it hung upright amid the dim haze of the lowland and the smoke of the sugar-works. Impressive as was, and always must be, the first sight of that famous constellation, I could not but agree with those who say that they are disappointed by its inequality, both in shape and in the size of its stars. However, I had but little time to make up my mind about it; for in five minutes more it had melted away into a blaze of sunlight, which reminded us that we ought to have been on foot half an hour before.

So away we went over the dewy paddocks, through broad-leaved grasses, and the pink balls of the sensitive-plants and blue Commelyna, and the upright negro Ipecacuanha,[1] with its scarlet and yellow flowers, gayest and commonest of weeds; then down into a bamboo copse, and across a pebbly brook, and away toward the mountains.

Our party consisted of a bât-mule, with food and clothes, two or three Negroes, a horse for me, another for general use in case of break-down; and four gentlemen who preferred walking to riding. It seemed at first a serious undertaking on their part; but one had only to see them begin to move, long, lithe, and light as deer-hounds, in their flannel shirts and trousers, with cutlass and pouch at their waists, to be sure that they could both go and stay, and were as well able to get to Blanchisseuse as the horses beside which they walked.

The ward of Blanchisseuse, on the north coast, whither we were bound, was of old, I understand, called Blanchi Sali, or something to that effect, signifying the white cliffs. The French settlers degraded the name to its present form, and that so hopelessly, that the other day an old Negress in Port of Spain puzzled the officer of Crown property by informing him that she wanted to buy 'a carré in what you call de washerwoman's.' It had been described to me as possibly the remotest, loneliest, and unhealthiest spot in Her Majesty's tropical dominions. No white man can live there for more than two or three years without ruin to his health. In spite of the perpetual trade-wind, and the steepness of the hillsides, malaria hangs for ever at the mouth of each little mountain torrent, and crawls up inland to leeward to a considerable height above the sea.

But we did not intend to stay there long enough to catch

---

[1] *Asclepias curassavica.*

fever and ague. We had plenty of quinine with us; and cheerily we went up the valley of Caura, first over the great boulder and pebble ridges, not bare like those of the Moor of Dinnet, or other Deeside stone heap, but clothed with cane-pieces and richest rastrajo copses ; and then entered the narrow gorge, which we had to follow into the heart of the hills, as our leader, taking one parting look at the broad green lowland behind us, reminded us of Shelley's lines about the plains of Lombardy seen from the Euganean hills :—

> 'Beneath me lies like a green sea
> The waveless plain of Lombardy,
>
> . . . .
>
> Where a soft and purple mist,
> Like a vaporous amethyst,
> Or an air-dissolvèd stone,
> Mingling light and fragrance, far
> From the curved horizon's bound
> To the point of heaven's profound,
> Fills the overflowing sky ;
> And the plains that silent lie
> Underneath, the leaves unsodden
> Where the infant frost has trodden
> With his morning-wingèd feet,
> Whose bright fruit is gleaming yet ;
> And the red and golden vines
> Piercing with their trellised lines
> The rough dark-skirted wilderness.'

But there the analogy stopped. It hardly applied even so far. Between us and the rough dark-skirted wilderness of the high forests on Montserrat the infant frost had never trodden ; all basked in the equal heat of the perpetual summer ; awaiting, it may be, in ages to come, a civilisation higher even than that whose decay Shelley deplored as he looked down on fallen Italy.

No clumsy words of mine can give an adequate picture of the beauty of the streams and glens which run down from either slope of the Northern Mountain. The reader must fancy for himself the loveliest brook which he ever saw in Devonshire or Yorkshire, Ireland or Scotland ; crystal-clear, bedded with gray pebbles, broken into rapids by rock-ledges or great white quartz boulders, swirling under steep cliffs, winding through flats of natural meadow and copse. Then let him transport his stream into the great Palm-house at Kew, stretch out the house up hill and down dale, five miles in length and two thousand feet in height ; pour down on it from above a blaze which lights up every leaf into a gem, and deepens every shadow into blackness, and yet that very blackness full of inner light—and if his fancy can do as much as that, he can imagine to himself the stream up which we rode or walked, now winding along the narrow track a hundred feet or two above, looking down on the upper surface of the forest, on the crests of palms, and the broad sheets of the balisier copse, and often on the statelier fronds of true bananas, which had run wild along the stream-side, flowering and fruiting in the wilderness for the benefit of the parrots and agoutis; or on huge dark clumps of bamboo, which (probably not indigenous to the island) have in like manner spread themselves along all the streams in the lapse of ages.

Now we scrambled down into the brook, and waded our horses through, amid shoals of the little spotted sardine,[1] who are too fearless, or too unaccustomed to man, to get out of the way more than a foot or two. But near akin as they are to the trout, they are still nearer to the terrible Pirai,[2] of the Orinocquan waters, the larger of which snap off the legs of swimming ducks and the fingers of unwary boatmen, while the smaller surround the rash bather, and devour him piecemeal till he drowns, torn by a thousand tiny wounds, in water purpled with his own blood. These little fellows prove their kindred with the Pirai by merely nibbling at the bather's skin, making him tingle from head to foot, while he thanks Heaven that his visitors are but two inches, and not a foot in length.

At last we stopped for breakfast. The horses were tethered to a tree, the food got out, and we sat down on a pebbly beach after a bathe in a deep pool, so clear that it looked but four feet deep, though the bathers soon found it to be eight and more. A few dark logs, as usual, were lodged at the bottom, looking suspiciously like alligators or boa-constrictors. The alligator, however, does not come up the mountain streams; and the boa-constrictors are rare, save on the east coast: but it is as well, ere you jump into a pool, to look whether there be not a snake in it, of any length from three to twenty feet.

Over the pool rose a rock, carrying a mass of vegetation, to be seen, doubtless, in every such spot in the island, but of a richness and variety beyond description. Nearest to the water the primeval garden began with ferns and creeping Selaginella. Next, of course, the common Arum,[3] with snow-white spathe and spadix, mingled with the larger leaves of Balisier, wild Tania, and Seguine, some of the latter upborne on crooked fleshy stalks as thick as a man's leg, and six feet high. Above them was a tangle of twenty different bushes, with leaves of every shape; above them again, the arching shoots of a bamboo clump, forty feet high, threw a deep shade over pool and rock and herbage; while above it again enormous timber trees were packed, one behind the other, up the steep mountain-side. On the more level ground were the usual weeds; Ipomœas with white and purple flowers, Bignonias, Echites, and Allamandas, with yellow ones, scrambled and tumbled everywhere; and, if not just there, then often enough elsewhere, might be seen a

---

[1] *Hydrocyon.*   [2] *Serrasalmo.*   [3] *Spathiphyllum cannifolium.*

single Aristolochia scrambling up a low tree, from which hung, amid round leaves, huge flowers shaped like a great helmet with a ladle at the lower lip, a foot or more across, of purplish colour, spotted like a toad, and about as fragrant as a dead dog.

But the plants which would strike a botanist most, I think, the first time he found himself on a tropic burn-side, are the peppers, groves of tall herbs some ten feet high or more, utterly unlike any European plants I have ever seen. Some[1] have round leaves, peltate, that is, with the footstalk springing from inside the circumference, like a one-sided umbrella. They catch the eye at once, from the great size of their leaves, each a full foot across; but they are hardly as odd and foreign-looking as the more abundant forms of peppers,[2] usually so soft and green that they look as if you might make them into salad, stalks and all, yet with a quaint stiffness and primness, given by the regular jointing of their knotted stalks, and the regular tiling of their pointed, drooping, strong-nerved leaves, which are usually, to add to the odd look of the plant, all crooked, one side of the base (and that in each species always the same side) being much larger than the other, so that the whole head of the bush seems to have got a twist from right to left, or left to right. Nothing can look more unlike than they to the climbing true peppers, or even to the creeping pepper-weeds, which abound in all waste land. But their rat-tails of small green flowers prove them to be peppers nevertheless.

On we went, upward ever, past Cacao and Bois Immortelle orchards, and comfortable settlers' hamlets; and now and then through a strip of virgin forest, in which we began to see, for the first time, though not for the last, that 'resplendent Calycophyllum' as Dr. Krueger calls it, Chaconia as it is commonly called here, after poor Alonzo de Chacon, the last Spanish governor of this island. It is indeed the jewel of these woods. A low straggling tree carries, on long pendent branches, leaves like a Spanish chestnut, a foot and more in length; and at the ends of the branches, long corymbs of yellow flowers. But it is not the flowers themselves which make the glory of the tree. As the flower opens, one calyx-lobe, by a rich vagary of nature, grows into a leaf three inches long, of a splendid scarlet; and the whole end of each branch, for two feet or more in length, blazes among the green foliage till you can see it and wonder at it a quarter of a mile away. This is 'the resplendent Calycophyllum,' elaborated, most probably, by long physical processes of variation and natural selection into a form equally monstrous and beautiful. There are those who will smile at my superstition, if I state my belief that He who makes all things make themselves may have used those very processes

---

[1] *Pothomorphe.* [2] *Enckea* and *Artanthe.*

of variation and natural selection for a final cause; and that the final cause was, that He might delight Himself in the beauty of one more strange and new creation. Be it so. I can only assume that their minds are, for the present at least, differently constituted from mine.

We reached the head of the glen at last, and outlet from the amphitheatre of wood there seemed none. But now I began to find out what a tropic mountain-path can be, and what a West Indian horse can do. We arrived at the lower end of a narrow ditch full of rocks and mud, which wandered up the face of a hill as steep as the roofs of the Louvre or Château Chambord. Accustomed only to English horses, I confess I paused in dismay: but as men and horses seemed to take the hill as a matter of course, the only thing to be done was to give the stout little cob his head, and not to slip over his tail. So up we went, splashing, clawing, slipping, stumbling, but never falling down; pausing every now and then to get breath for a fresh rush, and then on again, up a place as steep as a Devonshire furze-bank for twenty or thirty feet, till we had risen a thousand feet, as I suppose, and were on a long and more level chine, in the midst of ghastly dead forests, the remains of last year's fires. Much was burnt to tinder and ash; much more was simply killed and scorched, and stood or hung in an infinite tangle of lianes and boughs, all gray and bare. Here and there some huge tree had burnt as it stood, and rose like a soot-grimed tower; here another had fallen right across the path, and we had to cut our way round it step by step, amid a mass of fallen branches sometimes much higher than our heads, or to lead the horses underneath boughs which were too large to cut through, and just high enough to let them pass. An English horse would have lost his nerve, and become restive from confusion and terror; but these wise brutes, like the pack-mule, seemed to understand the matter as well as we; waited patiently till a passage was cut; and then struggled gallantly through, often among logs, where I expected to see their leg-bones snapped in two. But my fears were needless; the deft gallant animals got safe through without a scratch. However, for them, as for us, the work was very warm. The burnt forest was utterly without shade; and wood-cutting under a perpendicular noonday sun would have been trying enough had not our spirits been kept up by the excitement, the sense of freedom and of power, and also by the magnificent scenery which began to break upon us. From one cliff, off which the whole forest had been burnt away, we caught at last a sight westward of Tocuche, from summit to base, rising out of a green sea of wood—for the fire, coming from the eastward, had stopped half-way down the cliff; and to the right of the picture the blue Northern Sea shone through a gap in the hills. What a view that was! To conceive it, the reader must fancy himself at Clovelly, on the north coast of Devon, if he ever has had the good fortune to see that most beautiful of English cliff-woodlands; he must magnify the whole scene four or five times; and then pour down on it a tropic sunshine and a tropic haze.

Soon we felt, and thankful we were to feel it, a rush of air, soft and yet bracing, cool, yet not chilly; the 'champagne atmosphere,' as some one called it, of the trade-wind: and all, even the very horses, plucked up heart; for that told us that we were at the summit of the pass, and that the worst of our day's work was over. In five minutes more we were aware, between the tree-stems, of a green misty gulf beneath our very feet, which seemed at the first glance boundless, but which gradually resolved itself into mile after mile of forest, rushing down into the sea. The hues of the distant woodlands, twenty miles away, seen through a veil of ultramarine, mingled with the pale greens and blues of the water: and they again with the pale sky, till the eye could hardly discern where land and sea and air parted from each other.

We stopped to gaze, and breathe; and then downward again for nigh two thousand feet toward Blanchisseuse. And so, leading our tired horses, we went cheerily down the mountain side in Indian file, hopping and slipping from ledge to mud and mud to ledge, and calling a halt every five minutes to look at some fresh curiosity: now a tree-fern, now a climbing fern; now some huge tree-trunk, whose name was only to be guessed at; now a fresh armadillo-burrow; now a parasol-ants' warren, which had to be avoided lest horse and man should sink in it knee-deep, and come out sorely bitten; now some glimpse of sea and forest far below; now we cut a water-vine, and had a long cool drink; now a great moth had to be hunted, if not caught; or a toucan or some other strange bird listened to; or an eagle watched as he soared high over the green gulf. Now all stopped together; for the ground was sprinkled thick with great beads, scarlet, with a black eye, which had fallen from some tree high overhead; and we all set to work like schoolboys, filling our pockets with them for the ladies at home. Now the path was lost, having vanished in the six months' growth of weeds; and we had to beat about for it over fallen logs, through tangles of liane and thickets of the tall Arouma,[1] a cane with a flat tuft of leaves atop, which is plentiful in these dark, damp, northern slopes. Now we struggled and hopped, horse and man, down and round a corner, at the head of a glen, where a few flagstones fallen across a gully gave an uncertain foothold, and paused, under damp rocks covered with white and pink Begonias and ferns of innumerable forms, to drink the clear mountain water out of cups extemporised from a Calathea leaf; and then struggled up again over roots and

---

[1] *Ischnosiphon.*

ledges, and round the next spur, in cool green darkness, on which it seemed the sun had never shone; and in a silence which, when our own voices ceased, was saddening, all but appalling.

At last, striking into a broader trace which came from the westward, we found ourselves some six or eight hundred feet above the sea, in scenery still like a magnified Clovelly, but amid a vegetation which—how can I describe? Suffice it to say, that right and left of the path, and arching together overhead, rose a natural avenue of Cocorite palms, beneath whose shade I rode for miles, enjoying the fresh trade-wind, the perfume of the Vanilla flowers, and last, but not least, the conversation of one who used his high post to acquaint himself thoroughly with the beauties, the productions, the capabilities of the island which he governed; and his high culture to make such journeys as this a continuous stream of instruction and pleasure to those who accompanied him. Under his guidance we stopped at one point, silent with delight and awe.

Through an arch of Cocorite boughs—ah that English painters would go to paint such pictures, set in such natural frames—we saw, nearly a thousand feet below us, the little bay of Fillette. The height of the horizon line told us how high we were ourselves; for the blue of the Caribbean Sea rose far above a point which stretched out on our right, covered with noble wood; while the dark olive cliffs along its base were gnawed by snowy surf. On our left, the nearer mountain woods rushed into the sea, cutting off the view; and under our very feet, in the centre of an amphitheatre of wood, as the eye of the whole picture, was a group—such as I cannot hope to see again. Out of a group of scarlet Bois Immortelles rose three Palmistes, and close to them a single Balata, whose height I hardly dare to estimate. So tall they were, that though they were perhaps a thousand feet below us, they stood out against the blue sea, far up toward the horizon line; the central palm a hundred and fifty feet at least, the two others, as we guessed, a hundred and twenty feet or more. Their stems were perfectly straight and motionless, while their dark crowns, even at that distance, could be seen to toss and rage impatiently before the rush of the strong trade-wind. The black glossy head of the Balata, almost as high aloft as they, threw off sheets of spangled light, which mingled with the spangles of the waves; and, above the tree-tops, as if poised in a blue hazy sky, one tiny white sail danced before the breeze. The whole scene swam in soft sea-air; and such combined grandeur and delicacy of form and of colour I never beheld before.

We rode on and downward, toward a spot where we expected to find water. Our Negroes had lagged behind with the provisions; and, hungry and thirsty, we tethered our horses to

FILLETTE.

the trees at the bottom of a gully, and went down through the bush toward a low cliff. As we went, if I recollect, we found on the ground many curious pods,[1] curled two or three times round, something like those of a Medic, and when they split, bright red inside, setting off prettily enough the bright blue seeds. Some animal or other, however, admired these seeds as much as we; for they had been stripped as soon as they opened, and out of hundreds of pods we only secured one or two beads.

We got to the cliff—a smugglers' crack in the rock, and peered down, with some disgust. There should have been a pole or two there, to get down by: but they were washed away; a canoe also: but it had been carried off, probably out of the way of the surf. To get down the crack, for active men, was easy enough: but to get up again seemed, the longer we looked at it, the more impossible, at least for me. So after scrambling down, holding on by wild pines, as far as we dare—during which process one of us was stung (not bitten) by a great hunting-ant, causing much pain and swelling —we turned away; for the heat of the little corner was intolerable. But wistful eyes did we cast back at the next point of rock, behind which broke out the tantalising spring, which we could just not reach.

We rode on, sick and sorry, to find unexpected relief. We entered a clearing, with Bananas and Tanias, Cacao and Bois Immortelle, and better still, Avocado pears and orange-tree, with fruit. A tall and stately dame was there; her only garment a long cotton-print gown, which covered her tall figure from throat to ankle and wrist, showing brown feet and hands which had once been delicate, and a brown face, half Spanish, half Indian, modest and serious enough. We pointed to a tall orange-tree overhead, laden with fruit of every hue from bright green to gold. She, on being appealed to in Spanish, answered with a courteous smile, and then a piercing scream of—'Candelaria, come hither, and get oranges for the Governor and other señors!' Candelaria, who might have been eighteen or twenty, came sliding down under the Banana-leaves,

AVOCADO PEAR.

---

[1] *Pithecolobium* (?).

all modest smiles, and blushes through her whity-brown skin. But having no more clothes on than her mother, she naturally hesitated at climbing the tree; and after ineffectual attempts to knock down oranges with a bamboo, screamed in her turn for some José or Juan. José or Juan made his appearance, in a ragged shirt. A lanky lad, about seventeen years old, he was evidently the oaf or hobbedehoy of the family, just as he would have been on this side of the sea; was treated as such; and was accustomed to be so treated. In a tone of angry contempt (the poor boy had done and said nothing) the two women hounded him up the tree. He obeyed in meek resignation, and in a couple of minutes we had more oranges than we could eat. And such oranges: golden-green, but rather more green than gold, which cannot be (as at home) bitten or sucked; for so strong is the fragrant essential-oil in the skin, that it would blister the lips and disorder the stomach; and the orange must be carefully stripped of the outer coat before you attack a pulp compared with which, for flavour, the orange of our shops is but bad sugar and water.

As I tethered my horse to a cacao-stem, and sat on a log among hothouse ferns, peeling oranges with a bowie-knife beneath the burning mid-day sun, the quaintest fancy came over me that it was all a dream, a phantasmagoria, a Christmas pantomime got up by my host for my special amusement; and that if I only winked my eyes hard enough, when I opened them again it would be all gone, and I should find myself walking with him on Ascot Heath, while the snow whirled over the heather, and the black fir-trees groaned in the northeast wind.

We soon rode on, with blessings on fair Candelaria and her stately mother, while the noise of the surf grew louder and louder in front of us. We took (if I remember right) a sudden turn to the left, to get our horses to the shore. Our pedestrians held straight on; there was a Mangrove swamp and a lagoon in front, for which they, bold lads, cared nothing.

We passed over a sort of open down, from which all vegetation had been cleared, save the Palmistes—such a wood of them as I had never seen before. A hundred or more, averaging at least a hundred feet in height, stood motionless in the full cut of the strong trade-wind. One would have expected them, when the wood round was felled, to feel the sudden nakedness. One would have expected the inrush of salt air and foam to have injured their foliage. But, seemingly, it was not so. They stood utterly unharmed; save some half-dozen who had had their tops snapped off by a gale—there are no hurricanes in Trinidad—and remained as enormous unmeaning pikes, or posts, fifty to eighty feet high, transformed, by that one blast, from one of the loveliest to one of the ugliest natural objects.

Through the Palmiste pillars; through the usual black

Roseau scrub; then under tangled boughs down a steep stony bank; and we were on a long beach of deep sand and quartz gravel. On our right the Shore-grapes with their green bunches of fruit, the Mahauts[1] with their poplar-like leaves and great yellow flowers, and the ubiquitous Matapalos, fringed the shore. On our left weltered a broad waste of plunging foam; in front green mountains were piled on mountains, blazing in sunlight, yet softened and shrouded by an air saturated with steam and salt. We waded our horses over the mouth of the little Yarra, which hurried down through the sand, brown and foul from the lagoon above. We sat down on bare polished logs, which floods had carried from the hills above, and ate and drank—for our Negroes had by now rejoined us; and then scrambled up the shore back again, and into a trace running along the low cliff, even more beautiful, if possible, than that which we had followed in the morning. Along the cliff tall Balatas and Palmistes, with here and there an equally tall Cedar, and on the inside bank a green wall of Balisiers, with leaves full fifteen feet long and heads of scarlet flowers, marked the richness of the soil. Here and there, too, a Cannon-ball tree rose, grand and strange, among the Balatas; and in one place the ground was strewn with large white flowers, whose peculiar shape told us at once of some other Lecythid tree high overhead. These Lecythids are peculiar to the hottest parts of South America; to the valleys of the Orinoco and Amazon; to Trinidad, as a fragment of the old Orinocquan land, and possibly to some of the southern Antilles. So now, as we are in their home, it may be worth our while to pause a little round these strange and noble forms.

CANNON-BALL TREE.

Botanists tell us that they are, or rather may have been in old times, akin to myrtles. If so, they have taken a grand and original line of their own, and persevered in it for ages, till they have specialised themselves to a condition far in advance of

---

[1] *Paritium* and *Thespesia.*

most myrtles, in size, beauty, and use. They may be known from all other trees by one mark—their large handsome flowers. A group of the innumerable stamens have grown together on one side of the flower into a hood, which bends over the stigma and the other stamens. Tall trees they are, and glorious to behold, when in full flower; but they are notorious mostly for their huge fruits and delicious nuts. One of their finest forms, and the only one which the traveller is likely to see often in Trinidad, is the Cannon-ball tree.[1] There is a grand specimen in the Botanic Garden; and several may be met with in any day's ride through the high woods, and distinguished at once from any other tree. The stem rises, without a fork, for sixty feet or more, and rolls out at the top into a head very like that of an elm trimmed up, and like an elm too in its lateral water-boughs. For the whole of the stem, from the very ground to the forks, and the larger fork-branches likewise, are feathered all over with numberless short prickly pendent branchlets, which roll outward, and then down, and then up again in graceful curves, and carry large pale crimson flowers, each with a pink hood in the middle, looking like a new-born baby's fist. Those flowers, when torn, turn blue on exposure to the light; and when they fall, leave behind them the cannon-ball, a rough brown globe, as big as a thirty-two pound shot, which you must get down with a certain caution, lest that befall you which befell a certain gallant officer on the mainland of America. For, fired with a post-prandial ambition to obtain a cannon-ball, he took to himself a long bamboo, and poked at the tree. He succeeded: but not altogether as he had hoped. For the cannon-ball, in coming down, avenged itself by dropping exactly on the bridge of his nose, felling him to the ground, and giving him such a pair of black eyes that he was not seen on parade for a fortnight.

The pulp of this cannon-ball is, they say, 'vinous and pleasant' when fresh; but those who are mindful of what befell our forefather Adam from eating strange fruits, will avoid it, as they will many more fruits eaten in the Tropics, but digestible only by the dura ilia of Indians and Negroes. Whatever virtue it may have when fresh, it begins, as soon as stale, to give out an odour too abominable to be even recollected with comfort.

More useful, and the fruit of an even grander tree, are those 'Brazil nuts' which are sold in every sweet-shop at home. They belong to *Bertholletia excelsa*, a tree which grows sparingly—I have never seen it wild—in the southern part of the island, but plentifully in the forests of Guiana, and which is said to be one of the tallest of all the forest giants. The fruit, round like the cannon-ball, and about the size of a twenty-four

---

[1] *Couroupita Guianensis*.

pounder, is harder than the hardest wood, and has to be battered to pieces with the back of a hatchet to disclose the nuts, which lie packed close inside. Any one who has hammered at a Bertholletia fruit will be ready to believe the story that the Indians, fond as they are of the nuts, avoid the 'totocke' trees till the fruit has all fallen, for fear of fractured skulls; and the older story which Humboldt gives out of old Laet,[1] that the Indians dared not enter the forests, when the trees were fruiting, without having their heads and shoulders covered with bucklers of hard wood. These 'Almendras de Peru' (Peru almonds), as they were called, were known in Europe as early as the sixteenth century, the seeds being carried up the Maragnon, and by the Cordilleras to Peru, men knew not from whence. To Humboldt himself, I believe, is due the re-discovery of the tree itself and its enormous fruit; and the name of *Bertholletia excelsa* was given by him. The tree, he says, 'is not more than two or three feet in diameter, but attains one hundred or one hundred and twenty feet in height. It does not resemble the Mammee, the star-apple, and several other trees of the Tropics, of which the branches, as in the laurels of the temperate zone, rise straight toward the sky. The branches of the Bertholletia are open, very long, almost entirely bare toward the base, and loaded at their summits with tufts of very close foliage. This disposition of the semicoriaceous leaves, a little silvery beneath and more than two feet long, makes the branches bend down toward the ground, like the fronds of the palm-trees.'

'The Capuchin monkeys,' he continues, 'are singularly fond of these "chestnuts of Brazil," and the noise made by the seeds, when the fruit is shaken as it fell from the tree, excites their appetency in the highest degree.' He does not, however, believe the 'tale, very current on the lower Oroonoco, that the monkeys place themselves in a circle, and by striking the shell with a stone succeed in opening it.' That they may try is possible enough; for there is no doubt, I believe, that monkeys—at least the South American—do use stones to crack nuts; and I have seen myself a monkey, untaught, use a stick to rake his food up to him when put beyond the reach of his chain. The impossibility in this case would lie, not in want of wits, but want of strength; and the monkeys must have too often to wait for these feasts till the rainy season, when the woody shell rots of itself, and amuse themselves meanwhile, as Humboldt describes them, in rolling the fruit about, vainly longing to get their paws in through the one little hole at its base. The Agoutis, however, and Pacas, and other rodents, says Humboldt, have teeth and perseverance to gnaw through the shell; and when the seeds are once out, 'all the animals of the forest, the

---

[1] *Personal Narrative*, vol. v. p. 537.

monkeys, the manaviris, the squirrels, the agoutis, the parrots, the macaws, hasten thither to dispute the prey. They have all strength enough to break the woody covering of the seeds; they get out the kernel and carry it to the tops of the trees. "It is their festival also," said the Indians who had returned from the nut-harvest; and on hearing their complaints of the animals you perceive that they think themselves alone the legitimate masters of the forest.'

But if Nature has played the poor monkeys a somewhat tantalising trick about Brazil nuts, she has been more generous to them in the case of some other Lecythids,[1] which go by the name of monkey-pots. Huge trees like their kinsfolk, they are clothed in bark layers so delicate that the Indians beat them out till they are as thin as satin-paper, and use them as cigarette-wrappers. They carry great urn-shaped fruits, big enough to serve for drinking-vessels, each kindly provided with a round wooden cover, which becomes loose and lets out the savoury sapucaya nuts inside, to the comfort of all our 'poor relations.' Ah, when will there arise a tropic Landseer to draw for us some of the strange fashions of the strange birds and beasts of these lands?—to draw, for instance, the cunning, selfish, greedy grin of delight on the face of some burly, hairy, goitred old red Howler, as he lifts off a 'tapa del cacao de monos' (a monkey-cacao cover), and looks defiance out of the corners of his winking eyes at his wives and children, cousins and grandchildren, who sit round jabbering and screeching, and, monkey fashion, twisting their heads upside down, as they put their arms round each other's waists to peer over each other's shoulders at the great bully, who must feed himself first as his fee for having roared to them for an hour at sunrise on a tree-top, while they sat on the lower branches and looked up, trembling and delighted at the sound and fury of the idiot sermon.

What an untried world is here for the artist of every kind, not merely for the animal painter, for the landscape painter, for the student of human form and attitude, if he chose to live awhile among the still untrained Indians of the Main, or among the graceful Coolies of Trinidad and Demerara, but also for the botanical artist, for the man who should study long and carefully the more striking and beautiful of these wonderful leaves and stems, flowers and fruits, and introduce them into ornamentation, architectural or other.

And so I end my little episode about these Lecythids, only adding that the reader must not confound with their nuts the butter-nuts, Caryocar, or Souari, which may be bought, I believe, at Fortnum and Mason's, and which are of all nuts the largest and the most delicious. They have not been found as yet in

---

[1] *Lecythis Ollaris*, etc.

Trinidad, though they abound in Guiana. They are the fruit also of an enormous tree [1]—there is a young one fruiting finely in the Botanic Garden at Port of Spain—of a quite different order; a cousin of the Matapalos and of the Soap-berries. It carries large threefold leaves on pointed stalks; spikes of flowers with innumerable stamens; and here and there a fruit something like the cannon-ball, though not quite as large. On breaking the soft rind you find it full of white meal, probably eatable, and in the meal three or four great hard wrinkled nuts, rounded on one side, wedge-shaped on the other, which, cracked, are found full of almond-like white jelly, so delicious that one can well believe travellers when they tell us that the Indian tribes wage war against each other for the possession of the trees which bear these precious vagaries of bounteous nature.

And now we began to near the village, two scattered rows of clay and timber bowers right and left of the trace, each half buried in fruit-trees and vegetables, and fenced in with hedges of scarlet Hibiscus; the wooded mountains shading them to the south, the sea thundering behind them to the north. As we came up we heard a bell, and soon were aware of a brown mob running, with somewhat mysterious in the midst. Was it the Host? or a funeral? or a fight? Soon the mob came up with profound salutations, and smiles of self-satisfaction, evidently thinking that they had done a fine thing; and disclosed, hanging on a long bamboo, their one church-bell. Their old church (a clay and timber thing of their own handiwork) had become ruinous; and they dared not leave their bell aloft in it. But now they were going to build themselves a new and larger church, Government giving them the site; and the bell, being on furlough, was put into requisition to ring in His Excellency the Governor and his muddy and quaintly attired—or unattired —suite.

Ah, that I could have given a detailed picture of the scene before the police court-house—the coloured folk, of all hues of skin, all types of feature, and all gay colours of dress, crowding round, the tall stately brown policeman, Thompson, called forward and receiving with a military salute the Governor's commendations for having saved, at the risk of his life, some shipwrecked folk out of the surf close by; and the flash of his eye when he heard that he was to receive the Humane Society's medal from England, and to have his name mentioned, probably to the Queen herself; the greetings, too, of almost filial respect which were bestowed by the coloured people on one who, though still young, had been to them a father; who, indeed, had set the policeman the example of gallantry by saving, in another cove near by, other shipwrecked folk out of a still worse surf, by swimming out beyond a ledge of rock swarming with sharks,

---

[1] *Caryocar butyrosum.*

at the risk every moment of a hideous death. There, as in other places since, he had worked, like his elder brother at Montserrat, as a true civiliser in every sense of the word; and, when his health broke down from the noxious climate, had moved elsewhere to still harder and more extensive work, belying, like his father and his brothers, the common story that the climate forbids exertion, and that the Creole gentleman cannot or will not, when he has a chance, do as good work as the English gentleman at home. I do not mention these men's names. In England it matters little; in Trinidad there is no need to mention those whom all know.; all I shall say is, Heaven send the Queen many more such public servants, and me many more such friends.

Then up hurried the good little priest, and set forth in French—he was very indignant, by the by, at being taken for a Frenchman, and begged it to be understood that he was Belgian born and bred—setting forth how His Excellency had not been expected till next day, or he would have had ready an address from the loyal inhabitants of Blanchisseuse testifying their delight at the honour of, etc. etc.; which he begged leave to present in due form next day; and all the while the brown crowd surged round and in and out, and the naked brown children got between every one's legs, and every one was in a fume of curiosity and delight—anything being an event in Blanchisseuse—save the one Chinaman, if I recollect right, who stood in his blue jacket and trousers, his hands behind his back, with visage unimpassioned, dolorous, seemingly stolid, a creature of the earth, earthy,—say rather of the dirt, dirty,—but doubtless by no means as stolid as he looked. And all the while the palms and bananas rustled above, and the surf thundered, and long streams of light poured down through the glens in the black northern wall, and flooded the glossy foliage of the mangoes and sapodillas, and rose fast up the palm-stems, and to their very heads, and then vanished; for the sun was sinking, and in half an hour more, darkness would have fallen on the most remote little paradise in Her Majesty's dominions.

But where was the warden, who was by office, as well as by courtesy, to have received us? He too had not expected us, and was gone home after his day's work to his new clearing inland: but a man had been sent on to him over the mountain; and over the mountain we must go, and on foot too, for the horses could do no more, and there was no stabling for them farther on. How far was the new clearing? Oh, perhaps a couple of miles—perhaps a league. And how high up? Oh, nothing—only a hundred feet or two. One knew what that meant; and, with a sigh, resigned oneself to a four or five miles' mountain walk at the end of a long day, and started up the steep zigzag, through cacao groves, past the loveliest gardens—I recollect in one an agave in flower, nigh thirty feet high, its spike all primrose and golden yellow in the fading sunlight—then up into rastrajo ; and then into high wood, and a world of ferns—tree ferns, climbing ferns, and all other ferns which ever delighted the eye in an English hothouse. For along these northern slopes, sheltered from the sun for the greater part of the year, and for ever watered by the steam of the trade-wind, ferns are far more luxuriant and varied than in any other part of the island.

Soon it grew dark, and we strode on up hill and down dale, at one time for a mile or more through burnt forest, with its ghastly spider-work of leafless decaying branches and creepers against the moonlit sky—a sad sight : but music enough we had to cheer us on our way. We did not hear the howl of a monkey, nor the yell of a tiger-cat, common enough on the mountains which lay in front of us ; but of harping, fiddling, humming, drumming, croaking, clacking, snoring, screaming, hooting, from cicadas, toads, birds, and what not, there was a concert at every step, which made the glens ring again, as the Brocken might ring on a Walpurgis-night.

At last, pausing on the top of a hill, we could hear voices on the opposite side of the glen. Shouts and 'cooeys' soon brought us to the party which were awaiting us. We hurried joyfully down a steep hillside, across a shallow ford, and then up another hillside — this time with care, for the felled logs and brushwood lay all about a path full of stumps, and we needed a guide to show us our way in the moonlight up to the hospitable house above. And a right hospitable house it was. Its owner, a French gentleman of ancient Irish family—whose ancestors probably had gone to France as one of the valiant 'Irish Brigade'; whose children may have emigrated thence to St. Domingo, and their children or grandchildren again to Trinidad —had prepared for us in the wilderness a right sumptuous feast : 'nor did any soul lack aught of the equal banquet.'

We went to bed ; or, rather, I did. For here, as elsewhere before and after, I was compelled, by the courtesy of the Governor, to occupy the one bed of the house, as being the oldest, least acclimatised, and alas ! weakliest of the party ; while he, his little suite, and the owner of the house slept anywhere upon the floor ; on which, between fatigue and enjoyment of the wild life, I would have gladly slept myself.

When we turned out before sunrise next morning, I found myself in perhaps the most charming of all the charming 'camps' of these forests. Its owner, the warden, fearing the unhealthy air of the sea-coast, had bought some hundreds of acres up here in the hills, cleared them, and built, or rather was building, in the midst. As yet the house was rudimentary. A cottage of precious woods cut off the clearing, standing, of course, on stilts, contained two rooms, an inner and an outer. There was no glass in the windows, which occupied half the

walls. Door or shutters, to be closed if the wind and rain were
too violent, are all that is needed in a climate where the temperature changes but little, day or night, throughout the year.
A table, unpolished, like the wooden walls, but, like them, of
some precious wood; a few chairs or benches, not forgetting, of
course, an American rocking-chair; a shelf or two, with books
of law and medicine, and beside them a few good books of devotion; a press; a 'perch' for hanging clothes—for they mildew
when kept in drawers—just such as would have been seen in a
mediæval house in England; a covered four-post bed, with
gauze curtains, indispensable for fear of vampires, mosquitoes,
and other forest plagues; these make up the furniture of such
a bachelor's camp as, to the man who lives doing good work all
day out of doors, leaves nothing to be desired. Where is the
kitchen? It consists of half a dozen great stones under yonder
shed, where as good meals are cooked as in any London kitchen.
Other sheds hold the servants and hangers-on, the horses and
mules; and as the establishment grows, more will be added, and
the house itself will probably expand laterally, like a peripheral
Greek temple, by rows of posts, probably of palm-stems thatched
over with wooden shingle or with the leaves of the Timit[1] palm.
If ladies come to inhabit the camp, fresh rooms will be partitioned off by boardings as high as the eaves, leaving the roof
within open and common, for the sake of air. Soon, no regular
garden, but beautiful flowering shrubs—Crotons, Dracænas, and
Cereuses, will be planted; great bushes of Bauhinia and blue
Petræa will roll their long curved shoots over and over each
other; Gardenias fill the air with fragrance; and the Bougainvillia or the Clerodendron cover some arbour with lilac or white
racemes.

But this camp had not yet arrived at so high a state of civilisation. All round it, almost up to the very doors, a tangle of
logs, stumps, branches, dead ropes and nets of liane lay still in
the process of clearing; and the ground was seemingly as waste,
as it was difficult—often impossible—to cross. A second glance,
however, showed that, amongst the stumps and logs, Indian corn
was planted everywhere; and that a few months would give a
crop which would richly repay the clearing, over and above the
fact that the whole materials of the house had been cut on the
spot, and cost nothing.

As for the situation of the little oasis in the wilderness, it
bespoke good sense and good taste. The owner had stumbled,
in his forest wanderings, on a spot where two mountain streams,
after nearly meeting, parted again, and enclosed in a ring a hill
some hundred feet high, before they finally joined each other
below. That ring was his estate; which was formally christened
on the occasion of our visit, Avoca—the meeting of the waters;

[1] *Manicaria.*

a name, as all agreed, full of remembrances of the Old World and the land of his remote ancestors; and yet like enough to one of the graceful and sonorous Indian names of the island not to seem barbarous and out of place. Round the clearing the mountain woods surged up a thousand feet aloft; but so gradually, and so far off, as to allow free circulation of air and a broad sheet of sky overhead; and as the camp stood on the highest point of the rise, it did not give that choking and crushing sensation of being in a ditch, which makes houses in most mountain valleys—to me at least—intolerable. Up one glen, toward the south, we had a full view of the green Cerro of Arima, three thousand feet in height; and down another, to the north-east, was a great gate in the mountains, through which we could hear— though not see—the surf rolling upon the rocks three miles away.

I was woke that morning, as often before and afterwards, by a clacking of stones; and, looking out, saw in the dusk a Negro squatting, and hammering, with a round stone on a flat one, the coffee which we were to drink in a quarter of an hour. It was turned into a tin saucepan; put to boil over a firestick between two more great stones; clarified, by some cunning island trick, with a few drops of cold water; and then served up, bearing, in fragrance and taste, the same relation to average English coffee as fresh things usually do to stale ones, or live to dead. After which 'mañana,' and a little quinine for fear of fever, we lounged about waiting for breakfast, and for the arrival of the horses from the village.

Then we inspected a Coolie's great toe, which had been severely bitten by a vampire in the night. And here let me say, that the popular disbelief of vampire stories is only owing to English ignorance, and disinclination to believe any of the many quaint things which John Bull has not seen, because he does not care to see them. If he comes to these parts, he must be careful not to leave his feet or hands out of bed without mosquito curtains; if he has good horses, he ought not to leave them exposed at night without wire-gauze round the stable-shed —a plan which, to my surprise, I never saw used in the West Indies. Otherwise, he will be but too likely to find in the morning a triangular bit cut out of his own flesh, or even worse, out of his horse's withers or throat, where twisting and lashing cannot shake the tormentor off; and must be content to have himself lamed, or his horses weakened to staggering and thrown out of collar-work for a week, as I have seen happen more than once or twice. The only method of keeping off the vampire yet employed in stables is light; and a lamp is usually kept burning there. But the Negro—not the most careful of men—is apt not to fill and trim it; and if it goes out in the small hours, the horses are pretty sure to be sucked, if there is a forest near. So numerous and troublesome, indeed, are the vampires, that there are pastures in Trinidad in which, at least till the adjoining woods were cleared, the cattle would not fatten, or even thrive; being found, morning after morning, weak and sick from the bleedings which they had endured at night.

After looking at the Coolie's toe, of which he made light, though the bleeding from the triangular hole would not stop, any more than that from the bite of a horse-leech, we feasted our ears on the notes of delicate songsters, and our eyes on the colours and shapes of the forest, which, rising on the opposite side of the streams right and left, could be seen here more thoroughly than at any spot I yet visited. Again and again were the opera-glasses in requisition, to make out, or try to make out, what this or that tree might be. Here and there a Norantea, a mile or two miles off, showed like a whole crimson flower-bed in the tree-tops; or a Poui, just coming into flower, made a spot of golden yellow—'a guinea stuck against the mountain-side,' as some one said; or the head of a palm broke the monotony of the broad-leaved foliage with its huge star of green.

Near us we descried several trees covered with pale yellow flowers, conspicuous enough on the hillside. No one knew what they were; and a couple of Negroes (who are admirable woodmen) were sent off to cut one down and see. What mattered a tree or two less amid a world of trees? It was a quaint sight, —the two stalwart black figures struggling down over the fallen logs, and with them an Englishman, who thought he discerned which tree the flowers belonged to; while we at the house guided them by our shouts, and scanned the trunks through the glasses to make out in our turn which tree should be felled. From the moment that they entered under the green cloud, they of course could see little or nothing over their heads. Animated were the arguments—almost the bets—as to which tree-top belonged to which tree-trunk. Many were the mistakes made; and had it not been for the head of a certain palm, which served as a fixed point which there was no mistaking, three or four trees would have been cut before the right one was hit upon. At last the right tree came crashing down, and a branch of the flowers was brought up, to be carried home, and verified at Port of Spain; and meanwhile, disturbed by the axe-strokes, pair after pair of birds flew screaming over the tree-tops, which looked like rooks, till, as they turned in the sun, their colour—brilliant even at that distance—showed them to be great green parrots.

After breakfast—which among French and Spanish West Indians means a solid and elaborate luncheon—our party broke up. . . . I must be excused if I am almost prolix over the events of a day memorable to me.

The majority went down, on horse and foot, to Blanchisseuse again on official business. The site of the new church, an address from the inhabitants to the Governor, inspection of roads, examination of disputed claims, squatter questions, enclosure questions, and so forth, would occupy some hours in hard work. But the *pièce de résistance* of the day was to be the examination and probable committal of the Obeah-man of those parts. That worthy, not being satisfied with the official conduct of our host the warden, had advised himself to bribe, with certain dollars, a Coolie servant of his to 'put Obeah upon him'; and had, with that intent, entrusted to him a charm to be buried at his door, consisting, as usual, of a bottle containing toad, spider, rusty nails, dirty water, and other terrible jumbiferous articles. In addition to which attempt on the life and fortunes of the warden, he was said to have promised the Coolie forty dollars if he would do the business thoroughly for him. Now the Coolie well understood what doing the business thoroughly for an Obeah-man involved; namely, the putting Brinvilliers or other bush-poison into his food; or at least administering to him sundry dozes of ground glass, in hopes of producing that 'dysentery of the country' which proceeds in the West Indies, I am sorry to say, now and then, from other causes than that of climate. But having an affection for his master, and a conscience likewise, though he was but a heathen, he brought the bottle straight to the intended victim; and the Obeah-man was now in durance vile, awaiting further examination, and probably on his way to a felon's cell.

A sort of petition, or testimonial, had been sent up to the Governor, composed apparently by the hapless wizard himself, who seemed to be no mean penman, and signed by a dozen or more of the coloured inhabitants: setting forth how he was known by all to be far too virtuous a personage to dabble in that unlawful practice of Obeah, of which both he and his friends testified the deepest abhorrence. But there was the bottle, safe under lock and key; and as for the testimonial, those who read it said that it was not worth the paper it was written on. Most probably every one of these poor fellows had either employed the Obeah-man themselves to avert thieves or evil eye from a particularly fine fruit-tree, by hanging up thereon a somewhat similar bottle—such as may be seen, and more than one of them, in any long day's march. It was said again, that if asked by an Obeah-man to swear to his good character, they could not well refuse, under penalty of finding some fine morning a white cock's head—sign of all supernatural plagues—in their garden path, the beak pointing to their door; or an Obeah bottle under their doorstep; and either Brinvilliers in their pottage, or such an expectation of it, and of plague and ruin to them and all their worldly belongings, in their foolish souls, as would be likely enough to kill them, in a few months, of simple mortal fear.

Here perhaps I may be allowed to tell what I know about this curious custom of Obeah, or Fétish-worship. It appears to me, on closer examination, that it is not a worship of natural objects; not a primeval worship; scarcely a worship at all: but simply a system of incantation, carried on by a priesthood, or rather a sorcerer class; and this being the case, it seems to me unfortunate that the term Fêtish-worship should have been adopted by so many learned men as the general name for the supposed primeval Nature-worship. The Negro does not, as the primeval man is supposed to have done, regard as divine (and therefore as Fêtish, or Obeah) any object which excites his imagination; anything peculiarly beautiful, noble, or powerful; anything even which causes curiosity or fear. In fact, a Fêtish is no natural object at all; it is a spirit, an Obeah, Jumby, Duppy, like the 'Duvvels' or spirits of the air, which are the only deities of which our Gipsies have a conception left. That spirit belongs to the Obeah, or Fêtish-man; and he puts it, by magic ceremonies, into any object which he chooses. Thus anything may become Obeah, as far as I have ascertained. In a case which happened very lately, an Obeah-man came into the country, put the Obeah into a fresh monkey's jaw-bone, and made the people offer to it fowls and plantains, which of course he himself ate. Such is Obeah now; and such it was, as may be seen by De Bry's plates, when the Portuguese first met with it on the African coast four hundred years ago.

But surely it is an idolatry, and not a nature-worship. Just so does the priest of Southern India, after having made his idol, enchant his god into it by due ceremonial. It may be a very ancient system: but as for its being a primeval one, as neither I, nor any one else, ever had the pleasure of meeting a primeval man, it seems to me somewhat rash to imagine what primeval man's creeds and worships must have been like; more rash still to conclude that they must have been like those of the modern Negro. For if, as is probable, the Negro is one of the most ancient varieties of the human race; if, as is probable, he has remained—to his great misfortune—till the last three hundred years isolated on that vast island of Central Africa, which has probably continued as dry land during ages which have seen the whole of Europe, and Eastern and Southern Asia, sink more than once beneath the sea: then it is possible, and even probable, that during these long ages of the Negro's history, creed after creed, ceremonial after ceremonial, may have grown up and died out among the different tribes; and that any worship, or quasi-worship, which may linger among the Negroes now, are likely to be the mere dregs and fragments of those older superstitions.

As a fact, Obeah is rather to be ranked, it seems to me, with those ancient Eastern mysteries, at once magical and profligate, which troubled society and morals in later Rome, when

'In Tiberim defluxit Orontes.'

If so, we shall not be surprised to find that a very important, indeed the most practically important element of Obeah, is poisoning. This habit of poisoning has not (as one might well suppose) sprung up among the slaves desirous of revenge against their white masters. It has been imported, like the rest of the system, from Africa. Travellers of late have told us enough— and too much for our comfort of mind—of that prevailing dread of poison as well as of magic which urges the African Negroes to deeds of horrible cruelty; and the fact that these African Negroes, up to the very latest importations, are the special practisers of Obeah, is notorious through the West Indies. The existence of this trick of poisoning is denied, often enough. Sometimes Europeans, willing to believe the best of their fellow-men—and who shall blame them?—simply disbelieve it because it is unpleasant to believe. Sometimes, again, white West Indians will deny it, and the existence of Obeah beside, simply because they believe in it a little too much, and are afraid of the Negroes knowing that they believe in it. Not two generations ago there might be found, up and down the islands, respectable white men and women who had the same half-belief in the powers of an Obeah-man as our own ancestors, especially in the Highlands and in Devonshire, had in those of witches: while as to poisoning, it was, in some islands, a matter on which the less said the safer. It was but a few years ago that in a West Indian city an old and faithful free servant, in a family well known to me, astonished her master, on her death-bed, by a voluntary confession of more than a dozen murders.

'You remember such and such a party, when every one was ill? Well, I put something in the soup.'

As another instance; a woman who died respectable, a Christian and a communicant, told this to her clergyman :—She had lived from youth, for many years, happily and faithfully with a white gentleman who considered her as his wife. She saw him pine away and die from slow poison, administered, she knew, by another woman whom he had wronged. But she dared not speak. She had not courage enough to be poisoned herself likewise.

It is easy to conceive the terrorism, and the exactions in the shape of fowls, plantains, rum, and so forth, which are at the command of an Obeah practitioner, who is believed by the Negro to be invulnerable himself, while he is both able and willing to destroy them. Nothing but the strong arm of English law can put down the sorcerer; and that seldom enough, owing to the poor folks' dread of giving evidence. Thus a woman, Madame Phyllis by name, ruled in a certain forest-hamlet of Trinidad. Like Deborah of old, she sat under her own palm-tree, and judged her little Israel—by the Devil's law instead of God's. Her murders (or supposed murders) were notorious: but no evidence could be obtained; Madame Phyllis dealt in poisons, charms, and philtres; and waxed fat on her trade for many a year. The first shock her reputation received was from a friend of mine, who, in his Government duty, planned out a road which ran somewhat nearer her dwelling than was pleasant or safe for her privacy. She came out denouncing, threatening. The coloured workmen dared not proceed. My friend persevered coolly; and Madame, finding that the Government official considered himself Obeah-proof, tried to bribe him off, with the foolish cunning of a savage, with a present of—bottled beer. To the horror of his workmen, he accepted—for the day was hot, as usual—a single bottle; and drank it there and then. The Negroes looked—like the honest Maltese at St. Paul—'when he should have swollen, or fallen down dead suddenly': but nothing happened; and they went on with their work, secure under a leader whom even Madame Phyllis dared not poison. But he ran a great risk; and knew it.

'I took care,' said he, 'to see that the cork had not been drawn and put back again; and then, to draw it myself.'

At last Madame Phyllis's cup was full, and she fell into the snare which she had set for others. For a certain coloured policeman went off to her one night; and having poured out his love-lorn heart, and the agonies which he endured from the cruelty of a neighbouring fair, he begged for, got, and paid for a philtre to win her affections. On which, saying with Danton —'Que mon nom soit flétri, mais que la patrie soit libre,' he carried the philtre to the magistrate; laid his information; and Madame Phyllis and her male accomplice were sent to gaol as rogues and impostors.

Her coloured victims looked on aghast at the audacity of English lawyers. But when they found that Madame was actually going to prison, they rose—just as if they had been French Republicans—deposed their despot after she had been taken prisoner, sacked her magic castle, and levelled it with the ground. Whether they did, or did not, find skeletons of children buried under the floor, or what they found at all, I could not discover; and should be very careful how I believed any statement about the matter. But what they wanted specially to find was the skeleton of a certain rival Obeah-man, who having, some years before, rashly challenged Madame to a trial of skill, had gone to visit her one night, and never left her cottage again.

The chief centre of this detestable system is St. Vincent, where—so I was told by one who knows that island well—some sort of secret College, or School of the Prophets Diabolic, exists. Its emissaries spread over the islands, fattening themselves at the expense of their dupes, and exercising no small political authority, which has been ere now, and may be again, dangerous to society. In Jamaica, I was assured by a Nonconformist missionary who had long lived there, Obeah is by no means on the decrease; and in Hayti it is probably on the increase, and taking—at least until the fall and death of Salnave—shapes which, when made public in the civilised world, will excite more than mere disgust. But of Hayti I shall be silent; having heard more of the state of society in that unhappy place than it is prudent, for the sake of the few white residents, to tell at present.

The same missionary told me that in Sierra Leone, also, Obeah and poisoning go hand in hand. Arriving home one night, he said, with two friends, he heard hideous screams from the house of a Portuguese Negro, a known Obeah-man. Fearing that murder was being done, they burst open his door, and found that he had tied up his wife hand and foot, and was flogging her horribly. They cut the poor creature down, and placed her in safety.

A day or two after, the missionary's servant came in at sunrise with a mysterious air.

'You no go out just now, massa.'

There was something in the road: but what, he would not tell. My friend went out, of course, in spite of the faithful fellow's entreaties; and found, as he expected, a bottle containing the usual charms, and round it—sight of horror to all Negroes of the old school—three white cocks' heads—an old remnant, it is said, of a worship 'de quo sileat musa'—pointing their beaks, one to his door, one to the door of each of his friends. He picked them up, laughing, and threw them away, to the horror of his servant.

But the Obeah-man was not so easily beaten. In a few days the servant came in again with a wise visage.

'You no drink a milk to-day, massa.'

'Why not?'

'Oh, perhaps something bad in it. You give it a cat.'

'But I don't want to poison the cat!'

'Oh, dere a strange cat in a stable; me give it her.'

He did so; and the cat was dead in half an hour.

Again the fellow tried, watching when the three white men, as was their custom, should dine together, that he might poison them all. And again the black servant foiled him, though afraid to accuse him openly. This time it was—'You no drink a water in a filter.' And when the filter was searched, it was full of poison-leaves.

A third attempt the rascal made with no more success; and then vanished from Sierra Leone; considering—as the Obeah-men in the West Indies are said to hold of the Catholic priests—that 'Buccra Padre's Obeah was too strong for his Obeah.'

I know not how true the prevailing belief is, that some of these Obeah-men carry a drop of snake's poison under a sharpened finger-nail, a scratch from which is death. A similar story was told to Humboldt of a tribe of Indians on the Orinoco; and the thing is possible enough. One story, which seemingly corroborates it, I heard, so curiously illustrative of Negro manners in Trinidad during the last generation, that I shall give it at length. I owe it—as I do many curious facts—to the kindness of Mr. Lionel Fraser, chief of police of the Port of Spain, to whom it was told, as it here stands, by the late Mr. R——, stipendiary magistrate; himself a Creole and a man of colour:—

'When I was a lad of about seventeen years of age, I was very frequently on a sugar-estate belonging to a relation of mine; and during crop-time particularly I took good care to be there.

'Owing to my connection with the owner of the estate, I naturally had some authority with the people; and I did my best to preserve order amongst them, particularly in the boiling-house, where there used to be a good deal of petty theft, especially at night; for we had not then the powerful machinery which enables the planter to commence his grinding late and finish it early.

'There was one African on the estate who was the terror of the Negroes, owing to his reputed supernatural powers as an Obeah-man.

'This man, whom I will call Martin, was a tall, powerful Negro, who, even apart from the mysterious powers with which he was supposed to be invested, was a formidable opponent from his mere size and strength.

'I very soon found that Martin was determined to try his authority and influence against mine; and I resolved to give him the earliest possible opportunity for doing so.

'I remember the occasion when we first came into contact perfectly well. It was a Saturday night, and we were boiling off. The boiling-house was but very dimly lighted by two murky oil-lamps, the rays from which could scarcely penetrate through the dense atmosphere of steam which rose from the seething coppers. Occasionally a bright glow from the furnace-mouths lighted up the scene for a single instant, only to leave it the next moment darker than ever.

'It was during one of these flashes of light that I distinctly saw Martin deliberately filling a large tin pan with sugar from one of the coolers.

'I called out to him to desist; but he never deigned to take the slightest notice of me. I repeated my order in a louder and more angry tone; whereupon he turned his eyes upon me, and said, in a most contemptuous tone, "Chut, ti bequé: quitté moué tranquille, ou tende sinon malheur ka rivé ou." (Pshaw, little white boy: leave me alone, or worse will happen to you.)

'It was the tone more than the words themselves that enraged me; and without for one moment reflecting on the great disparity between us, I made a spring from the sort of raised platform on which I stood, and snatching the panful of sugar from

R   AT L.

his hand, I flung it, sugar and all, into the tache, from which I knew nothing short of a miracle could recover it.

'For a moment only did Martin hesitate; and then, after fumbling for one instant with his right hand in his girdle, he made a rush at me. Fortunately for me, I was prepared; and springing back to the spot where I had before been standing, I took up a light cutlass, which I always carried about with me, and stood on the defensive.

'I had, however, no occasion to use the weapon; for, in running towards me, Martin's foot slipped in some molasses which had been spilt on the ground, and he fell heavily to the floor, striking his head against the corner of one of the large wooden sugar-coolers.

'The blow stunned him for the time, and before he recovered I had left the boiling-house.

'The next day, to my surprise, I found him excessively civil, and almost obsequious: but I noticed that he had taken a violent dislike to our head overseer, whom I shall call Jean Marie, and whom he seemed to suspect as the person who had betrayed him to me when stealing the sugar.

'Things went on pretty quietly for some weeks, till the crop was nearly over.

'One afternoon Jean Marie told me there was to be a Jumby-dance amongst the Africans on the estate that very night. Now Jumby-dances were even then becoming less frequent, and I was extremely anxious to see one; and after a good deal of difficulty, I succeeded in persuading Jean Marie to accompany me to the hut wherein it was to be held.

'It was a miserable kind of an ajoupa near the river-side; and we had some difficulty in making our way to it through the tangled dank grass and brushwood which surrounded it. Nor was the journey rendered more pleasant by the constant rustling among this undergrowth, that reminded us that there were such things as snakes and other ugly creatures to be met with on our road.

'Curiosity, however, urged us on; and at length we reached the ajoupa, which was built on a small open space near the river, beneath a gigantic silk-cotton tree.

'Here we found assembled some thirty Africans, men and women, very scantily dressed, and with necklaces of beads, sharks' teeth, dried frogs, etc., hung round their necks. They were all squatted on their haunches outside the hut, apparently waiting for a signal to go in.

'They did not seem particularly pleased at seeing us; and one of the men said something in African, apparently addressed to some one inside the house; for an instant after the door was flung open, and Martin, almost naked, and with his body painted to represent a skeleton, stalked forth to meet us.

'He asked us very angrily what we wanted there, and seemed

particularly annoyed at seeing Jean Marie. However, on my repeated assurances that we only came to see what was going on, he at last consented to our remaining to see the dance ; only cautioning us that we must keep perfect silence, and that a word, much more a laugh, would entail most serious consequences.

'As long as I live I shall never forget that scene. The hut was lighted by some eight or ten candles or lamps ; and in the centre, dimly visible, was a Fêtish, somewhat of the appearance of a man, but with the head of a cock. Everything that the coarsest fancy could invent had been done to make this image horrible ; and yet it appeared to be the object of special adoration to the devotees assembled.

'Jean Marie, to be out of the way, clambered on to one of the cross-beams that supported the roof, whilst I leaned against the side wall, as near as I could get to the aperture that served for a window, to avoid the smells, which were overpowering.

'Martin took his seat astride of an African tom-tom or drum ; and I noticed at the time that Jean Marie's naked foot hung down from the cross-beam almost directly over Martin's head.

'Martin now began to chant a monotonous African song, accompanying with the tom-tom.

'Gradually he began to quicken the measure ; quicker went the words ; quicker beat the drum ; and suddenly one of the women sprang into the open space in front of the Fêtish. Round and round she went, keeping admirable time with the music.

'Quicker still went the drum. And now the whole of the woman's body seemed electrified by it ; and, as if catching the infection, a man now joined her in the mad dance. Couple after couple entered the arena, and a true sorcerers' sabbath began ; while light after light was extinguished, till at last but one remained ; by whose dim ray I could just perceive the faint outlines of the remaining persons.

'At this moment, from some cause or other, Jean Marie burst into a loud laugh.

'Instantly the drum stopped ; and I distinctly saw Martin raise his right hand, and, as it appeared to me, seize Jean Marie's naked foot between his finger and thumb.

'As he did so, Jean Marie, with a terrible scream, which I shall never forget, fell to the ground in strong convulsions.

'We succeeded in getting him outside. But he never spoke again ; and died two hours afterwards, his body having swollen up like that of a drowned man.

'In those days there were no inquests ; and but little interest was created by the affair. Martin himself soon after died.'

But enough of these abominations, of which I am forced to omit the worst.

That day—to go on with my own story—I left the rest of the party to go down to the court-house, while I stayed at the camp, sorry to lose so curious a scene, but too tired to face a crowded tropic court, and an atmosphere of perspiration and perjury.

Moreover, that had befallen me which might never befall me again—I had a chance of being alone in the forests; and into them I would wander, and meditate on them in silence.

So, when all had departed, I lounged awhile in the rocking-chair, watching two Negroes astride on the roof of a shed, on which they were nailing shingles. Their heads were bare; the sun was intense; the roof on which they sat must have been of the temperature of an average frying-pan on an English fire: but the good fellows worked on, steadily and carefully, though not fast, chattering and singing, evidently enjoying the very act of living, and fattening in the genial heat. Lucky dogs: who had probably never known hunger, certainly never known cold; never known, possibly, a single animal want which they could not satisfy. I could not but compare their lot with that of an average English artisan. Ah, well: there is no use in fruitless comparisons; and it is no reason that one should grudge the Negro what he has, because others, who deserve it certainly as much as he, have it not. After all, the ancestors of these Negroes have been, for centuries past, so hard-worked, ill-fed, ill-used too—sometimes worse than ill-used—that it is hard if the descendants may not have a holiday, and take the world easy for a generation or two.

The perpetual Saturnalia in which the Negro, in Trinidad at least, lives, will surely give physical strength and health to the body, and something of cheerfulness, self-help, independence to the spirit. If the Saturnalia be prolonged too far, and run, as they seem inclined to run, into brutality and licence, those stern laws of Nature which men call political economy will pull the Negro up short, and waken him out of his dream, soon enough and sharply enough—a 'judgment' by which the wise will profit and be preserved, while the fools only will be destroyed. And meanwhile, what if in these Saturnalia (as in Rome of old) the new sense of independence manifests itself in somewhat of self-assertion and rudeness, often in insolence, especially disagreeable, because deliberate? What if 'You call me black fellow? I mash you white face in,' were the first words one heard at St. Thomas's from a Negro, on being asked, civilly enough, by a sailor to cast off from a boat to which he had no right to be holding on? What if a Negro now and then addresses you as simple 'Buccra,' while he expects you to call him 'Sir'; or if a Negro woman, on being begged by an English lady to call to another Negro woman, answers at last, after long pretences not to hear, 'You coloured lady! you hear dis white woman a wanting of you'? Let it be. We white people bullied these black people quite enough for three hundred years, to be able to allow them to play (for it is no more) at bullying us. As long as the Negroes are decently loyal and peaceable, and do not murder their magistrates and drink their brains mixed with rum, nor send delegates to the President of Hayti to ask if he will assist them, in case of a general rising, to exterminate the whites—tricks which the harmless Negroes of Trinidad, to do them justice, never have played, or had a thought of playing—we must remember that we are very seriously in debt to the Negro, and must allow him to take out instalments of his debt, now and then, in his own fashion. After all, we brought him here, and we have no right to complain of our own work. If, like Frankenstein, we have tried to make a man, and made him badly; we must, like Frankenstein, pay the penalty.

So much for the Negro. As for the coloured population—especially the educated and civilised coloured population of the towns—they stand to us in an altogether different relation. They claim to be, and are, our kinsfolk, on another ground than that of common humanity. We are bound to them by a tie more sacred, I had almost said more stern, than we are to the mere Negro. They claim, and justly, to be considered as our kinsfolk and equals; and I believe, from what I have seen of them, that they will prove themselves such, whenever they are treated as they are in Trinidad. What faults some of them have, proceed mainly from a not dishonourable ambition, mixed with uncertainty of their own position. Let them be made to feel that they are now not a class; to forget, if possible, that they ever were one. Let any allusion to the painful past be treated, not merely as an offence against good manners, but as what it practically is, an offence against the British Government; and that Government will find in them, I believe, loyal citizens and able servants.

But to go back to the forest. I sauntered forth with cutlass and collecting-box, careless whither I went, and careless of what I saw; for everything that I could see would be worth seeing. I know not that I found many rare or new things that day. I recollect, amid the endless variety of objects, Film-ferns of various delicate species, some growing in the moss tree-trunks, some clasping the trunk itself by horizontal lateral fronds, while the main rachis climbed straight up many feet, thus embracing the stem in a network of semi-transparent green Guipure lace. I recollect, too, a coarse low fern[1] on stream-gravel which was remarkable, because its stem was set with thick green prickles. I recollect, too, a dead giant tree, the ruins of which struck me with awe. The stump stood some thirty feet high, crumbling into tinder and dust, though its death was so recent that the creepers and parasites had not yet had time to lay hold of it, and around its great spur-roots lay what had been its trunk

[1] *Pteris podophylla.*

and head, piled in stacks of rotten wood, over which I scrambled with some caution, for fear my leg, on breaking through, might be saluted from the inside by some deadly snake. The only sign of animal life, however, I found about the tree, save a few millipedes and land snails, were some lizard-eggs in a crack, about the size of those of a humming-bird.

I scrambled down on gravelly beaches, and gazed up the green avenues of the brooks. I sat amid the Balisiers and Aroumas, above still blue pools, bridged by huge fallen trunks, or with wild Pines of half a dozen kinds set in rows: I watched the shoals of fish play in and out of the black logs at the bottom: I gave myself up to the simple enjoyment of looking, careless of what I looked at, or what I thought about it all. There are times when the mind, like the body, had best feed, gorge if you will, and leave the digestion of its food to the unconscious alchemy of nature. It is as unwise to be always saying to oneself, 'Into what pigeon-hole of my brain ought I to put this fact, and what conclusion ought I to draw from it?' as to ask your teeth how they intend to chew, and your gastric juice how it intends to convert your three courses and a dessert into chyle. Whether on a Scotch moor or in a tropic forest, it is well at times to have full faith in Nature; to resign yourself to her, as a child upon a holiday; to be still and let her speak. She knows best what to say.

And yet I could not altogether do it that day. There was one class of objects in the forest which I had set my heart on examining, with all my eyes and soul; and after a while, I scrambled and hewed my way to them, and was well repaid for a quarter of an hour's very hard work.

I had remarked, from the camp, palms unlike any I had seen before, starring the opposite forest with pale gray-green leaves. Long and earnestly I had scanned them through the glasses. Now was the time to see them close, and from beneath. I soon guessed (and rightly) that I was looking at that Palma de Jagua,[1] which excited—and no wonder—the enthusiasm of the usually unimpassioned Humboldt. Magnificent as the tree is when its radiating leaves are viewed from above, it is even more magnificent when you stand beneath it. The stem, like that of the Coco-nut, usually curves the height of a man ere it rises in a shaft for fifty or sixty feet more. From the summit of that shaft springs a crown—I had rather say, a fountain—of pinnated leaves; only eight or ten of them; but five-and-twenty feet long each. For three-fourths of their length they rise at an angle of 45° or more; for the last fourth they fall over, till the point hangs straight down; and each leaflet, which is about two feet and a half long, falls over in a similar curve, completing the likeness of the whole to a foun-

---

[1] *Jessenia.*

tain of water, or a gush of rockets. I stood and looked up, watching the innumerable curled leaflets, pale green above and silver-gray below, shiver and rattle amid the denser foliage of the broad-leaved trees; and then went on to another and to another, to stare up again, and enjoy the mere shape of the most beautiful plant I had ever beheld, excepting always the Mûsa Ensete, from Abyssinia, in the Palm-house at Kew. Truly spoke Humboldt, of this or a closely allied species, 'Nature has lavished every beauty of form on the Jagua Palm.'

But here, as elsewhere to my great regret, I looked in vain for that famous and beautiful tree, the Piriajo,[1] or 'Peach Palm,' which is described in Mr. Bates's book, vol ii. p. 218, under the name of Pupunha. It grows here and there in the island, and always marks the site of an ancient Indian settlement. This is probable enough, for 'it grows,' says Mr. Bates, 'wild nowhere on the Amazons. It is one of those few vegetable productions (including three kinds of Manioc and the American species of Banana) which the Indians have cultivated from time immemorial, and brought with them in their original migration to Brazil.' From whence? It has never yet been found wild; 'its native home may possibly,' Mr. Bates thinks, 'be in some still unexplored tract on the eastern slopes of the Æquatorial Andes.' Possibly so: and possibly, again, on tracts long sunk beneath the sea. He describes the tree as 'a noble ornament, from fifty to sixty feet in height, and often as straight as a scaffold-pole. The taste of the fruit may be compared to a mixture of chestnuts and cheese. Vultures devour it greedily, and come in quarrelsome flocks to the trees when it is ripe. Dogs will also eat it. I do not recollect seeing cats do the same, though they will go into the woods to eat Tucuma, another kind of palm fruit.'

'It is only the more advanced tribes,' says Mr. Bates, 'who have kept up the cultivation. . . . Bunches of sterile or seedless fruits'—a mark of very long cultivation, as in the case of the Plantain—'occur. . . . It is one of the principal articles of food at Ega when in season, and is boiled and eaten with treacle or salt. A dozen of the seedless fruits make a good nourishing meal for a full-grown person. It is the general belief that there is more nutriment in Pupunha than in fish, or Vacca Marina (Manati).'

My friend Mr. Bates will, I am sure, excuse my borrowing so much from him about a tree which must be as significant in his eyes as it is in mine.

So passed many hours, till I began to be tired of—I may almost say, pained by—the appalling silence and loneliness; and I was glad to get back to a point where I could hear the click of the axes in the clearing. I welcomed it just as, after a

---

[1] *Guliclma speciosa.*

long night on a calm sea, when one nears the harbour again, one welcomes the sound of the children's voices and the stir of life about the quay, as a relief from the utter blank, and feels oneself no longer a bubble afloat on an infinity which knows one not, and cares nothing for one's existence. For in the dead stillness of mid-day, when not only the deer, and the agoutis, and the armadillos, but the birds and insects likewise, are all asleep, the crack of a falling branch was all that struck my ear, as I tried in vain to verify the truth of that beautiful passage of Humboldt's — true, doubtless, in other forests, or for ears more acute than mine. 'In the mid-day,' he says,[1] 'the larger animals seek shelter in the recesses of the forest, and the birds hide themselves under the thick foliage of the trees, or in the clefts of the rocks: but if, in this apparent entire stillness of nature, one listens for the faintest tones which an attentive ear can seize, there is perceived an all-pervading rustling sound, a humming and fluttering of insects close to the ground, and in the lower strata of the atmosphere. Everything announces a world of organic activity and life. In every bush, in the cracked bark of the trees, in the earth undermined by hymenopterous insects, life stirs audibly. It is, as it were, one of the many voices of Nature, and can only be heard by the sensitive and reverent ear of her true votaries.'

Be not too severe, great master. A man's ear may be reverent enough: but you must forgive its not being sensitive while it is recovering from that most deafening of plagues, a tropic cold in the head.

Would that I had space to tell at length of our long and delightful journey back the next day, which lay for several miles along the path by which we came, and then, after we had looked down once more on the exquisite bay of Fillette, kept along the northern wall of the mountains, instead of turning up to the slope which we came over out of Caura. For miles we paced a mule-path, narrow, but well kept—as it had need to be; for a fall would have involved a roll into green abysses, from which we should probably not have reascended. Again the surf rolled softly far below; and here and there a vista through the trees showed us some view of the sea and woodlands almost as beautiful as that at Fillette. Ever and anon some fresh valuable tree or plant, wasting in the wilderness, was pointed out. More than once we became aware of a keen and dreadful scent, as of a concentrated essence of unwashed tropic humanity, which proceeded from that strange animal, the porcupine with a prehensile tail,[2] who prowls in the tree-tops all night, and sleeps in them all day, spending his idle hours in making this hideous smell. Probably he or his ancestors have found it pay as a protection; for no jaguar or tiger-cat, it is to be presumed,

---

[1] *Aspects of Nature*, vol. ii. p. 272. [2] *Synetheres*.

would care to meddle with anything so exquisitely nasty, especially when it is all over sharp prickles.

Once—I should know the spot again among a thousand—where we scrambled over a stony brook just like one in a Devonshire wood, the boulders and the little pools between them swarmed with things like scarlet and orange fingers, or sticks of sealing-wax, which we recognised, and, looking up, saw a magnificent Bois Châtaigne,[1]—Pachira, as the Indians call it,—like a great horse-chestnut, spreading its heavy boughs overhead. And these were the fallen petals of its last-night's crop of flowers, which had opened there, under the moonlight, unseen and alone. Unseen and alone? How do we know that?

Then we emerged upon a beach, the very perfection of typical tropic shore, with little rocky coves, from one to another of which we had to ride through rolling surf, beneath the welcome shade of low shrub-fringed cliffs; while over the little mangrove-swamp at the mouth of the glen, Tocuche rose sheer, like M'Gillicuddy's Reeks transfigured into one huge emerald.

We turned inland again, and stopped for luncheon at a clear brook, running through a grove of Cacao and Bois Immortelles. We sat beneath the shade of a huge Bamboo clump; cut ourselves pint-stoups out of the joints; and then, like great boys, got, some of us at least, very wet in fruitless attempts to catch a huge cray-fish nigh eighteen inches long, blue and gray, and of a shape something between a gnat and a spider, who, with a wife and child, had taken up his abode in a pool among the spurs of a great Bois Immortelle. However, he was too nimble for us; and we went on, and inland once more, luckily not leaving our bamboo stoups behind.

We descended, I remember, to the sea-shore again, at a certain Maraccas Bay, and had a long ride along bright sands, between surf and scrub; in which ride, by the by, the civiliser of Montserrat and I, to avoid the blinding glare of the sand, rode along the firm sand between the sea and the lagoon, through the low wood of Shore Grape and Mahaut, Pinguin and Swamp Seguine[2] —which last is an Arum with a knotted stem, from three to twelve feet high. We brushed our way along with our cutlasses, as we sat on our saddles, enjoying the cool shade; till my companion's mule found herself jammed tight in scrub, and unable to forge either ahead or astern. Her rider was jammed too, and unable to get off; and the two had to be cut out of the bush by fair hewing, amid much laughter, while the wise old mule, as the cutlasses flashed close to her nose, never moved a muscle, perfectly well aware of what had happened, and how she was to be got out of the scrape, as she had been probably fifty times before.

We stopped at the end of the long beach, thoroughly tired

[1] *Carolinea insignis.*   [2] *Montrichardia.*

and hungry, for we had been on the march many hours; and discovered for the first time that we had nothing left to eat. Luckily, a certain little pot of 'Ramornie' essence of soup was recollected and brought out. The kettle was boiling in five minutes, and half a teaspoonful per man of the essence put on a knife's point, and stirred with a cutlass, to the astonishment of the grinning and unbelieving Negroes, who were told that we were going to make Obeah soup, and were more than half of that opinion themselves. Meanwhile, I saw the wise mule led up into the bush; and, on asking its owner why, was told that she was to be fed—on what, I could not see. But, much to my amusement, he cut down a quantity of the young leaves of the Cocorite palm; and she began to eat them greedily, as did my police-horse. And, when the bamboo stoups were brought out, and three-quarters of a pint of good soup was served round— not forgetting the Negroes, one of whom, after sucking it down, rubbed his stomach, and declared, with a grin, that it was very good Obeah—the oddness of the scene came over me. The blazing beach, the misty mountains, the hot trade-wind, the fantastic leaves overhead, the black limbs and faces, the horses eating palm-leaves, and we sitting on logs among the strange ungainly Montrichardias, drinking 'Ramornie' out of bamboo, washing it down with milk from green coco-nuts—was this, too, a scene in a pantomime? Would it, too, vanish if one only shut one's eyes and shook one's head?

We turned up into the loveliest green trace, where, I know not how, the mountain vegetation had, some of it, come down to the sea-level. Nowhere did I see the Melastomas more luxuriant; and among them, arching over our heads like parasols of green lace, between us and the sky, were tall tree-ferns, as fine as those on the mountain slopes.

In front of us opened a flat meadow of a few acres; and beyond it, spur upon spur, rose a noble mountain, in so steep a wall that it was difficult to see how we were to ascend.

Ere we got to the mountain foot, some of our party had nigh come to grief. For across the Savanna wandered a deep lagoon brook. The only bridge had been washed away by rains; and we had to get the horses through as we could, all but swimming them, two men on each horse; and then to drive the poor creatures back for a fresh double load, with fallings, splashings, much laughter, and a qualm or two at the recollection that there might be unpleasant animals in the water. Electric eels, happily, were not invented at the time when Trinidad parted from the Main, or at least had not spread so far east: but alligators had been by that time fully developed, and had arrived here in plenty; and to be laid hold of by one, would have been undesirable; though our party was strong enough to have made very short work with the monster.

So over we got, and through much mud, and up mountains

A TROPIC BEACH.

some fifteen hundred feet high, on which the vegetation was even richer than any we had seen before ; and down the other side, with the great lowland and the Gulf of Paria opening before us. We rested at a police-station—always a pleasant sight in Trinidad, for the sake of the stalwart soldier-like brown policemen and their buxom wives, and neat houses and gardens a focus of discipline and civilisation amid what would otherwise relapse too soon into anarchy and barbarism ; we whiled away the time by inspecting the ward police reports, which were kept as neatly, and worded as well, as they would have been in England ; and then rolled comfortably in the carriage down to Port of Spain, tired and happy, after three such days as had made old blood and old brains young again.

CHAPTER XII

THE SAVANNA OF ARIPO

THE last of my pleasant rides, and one which would have been perhaps the pleasantest of all, had I had (as on other occasions) the company of my host, was to the Cocal, or Coco-palm grove, of the east coast, taking on my way the Savanna of Aripo. It had been our wish to go up the Orinoco, as far as Ciudad Bolivar (the Angostura of Humboldt's travels), to see the new capital of Southern Venezuela, fast rising into wealth and importance under the wise and pacific policy of its president, Señor Dalla Costa, a man said to possess a genius and an integrity far superior to the average of South American Republicans—of which latter the less said the better; to push back, if possible, across those Llanos which Humboldt describes in his *Personal Narrative*, vol. iv. p. 295; it may be to visit the Falls of the Caroni. But that had to be done by others, after we were gone. My days in the island were growing short; and the most I could do was to see at Aripo a small specimen of that peculiar Savanna vegetation, which occupies thousands of square miles on the mainland.

If, therefore, the reader cares nothing for botanical and geological speculations, he will be wise to skip this chapter. But those who are interested in the vast changes of level and distribution of land which have taken place all over the world since the present forms of animals and vegetables were established on it, may possibly find a valuable fact or two in what I thought I saw at the Savanna of Aripo.

My first point was, of course, the little city of San Josef. To an Englishman, the place will be always interesting as the scene of Raleigh's exploit, and the capture of Berreos; and, to one who has received the kindness which I have received from the Spanish gentlemen of the neighbourhood, a spot full of most grateful memories. It lies pleasantly enough, on a rise at the southern foot of the mountains, and at the mouth of a torrent which comes down from the famous 'Chorro,' or waterfall, of Maraccas. In going up to that waterfall, just at the back of the town, I found buried, in several feet of earth, a great number of seemingly recent but very ancient shells. Whether they be remnants of an elevated sea-beach, or of some Indian 'kitchen-midden,' I dare not decide. But the question is well worth the attention of any geologist who may go that way. The waterfall, and the road up to it, are best described by one who, after fourteen years of hard scientific work in the island, now lies lonely in San Fernando churchyard, far from his beloved Fatherland—he, or at least all of him that could die. I wonder whether that of him which can never die, knows what his Fatherland is doing now? But to the waterfall of Maraccas, or rather to poor Dr. Krueger's description of it:—

'The northern chain of mountains, covered nearly everywhere with dense forests, is intersected at various angles by numbers of valleys presenting the most lovely character. Generally each valley is watered by a silvery stream, tumbling here and there over rocks and natural dams, ministering in a continuous rain to the strange-looking river-canes, dumb-canes, and balisiers that voluptuously bend their heads to the drizzly shower which plays incessantly on their glistening leaves, off which the globules roll in a thousand pearls, as from the glossy plumage of a stately swan.

'One of these falls deserves particular notice—the Cascade of Maraccas—in the valley of that name. The high road leads up the valley a few miles, over hills, and along the windings of the river, exhibiting the varying scenery of our mountain district in the fairest style. There, on the river-side, you may admire the gigantic pepper-trees, or the silvery leaves of the Calathea, the lofty bamboo, or the fragrant Pothos, the curious Cyclanthus, or frowning nettles, some of the latter from ten to twelve feet high. But how to describe the numberless treasures which everywhere strike the eye of the wandering naturalist?

'To reach the Chorro, or Cascade, you strike to the right into a "path" that brings you first to a cacao plantation, through a few rice or maize fields, and then you enter the shade of the virgin forest. Thousands of interesting objects now attract your attention: here, the wonderful Norantea or the resplendent Calycophyllum, a Tabernæmontana or a Faramea filling the air afar off with the fragrance of their blossoms; there, a graceful Heliconia winking at you from out some dark ravine. That shrubbery above is composed of a species of Bœhmeria or Ardisia, and that scarlet flower belongs to our native Aphelandra. In the rear are one or two Philodendrons—disagreeable guests, for their smell is bad enough, and they blister when imprudently touched. There also you may see a tree-fern, though a small one. Nearer to us, and low down beneath our feet, that rich panicle of flowers belongs to a Begonia; and here also is an assemblage of ferns of the genera Asplenium, Hymenophyllum, and Trichomanes, as well as of Hepaticæ and Mosses.

But what are those yellow and purple flowers hanging above our heads? They are Bignonias and Mucunas—creepers straying from afar which have selected this spot, where they may, under the influence of the sun's beams, propagate their race. Those chain-like, fantastic, strange-looking lianes, resembling a family of boas, are Bauhinias; and beyond, through the opening you see, in the abandoned ground of some squatter's garden, the trumpet-tree (Cecropia) and the groo-groo, the characteristic plants of the rastrajo.

'Now, let us proceed on our walk; we mean the cascade:— Here it is, opposite to you, a grand spectacle indeed! From a perpendicular wall of solid rock, of more than three hundred feet, down rushes a stream of water, splitting in the air, and producing a constant shower, which renders this lovely spot singularly and deliciously cool. Nearly the whole extent of this natural wall is covered with plants, among which you can easily discern numbers of ferns and mosses, two species of Pitcairnia with beautiful red flowers, some Aroids, various nettles, and here and there a Begonia. How different such a spot would look in cold Europe! Below, in the midst of a never-failing drizzle, grow luxuriant Ardisias, Aroids, Ferns, Costas, Heliconias, Centropogons, Hydrocotyles, Cyperoids, and Grasses of various genera, Tradescantias and Commelynas, Billbergias, and, occasionally, a few small Rubiaceæ and Melastomaceæ.'

The cascade, when I saw it, was somewhat disfigured above and below. Above, the forest-fires of last year had swept the edge of the cliff, and had even crawled half-way down, leaving blackened rocks and gray stems; and below, loyal zeal had cut away only too much of the rich vegetation, to make a shed or stable, in anticipation of a visit from the Duke of Edinburgh, who did not come. A year or two, however, in this climate will heal these temporary scars, and all will be as luxuriant as ever. Indeed such scars heal only too fast here. For the paths become impassable from brush and weeds every six months, and have to be cutlassed out afresh; and when it was known that we were going up to the waterfall, a gang had to be set to work to save the lady of the party being wetted through by leaf-dew up to her shoulders, as she sat upon her horse. Pretty it was— a bit out of an older and more simple world—to see the yeoman-gentleman who had contracted for the mending of the road, and who counts among his ancestors the famous Ponce de Leon, meeting us half-way on our return; dressed more simply, and probably much poorer, than an average English yeoman: but keeping untainted the stately Castilian courtesy, as with hat in hand—I hope I need not say that my hat was at my saddle-bow all the while—he inquired whether La Señorita had found the path free from all obstructions, and so forth.

> 'The old order changes, giving place to the new:
> Lest one good custom should corrupt the world.'

But when, two hundred years hence, there are no more such gentlemen of the old school left in the world, what higher form of true civilisation shall we have invented to put in its place? None as yet. All our best civilisation, in every class, is derived from that; from the true self-respect which is founded on respect for others.

From San Josef, I was taken on in the carriage of a Spanish gentleman through Arima, a large village where an Indian colony makes those baskets and other wares from the Aroumaleaf for which Trinidad is noted; and on to his estate at Guanapo, a pleasant lowland place, with wide plantations of Cacao, only fourteen years old, but in full and most profitable bearing; rich meadows with huge clumps of bamboo; and a roomy timber-house, beautifully thatched with palm, which serves as a retreat, in the dry season, for him and his ladies, when baked out of dusty San Josef. On my way there, by the by, I espied, and gathered for the first and last time, a flower very dear to me—a crimson Passion-flower, rambling wild over the bush.

When we arrived, the sun was still so high in heaven that the kind owner offered to push on that very afternoon to the Savanna of Aripo, some five miles off. Police-horses had arrived from Arima, in one of which I recognised my trusty old brown cob of the Northern Mountains, and laid hands on him at once; and away three or four of us went, the squire leading the way on his mule, with cutlass and umbrella, both needful enough.

We went along a sandy high road, bordered by a vegetation new to me. Low trees, with wiry branches and shining evergreen leaves, which belonged, I was told, principally to the myrtle tribe, were overtopped by Jagua palms, and packed below with Pinguins; with wild pine-apples, whose rose and purple flower-heads were very beautiful; and with a species of palm of which I had often heard, but which I had never seen before, at least in any abundance, namely, the Timit,[1] the leaves of which are used as thatch. A low tree, seldom rising more than twenty or thirty feet, it throws out wedge-shaped leaves some ten or twelve feet long, sometimes all but entire, sometimes irregularly pinnate, because the space between the straight and parallel side nerves has not been filled up. These flat wedge-shaped sheets, often six feet across, and the oblong pinnæ, some three feet long by six inches to a foot in breadth, make admirable thatch; and on emergency, as we often saw that day, good umbrellas. Bundles of them lay along the roadside, tied up, ready for carrying away, and each Negro or Negress whom we passed carried a Timit-leaf, and hooked it on to his head when a gush of rain came down.

After a while we turned off the high road into a forest path, which was sound enough, the soil being one sheet of poor sand

---

[1] *Manicaria.*

and white quartz gravel, which would in Scotland, or even Devonshire, have carried nothing taller than heath, but was here covered with impenetrable jungle. The luxuriance of this jungle, be it remembered, must not delude a stranger, as it has too many ere now, into fancying that the land would be profitable under cultivation. As long as the soil is shaded and kept damp, it will bear an abundant crop of woody fibre, which, composed almost entirely of carbon and water, drains hardly any mineral constituents from the soil. But if that jungle be once cleared off, the slow and careful work of ages has been undone in a moment. The burning sun bakes up everything; and the soil, having no mineral staple wherewith to support a fresh crop if planted, is reduced to aridity and sterility for years to come. Timber, therefore, I believe, and timber only, is the proper crop for these poor soils, unless medicinal or otherwise useful trees should be discovered hereafter worth the planting. To thin out the useless timbers—but cautiously, for fear of letting in the sun's rays—and to replace them by young plants of useful timbers, is all that Government can do with the poorer bits of these Crown lands, beyond protecting (as it does now to the best of its power) the natural crop of Timit-leaves from waste and destruction. So much it ought to do; and so much it can and will do in Trinidad, which—happily for it—possesses a Government which governs, instead of leaving every man, as in the Irishman's paradise, to 'do what is right in the sight of his own eyes, and what is wrong too, av he likes.' Without such wise regulation, and even restraint, of the ignorant greediness of human toil, intent only (as in the too exclusive cultivation of the sugar-cane and of the cotton-plant) on present profits, without foresight or care for the future, the lands of warmer climates will surely fall under that curse, so well described by the venerable Elias Fries, of Lund.[1]

'A broad belt of waste land follows gradually in the steps of cultivation. If it expands, its centre and its cradle dies, and on the outer borders only do we find green shoots. But it is not impossible, only difficult, for man, without renouncing the advantage of culture itself, one day to make reparation for the injury which he has inflicted; he is the appointed lord of creation. True it is that thorns and thistles, ill-favoured and poisonous plants, well named by botanists "rubbish-plants," mark the track which man has proudly traversed through the earth. Before him lay original Nature in her wild but sublime beauty. Behind him he leaves the desert, a deformed and ruined land; for childish desire of destruction or thoughtless squandering of vegetable treasures has destroyed the character of Nature; and, terrified, man himself flies from the arena of his actions, leaving the impoverished earth to barbarous races or to animals,

---

[1] Schleiden's *Plant: a Biography.* End of Lecture xi.

so long as yet another spot in virgin beauty smiles before him. Here, again, in selfish pursuit of profit, and, consciously or unconsciously, following the abominable principle of the great moral vileness which one man has expressed—"Après nous le déluge"—he begins anew the work of destruction. Thus did cultivation, driven out, leave the East, and perhaps the Deserts formerly robbed of their coverings: like the wild hordes of old over beautiful Greece, thus rolls the conquest with fearful rapidity from east to west through America; and the planter now often leaves the already exhausted land, the eastern climate becomes infertile through the demolition of the forests, to introduce a similar revolution into the far West.'

For a couple of miles or more we trotted on through this jungle, till suddenly we saw light ahead; and in five minutes the forest ended, and a scene opened before us which made me understand the admiration which Humboldt and other travellers have expressed at the far vaster Savannas of the Orinoco.

A large sheet of gray-green grass, bordered by the forest wall, as far as the eye could see, and dotted with low bushes, weltered in mirage; while stretching out into it, some half a mile off, a gray promontory into a green sea, was an object which filled me with more awe and admiration than anything which I had seen in the island.

It was a wood of Moriche palms; like a Greek temple, many hundred yards in length, and, as I guessed, nearly a hundred feet in height; and, like a Greek temple, ending abruptly at its full height. The gray columns, perfectly straight and parallel, supported a dark roof of leaves, gray underneath, and reflecting above, from their broad fans, sheets of pale glittering light. Such serenity of grandeur I never saw in any group of trees; and when we rode up to it, and tethered our horses in its shade, it seemed to me almost irreverent not to kneel and worship in that temple not made with hands.

When we had gazed our fill, we set hastily to work to collect plants, as many as the lateness of the hour and the scalding heat would allow. A glance showed the truth of Dr. Krueger's words:—

'It is impossible to describe the feelings of the botanist when arriving at a field like this, so much unlike anything he has seen before. Here are full-blowing large Orchids, with red, white, and yellow flowers; and among the grasses, smaller ones of great variety, and as great scientific interest—Melastomaceous plants of various genera; Utricularias, Droseras, rare and various grasses, and Cyperoids of small sizes and fine kinds, with a species of Cassytha; in the water, Ceratophyllum (the well-known hornwort of the English ponds) and bog-mosses. Such a variety of forms and colours is nowhere else to be met with in the island.'

Of the Orchids, we only found one in flower; and of the rest, of course, we had time only to gather a very few of the more remarkable, among which was that lovely cousin of the Clerodendrons, the crimson Amasonia, which ought to be in all hothouses. The low bushes, I found, were that curious tree the Chaparro,[1] but not the Chaparro[2] so often mentioned by Humboldt as abounding on the Llanos. This Chaparro is remarkable, first, for the queer little Natural Order to which it belongs; secondly, for its tanning properties; thirdly, for the very nasty smell of its flowers; fourthly, for the roughness of its leaves, which make one's flesh creep, and are used, I believe, for polishing steel; and lastly, for its wide geographical range, from Isla de Pinos, near Cuba—where Columbus, to his surprise, saw true pines growing in the Tropics—all over the Llanos, and down to Brazil; an ancient, ugly, sturdy form of vegetation, able to get a scanty living out of the poorest soils, and consequently triumphant, as yet, in the battle of life.

The soil of the Savanna was a poor sandy clay, treacherous, and often impassable for horses, being half dried above and wet beneath. The vegetation grew, not over the whole, but in innumerable tussocks, which made walking very difficult. The type of the rushes and grasses was very English; but among them grew, here and there, plants which excited my astonishment; above all, certain Bladder-worts,[3] which I had expected to find, but which, when found, were so utterly unlike any English ones, that I did not recognise at first what they were. Our English Bladder-worts, as everybody knows, float in stagnant water on tangles of hair-like leaves, something like those of the Water-Ranunculus, but furnished with innumerable tiny bladders; and this raft supports the little scape of yellow snapdragon-like flowers. There are in Trinidad and other parts of South America Bladder-worts of this type. But those which we found to-day, growing out of the damp clay, were more like in habit to a delicate stalk of flax, or even a bent of grass, upright, leafless or all but leafless, with heads of small blue or yellow flowers, and carrying, in one species, a few very minute bladders about the roots, in another none at all. A strange variation from the normal type of the family; yet not so strange, after all, as that of another variety in the high mountain woods, which, finding neither ponds to float in nor swamp to root in, has taken to lodging as a parasite among the wet moss on tree-trunks; not so strange, either, as that of yet another, which floats, but in the most unexpected spots, namely, in the water which lodges between the leaf-sheaths of the wild pines, perched on the tree-boughs, a parasite on parasites; and sends out long runners, as it grows, along the bough, in search of the next wild pine and its tiny reservoirs.

---

[1] *Curatella Americana.*   [2] *Rhopala.*   [3] *Utricularia.*

In the face of such strange facts, is it very absurd to guess that these Utricularias, so like each other in their singular and highly specialised flowers, so unlike each other in the habit of the rest of the plant, have started from some one original type, perhaps long since extinct; and that, carried by birds into quite new situations, they have adapted themselves, by natural selection, to new circumstances, changing the parts which required change—the leaves and stalks; but keeping comparatively unchanged those which needed no change—the flowers?

But I was not prepared, as I should have been had I studied my Griesbach's *West Indian Flora* carefully enough beforehand, for the next proof of the wide distribution of water-plants. For as I scratched and stumbled among the tussocks, 'larding the lean earth as I stalked along,' my kind guide put into my hand, with something of an air of triumph, a little plant, which was—there was no denying it—none other than the long-leaved Sundew,[1] with its clammy-haired paws full of dead flies, just as they would have been in any bog in Devonshire or in Hampshire, in Wales or in Scotland. But how came it here? And more, how has it spread, not only over the whole of Northern Europe, Canada, and the United States, but even as far south as Brazil? Its being common to North America and Europe is not surprising. It may belong to that comparatively ancient Flora which existed when there was landway between the two continents by way of Greenland, and the bison ranged from Russia to the Rocky Mountains. But its presence within the Tropics is more probably explained by supposing that it, like the Bladder-worts, has been carried on the feet or in the crop of birds.

The Savanna itself, like those of Caroni and Piarco, offers, I suspect, a fresh proof that a branch of the Orinoco once ran along the foot of the northern mountains of Trinidad.

'It is impossible,' says Humboldt,[2] 'to cross the burning plains' (of the Orinocquan Savannas) 'without inquiring whether they have always been in the same state; or whether they have been stripped of their vegetation by some revolution of nature. The stratum of mould now found on them is very thin.... The plains were, doubtless, less bare in the fifteenth century than they are now; yet the first Conquistadores, who came from Coro, described them then as Savannas, where nothing could be perceived save the sky and the turf; which were generally destitute of trees, and difficult to traverse on account of the reverberation of heat from the soil. Why does not the great forest of the Oroonoco extend to the north, or the left bank of that river? Why does it not fill that vast space

---

[1] *Drosera longifolia.*
[2] *Personal Narrative*, vol. iv. p. 336 of H. M. Williams's translation.

that reaches as far as the Cordillera of the coast, and which is fertilised by various rivers? This question is connected with all that relates to the history of our planet. If, indulging in geological reveries, we suppose that the Steppes of America and the desert of Sahara have been stripped of their vegetation by an irruption of the ocean, or that they formed the bottom of an inland lake'—(the Sahara, as is now well known, is the quite recently elevated bed of a great sea continuous with the Atlantic)—'we may conceive that thousands of years have not sufficed for the trees and shrubs to advance toward the centre from the borders of the forests, from the skirts of the plains either naked or covered with turf, and darken so vast a space with their shade. It is more difficult to explain the origin of bare savannas enclosed in forests, than to recognise the causes which maintain forests and savannas within their ancient limits like continents and seas.'

With these words in my mind, I could not but look on the Savanna of Aripo as one of the last-made bits of dry land in Trinidad, still unfurnished with the common vegetation of the island. The two invading armies of tropical plants—one advancing from the north, off the now almost destroyed land which connected Trinidad and the Cordillera with the Antilles; the other from the south-west, off the utterly destroyed land which connected Trinidad with Guiana—met, as I fancy, ages since, on the opposite banks of a mighty river, or estuary, by which the Orinoco entered the ocean along the foot of the northern mountains. As that river-bed rose and became dry land, the two Floras crossed and intermingled. Only here and there, as at Aripo, are left patches, as it were, of a third Flora, which once spread uninterruptedly along the southern base of the Cordillera and over the lowland which is now the Gulf of Paria, along the alluvial flats of the mighty stream; and the Moriche palms of Aripo may be the lineal descendants of those which now inhabit the Llanos of the main; as those again may be the lineal descendants of the Moriches which Schomburgk found forming forests among the mountains of Guiana, up to four thousand feet above the sea. Age after age the Moriche apples floated down the stream, settling themselves on every damp spot not yet occupied by the richer vegetation of the forests, and ennobled, with their solitary grandeur, what without them would have been a dreary waste of mud and sand.

These Savannas of Trinidad stand, it must be remembered, in the very line where, on such a theory, they might be expected to stand, along the newest deposit; the great band of sand, gravel, and clay rubbish which stretches across the island at the mountain-foot, its highest point in thirty-six miles being only two hundred and twenty feet—an elevation far less than the corresponding depression of the Bocas, which has parted Trinidad from the main Cordillera. That the rubbish on this line was deposited by a river or estuary is as clear to me as that the river was either a very rapid one, or subject to violent and lofty floods, as the Orinoco is now. For so are best explained, not merely the sheets of gravel, but the huge piles of boulder which have accumulated at the mouth of the mountain gorges on the northern side.

As for the southern shore of this supposed channel of the Orinoco, it at once catches the eye of any one standing on the northern range. He must see that he is on one shore of a vast channel, the other shore of which is formed by the Montserrat, Tamana, and Manzanilla hills; far lower now than the northern range, Tamana only being over a thousand feet, but doubtless, in past ages, far higher than now. No one can doubt this who has seen the extraordinary degradation going on still about the summits, or who remembers that the strata, whether tertiary or lower chalk, have been, over the greater part of the island, upheaved, faulted, set on end, by the convulsions seemingly so common during the Miocene epoch, and since then sawn away by water and air into one rolling outline, quite independent of the dip of the strata. The whole southern two-thirds of Trinidad represent a wear and tear which is not to be counted by thousands, or hundreds of thousands, of years; and yet which, I verily believe, has taken place since the average plants, trees, and animals of the island dwelt therein.

This elevation may have well coincided with the depression of the neighbouring Gulf of Paria. That the southern portion of that gulf was once dry land; that the Serpent's Mouth did not exist when the present varieties of plants and animals were created, is matter of fact, proven by the identity of the majority of plants and animals on both shores. How else—to give a few instances out of hundreds—did the Mora, the Brazil-nut, the Cannon-ball tree: how else did the Ant-eater, the Coendou, the two Cuencos, the Guazupita deer, enter Trinidad? Humboldt —though, unfortunately, he never visited the island—saw this at a glance. While he perceived that the Indian story, how the Boca Drago to the north had been only lately broken through, had a foundation of truth, 'It cannot be doubted,' he says, 'that the Gulf of Paria was once an inland basin, and the Punta Icacque (its south-western extremity) united to the Punta Toleto, east of the Boca de Pedernales.'[1] In which case there may well have been—one may almost say there must have been—an outlet for that vast body of water which pours, often in tremendous floods, from the Pedernales' mouth of the Orinoco, as well as from those of the Tigre, Guanipa, Caroli, and other streams between it and the Cordillera on the north; and this outlet probably lay along the line now occupied by the northern Savannas of Trinidad.

[1] *Personal Narrative*, vol. v. p. 725.

So much this little natural park of Aripo taught, or seemed to teach me. But I did not learn the whole of the lesson that afternoon, or indeed till long after. There was no time then to work out such theories. The sun was getting low, and more intolerable as he sank; and to escape a sunstroke on the spot, or at least a dark ride home, we hurried off into the forest shade, after one last look at the never-to-be-forgotten Morichal, and trotted home to luxury and sleep.

CHAPTER XIII

THE COCAL

NEXT day, like the 'Young Muleteers of Grenada,' a good song which often haunted me in those days,

> 'With morning's earliest twinkle
> Again we are up and gone,'

with two horses, two mules, and a Negro and a Coolie carrying our scanty luggage in Arima baskets: but not without an expression of pity from the Negro who cleaned my boots. 'Where were we going?' To the east coast. Cuffy turned up what little nose he had. He plainly considered the east coast, and indeed Trinidad itself, as not worth looking at. 'Ah! you should go Barbadoes, sa. Dat de country to see. I Barbadian, sa.' No doubt. It is very quaint, this self-satisfaction of the Barbadian Negro. Whether or not he belonged originally to some higher race—for there are as great differences of race among Negroes as among any white men—he looks down on the Negroes, and indeed on the white men, of other islands, as beings of an inferior grade; and takes care to inform you in the first five minutes that he is 'neider C'rab nor Creole, but true Barbadian barn.' This self-conceit of his, meanwhile, is apt to make him unruly, and the cause of unruliness in others when he emigrates. The Barbadian Negroes are, I believe, the only ones who give, or ever have given, any trouble in Trinidad; and in Barbadoes itself, though the agricultural Negroes work hard and well, who that knows the West Indies knows not the insubordination of the Bridgetown boatmen, among whose hands a traveller and his luggage are, it is said, likely enough to be pulled in pieces? However, they are rather more quiet just now; for not a thousand years ago a certain steamer's captain, utterly unable to clear his quarter of the fleet of fighting, jabbering brown people, turned the steam-pipe on them. At which quite unexpected artillery they fled precipitately; and have had some rational respect for a steamer's quarter ever since.

After all, I do not deny that this man's being a Barbadian opened my heart to him at once, for old sakes' sake.

Another specimen of Negro character I was to have analysed, or tried to analyse, at the estate where I had slept. M. F—— had lately caught a black servant at the brook-side busily washing something in a calabash, and asked him what was he doing there? The conversation would have been held, of course, in French-Spanish-African—Creole patois, a language which is becoming fixed, with its own grammar and declensions, etc. A curious book on it has lately been published in Trinidad by Mr. Thomas, a coloured gentleman, who seems to be at once no mean philologer and no mean humorist. The substance of the Negro's answer was, 'Why, sir, you sent me to the town to buy a packet of sugar and a packet of salt; and coming back it rained so hard, the packets burst, and the salt was all washed into the sugar. And so—I am washing it out again.' ...

This worthy was to have been brought to me, that I might discover, if possible, by what processes of 'that which he was pleased to call his mind' he had arrived at the conclusion that such a thing could be done. Clearly, he could not plead unavoidable ignorance of the subject-matter, as might the old cook at San Josef, who, the first time her master brought home Wenham Lake ice from Port of Spain, was scandalised at the dirtiness of the 'American water,' washed off the sawdust, and dried the ice in the sun. His was a case of Handy-Andyism, as that intellectual disease may be named, after Mr. Lover's hero; like that of the Obeah-woman, when she tried to bribe the white gentleman with half a dozen of bottled beer; a case of muddleheaded craft and elaborate silliness, which keeps no proportion between the means and the end; so common in insane persons; frequent, too, among the lower Irish, such as Handy Andy; and very frequent, I am afraid, among the Negroes. But—as might have been expected—the poor boy's moral sense had proved as shaky as his intellectual powers. He had just taken a fancy to some goods of his master's; and had retreated, to enjoy them the more securely, into the southern forests, with a couple of brown policemen on his track. So he was likely to undergo a more simple investigation than that which was submitted to my analysis, viz. how he proposed to wash the salt out of the sugar.

We arrived after a while at Valencia, a scattered hamlet in the woods, with a good shop or 'store' upon a village green, under the verandah whereof lay, side by side with bottled ale and biscuit tins, bags of Carapo[1] nuts; trapezoidal brown nuts —enclosed originally in a round fruit—which ought some day to form a valuable article of export. Their bitter anthelminthic oil is said to have medicinal uses; but it will be still more useful for machinery, as it has—like that curious flat gourd the

---

[1] *Carapa Guianensis.*

Sequa[1]—the property of keeping iron from rust. The tree itself, common here and in Guiana, is one of the true Forest Giants; we saw many a noble specimen of it in our rides. Its timber is tough, not over heavy, and extensively used already in the island; while its bark is a febrifuge and tonic. In fact, it possesses all those qualities which make its brethren, the Meliaceæ, valuable throughout the Tropics. But it is not the only tree of South America whose bark may be used as a substitute for quinine. They may be counted possibly by dozens. A glance at the excellent enumerations of the uses of vegetable products to be found in Lindley's *Vegetable Kingdom* (a monument of learning) will show how God provides, how man neglects and wastes. As a single instance, the Laurels alone are known already to contain several valuable febrifuges, among which the Demerara Greenheart, or Bibiri,[2] claims perhaps the highest rank. 'Dr. Maclagan has shown,' says Dr. Lindley, 'that sulphate of Bibiri acts with rapid and complete success in arresting ague.' This tree spreads from Jamaica to the Spanish Main. It is plentiful in Trinidad; still more plentiful in Guiana; and yet all of it which reaches Europe is a little of its hard beautiful wood for the use of cabinetmakers; while in Demerara, I am assured by an eye-witness, many tons of this precious Greenheart bark are thrown away year by year. So goes the world; and man meanwhile at once boasts of his civilisation, and complains of the niggardliness of Nature.

But if I once begin on this subject I shall not know where to end.

Our way lay now for miles along a path which justified all that I had fancied about the magnificent possibilities of landscape gardening in the Tropics. A grass drive, as we should call it in England—a 'trace,' as it is called in the West Indies—some sixty feet in width, and generally carpeted with short turf, led up hill and down dale; for the land, though low, is much ridged and gullied, and there has been as yet no time to cut down the hills, or to metal the centre of the road. It led, as the land became richer, through a natural avenue even grander than those which I had already seen. The light and air, entering the trace, had called into life the undergrowth and lower boughs, till from the very turf to a hundred and fifty feet in height rose one solid green wall, spangled here and there with flowers. Below was Mamure, Roseau, Timit, Aroumas, and Tulumas,[3] mixed with Myrtles and Melastomas; then the copper Bois Mulatres among the Cocorite and Jagua palms; above them the heads of enormous broad-leaved trees of I know not how many species; and the lianes festooning all from cope to base. The crimson masses of Norantea on the highest tree-tops were here most gorgeous; but we had to

---

[1] *Feuillea cordifolia.*   [2] *Nectandra Rodiæi.*   [3] *Manna.*

beware of staring aloft too long, for fear of riding into mudholes—for the wet season would not end as yet, though dry weather was due—or, even worse, into the great Parasol-ant warrens, which threatened, besides a heavy fall, stings innumerable. At one point, I recollect, a gold-green Jacamar sat on a log and looked at me till I was within five yards of her. At another we heard the screams of Parrots; at another, the double note of the Toucan; at another, the metallic clank of the Bell-bird, or what was said to be the Bell-bird. But this note was not that solemn and sonorous toll of the Campanese of the mainland which is described by Waterton and others. It resembled rather the less poetical sound of a woman beating a saucepan to make a swarm of bees settle.

At one point we met a gang of Negroes felling timber to widen the road. Fresh fallen trees, tied together with lianes, lay everywhere. What a harvest for the botanist was among them! I longed to stay there a week to examine and collect. But time pressed; and, indeed, collecting plants in the wet season is a difficult and disappointing work. In an air saturated with moisture specimens turn black and mouldy, and drop to pieces; and unless turned over and exposed to every chance burst of sunshine, the labour of weeks is lost, if indeed meanwhile the ants, and other creeping things, have not eaten the whole into rags.

Among these Negroes was one who excited my astonishment; not merely for his size, though he was perhaps the tallest man whom I saw among the usually tall Negroes of Trinidad; but for his features, which were altogether European of the highest type; the forehead high and broad, the cheek-bones flat, the masque long and oval, and the nose aquiline and thin enough for any prince. Conscious of his own beauty and strength, he stood up among the rest as an old Macedonian might have stood up among the Egyptians he had conquered. We tried to find out his parentage. My companions presumed he was an 'African,' *i.e.* imported during the times of slavery. He said No: that he was a Creole, island born; but his father, it appeared, had been in one of our Negro regiments, and had been settled afterwards on a Government grant of land. Whether his beauty was the result of 'atavism'—of the reappearance, under the black skin and woolly hair, of some old stain of white blood; or whether, which is more probable, he came of some higher African race; one could not look at him without hopeful surmises as to the possible rise of the Negro, and as to the way in which it will come about—the only way in which any race has permanently risen, as far as I can ascertain; namely, by the appearance among them of sudden sports of nature; individuals of an altogether higher type; such a man as that terrible Dâaga, whose story has been told. If I am any judge of physiognomy, such a man as that, having—

what the Negro has not yet had — 'la carrière ouverte aux talents,' might raise, not himself merely, but a whole tribe, to an altogether new level in culture and ability.

Just after passing this gang we found, lying by the road, two large snakes, just killed, which I would gladly have preserved had it been possible. They were, the Negroes told us, 'Dormillons,' or 'Mangrove Cascabel,' a species as yet, I believe, undescribed; and, of course, here considered as very poisonous, owing to their likeness to the true Cascabel,[1] whose deadly fangs are justly dreaded by the Lapo hunter. For the Cascabel has a fancy for living in the Lapo's burrow, as does the rattlesnake in that of the prairie dog in the Western United States, and in the same friendly and harmless fashion; and is apt, when dug out, to avenge himself and his host by a bite which is fatal in a few hours. But these did not seem to me to have the heads of poisonous snakes; and, in spite of the entreaties of the terrified Negroes, I opened their mouths to judge for myself, and found them, as I expected, utterly fangless and harmless. I was not aware then that Dr. De Verteuil had stated the same fact in print; but I am glad to corroborate it, for the benefit of at least the rational people in Trinidad: for snakes, even poisonous ones, should be killed as seldom as possible. They feed on rats and vermin, and are the farmer's good friend, whether in the Tropics or in England; and to kill a snake, or even an adder—who never bites any one if he is allowed to run away—is, in nineteen cases out of twenty, mere wanton mischief.

The way was beguiled, if I recollect rightly, for some miles on, by stories about Cuba and Cuban slavery from one of our party. He described the political morality of Cuba as utterly dissolute; told stories of great sums of money voted for roads which are not made to this day, while the money had found its way into the pockets of Government officials; and, on the whole, said enough to explain the determination of the Cubans to shake off Spanish misrule, and try what they could do for themselves on this earth. He described Cuban slavery as, on the whole, mild; corporal punishment being restricted by law to a few blows, and very seldom employed: but the mildness seemed dictated rather by self-interest than by humanity. 'Ill-use our slaves?' said a Cuban to him. 'We cannot afford it. You take good care of your four-legged mules: we of our two-legged ones.' The children, it seems, are taken away from the mothers, not merely because the mothers are needed for work, but because they neglect their offspring so much that the children have more chance of living—and therefore of paying—if brought up by hand. So each estate has, or had, its crêche, as the French would call it—a great nursery, in which the little black things are reared, kindly enough, by the elder ladies of the estate. To

---

[1] *Trigonocephalus Jararaca.*

one old lady, who wearied herself all day long in washing, doctoring, and cramming the babies, my friend expressed pity for all the trouble she took about her human brood. 'Oh dear no,' answered she; 'they are a great deal easier to rear than chickens.' The system, however, is nearly at an end. Already the Cuban Revolution has produced measures of half-emancipation; and in seven years' time probably there will not be a slave in Cuba.

We waded stream after stream under the bamboo clumps, and in one of them we saw swimming a green rigoise, or whip-snake, which must have been nearly ten feet long. It swam with its head and the first two feet of its body curved aloft like a swan, while the rest of the body lay along the surface of the water in many curves—a most graceful object as it glided away into dark shadow along an oily pool. At last we reached an outlying camp, belonging to one of our party who was superintending the making of new roads in that quarter, and there rested our weary limbs, some in hammock, some on the tables, some, again, on the clay floor. Here I saw, as I saw every ten minutes, something new—that quaint vegetable plaything described by Humboldt and others; namely, the spathe of the Timit palm. It encloses, as in most palms, a branched spadix covered with innumerable round buds, most like a head of millet, two feet and a half long: but the spathe, instead of splitting and forming a hood over the flowers, as in the Cocorite and most palms, remains entire, and slips off like the finger of a glove. When slipped off, it is found to be made of two transverse layers of fibre—a bit of veritable natural lace, similar to, though far less delicate than, the famous lace-bark of the Lagetta-tree, peculiar, I believe, to one district in the Jamaica mountains. And as it is elastic and easily stretched, what hinders the brown child from pulling it out till it makes an admirable fool's cap, some two feet high, and exactly the colour of his own skin, and dancing about therein, the fat oily little Cupidon, without a particle of clothing beside? And what wonder if we grown-up whites made fools' caps too, for children on the other side of the Atlantic? During which process we found — what all said they had never seen before—that one of the spadices carried two caps, one inside the other, and one exactly like the other; a wanton superfluity of Nature, which I should like to hear explained by some morphologist.

We rode away from that hospitable group of huts, whither we were to return in two or three days; and along the green trace once more. As we rode, M—— the civiliser of Montserrat and I side by side, talking of Cuba, and staring at the Noranteas overhead, a dull sound was heard, as if the earth had opened; as indeed it had, engulfing in the mud the whole forehand of M——'s mule; and there he knelt, his beard outspread upon the clay, while the mule's visage looked patiently out from under his left arm. However, it was soft falling there. The mule was hauled out by main force. As for cleaning either her or the rider, that was not thought of in a country where they were sure to be as dirty as ever in an hour ; and so we rode on, after taking a note of the spot, and, as it happened, forgetting it again—one of us at least.

On again, along the green trace, which rose now to a ridge, with charming glimpses of wooded hills and glens to right and left; past comfortable squatters' cottages, with cacao drying on sheets at the doors or under sheds; with hedges of dwarf Erythrina, dotted with red jumby beads, and here and there that pretty climbing vetch, the Overlook.[1] I forgot, by the by, to ask whether it is planted here, as in Jamaica, to keep off the evil eye, or 'overlook'; whence its name. Nor can I guess what peculiarity about the plant can have first made the Negro fix on it as a fêtish. The genesis of folly is as difficult to analyse as the genesis of most other things.

All this while the dull thunder of the surf was growing louder and louder ; till, not as in England over a bare down, but through thickest foliage down to the high-tide mark, we rode out upon the shore, and saw before us a right noble sight ; a flat, sandy, surf-beaten shore, along which stretched, in one grand curve, lost at last in the haze of spray, fourteen miles of Coco palms.

This was the Cocal; and it was worth coming all the way from England to see it alone. I at once felt the truth of my host's saying, that if I went to the Cocal I should find myself transported suddenly from the West Indies to the East. Just such must be the shore of a Coral island in the Pacific.

These Cocos, be it understood, are probably not indigenous. They spread, it is said, from an East Indian vessel which was wrecked here. Be that as it may, they have thoroughly naturalised themselves. Every nut which falls and lies, throws out, during the wet season, its roots into the sand ; and is ready to take the place of its parent when the old tree dies down.

About thirty to fifty feet is the average height of these Coco palms, which have all, without exception, a peculiarity which I have noticed to a less degree in another sand- and shore-growing tree, the Pinaster of the French Landes. They never spring upright from the ground. The butt curves, indeed lies almost horizontal in some cases, for the lowest two or three yards ; and the whole stem, up to the top, is inclined to lean ; it matters not toward which quarter, for they lean as often toward the wind as from it, crossing each other very gracefully. I am not

---

[1] *Canavalia.*

mechanician enough to say how this curve of the stem increases their security amid loose sands and furious winds. But that it does so I can hardly doubt, when I see a similar habit in the Pinaster. Another peculiarity was noteworthy: their innumerable roots, long, fleshy, about the thickness of a large string, piercing the sand in every direction, and running down to high-tide mark, apparently enjoying the salt water, and often piercing through bivalve shells, which remained strung upon the roots. Have they a fondness for carbonate of lime, as well as for salt?

The most remarkable, and to me unexpected, peculiarity of

YOUNG COCO PALM.

a Cocal is one which I am not aware whether any writer has mentioned; namely, the prevalence of that amber hue which we remarked in the very first specimens seen at St. Thomas's. But this is, certainly, the mark which distinguishes the Coco palm, not merely from the cold dark green of the Palmiste, or the silvery gray of the Jagua, but from any other tree which I have ever seen.

When inside the Cocal, the air is full of this amber light. Gradually the eye analyses the cause of it, and finds it to be the resultant of many other hues, from bright vermilion to bright green. Above, the latticed light which breaks between

THE COCAL.

and over the innumerable leaflets of the fruit fronds comes down in warmest green. It passes not over merely, but through, the semi-transparent straw and amber of the older leaves. It falls on yellow spadices and flowers, and rich brown spathes, and on great bunches of green nuts, to acquire from them more yellow yet; for each fruit-stalk and each flower-scale at the base of the nut is veined and tipped with bright orange. It pours down the stems, semi-gray on one side, then yellow, and then, on the opposite side, covered with a powdery lichen varying in colour from orange up to clear vermilion, and spreads itself over a floor of yellow sand and brown fallen nuts, and the only vegetation of which, in general, is a long crawling Echites, with pairs of large cream-white flowers. Thus the transparent shade is flooded with gold. One looks out through it at the chequer-work of blue sky, all the more intense from its contrast; or at a long whirl of white surf and gray spray; or, turning the eyes inland toward the lagoon, at dark masses of mangrove, above which rise, black and awful, the dying balatas, stag-headed, blasted, tottering to their fall; and all as through an atmosphere of Rhine wine, or from the inside of a topaz.

We rode along, mile after mile, wondering at many things. First, the innumerable dry fruits of Timit palm, which lay everywhere; mostly single, some double, a few treble, from coalition, I suppose, of the three carpels which every female palm flower ought to have, but of which it usually develops only one. They may have been brought down the lagoon from inland by floods; but the common belief is, that most of them come from the Orinoco itself, as do also the mighty logs which lie about the beach in every stage of wear and tear; and which, as fast as they are cut up and carried away, are replaced by fresh ones. Some of these trees may actually come from the mainland, and, drifting into this curving bay, be driven on shore by the incessant trade-wind. But I suspect that many of them are the produce of the island itself; and more, that they have grown, some of them, on the very spot where they now lie. For there are, I think, evidences of subsidence going on along this coast. Inside the Cocal, two hundred yards to the westward, stretches inland a labyrinth of lagoons and mangrove swamps, impassable to most creatures save alligators and boa-constrictors. But amid this labyrinth grow everywhere mighty trees—balatas in plenty among them, in every stage of decay; dying, seemingly, by gradual submergence of their roots, and giving a ghastly and ragged appearance to the forest. At the mouth of the little river Nariva, a few miles down, is proof positive, unless I am much mistaken, of similar subsidence. For there I found trees of all sizes—roseau scrub among them—standing rooted below high-tide mark; and killed where they grew.

So we rode on, stopping now and then to pick up shells; chip-chips,[1] which are said to be excellent eating; a beautiful purple bivalve,[2] to which, in almost every case, a coralline[3] had attached itself, of a form quite new to me. A lash some eighteen inches long, single or forked; purplish as long as its coat of lime—holding the polypes—still remained, but when that was rubbed off a mere round strip of dark horn; and in both cases flexible and elastic, so that it can be coiled up and tied in knots; a very curious and graceful piece of Nature's workmanship. Among them were curious flat cake-urchins, with oval holes punched in them, so brittle that, in spite of all our care, they resolved themselves into the loose sand of which they had been originally compact; and I could therefore verify neither their genus nor their species.

These were all, if I recollect, that we found that day. The next day we came on hundreds of a most beautiful bivalve,[4] their purple colour quite fresh, their long spines often quite uninjured. Some change of the sandy bottom had unearthed a whole warren of the lovely things; and mixed with chip-chips innumerable, and with a great bivalve[5] with a thin wing along the anterior line of the shell, they strewed the shore for a quarter of a mile and more.

We came at last to a little river, or rather tideway, leading from the lagoon to the sea, which goes by the name of Doubloon River. Some adventurous Spaniard, the story goes, contracted to make a cutting which would let off the lagoon water in time of flood for the sum of one doubloon—some three pound five; spent six times the money on it; and found his cutting, when once the sea had entered, enlarge into a roaring tideway, dangerous, often impassable, and eating away the Cocal rapidly toward the south; Mother Earth, in this case at least, having known her own business better than the Spaniard.

How we took off our saddles, sat down on the sand, hallooed, waited; how a black policeman—whose house was just being carried away by the sea—appeared at last with a canoe; how we and our baggage got over one by one in the hollow log without—by seeming miracle—being swept out to sea or upset; how some horses would swim, and others would not; how the Negroes held on by the horses till they all went head over ears under the surf; and how, at last, breathless with laughter and anxiety for our scanty wardrobes, we scrambled ashore one by one into prickly roseau, re-saddled our horses in an atmosphere of long thorns, and then cut our way and theirs out through scrub into the Cocal;—all this should not be written in these pages, but drawn for the benefit of *Punch*, by him who drew the egg-stealing frog—whose pencil I longed for again and again amid the delightful mishaps of those forest rambles, in all of

---

[1] *Trigonia.* [2] *Tellina rosea.* [3] *Xiphogorgia setacea* (Milne-Edwards).
[4] *Cytherea Dione.* [5] *Mactrella alata.*

which I never heard a single grumble, or saw temper lost for a moment. We should have been rather more serious, though, than we were, had we been aware that the river-god, or presiding Jumby, of the Doubloon was probably watching us the whole time, with the intention of eating any one whom he could catch, and only kept in wholesome awe by our noise and splashing.

At last, after the sun had gone down, and it was ill picking our way among logs and ground-creepers, we were aware of lights; and soon found ourselves again in civilisation, and that of no mean kind. A large and comfortable house, only just rebuilt after a fire, stood among the palm-trees, between the sea and the lagoon; and behind it the barns, sheds, and engine-houses of the coco-works; and inside it a hearty welcome from a most agreeable German gentleman and his German engineer. A lady's hand—I am sorry to say the lady was not at home—was evident enough in the arrangements of the central room. Pretty things, a piano, and good books, especially Longfellow and Tennyson, told of cultivation and taste in that remotest wilderness. The material hospitality was what it always is in the West Indies; and we sat up long into the night around the open door, while the surf roared, and the palm-trees sighed, and the fireflies twinkled, talking of dear old Germany, and German unity, and the possibility of many things which have since proved themselves unexpectedly most possible. I went to bed, and to somewhat intermittent sleep. First, my comrades, going to bed romping, like English schoolboys, and not in the least like the effeminate and luxurious Creoles who figure in the English imagination, broke a four-post bedstead down among them with hideous roar and ruin; and had to be picked up and called to order by their elders. Next, the wind, which ranged freely through the open roof, blew my bedclothes off. Then the dogs exploded outside, probably at some henroost-robbing opossum, and had a chevy through the cocos till they tree'd their game, and bayed it to their hearts' content. Then something else exploded—and I do not deny it set me more aghast than I had been for many a day—exploded, I say, under the window, with a shriek of Hut-hut-tut-tut, hut-tut, such as I hope never to hear again. After which, dead silence; save of the surf to the east and the toads to the west. I fell asleep, wondering what animal could own so detestable a voice; and in half an hour was awoke again by another explosion; after which, happily, the thing, I suppose, went its wicked way, for I heard it no more.

I found out the next morning that the obnoxious bird was not an owl, but a large goat-sucker, a Nycteribius, I believe, who goes by the name of jumby-bird among the English Negroes: and no wonder; for most ghostly and horrible is his cry. But worse: he has but one eye, and a glance from that glaring eye, as from the basilisk of old, is certain death : and worse still, he can turn off its light as a policeman does his lantern, and become instantly invisible : opinions which, if verified by experiment, are not always found to be in accordance with facts. But that is no reason why they should not be believed.

In St. Vincent, for instance, the Negroes one evening rushed shrieking out of a boiling-house, 'Oh! Massa Robert, we all killed. Dar one great jumby-bird come in a hole a-top a roof. Oh! Massa Robert, you no go in; you killed, we killed,' etc. etc. Massa Robert went in, and could see no bird. 'Ah, Massa Robert, him darky him eye, but him see you all da same. You killed, we killed,' etc. *Da capo.*

Massa Robert was not killed: but lives still, to the great benefit of his fellow-creatures, Negroes especially. Nevertheless, the Negroes held to their opinion. He might, could, would, or should have been killed ; and was not that clear proof that they were right?

After this, who can deny that the Negro is a man and a brother, possessing the same reasoning faculties, and exercising them in exactly the same way, as three out of four white persons?

But if the night was disturbed, pleasant was the waking next morning ; pleasant the surprise at finding that the whistling and howling air-bath of the night had not given one a severe cold, or any cold at all ; pleasant to slip on flannel shirt and trousers—shoes and stockings were needless—and hurry down through a stampede of kicking, squealing mules, who were being watered ere their day's work began, under the palms to the sea; pleasant to bathe in warm surf, into which the four-eyes squattered in shoals as one ran down, and the moment they saw one safe in the water, ran up with the next wave to lie staring at the sky ; pleasant to sit and read one's book upon a log, and listen to the soft rush of the breeze in the palm-leaves, and look at a sunrise of green and gold, pink and orange, and away over the great ocean, and to recollect, with a feeling of mingled nearness and loneliness, that there was nothing save that watery void between oneself and England, and all that England held; and then, when driven in to breakfast by the morning shower, to begin a new day of seeing, and seeing, and seeing, certain that one would learn more in it than in a whole week of book-reading at home.

We spent the next morning in inspecting the works. We watched the Negroes splitting the coco-nuts with a single blow of that all-useful cutlass, which they handle with surprising dexterity and force, throwing the thick husk on one side, the fruit on the other. We saw the husk carded out by machinery into its component fibres, for coco-rope matting, coir-rope, saddle-stuffing, brushes, and a dozen other uses ; while the fruit was crushed down for the sake of its oil ; and could but wish all success to an industry which would be most profitable, both to the projectors and to the island itself, were it not for the uncertainty, rather than the scarcity, of labour. Almost everything is done, of course, by piecework. The Negro has the price of his labour almost at his own command; and when, by working really hard and well for a while, he has earned a little money, he throws up his job and goes off, careless whether the whole works stand still or not. However, all prosperity to the coco-works of Messrs. Uhrich and Gerold; and may the day soon come when the English of Trinidad, like the Ceylonese and the Dutch of Java, shall count by millions the coco-palms which they have planted along their shores, and by thousands of pounds the profit which accrues from them.

After breakfast—call it luncheon rather—we started for the lagoon. We had set our hearts on seeing Manatis ('sea-cows'), which are still not uncommon on the east coast of this island, though they have been exterminated through the rest of the West Indies since the days of Père Labat. That good missionary speaks of them in his delightful journal as already rare in the year 1695; and now, as far as I am aware, none are to be found north of Trinidad and the Spanish Main, save a few round Cuba and Jamaica. We were anxious, too, to see, if not to get, a boa-constrictor of one kind or other. For there are two kinds in the island, which may be seen alive at the Zoological Gardens in the same cage. The true Boa,[1] which is here called Mahajuel, is striped as well as spotted with two patterns, one over the other. The Huillia, Anaconda, or Water-boa,[2] bears only a few large round spots. Both are fond of the water, the Huillia living almost entirely in it; both grow to a very large size; and both are dangerous, at least to children and small animals. That there were Huillias about the place, possibly within fifty yards of the house, there was no doubt. One of our party had seen with his own eyes one of seven-and-twenty feet long killed, with a whole kid inside it, only a few miles off. The brown policeman, crossing an arm of the Guanapo only a month or two before, had been frightened by meeting one in the ford, which his excited imagination magnified so much that its head was on the one bank while its tail was on the other—a measurement which must, I think, be divided at least by three. But in the very spot in which we stood, some four years since, happened what might have been a painful tragedy. Four young ladies, whose names were mentioned to me, preferred, not wisely, a bathe in the still lagoon to one in the surf outside; and as they disported themselves, one of them felt herself seized from behind. Fancying that one of her sisters was playing tricks, she called out to her to let her alone; and looking up, saw, to her astonishment, her three sisters sitting on the bank, and herself alone.

[1] Boa-constrictor.   [2] *Eunec urnus.*

She looked back, and shrieked for help : and only just in time ; for the Huillia had her. The other three girls, to their honour, dashed in to her assistance. The brute had luckily got hold, not of her poor little body, but of her bathing-dress, and held on stupidly. The girls pulled ; the bathing-dress, which was, luckily, of thin cotton, was torn off ; the Huillia slid back again with it in his mouth into the dark labyrinth of the mangrove-roots ; and the girl was saved. Two minutes' delay, and his coils would have been round her ; and all would have been over.

The sudden daring of these lazy and stupid animals is very great. Their brain seems to act like that of the alligator or the pike, paroxysmally, and by rare fits and starts, after lying for hours motionless as if asleep. But when excited, they will attempt great deeds. Dr. De Verteuil tells a story—and if he tells it, it must be believed—of some hunters who wounded a deer. The deer ran for the stream down a bank ; but the hunters had no sooner heard it splash into the water than they heard it scream. They leapt down to the place, and found it in the coils of a Huillia, which they killed with the deer. And yet this snake, which had dared to seize a full-grown deer, could have had no hope of eating her ; for it was only seven feet long.

We set out down a foul porter-coloured creek, which soon opened out into a river, reminding us, in spite of all differences, of certain alder and willow-fringed reaches of the Thames. But here the wood which hid the margin was altogether of mangrove ; the common Rhizophoras, or black mangroves, being, of course, the most abundant. Over them, however, rose the statelier Avicennias, or white mangroves, to a height of fifty or sixty feet, and poured down from their upper branches whole streams of air-roots, which waved and creaked dolefully in the breeze overhead. But on the water was no breeze at all. The lagoon was still as glass ; the sun was sickening ; and we were glad to put up our umbrellas and look out from under them for Manatis and Boas. But the Manatis usually only come in at night, to put their heads out of water and browse on the lowest mangrove leaves ; and the Boas hide themselves so cunningly, either altogether under water, or with only the head above, that we might have passed half a dozen without seeing them. The only chance, indeed, of coming across them, is when they are travelling from lagoon to lagoon, or basking on the mud at low tide.

So all the game which we saw was a lovely white Egret,[1] its back covered with those stiff pinnated plumes which young ladies—when they can obtain them—are only too happy to wear in their hats. He, after being civil enough to wait on a bough till one of us got a sitting shot at him, heard the cap snap, thought it as well not to wait till a fresh one was put on, and

---

[1] *Ardea Garzetta.*

flapped away. He need not have troubled himself. The Negroes —but too apt to forget something or other—had forgotten to bring a spare supply; and the gun was useless.

As we descended, the left bank of the river was entirely occupied with cocos; and the contrast between them and the mangroves on the right was made all the more striking by the afternoon sun, which, as it sank behind the forest, left the mangrove wall in black shadow, while it bathed the palm-groves opposite with yellow light. In one of these palm-groves we landed, for we were right thirsty; and to drink lagoon water would be to drink cholera or fever. But there was plenty of pure water in the coco-trees, and we soon had our fill. A Negro walked—not climbed—up a stem like a four-footed animal, his legs and arms straight, his feet pressed flat against it, his hands clinging round it—a feat impossible, as far as I have seen, to an European—tossed us down plenty of green nuts; and our feast began.

Two or three blows with the cutlass, at the small end of the nut, cut off not only the pith-coat, but the point of the shell; and disclose—the nut being held carefully upright meanwhile—a cavity full of perfectly clear water, slightly sweet, and so cold (the pith-coat being a good non-conductor of heat) that you are advised, for fear of cholera, to flavour it with a little brandy. After draining this natural cup, you are presented with a natural spoon of rind, green outside and white within, and told to scoop out and eat the cream which lines the inside of the shell, a very delicious food in the opinion of Creoles. After which, if you are as curious as some of us were, you will sit down under the amber shade, and examine at leisure the construction and germination of these famous and royal nuts. Let me explain it, even at the risk of prolixity. The coat of white pith outside, with its green skin, will gradually develop and harden into that brown fibre of which matting is made. The clear water inside will gradually harden into that sweetmeat which little boys eat off stalls and barrows in the street; the first delicate deposit of which is the cream in the green nut. This is albumen, intended to nourish the young palm till it has grown leaves enough to feed on the air, and roots enough to feed on the soil; and the birth of that young palm is in itself a mystery and a miracle, well worth considering. Much has been written on it, of which I, unfortunately, have read very little; but I can at least tell what I have seen with my own eyes.

If you search among the cream-layer at the larger end of the nut, you will find, gradually separating itself from the mass, a little white lump, like the stalk of a very young mushroom. That is the ovule. In that lies the life, the 'forma formativa,' of the future tree. How that life works, according to its kind, who can tell? What it does, is this: it is locked up inside a hard woody shell, and outside that shell are several inches of tough tangled fibre. How can it get out, as soft and seemingly helpless as a baby's finger?

All know that there are three eyes in the monkey's face, as the children call it, at the butt of the nut. Two of these eyes are blind, and filled up with hard wood. They are rudiments—hints—that the nut ought to have, perhaps had uncounted ages since, not one ovule, but three, the type-number in palms. One ovule alone is left; and that is opposite the one eye which is less blind than the rest; the eye which a schoolboy feels for with his knife, when he wants to get out the milk.

As the nut lies upon the sand, in shade, and rain, and heat, that baby's finger begins boring its way, with unerring aim, out of the weakest eye. Soft itself, yet with immense wedging power, from the gradual accretion of tiny cells, it pierces the wood, and then rends right and left the tough fibrous coat. Just so may be seen—I have seen—a large flagstone lifted in a night by a crop of tiny soft toadstools which have suddenly blossomed up beneath it. The baby's finger protrudes at last, and curves upward toward the light, to commence the campaign of life: but it has meanwhile established, like a good strategist, a safe base of operations in its rear, from which it intends to draw supplies. Into the albuminous cream which lines the shell, and into the cavity where the milk once was, it throws out white fibrous vessels, which eat up the albumen for it, and at last line the whole inside of the shell with a white pith. The albumen gives it food wherewith to grow, upward and downward. Upward, the white plumule hardens into what will be a stem; the one white cotyledon which sheaths it develops into a flat, ribbed, forked, green leaf, sheathing it still; and above it fresh leaves, sheathing always at their bases, begin to form a tiny crown; and assume each, more and more, the pinnate form of the usual coco-leaf. But long ere this, from the butt of the white plumule, just outside the nut, white threads of root have struck down into the sand; and so the nut lies, chained to the ground by a bridge-like chord, which drains its albumen, through the monkey's eye, into the young plant. After a while—a few months, I believe—the draining of the nut is complete; the chord dries up—I know not how, for I had neither microscope nor time wherewith to examine—and parts; and the little plant, having got all it can out of its poor wet-nurse, casts her ungratefully off to wither on the sand; while it grows up into a stately tree, which will begin to bear fruit in six or seven years, and thenceforth continue, flowering and fruiting the whole year round without a pause, for sixty years and more.

I think I have described this—to me—'miraculum' simply enough to be understood by the non-scientific reader, if only he or she have first learned the undoubted fact—known, I find, to very few 'educated' English people—that the coco-palm which produces coir-rope, and coco-nuts, and a hundred other useful things, is not the same plant as the cacao-bush which produces chocolate, nor anything like it. I am sorry to have to insist upon this fact: but till Professor Huxley's dream—and mine—is fulfilled, and our schools deign to teach, in the intervals of Latin and Greek, some slight knowledge of this planet, and of those of its productions which are most commonly in use, even this fact may need to be re-stated more than once.

We re-embarked again, and rowed down to the river-mouth to pick up shells, and drink in the rich roaring trade breeze, after the choking atmosphere of the lagoon; and then rowed up home, tired, and infinitely amused, though neither Manati nor Boa-constrictor had been seen; and then we fell to siesta; during which—with Mr. Tennyson's forgiveness—I read myself to sleep with one of his best poems; and then went to dinner, not without a little anxiety.

For M—— (the civiliser of Montserrat) had gone off early, with mule, cutlass, and haversack, back over the Doubloon and into the wilds of Manzanilla, to settle certain disputed squatter claims, and otherwise enforce the law; and now the night had fallen, and he was not yet home. However, he rode up at last, dead beat, with a strong touch of his old swamp-fever, and having had an adventure, which had like to have proved his last. For as he rode through the Doubloon at low tide in the morning, he espied in the surf that river-god, or Jumby, of which I spoke just now; namely, the gray back-fin of a shark; and his mule espied it too, and laid back her ears, knowing well what it was. M—— rode close up to the brute. He seemed full seven feet long, and eyed him surlily, disinclined to move off; so they parted, and M—— went on his way. But his business detained him longer than he expected; when he got back to the river-mouth it was quite dark, and the tide was full high. He must either sleep on the sands, which with fever upon him would not have been over-safe, or try the passage. So he stripped, swam the mule over, tied her up, and then went back, up to his shoulders in surf; and cutlass in hand too, for that same shark might be within two yards of him. But on his second journey he had to pile on his head, first his saddle, and then his clothes and other goods; few indeed, but enough to require both hands to steady them: and so walked helpless through the surf, expecting every moment to be accosted by a set of teeth, from which he would hardly have escaped with life.

To have faced such a danger, alone and in the dark, and thoroughly well aware, as an experienced man, of its extremity, was good proof (if any had been needed) of the indomitable Scots courage of the man. Nevertheless, he said, he never felt so cold down his back as he did during that last wade. By God's blessing the shark was not there, or did not see him; and he got safe home, thankful for dinner and quinine.

Going back the next morning at low tide, we kept a good look-out for M——'s shark, spreading out, walkers and riders, in hopes of surrounding him and cutting him up. There were half a dozen weapons among us, of which my heavy bowie-knife was not the worst; and we should have given good account of him had we met him, and got between him and the deep water. But our valour was superfluous. The enemy was nowhere to be seen; and we rode on, looking back wistfully, but in vain, for a gray fin among the ripples.

So we rode back, along the Cocal and along that wonderful green glade, where I, staring at Noranteas in tree-tops, instead of at the ground beneath my horse's feet, had the pleasure of being swallowed up—my horse's hindquarters at least—in the very same slough which had engulfed M——'s mule three days before, and got a roll in much soft mud. Then up to ——'s camp, where we expected breakfast, not with greediness, though we had been nigh six hours in the saddle, but with curiosity. For he had promised to send out the hunters for all game that could be found, and give us a true forest meal; and we were curious to taste what lapo, quenco, guazupita-deer, and other strange meats might be like. Nay, some of us agreed, that if the hunters had but brought in a tender young red monkey,[1] we would surely eat him too, if it were but to say that we had done it. But the hunters had had no luck. They had brought in only a Pajui,[2] an excellent game bird; an Ant-eater,[3] and a great Cachicame, or nine-banded Armadillo. The ant-eater the foolish fellows had eaten themselves—I would have given them what they asked for his skeleton; but the Armadillo was cut up and hashed for us, and was eaten to the last scrap, being about the best game I ever tasted. I fear he is a foul feeder at times, who by no means confines himself to roots, or even worms. If what I was told be true, there is but too much probability for Captain Mayne Reid's statement, that he will eat his way into the soft parts of a dead horse, and stay there until he has eaten his way out again. But, to do him justice, I never heard him accused, like the giant Armadillo[4] of the Main, of digging dead bodies out of their graves, as he is doing in a very clever drawing in Mr. Wood's *Homes without Hands*. Be that as it may, the Armadillo, whatever he feeds on, has the power of transmuting it into most delicate and wholesome flesh.

Meanwhile—and hereby hangs a tale—I was interested, not merely in the Armadillo, but in the excellent taste with which it, and everything else, was cooked in a little open shed over a few stones and firesticks. And complimenting my host thereon, I found that he had, there in the primeval forest, an

---

[1] *Mycetes ursinus.*
[3] *Myrmecophaga tridactyla.*
[2] *Penelope.*
[4] *Priodonta gigas.*

admirable French cook, to whom I begged to be introduced at once. Poor fellow! A little lithe Parisian, not thirty years old, he had got thither by a wild road. Cook to some good bourgeois family in Paris, he had fallen in love with his master's daughter, and she with him. And when their love was hopeless, and discovered, the two young foolish things, not having—as is too common in France—the fear of God before their eyes, could think of no better resource than to shut themselves up with a pan of lighted charcoal, and so go they knew not whither. The poor girl went—and was found dead. But the boy recovered; and was punished with twenty years of Cayenne; and here he was now, on a sort of ticket-of-leave, cooking for his livelihood. I talked a while with him, cheered him with some compliments about the Parisians, and so forth, dear to the Frenchman's heart—what else was there to say?—and so left him, not without the fancy that, if he had had but such an education as the middle classes in Paris have not, there were the makings of a man in that keen eye, large jaw, sharp chin. 'The very fellow,' said some one, 'to have been a first-rate Zouave.' Well: perhaps he was a better man, even as he was, than as a Zouave.

And so we rode away again, and through Valencia, and through San Josef, weary and happy, back to Port of Spain.

I would gladly, had I been able, have gone farther due westward into the forests which hide the river Oropuche, that I might have visited the scene of a certain two years' Idyll, which was enacted in them some forty years and more ago.

In 1827 cacao fell to so low a price (two dollars per cwt.) that it was no longer worth cultivating; and the head of the F—— family, leaving his slaves to live at ease on his estates, retreated, with a household of twelve persons, to a small property of his own, which was buried in the primeval forests of Oropuche. With them went his second son, Monsignor F——, then and afterwards curé of San Josef, who died shortly before my visit to the island. I always heard him spoken of as a gentleman and a scholar, a saintly and cultivated priest of the old French School, respected and beloved by men of all denominations. His church of San Josef, though still unfinished, had been taxed, as well as all the Roman Catholic churches of the island, to build the Roman Catholic Cathedral at Port of Spain; and he, refusing to obey an order which he considered unjust, threw up his cure, and retreated with the rest of the family to the palm-leaf ajoupas in the forest.

M. F—— chose three of his finest Negroes as companions. Melchior was to go out every day to shoot wild pigeons, coming every morning to ask how many were needed, so as not to squander powder and shot. The number ordered were always punctually brought in, besides sometimes a wild turkey—Pajui —or other fine birds. Alejos, who is now a cacao proprietor, and owner of a house in Arima, was chosen to go out every day, except Sundays, with the dogs; and scarcely ever failed to bring in a lapo or quenco. Aristobal was chosen for the fishing, and brought in good loads of river fish, some sixteen pounds weight: and thus the little party of cultivated gentlemen and ladies were able to live, though in poverty, yet sumptuously.

The Bishop had given Monsignor F—— permission to perform service on any of his father's estates. So a little chapel was built; the family and servants attended every Sunday, and many days in the week; and the country folk from great distances found their way through the woods to hear Mass in the palm-thatched sanctuary of 'El Riposo.'

So did that happy family live 'the gentle life' for some two years; till cacao rose again in price, the tax on the churches was taken off, and the F——s returned again to the world: but not to civilisation and Christianity. Those they had carried with them into the wilderness; and those they brought back with them unstained.

CHAPTER XIV

THE 'EDUCATION QUESTION' IN TRINIDAD

WHEN I arrived in Trinidad, the little island was somewhat excited about changes in the system of education, which ended in a compromise like that at home, though starting from almost the opposite point.

Among the many good deeds which Lord Harris did for the colony was the establishment throughout it of secular elementary ward schools, helped by Government grants, on a system which had, I think, but two defects. First, that attendance was not compulsory; and next, that it was too advanced for the state of society in the island.

In an ideal system, secular and religious education ought, I believe, to be strictly separate, and given, as far as possible, by different classes of men. The first is the business of scientific men and their pupils; the second, of the clergy and their pupils: and the less either invades the domain of the other, the better for the community. But, like all ideals, it requires not only first-rate workmen, but first-rate material to work on; an intelligent and high-minded populace, who can and will think for themselves upon religious questions; and who have, moreover, a thirst for truth and knowledge of every kind. With such a populace, secular and religious education can be safely parted. But can they be safely parted in the case of a populace either degraded or still savage; given up to the 'lusts of the flesh'; with no desire for improvement, and ignorant of that 'moral ideal,' without the influence of which, as my friend Professor Huxley well says, there can be no true education? It is well if such a people can be made to submit to one system of education. Is it wise to try to burden them with two at once? But if one system is to give way to the other, which is the more important: to teach them the elements of reading, writing, and arithmetic; or the elements of duty and morals? And how these latter can be taught without religion is a problem as yet unsolved.

So argued some of the Protestant and the whole of the

Roman Catholic clergy of Trinidad, and withdrew their support from the Government schools, to such an extent that at least three-fourths of the children, I understand, went to no school at all.

The Roman Catholic clergy had, certainly, much to urge on their own behalf. The great majority of the coloured population of the island, besides a large proportion of the white, belonged to their creed. Their influence was the chief (I had almost said the only) civilising and Christianising influence at work on the lower orders of their own coloured people. They knew, none so well, how much the Negro required, not merely to be instructed, but to be reclaimed from gross and ruinous vices. It was not a question in Port of Spain, any more than it is in Martinique, of whether the Negroes should be able to read and write, but of whether they should exist on the earth at all for a few generations longer. I say this openly and deliberately; and clergymen and police magistrates know but too well what I mean. The priesthood were, and are, doing their best to save the Negro; and they naturally wished to do their work, on behalf of society and of the colony, in their own way; and to subordinate all teaching to that of religion, which includes, with them, morality and decency. They therefore opposed the Government schools; because they tended, it was thought, to withdraw the Negro from his priest's influence.

I am not likely, I presume, to be suspected of any leaning toward Romanism. But I think a Roman Catholic priest would have a right to a fair and respectful hearing, if he said:—

'You have set these people free, without letting them go through that intermediate stage of feudalism, by which, and by which alone, the white races of Europe were educated into true freedom. I do not blame you. You could do no otherwise. But will you hinder their passing through that process of religious education under a priesthood, by which, and by which alone, the white races of Europe were educated up to something like obedience, virtue, and purity?

'These last, you know, we teach in the interest of the State, as well as of the Negro: and if we should ask the State for aid, in order that we may teach them, over and above a little reading and writing—which will not be taught save by us, for we only shall be listened to—are we asking too much, or anything which the State will not be wise in granting us? We can have no temptation to abuse our power for political purposes. It would not suit us—to put the matter on its lowest ground—to become demagogues. For our congregations include persons of every rank and occupation; and therefore it is our interest, as much as that of the British Government, that all classes should be loyal, peaceable, and wealthy.

'As for our peculiar creed, with its vivid appeals to the

senses: is it not a question whether the utterly unimaginative and illogical Negro can be taught the facts of Christianity, or indeed any religion at all, save through his senses? Is it not a question whether we do not, on the whole, give him a juster and clearer notion of the very truths which you hold in common with us, than an average Protestant missionary does?

'Your Church of England'—it must be understood that the relations between the Anglican and the Romish clergy in Trinidad are, as far as I have seen, friendly and tolerant—'does good work among its coloured members. But it does so by speaking, as we speak, with authority. It, too, finds it prudent to keep up in its services somewhat at least of that dignity, even pomp, which is as necessary for the Negro as it was for the half-savage European of the early Middle Age, if he is to be raised above his mere natural dread of spells, witches, and other harmful powers, to somewhat of admiration and reverence.

'As for the merely dogmatic teaching of the Dissenters: we do not believe that the mere Negro really comprehends one of those propositions, whether true or false, Catholic or Calvinist, which have been elaborated by the intellect and the emotions of races who have gone through a training unknown to the Negro. With all respect for those who disseminate such books, we think that the Negro can no more conceive the true meaning of an average Dissenting Hymn-book, than a Sclavonian of the German Marches a thousand years ago could have conceived the meaning of St. Augustine's Confessions. For what we see is this—that when the personal influence of the white missionary is withdrawn, and the Negro left to perpetuate his sect on democratic principles, his creed merely feeds his inordinate natural vanity with the notion that everybody who differs from him is going to hell, while he is going to heaven whatever his morals may be.'

If a Roman Catholic priest should say all this, he would at least have a right, I believe, to a respectful hearing.

Nay, more. If he were to say, 'You are afraid of our having too much to do with the education of the Negro, because we use the Confessional as an instrument of education. Now how far the Confessional is needful, or useful, or prudent, in a highly civilised and generally virtuous community, may be an open matter. But in spite of all your English dislike of it, hear our side of the question, as far as Negroes and races in a similar condition are concerned. Do you know why and how the Confessional arose? Have you looked, for instance, into the old middle-age Penitentials? If so, you must be aware that it arose in an age of coarseness, which seems now inconceivable; in those barbarous times when the lower classes of Europe, slaves or serfs, especially in remote country districts, lived lives little better than those of the monkeys in the forest, and committed habitually the most fearful crimes, without any clear notion that they were doing wrong: while the upper classes, to judge from the literature which they have left, were so coarse, and often so profligate, in spite of nobler instincts and a higher sense of duty, that the purest and justest spirits among them had again and again to flee from their own class into the cloister or the hermit's cell.

'In those days, it was found necessary to ask Christian people perpetually—Have you been doing this, or that? For if you have, you are not only unfit to be called a Christian; you are unfit to be called a decent human being. And this, because there was every reason to suppose that they had been doing it; and that they would not tell of themselves, if they could possibly avoid it. So the Confessional arose, as a necessary element for educating savages into common morality and decency. And for the same reasons we employ it among the Negroes of Trinidad. Have no fears lest we should corrupt the minds of the young. They see and hear more harm daily than we could ever teach them, were we so devilishly minded. There is vice now, rampant and notorious, in Port of Spain, which eludes even our Confessional. Let us alone to do our best. God knows we are trying to do it, according to our light.'

If any Roman Catholic clergyman in Port of Spain spoke thus to me—and I have been spoken to in words not unlike these—I could only answer, 'God's blessing on you, and all your efforts, whether I agree with you in detail or not.'

The Roman Catholic inhabitants of the island are to the Protestant as about 2½ to 1.[1] The whole of the more educated portion of them, as far as I could ascertain, are willing to entrust the education of their children to the clergy. The Archbishop of Trinidad, Monsignor Gonin, who has jurisdiction also in St. Lucia, St. Vincent, Grenada, and Tobago, is a man not only of great energy and devotion, but of cultivation and knowledge of the world; having, I was told, attained distinction as a barrister elsewhere before he took Holy Orders. A group of clergy is working under him—among them a

[1] In 1858 they were computed as—

Roman Catholics	44,576
Church of England	16,350
Presbyterians	2,570
Baptists	449
Independents, etc.	239

From *Trinidad, its Geography*, etc., by L. A. De Verteuil, M.D.P., a very able and interesting book. I regret much that its accomplished author resists the solicitations of his friends, and declines to bring out a fresh edition of one of the most complete monographs of a colony which I have yet seen.

personal friend of mine—able and ready to do their best to mend a state of things in which most of the children in the island, born nominal Roman Catholics, but the majority illegitimate, were growing up not only in ignorance, but in heathendom and brutality. Meanwhile, the clergy were in want of funds. There were no funds at all, indeed, which would enable them to set up in remote forest districts a religious school side by side with the secular ward school; and the colony could not well be asked for Government grants to two sets of schools at once. In face of these circumstances, the late Governor thought fit to take action on the very able and interesting report of Mr. J. P. Keenan, one of the chiefs of inspection of the Irish National Board of Education, who had been sent out as special commissioner to inquire into the state of education in the island; to modify Lord Harris's plan, however excellent in itself; and to pass an Ordinance by which Government aid was extended to private elementary schools, of whatever denomination, provided they had duly certificated teachers; were accessible to all children of the neighbourhood without distinction of religion or race; and 'offered solid guarantees for abstinence from proselytism and intolerance, by subjecting their rules and course of teaching to the Board of Education, and empowering that Board at any moment to cancel the certificate of the teacher.' In the wards in which such schools were founded, and proved to be working satisfactorily, the secular ward schools were to be discontinued. But the Government reserved to itself the power of reopening a secular school in the ward, in case the private school turned out a failure.

Such is a short sketch of an Ordinance which seems, to me at least, a rational and fair compromise, identical, *mutatis mutandis*, with that embodied in Mr. Forster's new Education Act; and the only one by which the lower orders of Trinidad were likely to get any education whatever. It was received, of course, with applause by the Roman Catholics, and by a great number of the Protestants of the colony. But, as was to be expected, it met with strong expressions of dissent from some of the Protestant gentry and clergy; especially from one gentleman, who attacked the new scheme with an acuteness and humour which made even those who differed from him regret that such remarkable talents had no wider sphere than a little island of forty-five miles by sixty. An accession of power to the Roman Catholic clergy was, of course, dreaded; and all the more because it was known that the scheme met with the approval of the Archbishop; that it was, indeed, a compromise with the requests made in a petition which that prelate had lately sent in to the Governor; a petition which seems to me most rational and temperate. It was argued, too, that though the existing Act—that of 1851—had more or less failed, it might still succeed if Lord Harris's plan was fully carried out, and the choice of the ward schoolmaster, the selection of ward schoolbooks, and the direction of the course of instruction, were vested in local committees. The simple answer was, that eighteen years had elapsed, and the colony had done nothing in that direction ; that the great majority of children in the island did not go to school at all, while those who did attended most irregularly, and learnt little or nothing ;[1] that the secular system of education had not attracted, as it was hoped, the children of the Hindoo immigrants, of whom scarcely one was to be found in a ward school ; that the ward schoolmasters were generally inefficient, and the Central Board of Education inactive ; that there was no rigorous local supervision, and no local interest felt in the schools ; that there were fewer children in the ward schools in 1868 than there had been in 1863, in spite of the rapid increase of population : and all this for the simple reason which the Archbishop had pointed out—the want of religious instruction. As was to be expected, the good people of the island, being most of them religious people also, felt no enthusiasm about schools where little was likely to be taught beyond the three royal R's.

I believe they were wrong. Any teaching which involves moral discipline is better than mere anarchy and idleness. But they had a right to their opinion ; and a right too, being the great majority of the islanders, to have that opinion respected by the Governor. Even now, it will be but too likely, I think, that the establishment and superintendence of schools in remote districts will devolve — as it did in Europe during the Middle Age — entirely on the different clergies, simply by default of laymen of sufficient zeal for the welfare of the coloured people. Be that as it may, the Ordinance has become Law ; and I have faith enough in the loyalty of the good folk of Trinidad to believe that they will do their best to make it work.

If, indeed, the present Ordinance does not work, it is difficult to conceive any that will. It seems exactly fitted for the needs of Trinidad. I do not say that it is fitted for the needs of any and every country. In Ireland, for instance, such a system would be, in my opinion, simply retrograde. The Irishman, to his honour, has passed, centuries since, beyond the stage at which he requires to be educated by a priesthood in the primary laws of religion and morality. His morality is—on certain important points—superior to that of almost any people. What he needs is to be trained to loyalty and order ; to be brought more in contact with the secular science and civilisation of the rest of Europe : and that must be done by a secular, and not by an ecclesiastical system of education.

[1] See Mr. Keenan's Report, and other papers, printed by order of the House of Commons, 10th August 1870.

The higher education, in Trinidad, seems in a more satisfactory state than the elementary. The young ladies, many of them, go 'home'—*i.e.* to England or France—for their schooling; and some of the young men to Oxford, Cambridge, London, or Edinburgh. The Gilchrist Trust of the University of London has lately offered annually a Scholarship of £100 a year for three years, to lads from the West India colonies, the examinations for it to be held in Jamaica, Barbadoes, Trinidad, and Demerara; and in Trinidad itself two Exhibitions of £150 a year each, tenable for three years, are attainable by lads of the Queen's Collegiate School, to help them toward their studies at a British University.

The Collegiate School received aid from the State to the amount of £3000 per annum—less by the students' fees; and was open to all denominations. But in it, again, the secular system would not work. The great majority of Roman Catholic lads were educated at St. Mary's College, which received no State aid at all. 417 Catholic pupils at the former school, as against 111 at the latter, were—as Mr. Keenan says—'a poor expression of confidence or favour on the part of the colonists.' The Roman Catholic religion was the creed of the great majority of the islanders, and especially of the wealthier and better educated of the coloured families. Justice seemed to demand that if State aid were given, it should be given to all creeds alike; and prudence certainly demanded that the respectable young men of Trinidad should not be arrayed in two alien camps, in which the differences of creed were intensified by those of race, and—in one camp at least—by a sense of something very like injustice on the part of a Protestant, and, it must always be remembered, originally conquering, Government. To give the lads as much as possible the same interests, the same views; to make them all alike feel that they were growing up, not merely English subjects, but English men, was one of the most important social problems in Trinidad. And the simplest way of solving it was, to educate them as much as possible side by side in the same school, on terms of perfect equality.

The late Governor, therefore, with the advice and consent of his Council, determined to develop the Queen's Collegiate School into a new Royal College, which was to be open to all creeds and races without distinction: but upon such terms as will, it is hoped, secure the willing attendance of Roman Catholic scholars.[1] Not only it, but schools duly affiliated to it, are to receive Government aid; and four Exhibitions of £150 a year each, instead of two, are granted to young men going home to a British University. The College was inaugurated—I am sorry to say after I had left the island—in June 1870, by

---

[1] See *Papers on the State of Education in Trinidad*, p. 137 *et seq.*

the Governor, in the presence of (to quote the *Port of Spain Gazette*) the Council, consisting of—

>The Honourable the Chief Judge Needham.
>J. Scott Bushe (Colonial Secretary).
>Charles W. Warner, C.B.
>E. J. Eagles.
>F. Warner.
>Dr. L. A. A. Verteuil.
>Henry Court.
>M. Maxwell Philip.
>His Honour Mr. Justice Fitzgerald.
>André Bernard, Esq.

The last five of these gentlemen being, I believe, Roman Catholics. Most of the Board of Education were also present; the Principal and Masters of the Collegiate School, the Superiors and Reverend Professors of St. Mary's College, the Clergy of the Church of England in the island; the leading professional men and merchants, etc., and especially a large number of the Roman Catholic gentry of the island; 'MM. Ambard, O'Connor, Giuseppi, Laney, Farfan, Gillineau, Rat, Pantin, Léotaud, Besson, Fraser, Paüll, Hobson, Garcia, Dr. Padron,' etc. I quote their names from the *Gazette*, in the order in which they occur. Many of them I have not the honour of knowing: but judging of those whom I do not know by those whom I do, I should say that their presence at the inauguration was a solid proof that the foundation of the new College was a just and politic measure, opening, as the *Gazette* well says, a great future to the youth of all creeds in the colony.

The late Governor's speech on the occasion I shall print entire. It will explain the circumstances of the case far better than I can do; and it may possibly meet with interest and approval from those who like to hear sound sense spoken, even in a small colony.

'We are met here to-day to inaugurate the Royal College, an institution in which the benefits of a sound education, I trust, will be secured to Protestants and Roman Catholics alike, without the slightest compromise of their respective principles.

'The Queen's Collegiate School, of which this College is, in some sort, an out-growth and development, was founded with the same object: but, successful as it has been in other respects, it cannot be said to have altogether attained this.

'St. Mary's College was founded by private enterprise with a different view, and to meet the wants of those who objected to the Collegiate School.

'It has long been felt the existence of two Colleges—one, the smaller, almost entirely supported by the State; the other, the larger, wholly without State aid—was objectionable; and that the whole question of secondary education presented a most difficult problem.

'Some saw its solution in the withdrawal of all State aid from higher education; others in the establishment by the State of two distinct Denominational Colleges.

'I have elsewhere explained the reason why I consider both these suggestions faulty, and their probable effect bad; the one being certain to check and discourage superior education altogether, the other likely to substitute inefficient for efficient teaching, and small exclusive schools for a wide national institution.

'I knew that, whilst insuperable objections existed to a combined education in all subjects, that objection had its limits: that in America and in Germany I had seen Protestants and Catholics learning side by side; that in Mauritius, a College numbering 700 pupils, partly Protestants, partly Roman Catholics, existed; and that similar establishments were not uncommon elsewhere.

'I therefore determined to endeavour to effect the establishment of a College where combined study might be carried on in those branches of education with respect to which no objection to such a course was felt, and to support with Government aid, and bring under Government supervision, those establishments where those branches in which a separate education was deemed necessary were taught.

'I had, when last at home, some anxious conferences with the highest ecclesiastical authority of the Roman Catholic Church in England on the subject, and came to a complete understanding with him in respect to it. That distinguished prelate, himself a man of the highest University eminence, is not one to be indifferent to the interests of learning. His position, his known opinions, afford a guarantee that nothing sanctioned by him could, even by the most scrupulous, be considered in the least degree inconsistent with the interests of his Church or his religion.

'He expressed a strong preference for a totally separate education: but candidly admitted the objections to such a course in a small and not very wealthy island, and drew a wide distinction between combination for all purposes, and for some only.

'There were certain courses of instruction in which combined instruction could not possibly be given consistently with due regard to the faith of the pupils; there were others where it was difficult to decide whether it could or could not properly be given; there were others again where it might be certainly given without objection.

'On this understanding the plan carried into effect is based: but the Legislature have gone far beyond what was then agreed; and whilst Archbishop Manning would have assented to an arrangement which would have excluded certain branches only of education from the common course, the law, as now in force, allows exemption from attendance on all, provided competent instruction is given to the pupils in the same branches elsewhere; till, in fact, all that remains obligatory is attendance at examinations, and at the course of instruction in one or more of four given branches of education, if it should so happen that no adequate teaching in that particular branch is given in the pupil's own school.

'A scheme more liberal—a bond more elastic—could hardly have been devised, capable of effecting, if desired, the closest union—capable of being stretched to almost any degree of slight connection; and even if some Catholics would still prefer a wholly separate system, they must, if candid men, admit that the Protestant population here have a right to demand that they should not be called on to surrender, in order to satisfy a mere preference, the great advantages they derive from a united College under State control, with its efficient staff and national character.

'If religious difficulties are met, and conscientious scruples are not wounded, a sacrifice of preferences must often be made. Private wishes must often yield to the public good.

'In the first instance, all the boys of the former Collegiate School have become students of the College; but probably a school of a similar character, but affiliated to the College, will shortly be formed, in which a large number of those boys will be included.

'That the headship of the College should be entrusted to the Principal of the Queen's Collegiate School will, I am sure, be universally felt to be only a just tribute to the zeal, efficiency, and success with which he has hitherto laboured in his office, whilst, in addition to these qualifications, he possesses the no less important one for the post he is about to fill, of a mind singularly impartial, just, liberal, and candid.

'I hope that the other Professors of the College may be taken from affiliated schools indiscriminately, the lectures being given as may be most convenient, and as may be arranged by the College Council.

'It is intended by the College Council that the fees charged for attendance at the Royal College should be much lower than those heretofore charged at the Queen's Collegiate School. I do not believe that the mere financial loss will be great, whilst I believe a good education will, by this means, be placed within the reach of many who cannot now afford it.

'I hope—but I express only my own personal wish, not that of the Council, which, as yet, has pronounced no opinion—that some of the changes introduced in most states of modern education will be made here, and that especial attention will be given to the teaching of some of the Eastern languages.

'It is almost impossible to overrate the importance of this both to the Government and the community ;—to the Government, as enabling it to avail itself of the services of honest, competent, and trustworthy interpreters ; and to the general community, as relieving both employer and employed from the necessity of depending on the interpretation of men not always very competent, nor always very scrupulous, whose mistakes or errors, whether wilful or accidental, may often effect much injustice, and on whose fidelity life may not unfrequently depend.

'I thank the members of the College Council for having accepted a task which will, at first, involve much delicate tact, forbearance, caution, and firmness, and the exercise of talents I know them to possess, and which I am confident will be freely bestowed in working out the success of the institution committed to their care.

'I thank the Principal and his staff for their past exertions, and I count with confidence on their future labours.

'I thank the parents who, by their presence, have manifested their interest in our undertaking, and their wishes for its success, and I especially thank the ladies who have been drawn within these walls by graver attractions than those which generally bring us together at this building.

'I rejoice to see here the Superior of St. Mary's College, and the goodly array of those under his charge, and I do so for many reasons.

'I rejoice, because being not as yet affiliated or in any way officially connected with the Royal College, their presence is a spontaneous evidence of their goodwill and kindly feeling, and of the spirit in which they have been disposed to meet the efforts made to consult their feelings in the arrangements of this institution ; a spirit yet further evinced by the fact that the Superior has informed me that he is about voluntarily to alter the course of study pursued in St. Mary's College, so as more nearly to assimilate it to that pursued here.

'I rejoice, because in their presence I hail a sign that the affiliation which is, I believe, desired by the great body of the Roman Catholic community in this island, and to which it has been shown no insuperable religious obstacle exists, will take place at no more distant day than is necessary to secure the approval, the naturally requisite approval, of ecclesiastical authority elsewhere.

'I rejoice at their presence, because it enables me before this company to express my high sense of the courage and liberality which have maintained their College for years past without any aid whatever from the State, and, in spite of manifold obstacles and discouragements, have caused it to increase in numbers and efficiency.

'I rejoice at their presence, because I desire to see the youth of Trinidad of every race, without indifference to their respective creeds, brought together on all possible occasions, whether for recreation or for work; because I wish to see them engaged in friendly rivalry in their studies now, as they will hereafter be in the world, which I desire to see them enter, not as strangers to each other, but as friends and fellow-citizens.

'I rejoice, because their presence enables me to take a personal farewell of so many of those who will in the next generation be the planters, the merchants, the official and professional men of Trinidad. By the time that you are men all the petty jealousies, all the mean resentments of this our day, will have faded into the oblivion which is their proper bourn. But the work now accomplished will not, I trust, so fade. They will melt and perish as the snow of the north would before our tropical sun: but the College will, I trust, remain as the rock on which the snow rests, and which remains uninjured by the heat, unmoved by the passing storm. May it endure and strengthen as it passes from the first feeble beginnings of this its infancy to a vigorous youth and maturity. You will sometimes in days to come recall the inauguration of your College, and perhaps not forget that its founder prayed you to bear in mind the truth that you will find, even now, the truest satisfaction in the strict discharge of duty ; that he urged you to form high and unselfish aims—to seek noble and worthy objects ; and as you enter on the world and all its tossing sea of jealousies, strife, division and distrust, to heed the lesson which an Apostle, whose words we all alike revere, has taught us, "If ye bite and devour one another, take ye heed that ye be not consumed one of another."

'Here, we hope, a point of union has been found which may last through life, and that whilst every man cherishes a love for his own peculiar School, all alike will have an interest in their common College, all alike be proud of a national institution, jealous of its honour, and eager to advance its welfare.

'It is a common thing to hear the bitterness of religious discord here deplored. I for one, looking back on the history of past years, cannot think, as some seem to do, that it has increased. On the contrary, it seems to me that it has greatly diminished in violence when displayed, and that its displays are far less frequent. Such, I believe, will be more and more the case ; and that whilst religious distinctions will remain the same, and conscientious convictions unaltered, social and party differences consequent on those distinctions and convictions will daily diminish ; that all alike will more and more feel in how many things they can think and act together for the benefit of their common country, and of the community of which they all are members ; how they can be glad together in her prosperity, and be sad together in the day of her distress ; and work together at all times to promote her good. That this College is calculated to aid in a great degree in effecting this happy result, I for one cannot entertain the shadow of a doubt. "Esto perpetua!"'

'Esto perpetua.' But there remains, I believe, more yet to be done for education in the West Indies; and that is to carry out Mr. Keenan's scheme for a Central University for the whole of the West Indian Colonies,[1] as a focus of higher education; and a focus, also, of cultivated public opinion, round which all that is shrewdest and noblest in the islands shall rally, and find strength in moral and intellectual union. I earnestly recommend all West Indians to ponder Mr. Keenan's weighty words on this matter; believing that, as they do so, even stronger reasons than he has given for establishing such an institution will suggest themselves to West Indian minds.

I am not aware, nor would the reader care much to know, what schools there may be in Port of Spain for Protestant young ladies. I can only say that, to judge from the young ladies themselves, the schools must be excellent. But one school in Port of Spain I am bound in honour, as a clergyman of the Church of England, not to pass by without earnest approval, namely, 'The Convent,' as it is usually called. It was established in 1836, under the patronage of the Roman Catholic Bishop, the Right Rev. Dr. Macdonnel, and was founded by the ladies of St. Joseph, a religious Sisterhood which originated in France a few years since, for the special purpose of diffusing instruction through the colonies.[2] This institution, which Dr. De Verteuil says is 'unique in the West Indies,' besides keeping up two large girls' schools for poor children, gave in 1857 a higher education to 120 girls of the middle and upper classes, and the number has much increased since then. It is impossible to doubt that this Convent has been 'a blessing to the colony.' At the very time when, just after slavery was abolished, society throughout the island was in the greatest peril, these good ladies came to supply a want which, under the peculiar circumstances of Trinidad, could only have been supplied by the self-sacrifice of devoted women. The Convent has not only spread instruction and religion among the wealthier coloured class: but it has done more; it has been a centre of true civilisation, purity, virtue, where one was but too much needed; and has preserved, doubtless, hundreds of young creatures from serious harm; and that without interfering in any wise, I should think, with their duty to their parents. On the contrary, many a mother in Port of Spain must have found in the Convent a protection for her daughters, better than she herself could give, against influences to which she herself had been but too much exposed during the evil days of slavery; influences which are not yet, alas! extinct in Port of Spain.

[1] Mr. Keenan's Report, pp. 63-67.
[2] Dr. De Verteuil's *Trinidad*.

Creoles will understand my words; and will understand, too, why I, Protestant though I am, bid heartily God speed to the good ladies of St. Joseph.

To the Anglican clergy, meanwhile, whom I met in the West Indies, I am bound to offer my thanks, not for courtesies shown to me—that is a slight matter—but for the worthy fashion in which they seem to be upholding the honour of the good old Church in the colonies. In Port of Spain I heard and saw enough of their work to believe that they are in nowise less active —more active they cannot be—than if they were seaport clergymen in England. The services were performed thoroughly well; with a certain stateliness, which is not only allowable but necessary, in a colony where the majority of the congregation are coloured; but without the least foppery or extravagance. The very best sermon, perhaps, for matter and manner, which I ever heard preached to unlettered folk, was preached by a young clergyman—a West Indian born—in the Great Church of Port of Spain; and he had no lack of hearers, and those attentive ones. The Great Church was always a pleasant sight, with its crowded congregation of every hue, all well dressed, and with the universal West Indian look of comfort; and its noble span of roof overhead, all cut from island timber—another proof of what the wood-carver may effect in the island hereafter. Certainly distractions were frequent and troublesome, at least to a newcomer. A large centipede would come out and take a hurried turn round the Governor's seat; or a bat would settle in broad daylight in the curate's hood; or one had to turn away one's eyes lest they should behold—not vanity, but—the magnificent head of a Cabbage-palm just outside the opposite window, with the black vultures trying to sit on the footstalks in a high wind, and slipping down, and flopping up again, half the service through. But one soon got accustomed to the strange sights; though it was, to say the least, somewhat startling to find, on Christmas Day, the altar and pulpit decked with exquisite tropic flowers; and each doorway arched over with a single pair of coco-nut leaves, fifteen feet high.

The Christmas Day Communion, too, was one not easily to be forgotten. At least 250 persons, mostly coloured, many as black as jet, attended; and were, I must say for them, most devout in manner. Pleasant it was to see the large proportion of men among them, many young white men of the middle and upper class; and still more pleasant, too, to see that all hues and ranks knelt side by side without the least distinction. One trio touched me deeply. An old lady—I know not who she was— with the unmistakable long, delicate, once beautiful features of a high-bred West Indian of the 'Ancien Régime,' came and knelt reverently, feebly, sadly, between two old Negro women. One of them seemed her maid. Both of them might have been once her slaves. Here at least they were equals. True Equality

—the consecration of humility, not the consecration of envy—first appeared on earth in the house of God, and at the altar of Christ: and I question much whether it will linger long in any spot on earth where that house and that altar are despised. It is easy to propose an equality without Christianity; as easy as to propose to kick down the ladder by which you have climbed, or to saw off the bough on which you sit. As easy; and as safe.

But I must not forget, while speaking of education in Trinidad, one truly 'educational' establishment which I visited at Tacarigua; namely, a Coolie Orphan Home, assisted by the State, but set up and kept up almost entirely by the zeal of one man—the Rev. —— Richards, brother of the excellent Rector of Trinity Church, Port of Spain. This good man, having no children of his own, has taken for his children the little brown immigrants, who, losing father and mother, are but too apt to be neglected by their own folk. At the foot of the mountains, beside a clear swift stream, amid scenery and vegetation which an European millionaire might envy, he has built a smart little quadrangle, with a long low house, on one side for the girls, on the other for the boys; a schoolroom, which was as well supplied with books, maps, and pictures as any average National School in England; and, adjoining the buildings, a garden where the boys are taught to work. A matron—who seemed thoroughly worthy of her post—conducts the whole; and comfort, cleanliness, and order were visible everywhere. A pleasant sight; but the pleasantest sight of all was to see the little bright-eyed brown darlings clustering round him who was indeed their father in God; who had delivered them from misery and loneliness, and—in the case of the girls—too probably vice likewise; and drawn them, by love, to civilisation and Christianity. The children, as fast as they grow up, are put out to domestic service, and the great majority of the boys at least turn out well. The girls, I was told, are curiously inferior to the boys in intellect and force of character; an inferiority which is certainly not to be found in Negroes, among whom the two sexes are more on a par, not only intellectually, but physically also, than among any race which I have seen. One instance, indeed, we saw of the success of the school. A young creature, brought up there, and well married near by, came in during our visit to show off her first baby to the matron and the children; as pretty a mother and babe as one could well see. Only we regretted that, in obedience to the supposed demands of civilisation, and of a rise in life, she had discarded the graceful and modest Hindoo dress of her ancestresses, for a French bonnet and all that accompanies it. The transfiguration added, one must charitably suppose, to her self-respect; if so, it must be condoned on moral grounds: but in an æsthetic view, she had made a great mistake.

In remembrance of our visit, a little brown child, some three or four years old, who had been christened that day, was named after me; and I was glad to have my name connected, even in so minute an item, with an institution which at all events delivers children from the fancy that they can, without being good or doing good, conciliate the upper powers by hanging garlands on a trident inside a hut, or putting red dust on a stump of wood outside it, while they stare in and mumble prayers to they know not what of gilded wood.

The coolie temples are curious places to those who have never before been face to face with real heathendom. Their mark is, generally, a long bamboo with a pennon atop, outside a low dark hut, with a broad flat verandah, or rather shed, outside the door. Under the latter, opposite each door, if I recollect rightly, is a stone or small stump, on which offerings are made of red dust and flowers. From it the worshippers can see the images within. The white man, stooping, enters the temple. The attendant priest, so far from forbidding him, seems highly honoured, especially if the visitor give him a shilling; and points out, in the darkness—for there is no light save through the low doors—three or four squatting abominations, usually gilded. Sometimes these have been carved in the island. Sometimes the poor folk have taken the trouble to bring them all the way from India on board ship. Hung beside them on the walls are little pictures, often very well executed in the miniature-like Hindoo style by native artists in the island. Large brass pots, which have some sacred meaning, stand about, and with them a curious trident-shaped stand, about four feet high, on the horns of which garlands of flowers are hung as offerings. The visitor is told that the male figures are Mahadeva, and the female Kali: we could hear of no other deities. I leave it to those who know Indian mythology better than I do, to interpret the meaning—or rather the past meaning, for I suspect it means very little now—of all this trumpery and nonsense, on which the poor folk seem to spend much money. It was impossible, of course, even if one had understood their language, to find out what notions they attached to it all; and all I could do, on looking at these heathen idol chapels, in the midst of a Christian and civilised land, was to ponder, in sadness and astonishment, over a puzzle as yet to me inexplicable; namely, how human beings first got into their heads the vagary of worshipping images. I fully allow the cleverness and apparent reasonableness of M. Comte's now famous theory of the development of religions. I blame no one for holding it. But I cannot agree with it. The more of a 'saine appréciation,' as M. Comte calls it, I bring to bear on the known facts; the more I 'let my thought play freely around them,' the more it is inconceivable to me, according to any laws of the human intellect which I have seen at work, that savage or half-savage folk should have invented idolatries. I do not believe that Fêtishism is the parent of idolatry; but rather—as I have said elsewhere—that it is the dregs and remnants of idolatry. The idolatrous nations now, as always, are not the savage nations; but those who profess a very ancient and

COOLIE SACRIFICING

decaying civilisation. The Hebrew Scriptures uniformly represent the non-idolatrous and monotheistic peoples, from Abraham to Cyrus, as lower in what we now call the scale of civilisation, than the idolatrous and polytheistic peoples about them. May not the contrast between the Patriarchs and the Pharaohs, David and the Philistines, the Persians and the Babylonians, mark a law of history of wider application than we are wont to suspect? But if so, what was the parent of idolatry? For a natural genesis it must have had, whether it be a healthy and necessary development of the human mind—as some hold, not without weighty arguments on their side ; or whether it be a diseased and merely fungoid growth, as I believe it to be. I cannot hold that it originated in Nature-worship, simply because I can find no evidence of such an origin. There is rather evidence, if the statements of the idolaters themselves are to be taken, that it originated in the worship of superior races by inferior races; possibly also in the worship of works of art which those races, dying out, had left behind them, and which the lower race, while unable to copy them, believed to be possessed of magical powers derived from a civilisation which they had lost. After a while the priesthood, which has usually, in all ages and countries, proclaimed itself the depository of a knowledge and a civilisation lost to the mass of the people, may have gained courage to imitate these old works of art, with proper improvements for the worse, and have persuaded the people that the new idols would do as well as the old ones. Would that some truly learned man would 'let his thoughts play freely' round this view of the mystery, and see what can be made out of it. But whatever is made out, on either view, it will still remain a mystery—to me at least, as much as to Isaiah of old—how this utterly abnormal and astonishing animal called man first got into his foolish head that he could cut a thing out of wood or stone which would listen to him and answer his prayers. Yet so it is; so it has been for unnumbered ages. Man may be defined as a speaking animal, or a cooking animal. He is best, I fear, defined as an idolatrous animal; and so much the worse for him. But what if that very fact, diseased as it is, should be a sure proof that he is more than an animal?

CHAPTER XV

THE RACES—A LETTER

DEAR ——, I have been to the races: not to bet, nor to see the horses run: not even to see the fair ladies on the Grand Stand, in all the newest fashions of Paris *viâ* New York: but to wander *en mufti* among the crowd outside, and behold the humours of men. And I must say that their humours were very good humours; far better, it seemed to me, than those of an English race-ground. Not that I have set foot on one for thirty years; but at railway stations, and elsewhere, one cannot help seeing what manner of folk, beside mere holiday folk, rich or poor, affect English races; or help pronouncing them, if physiognomy be any test of character, the most degraded beings, even some of those smart-dressed men who carry bags with their names on them, which our pseudo-civilisation has yet done itself the dishonour of producing. Now, of that class I saw absolutely none. I do not suppose that the brown fellows who hung about the horses, whether Barbadians or Trinidad men, were of very angelic morals: but they looked like heroes compared with the bloated hangdog roughs and quasi-grooms of English races. As for the sporting gentlemen, not having the honour to know them, I can only say that they looked like gentlemen, and that I wish, in all courtesy, that they had been more wisely employed.

But the Negro, or the coloured man of the lower class, was in his glory. He was smart, clean, shiny, happy, according to his light. He got up into trees, and clustered there, grinning from ear to ear. He bawled about island horses and Barbadian horses—for the Barbadians mustered strong, and a fight was expected, which, however, never came off; he sang songs, possibly some of them extempore, like that which amused one's childhood concerning a once notable event in a certain island—

> 'I went to da Place
> To see da horse-race,
> I see Mr. Barton
> A-wipin' ob his face.

WAITING FOR THE BUCKS.

> 'Run, Allwright,
> Run for your life;
> See Mr. Barton
> A-comin' wid a knife.

> 'Oh, Mr. Barton,
> I sarry for your loss;
> If you no believe me,
> I tie my head across.'

That is—go into mourning. But no one seemed inclined to tie their heads across that day. The Coolies seemed as merry as the Negroes; even about the face of the Chinese there flickered, at times, a feeble ray of interest.

The coloured women wandered about, in showy prints, great crinolines, and gorgeous turbans. The Coolie women sat in groups on the grass—ah! Isle of the Blest, where people can sit on the grass in January—like live flower-beds of the most splendid and yet harmonious hues. As for jewels, of gold as well as silver, there were many there, on arms, ankles, necks, and noses, which made white ladies fresh from England break the tenth commandment.

I wandered about, looking at the live flower-beds, and giving passing glances into booths, which I longed to enter, and hear what sort of human speech might be going on therein: but I was deterred, first by the thought that much of the speech might not be over-edifying, and next by the smells, especially by that most hideous of all smells—new rum.

At last I came to a crowd; and in the midst of it, one of those great French merry-go-rounds, turned by machinery, with pictures of languishing ladies round the central column. All the way from the Champs Elysées the huge piece of fools' tackle had lumbered and creaked hither across the sea to Martinique, and was now making the round of the islands; and a very profitable round, to judge from the number of its customers. The hobby-horses swarmed with Negresses and Hindoos of the lower order. The Negresses, I am sorry to say, forgot themselves, kicked up their legs, shouted to the bystanders, and were altogether incondite. The Hindoo women, though showing much more of their limbs than the Negresses, kept them gracefully together, drew their veils round their heads, and sat coyly, half frightened, half amused, to the delight of their 'papas,' or husbands, who had in some cases to urge them to get up and ride, while they stood by, as on guard, with the long hardwood quarter-staff in hand.

As I looked on, considered what a strange creature man is, and wondered what possible pleasure these women could derive from being whirled round till they were giddy and stupid, I saw an old gentleman seemingly absorbed in the very same reflection. He was dressed in dark blue, with a straw hat. He stood with his hands behind his back, his knees a little bent, and a sort of wise, half-sad, half-humorous smile upon his aquiline high-cheek-boned features. I took him for an old Scot; a canny, austere man—a man, too, who had known sorrow, and profited thereby; and I drew near to him. But as he turned his head deliberately round to me, I beheld to my astonishment the unmistakable features of a Chinese. He and I looked each other full in the face, without a word; and I fancied that we understood each other about the merry-go-round, and many things besides. And then we both walked off different ways, as having seen enough, and more than enough. Was he, after all, an honest man and true? Or had he, like Ah Sin, in Mr. Bret Harte's delectable ballad, with 'the smile that was child-like and bland'—

> 'In his sleeves, which were large,
> Twenty-four packs of cards,
> And—On his nails, which were taper,
> What's common in tapers—that's wax'?

I know not; for the Chinese visage is unfathomable. But I incline to this day to the more charitable judgment; for the man's face haunted me, and haunts me still; and I am weak enough to believe that I should know the man and like him, if I met him in another planet, a thousand years hence.

Then I walked back under the blazing sun across the Savanna, over the sensitive plants and the mole-crickets' nests, while the great locusts whirred up before me at every step; toward the archway between the bamboo clumps, and the red sentry shining like a spark of fire beneath its deep shadow; and found on my way a dying racehorse, with a group of coloured men round him, whom I advised in vain to do the one thing needful—put a blanket over him to keep off the sun, for the poor thing had fallen from sunstroke; so I left them to jabber and do nothing: asking myself—Is the human race, in the matter of amusements, as civilised as it was—say three thousand years ago? People have, certainly—quite of late years—given up going to see cocks fight, or heretics burnt: but that is mainly because the heretics just now make the laws —in favour of themselves and the cocks. But are our amusements to be compared with those of the old Greeks, with the one exception of liking to hear really good music? Yet that fruit of civilisation is barely twenty years old; and we owe its introduction, be it always remembered, to the Germans. French civilisation signifies practically, certainly in the New World, little save ballet-girls, billiard-tables, and thin boots: English civilisation, little save horse-racing and cricket. The latter sport is certainly blameless; nay, in the West Indies, laudable and even heroic, when played, as on the Savanna here, under a noonday sun which feels hot enough to cook a mutton-chop. But with all respect for cricket, one cannot help looking back at the old games of Greece, and questioning whether man has advanced much in the art of amusing himself rationally and wholesomely.

I had reason to ask the same question that evening, as we sat in the cool verandah, watching the fireflies flicker about the tree-tops, and listening to the weary din of the tom-toms which came from all sides of the Savanna save our own, drowning the screeching and snoring of the toads, and even, at times, the screams of an European band, which was playing a 'combination tune,' near the Grand Stand, half a mile off.

To the music of tom-tom and chac-chac, the coloured folk would dance perpetually till ten o'clock, after which time the rites of Mylitta are silenced by the policeman, for the sake of quiet folk in bed. They are but too apt, however, to break out again with fresh din about one in the morning, under the excuse—'Dis am not last night, Policeman. Dis am 'nother day.'

Well: but is the nightly tom-tom dance so much more absurd than the nightly ball, which is now considered an integral element of white civilisation? A few centuries hence may not both of them be looked back on as equally sheer barbarisms?

These tom-tom dances are not easily seen. The only glance I ever had of them was from the steep slope of once beautiful Belmont. 'Sitting on a hill apart,' my host and I were discoursing, not 'of fate, free-will, free-knowledge absolute,' but of a question almost as mysterious—the doings of the Parasol-ants who marched up and down their trackways past us, and whether these doings were guided by an intellect differing from ours, only in degree, but not in kind. A hundred yards below we espied a dance in a negro garden; a few couples, mostly of women, pousetting to each other with violent and ungainly stampings, to the music of tom-tom and chac-chac, if music it can be called. Some power over the emotions it must have; for the Negroes are said to be gradually maddened by it; and white people have told me that its very monotony, if listened to long, is strangely exciting, like the monotony of a bagpipe drone, or of a drum. What more went on at the dance we could not see; and if we had tried, we should probably not have been allowed to see. The Negro is chary of admitting white men to his amusements; and no wonder. If a London ballroom were suddenly invaded by Phœbus, Ares, and Hermes, such as Homer drew them, they would probably be unwelcome guests; at least in the eyes of the gentlemen. The latter would, I suspect, thoroughly sympathise with the Negro in the old story, intelligible enough to those who know what is the favourite food of a West Indian chicken.

'Well, John, so they gave a dignity ball on the estate last night?'

'Yes, massa, very nice ball. Plenty of pretty ladies, massa.'

'Why did you not ask me, John? I like to look at pretty ladies as well as you.'

'Ah, massa: when cockroach give a ball, him no ask da fowls.'

Great and worthy exertions are made, every London Season, for the conversion of the Negro and the Heathen, and the abolition of their barbarous customs and dances. It is to be hoped that the Negro and the Heathen will some day show their gratitude to us, by sending missionaries hither to convert the London Season itself, dances and all; and assist it to take the beam out of its own eye, in return for having taken the mote out of theirs.

CHAPTER XVI

A PROVISION GROUND

THE 'provision grounds' of the Negroes were very interesting. I had longed to behold, alive and growing, fruits and plants which I had heard so often named, and seen so often figured, that I had expected to recognise many of them at first sight; and found, in nine cases out of ten, that I could not. Again, I had longed to gather some hints as to the possibility of carrying out in the West Indian islands that system of 'Petite Culture'—of small spade farming—which I have long regarded, with Mr. John Stuart Mill and others, as not only the ideal form of agriculture, but perhaps the basis of any ideal rustic civilisation. And what scanty and imperfect facts I could collect I set down here.

It was a pleasant sensation to have, day after day, old names translated for me into new facts. Pleasant, at least to me: not so pleasant, I fear, to my kind companions, whose courtesy I taxed to the uttermost by stopping to look over every fence, and ask, 'What is that? And that?' Let the reader who has a taste for the beautiful as well as the useful in horticulture, do the same, and look in fancy over the hedge of the nearest provision ground.

There are orange-trees laden with fruit: who knows not them? and that awkward-boughed tree, with huge green fruit, and deeply-cut leaves a foot or more across—leaves so grand that, as one of our party often suggested, their form ought to be introduced into architectural ornamentation, and to take the place of the Greek acanthus, which they surpass in beauty —that is, of course, a Bread-fruit tree.

That round-headed tree, with dark rich Portugal laurel foliage, arranged in stars at the end of each twig, is the Mango, always a beautiful object, whether in orchard or in open park. In the West Indies, as far as I have seen, the Mango has not yet reached the huge size of its ancestors in Hindostan. There —to judge, at least, from photographs—the Mango must be indeed the queen of trees; growing to the size of the largest

THE LAST OF THE GIANTS.

English oak, and keeping always the round oak-like form. Rich in resplendent foliage, and still more rich in fruit, the tree easily became encircled with an atmosphere of myth in the fancy of the imaginative Hindoo.

That tree with upright branches, and large, dark, glossy leaves tiled upwards along them, is the Mammee Sapota,[1] beautiful likewise. And what is the next, like an evergreen peach, shedding from the under side of every leaf a golden light—call it not shade? A Star-apple;[2] and that young thing which you may often see grown into a great timber-tree, with leaves like a Spanish chestnut, is the Avocado,[3] or, as some call it, alligator, pear. This with the glossy leaves, somewhat like the Mammee Sapota, is a Sapodilla,[4] and that with leaves like a great myrtle, and bright flesh-coloured fruit, a Malacca-apple, or perhaps a Rose-apple.[5] Its neighbour, with large leaves, gray and rough underneath, flowers as big as your two hands, with greenish petals and a purple eye, followed by fat scaly yellow apples, is the Sweet-sop;[6] and that privet-like bush with little flowers and green berries a Guava,[7] of which you may eat if you will, as you may of the rest.

BREAD-FRUIT.

The truth, however, must be told. These West Indian fruits are, most of them, still so little improved by careful culture and selection of kinds, that not one of them (as far as we have tried them) is to be compared with an average strawberry, plum, or pear.

But how beautiful they are all and each, after their kinds! What a joy for a man to stand at his door and simply look at them growing, leafing, blossoming, fruiting, without pause, through the perpetual summer, in his little garden of the Hesperides, where, as in those of the Phœnicians of old, 'pear grows ripe on pear, and fig on fig,' for ever and for ever!

Now look at the vegetables. At the Bananas and Plantains first of all. A stranger's eye would not distinguish them. The practical difference between them is, that the Plaintain[8] bears

---

[1] *Lucuma mammosa.*
[2] *Chrysophyllum cainito.*
[3] *Persea gratissima.*
[4] *Sapota achras.*
[5] *Jambosa malaccensis* and *vulgaris.*
[6] *Anona squamosa.*
[7] *Psidium Guava.*
[8] *Musa paradisiaca.*

large fruits which require cooking; the Banana[1] smaller and sweeter fruits, which are eaten raw. As for the plant on which they grow, no mere words can picture the simple grandeur and grace of a form which startles me whenever I look steadily at it. For however common it is—none commoner here—it is so unlike aught else, so perfect in itself, that, like a palm, it might well have become, in early ages, an object of worship.

And who knows that it has not? Who knows that there have not been races who looked on it as the Red Indians looked on Mondamin, the maize-plant; as a gift of a god—perhaps the incarnation of a god? Who knows? Whence did the ancestors of that plant come? What was its wild stock like ages ago? It is wild nowhere now on earth. It stands alone and unique in the vegetable kingdom, with distant cousins, but no brother kinds. It has been cultivated so long that though it flowers and fruits, it seldom or never seeds, and is propagated entirely by cuttings. The only spot, as far as I am aware, in which it seeds regularly and plentifully, is the remote, and till of late barbarous Andaman Islands in the Bay of Bengal.[2]

There it regularly springs up in the second growth, after the forest is cleared, and bears fruits full of seed as close together as they can be pressed. How did the plant get there? Was it once cultivated there by a race superior to the now utterly savage islanders, and at an epoch so remote that it had not yet lost the power of seeding? Are the Andamans its original home? or rather, was its original home that great southern continent of which the Andamans are perhaps a remnant? Does not this fact, as well as the broader fact that different varieties of the Plantain and Banana girdle the earth round at the Tropics, and have girdled it as long as records go back, hint at a time when there was a tropic continent or archipelago round the whole equator, and at a civilisation and a horticulture to which those of old Egypt are upstarts of yesterday? There are those who never can look at the Banana without a feeling of awe, as at a token of how ancient the race of man may be, and how little we know of his history.

Most beautiful it is. The lush fat green stem; the crown of huge leaves, falling over in curves like those of human limbs; and below, the whorls of green or golden fruit, with the purple heart of flowers dangling below them; and all so full of life, that this splendid object is the product of a few months. I am told that if you cut the stem off at certain seasons, you may see the young leaf—remember that it is an endogen, and grows

---

[1] *M. sapientum.*
[2] I owe these curious facts, and specimens of the seeds, to the courtesy of Dr. King, of the Bengal Army. The seeds are now in the hands of Dr. Hooker, at Kew.

from within, like a palm, or a lily, or a grass—actually move upward from within and grow before your eyes; and that each stem of Plantain will bear from thirty to sixty pounds of rich food during the year of its short life.

But, beside the grand Plantains and Bananas, there are other interesting plants, whose names you have often heard. The tall plant with stem unbranched, but knotty and zigzag, and leaves atop like hemp, but of a cold purplish tinge, is the famous Cassava,[1] or Manioc, the old food of the Indians, poisonous till its juice is squeezed out in a curious spiral grass basket. The young Laburnums (as they seem), with purple flowers, are Pigeon-peas,[2] right good to eat. The creeping vines, like our Tamus, or Black Bryony, are Yams,[3]—best of all roots.

The branching broad-leaved canes, with strange white flowers, is Arrowroot.[4] The tall mallow-like shrub, with large pale yellowish-white flowers, Cotton. The huge grass with beads on it[5] is covered with the Job's tears, which are precious in children's eyes, and will be used as beads for necklaces. The castor-oil plants, and the maize —that last always beautiful—are of course well known. The arrow leaves, three feet long, on stalks three feet high, like gigantic Arums, are Tanias,[6] whose roots are excellent. The plot of creeping convolvulus-like plants, with purple flowers, is the Sweet, or true, Potato.[7]

And we must not overlook the French Physic-nut,[8] with its hemp-like leaves, and a little bunch of red coral in the midst, with which the Negro loves to adorn his garden, and uses it also as medicine; or the Indian Shot,[9] which may be seen planted out now in summer gardens in England. The Negro grows it, not for its pretty crimson flowers, but because its hard seed put into a bladder furnishes him with that detestable musical instrument the chac-chac, wherewith he accompanies nightly that equally detestable instrument the tom-tom.

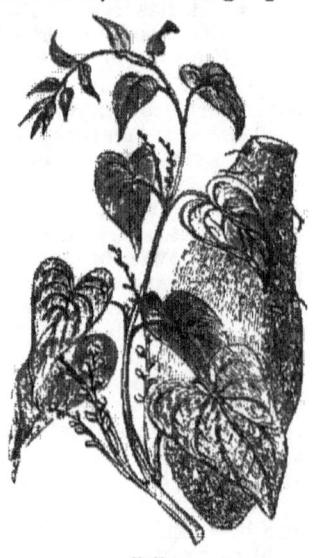

YAM.

The list of vegetables is already long: but there are a few more to be added to it. For there, in a corner, creep some

[1] *Janipha Manihot.* [2] *Cajanus Indicus.* [3] *Dioscorea.*
[4] *Maranta.* [5] *Coix lacryma.* [6] *Xanthosoma.*
[7] *Ipomœa Batatas.* [8] *Jatropha multifida.* [9] *Canna.*

plants of the Earth-nut,[1] a little vetch which buries its pods in the earth. The owner will roast and eat their oily seeds. There is also a tall bunch of Ochro[2]—a purple-stemmed mallow-flowered plant—whose mucilaginous seeds will thicken his soup. Up a tree, and round the house-eaves, scramble a large coarse Pumpkin, and a more delicate Granadilla,[3] whose large yellow fruits hang ready to be plucked, and eaten principally for a few seeds of the shape and colour of young cockroaches. If he be a prudent man (especially if he lives in Jamaica), he will have a plant of the pretty Overlook pea,[4] trailing aloft somewhere, to prevent his garden being 'overlooked,' *i.e.* bewitched by an evil eye, in case the Obeah-bottle which hangs from the Mango-tree, charged with toad and spider, dirty water, and so forth, has no terrors for his secret enemy. He will have a Libidibi[5] tree, too, for astringent medicine; and his hedge will be composed, if he be a man of taste—as he often seems to be —of Hibiscus bushes, whose magnificent crimson flowers contrast with the bright yellow bunches of the common Cassia, and the scarlet flowers of the Jumby-bead bush,[6] and blue and white and pink Convolvuluses. The sulphur and purple Neerembergia of our hothouses, which is here one mass of flower at Christmas, and the creeping Crab's-eye Vine,[7] will scramble over the fence; while, as a finish to his little Paradise, he will have planted at each of its four corners an upright Dragon's-blood[8] bush, whose violet and red leaves bedeck our dinner-tables in winter; and are here used, from their unlikeness to any other plant in the island, to mark boundaries.

SWEET POTATO.

I have not dared—for fear of prolixity—to make this catalogue as complete as I could have done. But it must be remembered that, over and above all this, every hedge and wood furnishes wild fruit more or less eatable; the high forests

[1] *Arachis hypogœa.*   [2] *Abelmoschus esculentus.*
[3] *Passiflora.*   [4] *Canavalia.*
[5] *Libidibia coriacea,* now largely imported into Liverpool for tanning.
[6] *Erythrina corallodendron.*   [7] *Abrus precatorius.*
[8] *Dracæna terminalis.*

plenty of oily seeds, in which the tropic man delights; and woods, forests, and fields medicinal plants uncounted. 'There is more medicine in the bush, and better, than in all the shops in Port of Spain,' said a wise medical man to me; and to the Exhibition of 1862 Mr. M'Clintock alone contributed, from British Guiana, one hundred and forty species of barks used as medicine by the Indians. There is therefore no fear that the tropical small farmer should suffer, either from want, or from monotony of food; and equally small fear lest, when his children have eaten themselves sick—as they are likely to do if, like the Negro children, they are eating all day long—he should be unable to find something in the hedge which will set them all right again.

At the amount of food which a man can get off this little patch I dare not guess. Well says Humboldt, that an European lately arrived in the torrid zone is struck with nothing so much as the extreme smallness of the spots under cultivation round a cabin which contains a numerous family. The plantains alone ought, according to Humboldt, to give one hundred and thirty-three times as much food as the same space of ground sown with wheat, and forty-four times as much as if it grew potatoes. True, the plantain is by no means as nourishing as wheat: which reduces the actual difference between their value per acre to twenty-five to one. But under his plantains he can grow other vegetables. He has no winter, and therefore some crop or other is always coming forward. From whence it comes, that, as I just hinted, his wife and children seem to have always something to eat in their mouths, if it be only the berries and nuts which abound in every hedge and wood. Neither dare I guess at the profit which he might make, and I hope will some day make, out of his land, if he would cultivate somewhat more for exportation, and not merely for home consumption. If any one wishes to know more on this matter, let him consult the catalogue of contributions from British Guiana to the London Exhibition of 1862; especially the pages from lix. to lxviii. on the starch-producing plants of the West Indies.

Beyond the facts which I have given as to the plantain, I have no statistics of the amount of produce which is usually raised on a West Indian provision ground. Nor would any be of use; for a glance shows that the limit of production has not been nearly reached. Were the fork used instead of the hoe; were the weeds kept down; were the manure returned to the soil, instead of festering about everywhere in sun and rain: in a word, were even as much done for the land as an English labourer does for his garden; still more, if as much were done for it as for a suburban market-garden, the produce might be doubled or trebled, and that without exhausting the soil.

The West Indian peasant can, if he will, carry 'la petite culture' to a perfection and a wealth which it has not yet attained even in China, Japan, and Hindostan, and make every rood of ground not merely maintain its man, but its civilised man. This, however, will require a skill and a thoughtfulness which the Negro does not as yet possess. If he ever had them, he lost them under slavery, from the brutalising effects of a rough and unscientific 'grande culture'; and it will need several generations of training ere he recovers them. Garden-tillage and spade-farming are not learnt in a day, especially when they depend—as they always must in temperate climates—for their main profit on some article which requires skilled labour to prepare it for the market—on flax, for instance, silk, wine, or fruits. An average English labourer, I fear, if put in possession of half a dozen acres of land, would fare as badly as the poor Chartists who, some twenty years ago, joined in Feargus O'Connor's land scheme, unless he knew half a dozen ways of eking out a livelihood which even our squatters around Windsor and the New Forest are, alas! forgetting, under the money-making and man-unmaking influences of the 'division of labour.' He is vanishing fast, the old bee-keeping, apple-growing, basket-making, copse-cutting, many-counselled Ulysses of our youth, as handy as a sailor: and we know too well what he leaves behind him; grandchildren better fed, better clothed, better taught than he, but his inferiors in intellect and in manhood, because—whatever they may be taught—they cannot be taught by schooling to use their fingers and their wits. I fear, therefore, that the average English labourer would not prosper here. He has not stamina enough for the hard work of the sugar plantation. He has not wit and handiness enough for the more delicate work of a little spade-farm: and he would sink, as the Negro seems inclined to sink, into a mere grower of food for himself; or take to drink—as too many of the white immigrants to certain West Indian colonies did thirty years ago—and burn the life out of himself with new rum. The Hindoo immigrant, on the other hand, has been trained by long ages to a somewhat scientific agriculture, and civilised into the want of many luxuries for which the Negro cares nothing; and it is to him that we must look, I think, for a 'petite culture' which will do justice to the inexhaustible wealth of the West Indian soil and climate.

As for the house, which is embowered in the little Paradise which I have been describing, I am sorry to say that it is, in general, the merest wooden hut on stilts; the front half altogether open and unwalled; the back half boarded up to form a single room, a passing glance into which will not make the stranger wish to enter, if he has any nose, or any dislike of vermin. The group at the door, meanwhile, will do anything but invite him to enter; and he will ride on, with something like a sigh at what man might be, and what he is.

Doubtless, there are great excuses for the inmates. A house in this climate is only needed for a sleeping or lounging place. The cooking is carried on between a few stones in the garden; the washing at the neighbouring brook. No store-rooms are needed, where there is no winter, and everything grows fresh and fresh, save the salt-fish, which can be easily kept—and I understand usually is kept—underneath the bed. As for separate bedrooms for boys and girls, and all those decencies and moralities for which those who build model cottages strive, and with good cause—of such things none dream. But it is not so very long ago that the British Isles were not perfect in such matters; some think that they are not quite perfect yet. So we will take the beam out of our own eye, before we try to take the mote from the Negro's. The latter, however, no man can do. For the Negro, being a freeholder and the owner of his own cottage, must take the mote out of his own eye, having no landlord to build cottages for him; in the meanwhile, however, the less said about his lodging the better.

In the villages, however, in Maraval, for instance, you see houses of a far better stamp, belonging, I believe, to coloured people employed in trades; long and low wooden buildings with jalousies instead of windows—for no glass is needed here; divided into rooms, and smart with paint, which is not as pretty as the native wood. You catch sight as you pass of prints, usually devotional, on the walls, comfortable furniture, looking-glasses, and sideboards, and other pleasant signs that a civilisation of the middle classes is springing up; and springing, to judge from the number of new houses building everywhere, very rapidly, as befits a colony whose revenue has risen, since 1855, from £72,300 to £240,000, beside the local taxation of the wards, some £30,000 or £40,000 more.

What will be the future of agriculture in the West Indian colonies I of course dare not guess. The profits of sugar-growing, in spite of all drawbacks, have been of late very great. They will be greater still under the improved methods of manufacture which will be employed now that the sugar duties have been at least rationally reformed by Mr. Lowe. And therefore, for some time to come, capital will naturally flow towards sugar-planting; and great sheets of the forest will be, too probably, ruthlessly and wastefully swept away to make room for canes. And yet one must ask, regretfully, are there no other cultures save that of cane which will yield a fair, even an ample, return, to men of small capital and energetic habits? What of the culture of bamboo for paper-fibre, of which I have spoken already? It has been, I understand, taken up successfully in Jamaica, to supply the United States' paper market. Why should it not be taken up in Trinidad? Why should not Plantain-meal[1] be hereafter largely exported for the use of the English working classes? Why should not Trinidad, and other islands, export fruits—preserved fruits especially? Surely such a trade might be profitable, if only a quarter as much care were taken in the West Indies as is taken in England to improve the varieties by selection and culture; and care taken also not to spoil the preserves, as now, for the English market, by swamping them with sugar or sling. Can nothing be done in growing the oil-producing seeds with which the Tropics abound, and for which a demand is rising in England, if it be only for use about machinery? Nothing, too, toward growing drugs for the home market? Nothing toward using the treasures of gutta-percha which are now wasting in the Balatas? Above all, can nothing be done to increase the yield of the cacao-farms, and the quality of Trinidad cacao?

For this latter industry, at least, I have hope. My friend—if he will allow me to call him so—Mr. John Law has shown what extraordinary returns may be obtained from improved cacao-growing; at least, so far to his own satisfaction that he is himself trying the experiment. He calculates[2] that 200 acres, at a maximum outlay of about 11,000 dollars spread over six years, and diminishing from that time till the end of the tenth year, should give, for fifty years after that, a net income of 6800 dollars; and then 'the industrious planter may sit down,' as I heartily hope Mr. Law will do, 'and enjoy the fruits of his labour.'

Mr. Law is of opinion that, to give such a return, the cacao must be farmed in a very different way from the usual plan; that the trees must not be left shaded, as now, by Bois Immortelles, sixty to eighty feet high, during their whole life. The trees, he says with reason, impoverish the soil by their roots. The shade causes excess of moisture, chills, weakens and retards the plants; encourages parasitic moss and insects; and, moreover, is least useful in the very months in which the sun is hottest, viz. February, March, and April, which are just the months in which the Bois Immortelles shed their leaves. He believes that the cacao needs no shade after the third year; and that, till then, shade would be amply given by plantains and maize set between the trees, which would, in the very first year, repay the planter some 6500 dollars on his first outlay of some 8000. It is not for me to give an opinion upon the correctness of his estimates: but the past history of Trinidad shows so many failures of the cacao crop, that even a practically ignorant man

---

[1] Directions for preparing it may be found in the catalogue of contributions from British Guiana to the International Exhibition of 1862. Preface, pp. lix. lxii.

[2] 'How to Establish and Cultivate an Estate of One Square Mile in Cacao:' a Paper read to the Scientific Association of Trinidad, 1865.

may be excused for guessing that there is something wrong in the old Spanish system; and that with cacao, as with wheat and every other known crop, improved culture means improved produce and steadier profits.

As an advocate of 'petite culture,' I heartily hope that such may be the case. I have hinted in these volumes my belief that exclusive sugar cultivation, on the large scale, has been the bane of the West Indies.

I went out thither with a somewhat foregone conclusion in that direction. But it was at least founded on what I believed to be facts. And it was, certainly, verified by the fresh facts which I saw there. I returned with a belief stronger than ever, that exclusive sugar cultivation had put a premium on unskilled slave-labour, to the disadvantage of skilled white-labour; and to the disadvantage, also, of any attempt to educate and raise the Negro, whom it was not worth while to civilise, as long as he was needed merely as an instrument exerting brute strength. It seems to me, also, that to the exclusive cultivation of sugar is owing, more than to any other cause, that frightful decrease throughout the islands of the white population, of which most English people are, I believe, quite unaware. Do they know, for instance, that Barbadoes could in Cromwell's time send three thousand white volunteers, and St. Kitts and Nevis a thousand, to help in the gallant conquest of Jamaica? Do they know that in 1676 Barbadoes was reported to maintain, as against 80,000 black, 70,000 free whites; while in 1851 the island contained more than 120,000 Negroes and people of colour, as against only 15,824 whites? That St. Kitts held, even as late as 1761, 7000 whites; but in 1826—before emancipation—only 1600? Or that little Montserrat, which held, about 1648, 1000 white families, and had a militia of 360 effective men, held in 1787 only 1300 whites, in 1828 only 315, and in 1851 only 150?

It will be said that this ugly decrease in the white population is owing to the unfitness of the climate. I believe it to have been produced rather by the introduction of sugar cultivation, at which the white man cannot work. These early settlers had grants of ten acres apiece; at least in Barbadoes. They grew not only provisions enough for themselves, but tobacco, cotton, and indigo—products now all but obliterated out of the British islands. They made cotton hammocks, and sold them abroad as well as in the island. They might, had they been wisely educated to perceive and use the natural wealth around them, have made money out of many other wild products. But the profits of sugar-growing were so enormous, in spite of their uncertainty, that, during the greater part of the eighteenth century, their little freeholds were bought up, and converted into cane-pieces by their wealthier neighbours, who could afford to buy slaves and sugar-mills. They sought their fortunes in other lands: and so was exterminated a race of yeomen, who might have been at this day a source of strength and honour, not only to the colonies, but to England herself.

It may be that the extermination was not altogether undeserved; that they were not sufficiently educated or skilful to carry out that 'petite culture' which requires—as I have said already—not only intellect and practical education, but a hereditary and traditional experience, such as is possessed by the Belgians, the Piedmontese, and, above all, by the charming peasantry of Provence and Languedoc, the fathers (as far as Western Europe is concerned) of all our agriculture. It may be, too, that as the sugar cultivation increased, they were tempted more and more, in the old hard drinking days, by the special poison of the West Indies—new rum, to the destruction both of soul and body. Be that as it may, their extirpation helped to make inevitable the vicious system of large estates cultivated by slaves; a system which is judged by its own results; for it was ruinate before emancipation; and emancipation only gave the *coup de grâce.* The 'Latifundia perdidere' the Antilles, as they did Italy of old. The vicious system brought its own Nemesis. The ruin of the West Indies at the end of the great French war was principally owing to that exclusive cultivation of the cane, which forced the planter to depend on a single article of produce, and left him embarrassed every time prices fell suddenly, or the canes failed from drought or hurricane. We all know what would be thought of an European farmer who thus staked his capital on one venture. 'He is a bad farmer,' says the proverb, 'who does not stand on four legs, and, if he can, on five.' If his wheat fails, he has his barley—if his barley, he has his sheep—if his sheep, he has his fatting oxen. The Provençal, the model farmer, can retreat on his almonds if his mulberries fail; on his olives, if his vines fail; on his maize, if his wheat fails. The West Indian might have had—the Cuban has—his tobacco; his indigo too; his coffee, or—as in Trinidad—his cacao and his arrowroot; and half a dozen crops more: indeed, had his intellect—and he had intellect in plenty—been diverted from the fatal fixed idea of making money as fast as possible by sugar, he might have ere now discovered in America, or imported from the East, plants for cultivation far more valuable than that Bread-fruit tree, of which such high hopes were once entertained, as a food for the Negro. As it was, his very green crops were neglected, till, in some islands at least, he could not feed his cattle and mules with certainty; while the sugar-cane, to which everything else had been sacrificed, proved sometimes, indeed, a valuable servant: but too often a tyrannous and capricious master.

But those days are past; and better ones have dawned, with better education, and a wider knowledge of the world and of science. What West Indians have to learn—some of them have learnt it already—is that if they can compete with other countries only by improved and more scientific cultivation and manufacture, as they themselves confess, then they can carry out the new methods only by more skilful labour. They therefore require now, as they never required before, to give the labouring classes a practical education; to quicken their intellect, and to teach them habits of self-dependent and originative action, which are—as in the case of the Prussian soldier, and of the English sailor and railway servant — perfectly compatible with strict discipline. Let them take warning from the English manufacturing system, which condemns a human intellect to waste itself in perpetually heading pins, or opening and shutting trap-doors, and punishes itself by producing a class of workpeople who alternate between reckless comfort and moody discontent. Let them be sure that they will help rather than injure the labour - market of the colony, by making the labourer also a small free-holding peasant. He will learn more in his own provision ground —properly tilled—than he will in the cane-piece: and he will take to the cane - piece and use for his employer the self-helpfulness which he has learnt in the provision ground. It

GUAVA.

is so in England. Our best agricultural day-labourers are, without exception, those who cultivate some scrap of ground, or follow some petty occupation, which prevents their depending entirely on wage-labour. And so I believe it will be in the West Indies. Let the land-policy of the late Governor be followed up. Let squatting be rigidly forbidden. Let no man hold possession of land without having earned, or inherited, money enough to purchase it, as a guarantee of his ability and respectability, or—as in the case of Coolies past their indentures —as a commutation for rights which he has earned in likewise. But let the coloured man of every race be encouraged to become a landholder and a producer in his own small way. He will thus, not only by what he produces, but by what he consumes, add largely to the wealth of the colony; while his increased wants, and those of his children, till they too can purchase land, will draw him and his sons and daughters to the sugar-estates, as intelligent and helpful day-labourers.

So it may be: and I cannot but trust, from what I have seen of the temper of the gentlemen of Trinidad, that so it will be.

CHAPTER XVII (AND LAST)

HOMEWARD BOUND

AT last we were homeward bound. We had been seven weeks in the island. We had promised to be back in England, if possible, within the three months ; and we had a certain pride in keeping our promise, not only for its own sake, but for the sake of the dear West Indies. We wished to show those at home how easy it was to get there ; how easy to get home again. Moreover, though going to sea in the *Shannon* was not quite the same 'as going to sea in a sieve,' our stay-at-home friends were of the same mind as those of the dear little Jumblies, whom Mr. Lear has made immortal in his *New Book of Nonsense;* and we were bound to come back as soon as possible, and not 'in twenty years or more,' if we wished them to say—

'If we live,
We too will go to sea in a sieve,
To the Hills of the Chankly bore.'

So we left. But it was sore leaving. People had been very kind ; and were ready to be kinder still ; while we, busy—perhaps too busy—over our Natural History collections, had seen very little of our neighbours ; had been able to accept very few of the invitations which were showered on us, and which would, I doubt not, have given us opportunities for liking the islanders still more than we liked them already.

Another cause made our leaving sore to us. The hunger for travel had been aroused—above all for travel westward—and would not be satisfied. Up the Orinoco we longed to go : but could not. To La Guayra and Caraccas we longed to go : but dared not. Thanks to Spanish Republican barbarism, the only regular communication with that once magnificent capital of Northern Venezuela was by a filthy steamer, the *Regos Ferreos*, which had become, from her very looks, a byword in the port. On board of her some friends of ours had lately been glad to sleep in a dog-hutch on deck, to escape the filth and vermin of the berths ; and went hungry for want of decent food. Caraccas itself was going through one of its periodic revolutions—it has not got through the fever fit yet—and neither life nor property was safe.

But the longing to go westward was on us nevertheless. It seemed hard to turn back after getting so far along the great path of the human race; and one had to reason with oneself— Foolish soul, whither would you go? You cannot go westward for ever. If you go up the Orinoco, you will long to go up the Meta. If you get to Sta. Fe de Bogota, you will not be content till you cross the Andes and see Cotopaxi and Chimborazo. When you look down on the Pacific, you will be craving to go to the Gallapagos, after Darwin; and then to the Marquesas, after Herman Melville; and then to the Fijis, after Seeman; and then to Borneo, after Brooke; and then to the Archipelago, after Wallace; and then to Hindostan, and round the world. And when you get home, the westward fever will be stronger on you than ever, and you will crave to start again. Go home at once, like a reasonable man, and do your duty, and thank God for what you have been allowed to see; and try to become of the same mind as that most brilliant of old ladies, who boasted that she had not been abroad since she saw the Apotheosis of Voltaire, before the French Revolution; and did not care to go, as long as all manner of clever people were kind enough to go instead, and write charming books about what they had seen for her.

But the westward fever was slow to cool: and with wistful eyes we watched the sun by day, and Venus and the moon by night, sink down into the gulf, to lighten lands which we should never see. A few days more, and we were steaming out to the Bocas—which we had begun to love as the gates of a new home —heaped with presents to the last minute, some of them from persons we hardly knew. Behind us Port of Spain sank into haze: before us Monos rose, tall, dark, and grim—if Monos could be grim—in moonless night. We ran on, and past the island; this time we were going, not through the Boca de Monos, but through the next, the Umbrella Bocas. It was too dark to see houses, palm-trees, aught but the ragged outline of the hills against the northern sky, and beneath, sparks of light in sheltered coves, some of which were already, to one of us, well-beloved nooks. There was the great gulf of the Boca de Monos. There was Morrison's—our good Scotch host of seven weeks since; and the glasses were turned on it, to see, if possible, through the dusk, the almond-tree and the coco-grove for the last time. Ah, well—When we next meet, what will he be, and where? And where the handsome Creole wife, and the little brown Cupid who danced all naked in the log canoe, till the white gentlemen, swimming round, upset him; and canoe, and boy, and men rolled and splashed about like a shoal of seals at play, beneath the cliff with the Seguines and Cereuses; while the ripple lapped the Moriche-nuts about the roots of the Manchineel bush, and the skippers leaped and flashed outside, like silver splinters? And here, where we steamed along, was the very spot where we had seen the shark's back-fin when we rowed back from the first Guacharo cave. And it was all over.

We are such stuff as dreams are made of. And as in a dream, or rather as part of a dream, and myself a phantom and a play-actor, I looked out over the side, and saw on the right the black walls of Monos, on the left the black walls of Huevos—a gate even grander, though not as narrow, as that of Monos; and the Umbrella Rock, capped with Matapalo and Cactus, and night-blowing Cereus, dim in the dusk. And now we were outside. The roar of the surf, the tumble of the sea, the rush of the trade-wind, told us that at once. Out in the great sea, with Grenada, and kind friends in it, ahead; not to be seen or reached till morning light. But we looked astern and not ahead. We could see into and through the gap in Huevos, through which we had tried to reach the Guacharo cave. Inside that notch in the cliffs must be the wooded bay, whence we picked up the shells among the fallen leaves and flowers. From under that dark wall beyond it the Guacharos must be just trooping out for their nightly forage, as they had trooped out since—He alone who made them knows how long. The outline of Huevos, the outline of Monos, were growing lower and grayer astern. A long ragged haze, far loftier than that on the starboard quarter, signified the Northern Mountains; and far off on the port quarter lay a flat bank of cloud, amid which rose, or seemed to rise, the Cordillera of the Main, and the hills where jaguars lie. Canopus blazed high astern, and Fomalhaut below him to the west, as if bidding us a kind farewell. Orion and Aldebaran spangled the zenith. The young moon lay on her back in the far west, thin and pale, over Cumana and the Cordillera, with Venus, ragged and red with earth mist, just beneath. And low ahead, with the pointers horizontal, glimmered the cold pole-star, for which we were steering, out of the summer into the winter once more. We grew chill as we looked at him; and shuddered, it may be, cowered for a moment, at the thought of 'Niflheim,' the home of frosts and fogs, towards which we were bound.

However, we were not yet out of the Tropics. We had still nearly a fortnight before us in which to feel sure there was a sun in heaven; a fortnight more of the 'warm champagne' atmosphere which was giving fresh life and health to us both. And up the islands we went, wiser, but not sadder, than when we went down them; casting wistful eyes, though, to windward, for there away—and scarcely out of sight—lay Tobago, to which we had a most kind invitation; and gladly would we have looked at that beautiful and fertile little spot, and have pictured to ourselves Robinson Crusoe and Man Friday pacing along the coral beach in one of its little southern coves. More wistfully still did we look to windward when we thought of Barbadoes, and of the kind people who were ready to welcome us into that prosperous and civilised little cane-garden, which deserves—and has deserved for now two hundred years, far more than poor old Ireland—the name of 'The Emerald Gem of the Western World.'

But it could not be. A few hours at Grenada, and a few hours at St. Lucia, were all the stoppages possible to us. The steamer only passes once a fortnight, and it is necessary to spend that time on each island which is visited, unless the traveller commits himself—which he cannot well do if he has a lady with him—to the chances and changes of coasting schooners. More frequent and easy intercommunication is needed throughout the Antilles. The good people, whether white or coloured, need to see more of each other, and more of visitors from home. Whether a small weekly steamer between the islands would pay in money, I know not. That it would pay morally and socially, I am sure. Perhaps, when the telegraph is laid down along the islands, the need of more steamers will be felt and supplied.

Very pleasant was the run up to St. Thomas's, not merely on account of the scenery, but because we had once more—contrary to our expectation—the most agreeable of captains. His French cultivation—he had been brought up in Provence—joined to brilliant natural talents, had made him as good a talker as he doubtless is a sailor; and the charm of his conversation, about all matters on earth, and some above the earth, will not be soon forgotten by those who went up with him to St. Thomas's, and left him there with regret.

We transhipped to the *Neva*, Captain Woolward—to whom I must tender my thanks, as I do to Captain Bax, of the *Shannon*, for all kinds of civility. We slept a night in the harbour, the town having just then a clean bill of health; and were very glad to find ourselves, during the next few days, none the worse for having done so. On remarking, the first evening, that I did not smell the harbour after all, I was comforted by the answer that—'When a man did, he had better go below and make his will.' It is a pity that the most important harbour in the Caribbean Sea should be so unhealthy. No doubt it offers advantages for traffic which can be found nowhere else: and there the steamers must continue to assemble, yellow fever or none. But why should not an hotel be built for the passengers in some healthy and airy spot outside the basin—on the south slope of Water Island, for instance, or on Buck Island—where they might land at once, and sleep in pure fresh air and sea-breeze? The establishment of such an hotel would surely, when once known, attract to the West Indies many travellers to whom St. Thomas's is now as much a name of fear as Colon or the Panama.

We left St. Thomas's by a different track from that by which we came to it. We ran northward up the magnificent land-locked channel between Tortola and Virgin Gorda, to pass to leeward of Virgin Gorda and Anegada, and so northward toward the Gulf Stream.

This channel has borne the name of Drake, I presume, ever since the year 1575. For in the account of that fatal, though successful voyage, which cost the lives both of Sir John Hawkins, who died off Porto Rico, and Sir Francis Drake, who died off Porto Bello, where Hosier and the greater part of the crews of a noble British fleet perished a hundred and fifty years afterward, it is written in Hakluyt how—after running up N. and N.W. past Saba—the fleet 'stood away S.W., and on the 8th of November, being a Saturday, we came to an anker some 7 or 8 leagues off among certain broken Ilands called Las Virgines, which have bene accounted dangerous: but we found there a very good rode, had it bene for a thousand sails of ships in 7 & 8 fadomes, fine sand, good ankorage, high Ilands on either side, but no fresh water that we could find: here is much fish to be taken with nets and hookes: also we stayed on shore and fowled. Here Sir John Hawkins was extreme sick' (he died within ten days), 'which his sickness began upon newes of the taking of the *Francis*' (his sternmost vessel). 'The 18th day wee weied and stood north and by east into a lesser sound, which Sir Francis in his barge discovered the night before; and ankored in 13 fadomes, having hie steepe hiles on either side, some league distant from our first riding.

'The 12 in the morning we weied and set sayle into the Sea due south through a small streit but without danger' —possibly the very gap in which the *Rhone's* wreck now lies— 'and then stode west and by north for S. Juan de Puerto Rico.'

This northerly course is, plainly, the most advantageous for a homeward-bound ship, as it strikes the Gulf Stream soonest, and keeps in it longest. Conversely, the southerly route by the Azores is best for outward-bound ships; as it escapes most of the Gulf Stream, and traverses the still Sargasso Sea, and even the extremity of the westward equatorial current.

Strange as these Virgin Isles had looked when seen from the south, outside, and at the distance of a few miles, they looked still more strange when we were fairly threading our way between them, sometimes not a rifle-shot from the cliffs, with the white coral banks gleaming under our keel. Had they ever carried a tropic vegetation? Had the hills of Tortola and Virgin Gorda, in shape and size much like those which surround a sea-loch in the Western Islands, ever been furred with forests like those of Guadaloupe or St. Lucia? The loftier were now mere mounds of almost barren earth; the lower were often, like 'Fallen Jerusalem,' mere long earthless moles, as of minute Cyclopean masonry. But what had destroyed their vegetation, if it ever existed? Were they not, too, the mere remnants of a submerged and destroyed land, connected now only by the coral shoals? So it seemed to us, as we ran out past the magnificent harbour at the back of Virgin Gorda, where, in the old war times, the merchantmen of all the West Indies used to collect, to be conveyed homeward by the naval squadron, and across a shallow sea white with coral beds. We passed to leeward of the island, or rather reef, of Anegada, so low that it could only be discerned, at a few miles' distance, by the breaking surf and a few bushes; and then plunged, as it were, suddenly out of shallow white water into deep azure ocean. An upheaval of only forty fathoms would, I believe, join all these islands to each other, and to the great mountain island of Porto Rico to the west. The same upheaval would connect with each other Anguilla, St. Martin, and St. Bartholomew, to the east. But Santa Cruz, though so near St. Thomas's, and the Virgin Gordas to the south, would still be parted from them by a gulf nearly two thousand fathoms deep—a gulf which marks still, probably, the separation of two ancient continents, or at least two archipelagoes.

Much light has been thrown on this curious problem since our return, by an American naturalist, Mr. Bland, in a paper read before the American Philosophical Society, on 'The Geology and Physical Geography of the West Indies, with reference to the distribution of Mollusca.' It is plain that of all animals, land-shells and reptiles give the surest tokens of any former connection of islands, being neither able to swim nor fly from one to another, and very unlikely to be carried by birds or currents. Judging, therefore, as he has a right to do, by the similarity of the land-shells, Mr. Bland is of opinion that Porto Rico, the Virgins, and the Anguilla group once formed continuous dry land, connected with Cuba, the Bahamas, and Hayti; and that their shell-fauna is of a Mexican and Central American type. The shell-fauna of the islands to the south, on the contrary, from Barbuda and St. Kitts down to Trinidad, is South American: but of two types, one Venezuelan, the other Guianan. It seems, from Mr. Bland's researches, that there must have existed once not merely an extension of the North American Continent south-eastward, but that very extension of the South American Continent northward, at which I have hinted more than once in these pages. Moreover—a fact which I certainly did not expect—the western side of this supposed land, namely, Trinidad, Tobago, Grenada, the Grenadines, St. Vincent, and St. Lucia, have, as far as land-shells are concerned, a Venezuelan fauna; while the eastern side of it, namely, Barbadoes, Martinique, Dominica, Guadaloupe, Antigua, etc., have, most strangely, the fauna of Guiana.

If this be so, a glance at the map will show the vast destruction of tropic land during almost the very latest geological epoch; and show, too, how little, in the present imperfect state of our knowledge, we ought to dare any speculations as to the absence of man, as well as of other creatures, on those great lands now destroyed. For, to supply the dry land which Mr. Bland's theory needs, we shall have to conceive a junction, reaching over at least five degrees of latitude, between the north of British Guiana and Barbadoes; and may freely indulge in the dream that the waters of the Orinoco, when they ran over the lowlands of Trinidad, passed east of Tobago; then northward between Barbadoes and St. Lucia; then turned westward between the latter island and Martinique; and that the mighty estuary formed—for a great part at least of that line—the original barrier which kept the land-shells of Venezuela apart from those of Guiana. A 'stretch of the imagination,' doubtless: but no greater stretch than will be required by any explanation of the facts whatsoever.

And so, thanking Mr. Bland heartily for his valuable contribution to the infant science of Bio-Geology—I take leave, in these pages at least, of the Earthly Paradise.

Our run homeward was quite as successful as our run out. The magnificent *Neva*, her captain and her officers, were what these Royal Mail steamers and their crews are—without, I believe, an exception—all that we could wish. Our passengers, certainly, were neither so numerous nor so agreeable as when going out; and the most notable personage among them was a keen-eyed, strong-jawed little Corsican, who had been lately hired—so ran his story—by the coloured insurgents of Hayti, to put down the President—*alias* (as usual in such Republics) Tyrant—Salnave.

He seemed, by his own account, to have done his work effectually. Seven thousand lives were lost in the attack on Salnave's quarters in Port au Prince. Whole families were bayonetted, to save the trouble of judging and shooting them. Women were not spared: and—if all that I have heard of Hayti be true—some of them did not deserve to be spared. The noble old French buildings of the city were ruined—the Corsican said, not by his artillery, but by Salnave's. He had slain Salnave himself; and was now going back to France to claim his rights as a French citizen, carrying with him Salnave's sword, which was wrapped in a newspaper, save when taken out to be brandished on the main deck. One could not but be interested in the valiant adventurer. He seemed a man such as Red Republics and Revolutions breed, and need; very capable of doing rough work, and not likely to be hampered by scruples as to the manner of doing it. If he is, as I take for granted, busy in France just now, he will leave his mark behind.

The voyage, however, seemed likely to be a dull one; and to relieve the monotony, a wild-beast show was determined on, ere the weather grew too cold. So one day all the new curiosities were brought on deck at noon; and if some great zoologist had been on board, he would have found materials in our show for more than one interesting lecture. The doctor contributed an Alligator, some two feet six inches long; another officer, a curiously-marked Ant-eater—of a species unknown to me. It was common, he said, in the Isthmus of Panama; and seemed the most foolish and helpless of beasts. As no ants were procurable, it was fed on raw yolk of egg, which it contrived to suck in with its long tongue—not enough, however, to keep it alive during the voyage.

The chief engineer exhibited a live 'Tarantula,' or bird-catching spider, who was very safely barred into its box with strips of iron, as a bite from it is rather worse than that of an English adder.

We showed a Vulturine Parrot and a Kinkajou. The Kinkajou, by the by, got loose one night, and displayed his natural inclination by instantly catching a rat, and dancing between decks with it in his mouth: but was so tame withal, that he let the stewardess stroke him in passing. The good lady mistook him for a cat; and when she discovered next morning that she had been handling a 'loose wild beast,' her horror was as great as her thankfulness for the supposed escape. In curious contrast to the natural tameness of the Kinkajou was the natural untameness of a beautiful little Night-Monkey, belonging to the purser. Its great owl's eyes were instinct with nothing but abject terror of everybody and everything; and it was a miracle that ere the voyage was over it did not die of mere fright. How is it, *en passant*, that some animals are naturally fearless and tamable, others not; and that even in the same family? Among the South American monkeys the Howlers are untamable; the Sapajous less so; while the Spider Monkeys are instinctively gentle and fond of man: as may be seen in the case of the very fine Marimonda (*Ateles Beelzebub*) now dying, I fear, in the Zoological Gardens at Bristol.

As we got into colder latitudes, we began to lose our pets. The Ant-eater departed first: then the doctor, who kept his alligator in a tub on his cabin floor, was awoke by doleful wails, as of a babe. Being pretty sure that there was not likely to be one on board, and certainly not in his cabin, he naturally struck a light, and discovered the alligator, who had never uttered a sound before, outside his tub on the floor, bewailing bitterly his fate. Whether he 'wept crocodile tears' besides, the doctor could not discover; but it was at least clear, that if swans sing before they die, alligators do so likewise: for the poor thing was dead next morning.

It was time, after this, to stow the pets warm between decks, and as near the galley-fires as they could be put. For now, as we neared the 'roaring forties,' there fell on us a gale from the north-west, and would not cease.

The wind was, of course, right abeam; the sea soon ran very high. The *Neva*, being a long screw, was lively enough, and too lively; for she soon showed a chronic inclination to roll, and that suddenly, by fits and starts. The fiddles were on the tables for nearly a week: but they did not prevent more than one of us finding his dinner suddenly in his lap instead of his stomach. However, no one was hurt, nor even frightened: save two poor ladies—not from Trinidad—who spent their doleful days and nights in screaming, telling their beads, drinking weak brandy-and-water, and informing the hunted stewardess that if they had known what horrors they were about to endure, they would have gone to Europe in—a sailing vessel. The foreigners—who are usually, I know not why, bad sailors—soon vanished to their berths: so did the ladies: even those who were not ill jammed themselves into their berths, and lay there, for fear of falls and bruises; while the Englishmen and a coloured man or two—the coloured men usually stand the sea well—had the deck all to themselves; and slopped about, holding on, and longing for a monkey's tail; but on the whole rather liking it.

For, after all, it is a glorious pastime to find oneself in a real gale of wind, in a big ship, with not a rock to run against within a thousand miles. One seems in such danger; and one is so safe. And gradually the sense of security grows, and grows into a sense of victory, as with the boy who fears his first fence, plucks up heart for the second, is rather pleased at the third, and craves for the triumph of the fourth and of all the rest, sorry at last when the run is over. And when a man—not being sea-sick—has once discovered that the apparent heel of the ship in rolling is at least four times less than it looks, and that she will jump upright again in a quarter of a minute like a fisher's float; has learnt to get his trunk out from under his berth, and put it back again, by jamming his forehead against the berth-side and his heels against the ship's wall; has learnt —if he sleep aft—to sleep through the firing of the screw, though it does shake all the marrow in his backbone; and has, above all, made a solemn vow to shave and bathe every morning, let the ship be as lively as she will: then he will find a full gale a finer tonic, and a finer stirrer of wholesome appetite, than all the drugs of Apothecaries' Hall.

This particular gale, however, began to get a little too strong. We had a sail or two set to steady the ship: on the second night one split with a crack like a cannon; and was tied up in an instant, cordage and strips, into inextricable knots.

The next night I was woke by a slap which shook the *Neva* from stem to stern, and made her stagger and writhe like a live thing struck across the loins. Then a dull rush of water which there was no mistaking. We had shipped a green sea. Well, I could not bale it out again; and there was plenty of room for it on board. So, after ascertaining that R—— was not frightened, I went back to my berth and slept again, somewhat wondering that the roll of the screw was all but silent.

Next morning we found that a sea had walked in over the bridge, breaking it, and washing off it the first officer and the look-out man—luckily they fell into a sail and not overboard; put out the galley-fires, so that we got a cold breakfast; and eased the ship; for the shock turned the indicator in the engine-room to 'Ease her.' The engineer, thinking that the captain had given the order, obeyed it. The captain turned out into the wet to know who had eased his ship, and then returned to bed, wisely remarking, that the ship knew her own business best; and as she had chosen to ease the engines herself, eased she should be, his orders being 'not to prosecute a voyage so as to endanger the lives of the passengers or the property of the Company.'

So we went on easily for sixteen hours, the wise captain judging—and his judgment proved true—that the centre of the storm was crossing our course ahead; and that if we waited, it would pass us. So, as he expected, we came after a day or two into an almost windless sea, where smooth mountainous waves, the relics of the storm, were weltering aimlessly up and down under a dark sad sky.

Soon we began to sight ship after ship, and found ourselves on the great south-western high-road of the Atlantic; and found ourselves, too, nearing Niflheim day by day. Colder and colder grew the wind, lower the sun, darker the cloud-world overhead; and we went on deck each morning, with some additional garment on, sorely against our wills. Only on the very day on which we sighted land, we had one of those treacherously beautiful days which occur, now and then, in an English February, mild, still, and shining, if not with keen joyful blaze, at least with a cheerful and tender gleam from sea and sky.

The Land's End was visible at a great distance; and as we neared the Lizard, we could see not only the lighthouses on the Cliff, and every well-known cove and rock from Mullion and Kynance round to St. Keverne, but far inland likewise. Breage Church, and the great tin-works of Wheal Vor, stood out hard against the sky. We could see up the Looe Pool to Helston Church, and away beyond it, till we fancied that we could almost discern, across the isthmus, the sacred hill of Carnbrea.

Along the Cornish shore we ran, through a sea swarming with sails: an exciting contrast to the loneliness of the wide ocean which we had left—and so on to Plymouth Sound.

The last time I had been on that water, I was looking up in awe at Sir Edward Codrington's fleet just home from the battle of Navarino. Even then, as a mere boy, I was struck by the grand symmetry of that ample basin: the breakwater—then unfinished—lying across the centre; the heights of Bovisand

and Cawsand, and those again of Mount Batten and Mount Edgecumbe, left and right; the citadel and the Hoe across the bottom of the Sound, the southern sun full on their walls, with the twin harbours and their forests of masts, winding away into dim distance on each side; and behind all and above all, the purple range of Dartmoor, with the black rain-clouds crawling along its top. And now, after nearly forty years, the place looked to me even more grand than my recollections had pictured it. The newer fortifications have added to the moral effect of the scene, without taking away from its physical beauty: and I heard without surprise — though not without pride — the foreigners express their admiration of this, their first specimen of an English port.

We steamed away again, after landing our letters, close past the dear old Mewstone. The warrener's hut stood on it still: and I wondered whether the old he-goat, who used to terrify me as a boy, had left any long-bearded descendants. Then under the Revelstoke and Bolt Head cliffs, with just one flying glance up into the hidden nooks of delicious little Salcombe, and away south-west into the night, bound for Cherbourg, and a very different scene.

We were awakened soon after midnight by the stopping of the steamer. Then a gun. After awhile another; and presently a third: but there was no reply, though our coming had been telegraphed from England; and for nearly six hours we lay in the heart of the most important French arsenal, with all our mails and passengers waiting to get ashore; and nobody deigning to notice us. True, we could do no harm there: but our delay, and other things which happened, were proofs—and I was told not uncommon ones — of that carelessness, unreadiness, and general indiscipline of French arrangements, which has helped to bring about, since then, an utter ruin.

As the day dawned through fog, we went on deck to find the ship lying inside a long breakwater bristling with cannon, which looked formidable enough: but the whole thing, I was told, was useless against modern artillery and ironclads: and there was more than one jest on board as to the possibility of running the Channel Squadron across, and smashing Cherbourg in a single night, unless the French learnt to keep a better look-out in time of war than they did in time of peace.

Just inside us lay two or three ironclads; strong and ugly: untidy, too, to a degree shocking to English eyes. All sorts of odds and ends were hanging over the side, and about the rigging; the yards were not properly squared, and so forth; till—as old sailors would say—the ships had no more decency about them than so many collier-brigs.

Beyond them were arsenals, docks, fortifications, of which of course we could not judge; and backing all, a cliff, some two hundred feet high, much quarried for building-stone. An ugly place it is to look at; and, I should think, an ugly place to get into, with the wind anywhere between N.W. and N.E.; an artificial and expensive luxury, built originally as a mere menace to England, in days when France, which has had too long a moral mission to fight some one, thought of fighting us, who only wished to live in peace with our neighbours. Alas! alas! 'Tu l'a voulu, George Dandin.' She has fought at last: but not us.

Out of Cherbourg we steamed again, sulky enough; for the delay would cause us to get home on the Sunday evening instead of the Sunday morning; and ran northward for the Needles. With what joy we saw at last the white wall of the island glooming dim ahead. With what joy we first discerned that huge outline of a visage on Freshwater Cliff, so well known to sailors, which, as the eye catches it in one direction, is a ridiculous caricature; in another, really noble, and even beautiful. With what joy did we round the old Needles, and run past Hurst Castle; and with what shivering, too. For the wind, though dead south, came to us as a continental wind, harsh and keen from off the frozen land of France, and chilled us to the very marrow all the way up to Southampton.

But there were warm hearts and kind faces waiting us on the quay, and good news too. The gentlemen at the Customhouse courteously declined the least inspection of our luggage; and we were at once away in the train home. At first, I must confess, an English winter was a change for the worse. Fine old oaks and beeches looked to us, fresh from ceibas and balatas, like leafless brooms stuck into the ground by their handles; while the want of light was for some days painful and depressing. But we had done it; and within the three months, as we promised. As the king in the old play says, 'What has been, has been, and I've had my hour.' At last we had seen it; and we could not unsee it. We could not not have been in the Tropics.

THE END

www.ingramcontent.com/pod-product-compliance
Lightning Source LLC
Chambersburg PA
CBHW032049220426
43664CB00008B/928